The Psychobiology of Mind-Body Healing

New Concepts of
Therapeutic Hypnosis

Revised Edition

Other Books by the Same Author

Dreams and the Growth of Personality (1972/1985)

Hypnotic Realities (1976, with Milton H. Erickson)

Hypnotherapy: An Exploratory Casebook (1979, with Milton H. Erickson)

Experiencing Hypnosis (1981, with Milton H. Erickson)

The Collected Papers of Milton H. Erickson on Hypnosis (1980, editor)
Volume I: *The Nature of Hypnosis and Suggestion*
Volume II: *Hypnotic Alteration of Sensory, Perceptual, and Psychophysiological Processes*
Volume III: *Hypnotic Investigation of Psychodynamic Processes*
Volume IV: *Innovative Hypnotherapy*

Healing in Hypnosis.
Volume 1: The Seminars, Workshops, and Lectures of Milton H. Erickson
(1984, edited with Margaret O. Ryan)

Life Reframing in Hypnosis.
Volume 2: The Seminars, Workshops, and Lectures of Milton H. Erickson
(1985, edited with Margaret O. Ryan)

Mind-Body Communication in Hypnosis.
Volume 3: The Seminars, Workshops, and Lectures of Erickson
(1986, edited with Margaret O. Ryan)

Creative Choice in Hypnosis.
Volume 4: The Seminars, Workshops, and Lectures of Erickson
(1991, edited with Margaret O. Ryan)

The Psychobiology of Mind-Body Healing: New Concepts of Therapeutic Hypnosis (1986)

Mind-Body Therapy: Ideodynamic Healing in Hypnosis (1988, with David Cheek)

The February Man: Evolving Consciousness and Identity in Hypnotherapy
(1989, with Milton H. Erickson)

The Twenty Minute Break: The Ultradian Healing Response (1991, with David Nimmons)

Ultradian Rhythms in Life Processes:
A Fundamental Inquiry into Chronobiology and Psychobiology
(1992, edited with David Lloyd)

A NORTON PROFESSIONAL BOOK

The Psychobiology of Mind-Body Healing

New Concepts of
Therapeutic Hypnosis

Revised Edition

ERNEST LAWRENCE ROSSI

W • W • NORTON & COMPANY, INC. • *NEW YORK* • *LONDON*

Permission to quote from the following is acknowledged:
J. Bodden, Accessing state-bound memories in the treatment of phobias: Two case studies. *American Journal of Clinical Hypnosis, 34,* 24–28, 1991. B. Klopfer (1957), Psychological variables in human cancer. *Journal of Projective Techniques, 21,* 331–340. Reprinted by permission of Lawrence Erlbaum Associates, Inc. W. Cannon, "Voodoo" death, *Psychosomatic Medicine, 19*(3), 182–190 © 1957, American Psychosomatic Society. Excerpt from *The Transformed Cell* by Steven Rosenberg reprinted by permission of The Putnam Publishing Group. Copyright © 1992 by Steven Rosenberg. K. Bowers (1977), Hypnosis: An informational approach. *Annals of the New York Academy of Sciences, 296,* 222–237. Reprinted by permission of The New York Academy of Sciences. K. Pribram, The cognitive revolution and mind-brain issues, *American Psychologist, 41,* 507–520. Copyright 1986 by the American Psychological Association. Reprinted by permission. C. Jung, *The Collected Works of Carl G. Jung.* Copyright © 1960 by Princeton University Press. Reprinted by permission of Princeton University Press. Excerpt from *Stress without Distress* by H. Selye. Copyright © 1974 by Hans Selye, M.D. Reprinted by permission of HarperCollins Publishers, Inc. Excerpt from *Paradoxical Strategies in Psychotherapy* by L. Seltzer, copyright © 1985 by L. Seltzer. Reprinted by permission of John Wiley & Sons, Inc. T. Hunter, A thousand and one protein kinases, *Cell, 50,* 823–829. Copyright © 1987 by Cell Press. T. Melnechuk (1985), Neuroimmunology: Crossroads between behavior and disease, *Advances, 2*(3), 54–58. Reprinted from *Advances: The Journal of Mind/Body Health.* Effectiveness of incentive in clinical hypnosis by David Cheek, reprinted with permission from The American College of Obstetricians and Gynecologists (*Obstetrics and Gynecology,* 1957, *9*(6), 720–724). N. Ischlondsky, The inhibitory process in the cerebrophysiological laboratory and in the clinic, *Journal of Nervous and Mental Diseases, 121,* 5–18 copyright © Williams and Wilkins, 1955. G. Smith et al., Psychologic modulation of the human immune response to varicella zoster, *Archives of Internal Medicine, 145,* 2110–2112, copyright © 1985, American Medical Association. Improving on the formula by F. Balkwill. Reprinted with permission from *Nature, 361,* 206–207. Copyright © 1993, Macmillan Magazines, Ltd. A. Kreinheder, The call to individuation, reprinted with permission from *Psychological Perspectives, 10*(1). Copyright © 1979 by the C. G. Jung Institute of Los Angeles (10349 W. Pico Blvd., Los Angeles, CA 90064).

Library of Congress Cataloging-in-Publication Data

Rossi, Ernest Lawrence.
   The psychobiology of mind-body healing : new concepts of therapeutic hypnosis / Ernest Lawrence Rossi.—Rev. ed.
      p.   cm.
   Includes bibliographical references and index.
   ISBN 0-393-70168-9
   1. Medicine, Psychosomatic.   2. Mind and body therapies.
3. Psychoneuroimmunology.   4. Hypnotism—Therapeutic use.
5. Psychobiology.   I. Title.
RC49.R674   1993
615.8'512—dc20   93-23757   CIP

W. W. Norton & Company, Inc., 500 Fifth Avenue, New York, NY 10110
   W. W. Norton & Company, Ltd., 10 Coptic Street, London WC1A 1PU

5   6   7   8   9   0

Dedicated to my father Angelo, who died of Alzheimer's,
and my mother Mary, who struggles with senile dementia.
So sorry this book and the legions to follow come too late for you.

Foreword
to the First Edition

THE *Psychobiology of Mind-Body Healing* supplies the missing link between the theory that the mind can make a significant difference in dealing with disease and the clinical observations of physicians that the theory works in enough cases to be taken seriously. This book identifies what the medical profession calls "pathways," that is, the way attitudes or emotions are processed by the body in creating physiological or biochemical change. The past ten years have seen extraordinary advances in the knowledge of such pathways—so much so, that the concept of a patient-physician partnership is rapidly becoming a dominant feature in contemporary medicine. In such a partnership the physician brings the best that medical science has to offer and the patient brings his or her resources in the form of a healing system and the confidence and determination to get the best out of what the physician has to offer.

This book provides state-of-the-art information on the interaction of the nervous system, the endocrine system and the immune system. The facts assembled and summarized in this work make it impossible any longer to say that "hard" evidence is lacking to support the belief that what we think and believe can sometimes have a profound effect on our ability to deal with major challenges, whether with respect to disease or the way we function in our daily lives.

Norman Cousins
August 1986

Contents

SECTION I
The Psychobiology of Mind-Body Communication

SECTION II
The Psychobiology of Mind-Body Healing

List of Teaching Tutorials

List of Boxes

List of Tables

List of Figures

Preface

THIS VOLUME BEGAN as a personal quest a few years ago. I wanted to learn something of what everyone was speculating about but no one really seemed to understand: Is it really possible to use mind and mental methods to heal body illness? The quest was intensely personal because, having reached a certain age, I was beginning to experience cardiac symptoms that might have a psychosomatic basis. The quest was also professional because, as a clinical psychologist trained in hypnotherapy by the late Milton H. Erickson, I was getting more and more requests with ever increasing expectations that I should be able to ameliorate all sorts of pain, cancer, arthritis, and a host of other body ills I had hardly ever heard of. Clearly, the trend of the times—the *zeitgeist*—was to explore more about the whole area of mind-body relationships.

By now there are thousands of correlational studies that report statistically significant relationships between attitudes of mind, mood, and "sociocultural" factors with the ills of the body. These studies tend to leave many of us vaguely unsatisfied, however: We all know that correlation is not causation. We really do not understand how something as insubstantial as "mind" can effect something as solid as our own flesh and blood. Where is the connection between mind and body? Can you see it under a microscope? Can you measure it in a test tube?

It was really a struggle that required a lot of dogged determination to plough through the new medical and psychophysiological texts that were buzzing about mind-body relationships, stress, psychoneuroimmunology, neuroendocrinology, molecular genetics, and the neurobiology of memory and learning. These fields all deal with concepts and data that most of us have not even heard of if we have been out of school for more than ten years.

What was most irritating in my investigations was the realization that none of the specialists who seemed to know something ever shared their knowledge with those outside their narrow area of expertise. As I put the facts and implications of the different specialty areas together, I kept coming up with what seemed to be bizarre notions that apparently were based on solid research but no one seemed willing to acknowledge.

For example: Is there really a mind-gene connection? Does mind move not only our emotions and blood pressure, but also the very genes and molecules that are generated within the microscopic cells of our body? Is there any real evidence for this? Well, if you push any endocrinologist hard enough, he/she will admit that, "Yes, it is really true!" Under "mental" stress, the limbic-hypothalamic system in the brain converts the neural messages of mind into the neurohormonal "messenger molecules" of the body. These, in turn, can direct the endocrine system to produce steroid hormones that can reach into the nucleus of different cells of the body to modulate the expression of genes. These genes then direct the cells to produce the various molecules that will regulate metabolism, growth, activity level, sexuality, and the immune response in sickness and health. There really is a mind-gene connection! Mind ultimately does modulate the creation and expression of the molecules of life!

Knowing that mind-body communication and healing involve a real process that can be seen and measured, the next question becomes, "How do we learn to utilize these natural processes of mind-body communication to facilitate our emotional and physical well-being? These processes of mind-body communication usually function autonomously on an unconscious level. When things are going well for us, mind-body healing takes place all by itself, without our having to give it a thought. When things are going badly for us, however, problems in the natural flow of mind-body communication—illness and symptoms—also happen all by themselves!

Can we learn to correct these malfunctioning mind-body patterns to facilitate our own healing and health when things are going badly for us? I'd like to believe that the explorations and approaches developed in this book are a significant step in learning to utilize our natural processes of mind-body communication for self-healing, just when we need it.

While much of the material of this book comes from historical and modern methods of therapeutic hypnosis, it should be recognized that the new approaches to mind-body healing developed herein are not limited to the formal induction of hypnosis or trance. Since the inception of hypnosis more than 200 years ago, it has been impossible to find general agreement among professionals on just exactly what hypnosis is. No definition or empirical test has ever been devised to accurately assess whether or not a hypnotic state even exists! It may be that our understanding of the healing inherent in what has been called "hypnosis" or "therapeutic trance" will continue to change as long as our conceptions of consciousness and the nature of mind continue to evolve. These processes of healing are a natural function of whatever mind, imagination, and life are.

This means that the psychobiological perspective and approaches to mind-body healing developed in this book can be used by therapists of any school or theoretical persuasion. These approaches are designed to supplement the therapeutic methodology of all health workers, whatever their fields of expertise. What this book offers is a broader frame of reference, a more effective language for accessing and facilitating the natural processes of healing that are an inherent characteristic of life itself. There is thus nothing fixed or final about these approaches; they are but steppingstones on a path of greater health and self-facilitation that will continue for as long as we are here to pursue it.

*****

The ever-increasing growth rate of research publications in the area of mind-body healing since the first edition of this book seven years ago is leading to profound changes in the ways we view ourselves. Information is rapidly becoming the common theme uniting physics, biology, psychology, sociology, and medicine; new views of the nature of life and healing as the evolution and flow of information are restructuring the scientific foundations of human knowledge.

We are still in the kindergarten of our understanding of these revolutionary changes. This book, more than ever, is a call for further exploration. While we are excited by all the new possibilities that are becoming available to us, we can now see with breathtaking clarity just how far off the mark all previous paradigms and methods of mind-body healing were. This must lead us to modesty about where we are now and what we believe we can actually accomplish at this time. As yet there are no methods of mind-body healing that have entirely satisfactory scientific documentation. Indeed, a major purpose of this second edition is to point out possibilities for more effective research and practice in our current daily work and better preparation for the future.

Ernest Lawrence Rossi
Malibu, 1993

Acknowledgments

I EXTEND THANKFUL appreciation to my colleagues for the support and feedback they have provided during the development of this volume:

Jeanne Achterberg
Jeffrey Auerback
Ira Black
Kenneth Bowers
Peter Brown
Kristina Erickson
Dabney Ewin
Stephen Gilligan
Robert Glaser
Melvin Gravitz
James Hall
Ernest Hilgard
Patrick Jichaku
Brian Lippincott

David Lloyd
Camillo Loriedo
Darlene Osowiec
Joyce Mills
Karl Pribram
Shirley Sanders
George Solomon
Carol Sommer
Tom Stonier
Lydia Temoshok
Lewis Wolberg
Sandra Wooten
Michael Yapko
Jeffrey K. Zeig

A special note of thanks to Frank Laughlin of desktopLAB for his clear and accurate medical artwork; and to Susan Barrows Munro, whose enthusiasm, support, and skill have made possible the rapid publication of this volume.

SECTION I

The Psychobiology of Mind-Body Communication

1

The Placebo Response:
A Rejected Cornerstone of
Mind-Body Healing

SOME INTERESTING STORIES have been told over and over again because they express truths that our thinking minds can understand in no other way. This certainly is the case with the many folktales, both ancient and modern, of how unexpected illness and "miracle cures" have taken place. Modern science tends to reject these anecdotal accounts as unreliable or, at best, as mere examples of the "placebo response": The person gets better only because of a cultural belief or suggestion that deludes everyone into thinking healing took place. The placebo response is rejected as a "nuisance factor" that no one understands; it is unreliable and therefore unreal. Let us begin this chapter by retelling a few of these healing tales—the ones reported by highly regarded medical experts—to learn if we can discern a common denominator in them. Perhaps it will turn out that the placebo response has been, in fact, the rejected cornerstone of what could become a practical approach to building a new understanding of mind-body communication and healing.

THE LIKABLE MR. WRIGHT: CANCER AND THE IMMUNE SYSTEM

One of my earliest teachers in these mysteries of mind and body was old Bruno Klopfer, a short, powerfully built gnome of a man who was so short-sighted he had to hold a book right up to his nose in order to read the print. His eyeglasses magnified his eyes to such a degree that I was usually too stupefied to say anything to him. Bruno was reputed to have been sort of a minor genius with the Rorschach Inkblot test, and he had written a standard three-volume work in the field. Yet his humble manner gave no hint of his interpretive wizardry, which went well beyond what he was able to write and teach.

Bruno's civility and perfect manners were a natural endowment from his European background; he was always poised to listen fully when anyone, particularly a student, was speaking. I would sometimes steal a long, sideward glance at him during the fireside seminars he organized for Jungian analysts in training on the California coast at Asilomar during the early 1960s. Yet always, it seemed, behind his outward attention, there was another part of him far, far away, communing with who-knows-what levels of imagination and wisdom. If he caught you looking at him, he would immediately "come back" with only the slightest eyeblink and a wan, collegial smile.

One of Bruno's well-documented feats was his ability to distinguish between the Rorschach records of patients who had rapid versus slowly progressing cancers. In his Presidential Address to the Society of Projective Techniques in 1957, he tried to impart something of his skills in this area by presenting his views on the psychological variables in human cancer. As I said, he was a humble man, so instead of talking about his successes, he chose to present a detailed case history of one of his failures. This was the case of the likable Mr. Wright, who so intrigued Bruno that he spoke of him often. I believe this case meant something important to that wise part of Bruno that was so often far away. I will therefore present it here, exactly as he published it. The original report on Mr. Wright was written by one of his personal physicians, Dr. Philip West, a reliable observer who played an important part in the story (Klopfer, 1957, pp. 337–339).

> Mr. Wright had a generalized far advanced malignancy involving the lymph nodes, lymphosarcoma. Eventually the day came when he developed resistance to all known palliative treatments. Also, his increasing anemia precluded any intensive efforts with X-rays or nitrogen mustard, which might otherwise have been attempted. Huge tumor masses the size of oranges were in the neck, axillas, groin, chest and abdomen. The spleen and liver were enormous. The thoracic duct was obstructed, and between 1 and 2 liters of milky fluid had to be drawn from his chest every other day. He was taking oxygen by mask frequently, and our impression was that he was in a terminal state, untreatable, other than to give sedatives to ease him on his way.
>
> In spite of all this, Mr. Wright was not without hope, even though his doctors most certainly were. The reason for this was that the new drug that he had expected to come along and save the day had already been reported in the newspapers! Its name was "Krebiozen" (subsequently shown to be a useless, inert preparation).

Then he heard in some way that our clinic was to be one of a hundred places chosen by the Medical Association for evaluation of this treatment. We were allotted supplies of the drug sufficient for treating 12 selected cases. Mr. Wright was not considered eligible, since one stipulation was that the patient must not only be beyond the point where standard therapies could benefit, but *also* must have a life expectancy of at least three, and preferably six, months. He certainly didn't qualify on the latter point, and to give him a prognosis of more than two weeks seemed to be stretching things.

However, a few days later, the drug arrived, and we began setting up our testing program which, of course, did *not* include Mr. Wright. When he heard we were going to begin treatment with Krebiozen, his enthusiasm knew no bounds, and as much as I tried to dissuade him, he begged so hard for this "golden opportunity," that against my better judgment, and against the rules of the Krebiozen committee, I decided I would have to include him.

Injections were to be given three times weekly, and I remember he received his first one on a Friday. I didn't see him again until Monday and thought as I came to the hospital he might be moribund or dead by that time, and his supply of the drug could then be transferred to another case.

What a surprise was in store for me! I had left him febrile, gasping for air, completely bedridden. Now, here he was, walking around the ward, chatting happily with the nurses, and spreading his message of good cheer to any who would listen. Immediately I hastened to see the others who had received their first injection at the same time. No change, or change for the worse, was noted. Only in Mr. Wright was there brilliant improvement. The tumor masses had melted like snowballs on a hot stove, and in only these few days, they were half their original size! This is, of course, far more rapid regression than the most radio-sensitive tumor could display under heavy X-ray given every day. And we already knew his tumor was no longer sensitive to irradiation. Also, he had had no other treatment outside of the single useless "shot."

This phenomenon demanded an explanation, but not only that, it almost insisted that we open our minds to learn, rather than to try to explain. So, the injections were given three times weekly as planned, much to the joy of the patient, but much to our bewilderment. Within 10 days [Mr. Wright] was able to be discharged from his "death-bed," practically all signs of his disease having vanished in this short time. Incredible as it sounds, this "terminal" patient, gasping his last breath through an oxygen mask, was now not only breathing normally, and fully active, he took off in his plane and flew at 12,000 feet with no discomfort!

This unbelievable situation occurred at the beginning of the "Krebiozen" evaluation, but within two months, conflicting reports began to appear in the news, all of the testing clinics reporting no results. At the same time, the originators of the treatment were still blindly contradicting the discouraging facts that were beginning to emerge.

This disturbed our Mr. Wright considerable as the weeks wore on. Although he had no special training, he was, at times, reasonably logical and scientific in his thinking. He began to lose faith in his last hope which so far had been life-saving and left nothing to be desired. As the reported results became increasingly dismal, his faith waned, and after two months of practically perfect health, he relapsed to his original state, and became very gloomy and miserable.

But here I saw the opportunity to *double-check* the drug and maybe, too, find out how the quacks can accomplish the results that they claim (and many of their claims are well substantiated). Knowing something of my patient's innate optimism by this time, I deliberately took advantage of him. This was for purely scientific reasons, in order to perform the perfect control experiment which could answer all the perplexing questions he had brought up. Furthermore, this scheme could not harm him in any way, I felt sure, and there was nothing I knew anyway that could help him.

When Mr. Wright had all but given up in despair with the recrudescence of his disease, in spite of the "wonder-drug" which had worked so well at first, I decided to take the chance and play the quack. So deliberately lying, I told him not to believe what he read in the papers, the drug was really most promising after all. "What then," he asked, "was the reason for his relapse?" "Just because the substance deteriorated on standing," I replied, "a new superrefined, double-strength product is due to arrive tomorrow which can more than reproduce the great benefits derived from the original injections."

The news came as a great revelation to him, and Mr. Wright, as ill as he was, became his optimistic self again, eager to start over. By delaying a couple of days before the "shipment" arrived, his anticipation of salvation had reached a tremendous pitch. When I announced that the new series of injections was about to begin, he was almost ecstatic and his faith was very strong.

With much fanfare, and putting on quite an act (which I deemed permissible under the circumstances), I administered the first injection of the doubly potent, *fresh* preparation—consisting of *fresh water* and nothing more. The results of this experiment were quite unbelievable to us at the time, although we must have had some suspicion of the remotely possible outcome to have even attempted it at all.

Recovery from his second near-terminal state was even more dramatic than the first. Tumor masses melted, chest fluid vanished, he became ambulatory, and even went back to flying again. At this time he was certainly the picture of health. The water injections were continued, since they worked such wonders. He then remained symptom-free for over two months. At this time the final AMA announcement appeared in the press—"nationwide tests show Krebiozen to be a worthless drug in treatment of cancer."

Within a few days of this report, Mr. wright was readmitted to the hospital *in extremis*. His faith was now gone, his last hope vanished, and he succumbed in less than two days.

Bruno Klopfer's summary of Mr. Wright's personality as revealed in his Rorschach record is as follows (Klopfer, 1957, p. 339):

> Mr. Wright's Rorschach record was obtained before his transformation from optimism to pessimism took place. It reflects the picture of a personality with what I called previously a "floating ego organization." This is reflected in his actual behavior and the great ease with which he followed first the suggestion of the drug advertisement and later on the deliberate experimentally motivated suggestion of his doctor without any sign of defensiveness or even criticalness. His ego was simply floating along and therefore left all available vital energy free to produce a response to the cancer treatment which seemed nothing short of miraculous.
>
> Unfortunately this situation could not last since it was not reinforced by any deep-rooted personality center with a long-range point of view which could have counteracted the catastrophic effect of his disappointment about the drug. To use a symbolic analogy, while he was floating along on the surface of the water under the influence of his optimistic auto-suggestion, he was transformed into a heavy stone and sank to the bottom without any resistance at the moment when the powers of this suggestion expired.

The case of Mr. Wright all too vividly illustrates the hope and failure of our attempts at mind-body communication and healing as they currently exist. We don't understand yet all the important factors in any individual situation, and we have only the vaguest ideas about how to facilitate mind-body healing in a *reliable* manner. Yet, we do know considerably more about it today than 30 years ago when Mr. Wright showed his doctors the power of optimism.

We know today, for example, that growth of some cancers can be controlled by the person's immune system; if you can improve the immune system, it can destroy the cancer. Obviously, Mr. Wright's immune system must have been activated by his belief in a cure. The incredible rapidity of his healing also suggests that his autonomic and endocrine systems must have been responsive to suggestion, enabling him to mobilize his blood system with such amazing efficiency to remove the toxic fluids and waste products of the fast diminishing cancer. As we shall learn later in this book, we now know a lot more about the "limbic-hypothalamic system" of the brain as the major mind-body connector modulating the biological activity of the autonomic, endocrine, and immune systems in response to mental suggestion and beliefs. In summary, Mr. Wright's experience tells us that it was his *total belief in the efficacy* of the worthless drug, Krebiozen, that mobilized a healing placebo response by activating *all* these major systems of mind-body communication and healing. But we are getting ahead of ourselves. First, let me tell you a story about another one of my teachers.

FRANZ ALEXANDER'S POSITIVE INTERPRETATIONS:
CONSCIOUSNESS, THE HYPOTHALAMUS,
AND THE ENDOCRINE SYSTEM

Franz Alexander, who was a world leader in psychosomatic medicine, made pioneering efforts to relate psychoanalysis to the physiology of the body (Alexander 1939/1984). He taught those of us who were lucky enough to be his students that it wasn't enough to simply understand and analyze patients. He had an inspired way of phrasing Freudian interpretations in a positive manner in order to evoke confidence, belief, and the placebo response as a natural form of mind-body healing.

Alexander was truly a master in his understanding of the relations between personality, emotional conflict, and the endocrine system. Like Klopfer, he was a gift to America, trained in the classical European intellectual tradition. Alexander was a patrician type, with beautifully tailored suits and well manicured fingernails. Those fingernails—they would occasionally drum silently on the conference table while a colleague droned on somewhere in the room. It didn't matter to Alexander; he also had the gift of quietly slipping into his own inner vision quest while apparently remaining with the rest of us who were stumbling about on the outside.

Alexander's recognition of the positive aspects of mind-body adaptations to even the most difficult environmental stressors is indicated by the following clinical examples of thyrotoxicosis (hyperthyroidism, or overactivity of the thyroid gland). In Alexander's time it was already well known that the thyroid gland was a part of the endocrine system that produces hormones that regulate metabolism and growth. Today we know that all hormones function as *messenger molecules* that carry information from one part of the body to another. Many of these messenger molecules also modulate psychological processes such as memory, learning, behavior, and personality, along with the biology of metabolism and growth. From our modern understanding of this *double duty of hormonal messenger molecules—the simultaneous regulation of the biological and psychological processes—*Alexander's case histories make even more sense than when they were first published two generations ago. Here are a few that show how early life stress can overstimulate the thyroid gland to produce a precocious though precarious sort of psychological maturity (Alexander, 1950, pp. 178–181):

Threat to security in childhood is a very common finding, both in neurotics and in healthy individuals. Characteristic of patients with thyrotoxicosis is their manner of handling this insecurity. Because of the external circumstances described above, these patients cannot overcome their anxiety by turning to their parents for help. Their dependent needs are constantly frustrated by fate or by parental attitudes, by loss of one or both parents, or by parental rejection, as well as by conflicts of more complex nature which involve guilt. Since they are frustrated in their dependent needs, they make a desperate attempt to identify themselves prematurely with one of the parents, usually the mother. ("If I cannot have her, I must become like her, so that I can dispense with her.") This precocious identification is beyond their physiological and psychological capacity and results in a persistent struggle to master the anxiety and insecurity by a pseudo self-reliance.

. . . Examples of premature need for self-sufficiency, manifested in active participation in the support of the family or in taking care of younger siblings, follow:

B.R., a 13-year-old white girl, is described by the mother as a "little old lady" because she is so prematurely grownup, obedient, and reliable. She learned to cook when she was six and has cooked and helped with the housework ever since. Whenever her mother became ill, she swept and cleaned the house and took care of the whole family. She acted as second mother to her younger brother.

H.D., a 35-year-old single man, the last of eight children, is the only surviving male. Two older brothers died at ages ten and three respectively, and one brother died at home one week after birth when the patient was two. His father was a puritanical man who was harsh and impersonal to hide his own weakness and insecurity. He was apparently demonstrative of affection and fondled his children as long as they were helpless infants but demanded adult behavior as soon as they were able to walk and talk. The mother was depreciated by the father because she had had an illegitimate child in her adolescence (patient's oldest sister) and was married "out of pity" by the patient's father. She was unable to stand up to the father and during the patient's infancy worked in the family store for several years. The father prevented the mother as well as the older sisters from giving the patient much attention. After the patient entered the first grade, his father insisted that no one read him the funny papers any more because he should learn to read for himself. Constant pressure was brought to bear on him to behave like an adult and yet he was constantly restricted in the active pursuit of his interests.

E.B., a 24-year-old single colored woman, was a prodigy and progressed rapidly in her school years. She was extremely conscientious, never truant. Her mother was a teacher and "a very intelligent and beautiful woman." The patient was obviously competing with her but never expressed her hostility openly. When her mother became ill, the patient took over the responsibility for her two younger sisters and assumed the function of mother toward them. She supported them financially even during her college years. She has always been self-sufficient and extremely ambitious and has controlled or repressed most of her feminine desires in order to reach her intellectual goals.

Alexander recognized that mental stress somehow interacted with the hypothalamus, which in turn stimulated the entire endocrine system via the pituitary and thyroid. The hypothalamus was the bridge between *psyche* and *soma*, and perhaps a mediator of consciousness itself. In Alexander and French's edited volume, Grinker quotes with approval Ingham's (1938) view of the situation (1948, p. 70):

> The neurologic concept of consciousness is that it is a state of activity of the entire nervous system, and in particular of the brain, which varies quantitatively from the maximum degree of mental action to complete inactivity, as in coma or general surgical anesthesia. Although all parts of the brain may contribute to the mental processes during consciousness, mental activity of all kinds appears to depend on the normal functioning of groups of neurons in the primitive diencephalon [i.e., the hypothalamus]. The normal cycles of sleeping and waking are evidences of the physiologic activity of this mechanism. As it would appear that energy liberated in the diencephalon is essential for the activation of all the rest of the nervous system so far as psychologic phenomena are concerned, it may be postulated that the "center" of consciousness is located in this region, and much clinical and experimental evidence supports this view. It is surely not accidental that other primitive functions of the nervous system related to the vegetative processes, instincts, and emotions have been found to be dependent on structures in the basal region of the brain in close proximity to those postulated as the center of consciousness. The application of this concept of consciousness to psychiatry seems obvious, since quantitative variations of consciousness are manifested in disturbances of behavior in terms of intelligence, emotions, and instinctive action.

Although these words may sound a bit antiquated, they are a prescient recognition of our current understanding of the cyclic or wave nature of mind-body communication and healing that is mediated by the biological clocks of the limbic-hypothalamic system that pulsate the flow of our hormonal messenger molecules throughout the day. I will document this new view with recent research in chronobiology, the biology of time (Lloyd & Rossi, 1992a & b), throughout this volume. This will lead us to a new psychobiological conception of "consciousness as a process of self-reflective information transduction" mediated by the messenger molecules of the mind-body.

Alexander had a high regard for the physiologist Walter Cannon who did related research in psychosomatic medicine and the psychobiological basis of the seemingly strange phenomenon of "voodoo death." As we shall see, this is another stress related psychobiological process where consciousness plays a crucial role in bridging the flow of information between a negative psychosocial suggestion, being cast under a "spell," and the excessive activation of the hormonal messenger molecules of the limbic-hypothalamic system that actually can result in death.

VOODOO DEATH AND LIFE!
THE "GIVING-UP" COMPLEX THE AUTONOMIC NERVOUS SYSTEM

Walton Cannon, who was regarded as one of the most creative and authoritative medical physiologists of his day, tells the following stories of voodoo death and recovery (1957, pp. 183–184):

> Dr. S. M. Lambert of the Western Pacific Health Service of the Rockefeller Foundation wrote to me that on several occasions he had seen evidence of death from fear. In one case there was a startling recovery. At a Mission at Mona Mona in North Queensland were many native converts, but on the outskirts of the Mission was a group of non-converts including one Nebo, a famous witch doctor. The chief helper of the missionary was Rob, a native who had been converted. When Dr. Lambert arrived at the Mission he learned that Rob was in distress and that the missionary wanted him examined. Dr. Lambert made the examination, and found no fever, no complaint of pain, no symptoms or signs of disease. He was impressed, however, by the obvious indications that Rob was seriously ill and extremely weak. From the missionary he learned that Rob had had a bone pointed at him by Nebo and was convinced that in consequence he must die. Thereupon Dr. Lambert and the missionary went for Nebo, threatened him sharply that his supply of food would be shut off if anything happened to Rob and that he and his people would be driven away from the Mission. At once Nebo agreed to go with them to see Rob. He leaned over Rob's bed and told the sick man that it was all a mistake, a mere joke—indeed, that he had not pointed a bone at all. The relief, Dr. Lambert testifies, was almost instantaneous; that evening Rob was back at work, quite happy again and in full possession of his physical strength.

And a less fortunate outcome:

> Dr. Lambert . . . wrote to me concerning the experience of Dr. P. S. Clarke with Kanakas working on the sugar plantations of North Queensland. One day a Kanaka came to his hospital and told him he would die in a few

days because a spell had been put upon him and nothing could be done to counteract it. The man and been known by Dr. Clarke for some time. He was given a very thorough examination, including an examination of the stool and the urine. All was found normal, but as he lay in bed he gradually grew weaker. Dr. Clarke called upon the foreman of the Kanakas to come to the hospital to give the man assurance, but on reaching the foot of the bed, the foreman leaned over, looked at the patient, and then turned to Dr. Clarke saying, "Yes, doctor, close up him he die" (i.e., he is nearly dead). The next day, at 11 o'clock in the morning, he ceased to live.

Cannon (1942, 1963) concluded that voodoo death was due to a heightened and prolonged exposure to the emotional stress of believing one was under the witch doctor's spell. The actual physiological cause was an overactivated sympathetic nervous system. Cannon believed that voodoo death was possible only because of the "profound ignorance and insecurity" of native populations who lived "in a haunted world." In a more recent study in our own society of the problem of "sudden and rapid death during psychological stress," Engel (1971) came to a similar conclusion in ascribing death to "rapid shifts between sympathetic and parasympathetic cardiovascular effects." Engel believed this "biological emergency pattern" (1968) becomes fatal when the person feels unable to cope and has lost all expectation that there will be any change or help from any other source. The person dies because of an acute "giving-up-given-in" complex. In a recent review of this area, Hahn (1985) describes the relation between voodoo death, the autonomic nervous system, and the selection of native healers as follows (p. 182):

> Lex (1974) similarly explains the pathogenesis of voodoo death and the therapy of curing rituals in terms of three stages of "tuning" of the sympathetic and parasympathetic processes of the autonomic nervous system. "Suggestion" passes a lowered threshold of analytic judgment to effect what is suggested. Lex also explains the common requirement of traditional medical systems that healers have suffered the conditions that they come to treat: Their prior illness gives these healers first-hand acquaintance with and sensitivity to the vagaries of the autonomic nervous system.

As we shall see in the successive chapters of this volume, the autonomic nervous system with its two branches, the sympathetic (which activates heart rate, respiration, blood pressure, tension, etc.) and the parasympathetic (with generally relaxing effects opposite to the sympathetic system), is, indeed, one of the major systems of mind-body communication and the placebo response in illness or healing. Many messenger molecules of the autonomic nervous system such as adrenaline are now know to encode *state-dependent memory, learning, and behavior* (SDMLB) during biological and psychological emergencies. In Chapter 3 we will outline how recent research in state-dependent memory, mood, and emotions can account for the amnesias and psychosomatic symptoms associated with traumatic life experiences. This new understanding will help us generate new psychotherapeutic approaches for the recovery of traumatically "dissociated memory" as well as the healing of the emotional problems and symptoms associated with sexual molestation, multiple personality, and the posttraumatic stress disorders.

The Healing Heart and Mind: Norman Cousins' Positive Emotions

Thus far in this chapter we have illustrated how negative life circumstances and attitudes can lead to illness and death via the mind's modulation of the autonomic, endocrine, and immune systems. Sensitive physicians have always known that the reverse is true as well, and wise observers in most cultures have recognized that a positive frame of mind can have a salutary effect in healing the gravest illness.

No one has done more in current American culture to illustrate this truth with well-documented and poignant examples from his own life than Norman Cousins in his two books, *Anatomy of an Illness* and *The Healing Heart*. Cousins' personal experience with mind-body healing began at the age of ten when he was misdiagnosed and sent to a tuberculosis sanitarium for six months. Left to their own devices, he and some of his fellow patients found a way to a positive attitude and healing, which Cousins describes as follows (1979, pp. 155–156):

> What was most interesting to me about that early experience was that patients divided themselves into two groups: those who were confident they would beat back the disease and be able to resume normal lives, and those who resigned themselves to a prolonged and even fatal illness. Those of use who held to the optimistic view became good friends, involved ourselves in creative activities, and had little to do with the patients who had resigned themselves to the worst. When newcomers arrived at the hospital, we did our best to recruit them before the bleak brigade went to work.
>
> I couldn't help being impressed with the fact that the boys in my group had a far higher percentage of "discharged as cured" outcomes than the kids in the other group. Even at the age of ten, I was being philosophically

conditioned; I became aware of the power of the mind in overcoming disease. The lessons I learned about hope at that time played an important part in my complete recovery [as an adult] and in the feelings I have had since about the preciousness of life.

This early life experience with the therapeutic value of optimistic views and creative activities led to a lifetime of accomplishment as the editor of one of America's leading periodicals, *The Saturday Review*, and later as Adjunct Professor at UCLA's School of Medicine. Cousins' carefully documented recovery (1979) from a serious arthritic and rheumatoid-like collagen disease of the connective tissues (diagnosed as *ankylosing spondylitis*) by treating himself with generous, positive doses of good humor (primarily in the form of old *Marx Brothers* movies and reruns of Allen Funt's *Candid Camera*) is becoming part of a new folklore of healing. His recovery from a heart attack involving both myocardial infarction and congestive heart failure (Cousins, 1983) was discussed by the four heart specialists and physicians most closely associated with the case. Among the factors they described as significant in Cousins' self-therapeutic attitude are:

1) The absence of panic in the face of the obviously grave symptoms of his heart attack. (Such panic is part of the emotional syndrome that kills victims of voodoo death.)
2) His unshakable confidence in his body's ability to utilize its own wisdom in facilitating healing.
3) An irrepressible good humor and cheerfulness that created an auspicious, healing environment for himself, as well as for the entire hospital staff.
4) Taking a full share of responsibility for his recovery by establishing a close "partner relationship" with his physicians.
5) His focus on creativity and meaningful goals, which made recovery worth fighting for and life worth living.

Cousins summarized his experiences of personal healing by emphasizing that positive attitudes and emotions can affect the biochemistry of the body to facilitate rejuvenation and health. Positive attitudes and emotions are the essence of well-being and the placebo response. As he aptly stated, "The placebo is the doctor who resides within" (Cousins, 1979, p. 69). This statement reflects a profound change from the traditional view of the placebo as a "nuisance factor."

Let us now take a closer look at what recent research on the placebo response can tell us about mind-body healing.

THE 55% PLACEBO CONNECTION

During the same time period when the anecdotal accounts of mind-body healing described previously were being assembled by early leaders in the field of psychosomatic medicine, more scientifically objective double-blind studies of clinical pain were being conducted. (In double-blind studies, neither doctors nor patients know who is getting real medication and who is getting inert placebos.) Beecher's analysis and review (1959) of 15 double-blind studies concluded that 35% of the patients with a wide variety of postoperative pain found significant relief with placebos (inert medication or "sugar pills"). In a more recent review (Evans, 1985), these conclusions were confirmed with 11 more double-blind studies in which it was found that 36% of the patients received at least 50% of pain relief from placebos. The most carefully controlled clinical studies of placebos with humans thus consistently find that about one-third of the patients receive more than 50% relief. Under the right circumstances, the medically inert placebo is somehow able to facilitate belief and expectation on the psychological level. This accesses and activates very real mind-body healing mechanisms that some now call the "placebo response."

The placebo response is not limited to pain relief. It has been found to be a mind-body healing factor in all of the following illnesses (items 1 through 3), therapeutic procedures (items 4 through 6), and even in the expectation of getting help (item 7):

1) Hypertension, stress, cardiac pain, blood cell counts, headaches, pupillary dilation (*implicating the autonomic nervous system*);
2) Adrenal gland secretion, diabetes, ulcers, gastric secretion and motility, colitis, oral contraceptives, menstrual pain, thyrotoxicosis (*implicating the endocrine system*);
3) The common cold, fever, vaccines, asthma, multiple sclerosis, rheumatoid arthritis, warts, cancer (*implicating the immune system*);
4) Surgical treatments (e.g., for angina pectoris or "heart pain");
5) Biofeedback instrumentation and medical devices of all sorts;
6) Psychological treatments such as conditioning (systematic desensitization) and perhaps all forms of psychotherapy;
7) Making an appointment to see a doctor.

In a review of these studies, most investigators (White, Tursky, & Schwartz, 1985) conclude that the placebo response, which has been demonstrated across such a wide range of problems and treatment modalities, must be a "true *general* ingredient in *all clinical* situations" (Wickramasekera, 1985). One of the most informative of these recent studies has been written by Fredrick Evans, a psychologist who has done a great deal of original experimental work in this area. Evans has brought together a mass of data to answer two basic questions about how the placebo response functions in a variety of medical situations (1985, p. 215):

1) How powerful is the placebo response in terms of its clinical effi-cacy?
2) To what extent is the placebo response mediated by verbal and nonverbal expectational factors?

To deal with the first question about the clinical efficacy of the placebo response, Evans studied the data on double-blind studies of drug anal-gesia, since these were the most numerous and carefully controlled examples of experimental research. As is indicated in Box 1, the efficacy of an unknown analgesic is determined by calculating an index of drug efficiency. *There is a remarkably consistent degree of placebo response, averag-ing about 55% of the therapeutic effect for all the analgesic drugs studied.*

That is, while morphine obviously has more potent analgesic effects than aspirin, about 55% of the potency of *each* is a placebo response. As Evans describes it (1985, p. 223):

> In other words, the effectiveness of a placebo compared to standard doses of different analgesic drugs under double-blind circumstances seems to be relatively constant. This is indeed a rather remarkable and unique characteris-tic for any therapeutic agent! The effectiveness of the placebo is proportional to the apparent effectiveness of the active analgesic agent.
>
> It is worth noting that this 56% effectiveness ratio is not limited to compar-ing placebo with analgesic drugs. It is also found in double-blind studies of nonpharmacological insomnia treatment techniques (58% from 13 studies) and psychotropic drugs for the treatment of depression such as tricyclics (59% from 93 studies reviewed by Morris & Beck, 1974) and lithium (62% from 13 studies reviewed in Marini, Sheard, Bridges & Wagner, 1976). Thus, it appears that placebo is about 55–60% as effective as active medications, irrespective of the potency of these active medications.

The implication of these findings is that *there may be a 55% placebo response in many, if not all, healing procedures.* Such a consistent degree of placebo response also suggests *there is a common, underlying mechanism*

BOX 1 Comparing Efficiency of Placebo and Analgesics

Illustration of Calculation of Index of Drug Efficiency for Evaluating
Placebo Efficiency Compared to Analgesic Drugs

Index of analgesic drug efficiency:

$$\frac{\text{Reduction in pain with unknown drug}}{\text{Reduction in pain with known analgesic (typically morphine)}}$$

Pain criterion:

Reduction in pain by 50% of initial level over drug level.
or
change in pain of 50% on rating scale (typically 10- or 5-point)

Index of placebo efficiency for morphine:
(averaged across six double-blind non-crossover-design studies)

$$\frac{\text{Reduction in pain with placebo}}{\text{Reduction in pain with morphine}} = 56\%$$

Index of Placebo Efficiency Comparing Placebo with Morphine,
Aspirin, Darvon, and Zomax (Derived from Available Single-Trial
Double-Blind Published Studies)

Number of double-blind studies	Placebo efficiency for	%
6	Morphine	56
9	Aspirin	54
2	Darvon	54
2	Codeine	56
3	Zomax	55

Used by permission from Evans (1985).

*or process that accounts for mind-body communication and healing, regardless
of the problem, symptom, or disease.*

This brings us to Evans' second question about the extent to which
the placebo response is mediated by verbal and nonverbal expectational
factors. He discusses three factors that have been found by investigators
to mediate the placebo response: (1) suggestion (or hypnosis); (2) anxi-

ety reduction; and (3) the expectancy aroused by cultural or medical belief systems. It has been assumed in the past the *placebo* and *suggestion* were essentially the same sort of phenomenon. The surprising conclusion from a variety of well-controlled experimental studies comparing the placebo response with hypnotic suggestion, however, is that there is no correlation or relationship between them (Evans, 1977, 1981; McGlashan, Evans, & Orne, 1969; Orne, 1974). During experimental conditions in the laboratory, hypnotic suggestion and the placebo response appeared to operate by different mechanisms or levels of response. One way of understanding the difference is to say that hypnotic responsiveness is a specific, innate ability and skill that involves the capacity to access or change one's own patterns of mind-body communication by the use of psychological suggestion alone. The placebo response, in contrast, is a more general, automatic mind-body communication that utilizes physical treatment methods to reduce anxiety and facilitate healing by marshalling powerful cultural expectations and beliefs in the treatment method. Other researchers, to be discussed in the next chapter, believe that while hypnotic and placebo responses appear to be different in the way they are facilitated on a social-cultural level, they are both mediated by the messenger molecules mediating communication between mind and body.

The issues raised in this section are complex. There are many ways of analyzing the statistical data on the placebo response. According to some estimates the contribution of psychological factors in illness and healing may be closer to 10% for the general population depending on many hidden psychosocial factors and the varying definitions of what a placebo response is (Glaser & Kiecolt-Glaser, 1991; Temoshok & Dreher, 1992). A basic premise of this book is that in the final analysis we will be able to clarify these complexities for a general theory of mind-body healing only when we understand more about the actual pathways of mind-body communication and healing on all levels. For now, it is enough to note that for at least one-third of the population a 55% placebo connection is a consistent healing factor operative with many different drugs, therapeutic procedures, and psychophysiological symptoms and problems. The consistency of this healing response across so many different conditions suggests that it is mediated by a common mechanism or communication link between mind and body. But what, precisely, is the nature of this communication link between mind and body? Our next story as told by Doctor Steven Rosenberg of the National Cancer Institute provides us with a most important clue.

THE NEW PSYCHOIMMUNOLOGY: MIND-BODY MESSENGERS OF THE IMMUNE SYSTEM

In his recent book, *The Transformed Cell*, Steven Rosenberg tells the remarkable story of how early in his training to become a surgeon an apparently bizarre case of spontaneous healing of cancer sent him on a pioneering path of clinical research. The tale begins with his first examination of Mr. DeAngelo's medical chart when he was admitted to the hospital (Rosenberg & Barry, 1992, pp. 14–15).

His chart recounted how, twelve years before, Mr. DeAngelo had walked into the hospital suffering from overall malaise, excessive tiredness and weight loss, and severe abdominal pain. He drank and smoked heavily, consuming three to four fifths of whiskey a week and two packs of cigarettes a day. Reading this, I thought he must have been a hard and troubled man; he seemed less so now. X-rays had revealed a large mass in his stomach. An exploratory laparotomy—abdominal surgery—was performed.

According to the chart, the surgeon discovered a life-threatening condition: a fist-size tumor in the patient's stomach, three smaller tumors on his liver, and suspiciously hardened lymph nodes. All of these findings are typical of advanced cancer. The surgeon's operative note stated that biopsies had been sent to the pathologist, who not only confirmed the diagnosis of cancer but added that the disease seemed particularly aggressive and fast-growing. In fact, tumor had already replaced part of the liver.

To alleviate Mr. DeAngelo's pain, the surgeon removed the largest mass along with two-thirds of his stomach, but left the cancers growing in the liver and elsewhere. Resecting them would have greatly increased the risk of killing him on the operating table in return for very little potential benefit. The cancer had spread so far and was advancing so rapidly that removal of more tumors might not have added to his life expectancy at all, while the strain of the additional surgery might have filled what time he had left with more suffering.

On the basis of the diagnosis, Mr. DeAngelo's case seemed hopeless. He should have died within a few months after the operation. But five months later, at a follow-up visit to the hospital, he was very much alive, had gained twenty pounds, and had returned to work.

Now, twelve years later, here he was again.

This did not seem possible. Among the tens of millions of cancer victims since medicine and science joined hands in precise diagnoses, there had been only four documented cases—not four a year in the United States, but four, ever, in the world—of spontaneous and complete remission of stomach cancer. Mr. DeAngelo had experienced a spontaneous and complete remission of stomach cancer.

Dr. Rosenberg immediately checked the pathology report written twelve years earlier and was able to check the original tissue slides under the microscope to confirm that there had been no mistake; Mr. DeAngelo really had a most aggressive cancer that is usually lethal. Mr. DeAngelo's current medical condition now warranted that he needed an operation to remove his gallbladder. Dr. Rosenberg seized this opportunity to explore DeAngelo's abdomen for any traces of the original cancer. He describes his findings with these words (Rosenberg & Barry, 1992, p. 17):

> A tumor is easy to identify by touch; it is tough, dense, unyielding, unlike the texture of normal tissue. It seems alien even. This man had had several large tumors on his liver twelve years earlier.
>
> There was nothing there.
>
> I repeated by exploration, certain my fingers must somehow have skipped over something, some roughness, some alteration in the texture, some nodule. Nothing. Absolutely nothing. I was excited now and explored the intestines rapidly but thoroughly, feeling about for lymph nodes, feeling for some sign, any sign, of cancer, going over the same area twice, asking the senior resident for his opinion and the knowledge of his fingers.
>
> Neither of us could find any evidence of cancer anywhere.
>
> This man had had a virulent and untreatable cancer that should have killed him quickly. He had received no treatment whatsoever for his disease from us or from anyone else. And he had been cured.
>
> I was fascinated. *How?* This man's body had cured cancer. *How?*

This question of *how* occupied Rosenberg for a quarter of a century and motivated innovative research into the way the immune system protects health by destroying invading bacteria and viruses as well as the body's natural breakdown products and errors at the molecular level. Over the years a picture emerged of how the immune system can even recognize when certain genes that normally regulate growth lose control and allow the unrestrained growth we call cancer to take over the body. Usually, however, a number of the immune system's many different types of cells (such as killer lymphocytes) will then coordinate an attack against the excessively proliferating cells of cancer and destroy them before they can form large tumors. What coordinates this attack? In brief, it is now known that all cells of the immune system communicate with each other with a variety of "messenger molecules" generally called cytokines. Rosenberg found a way of strengthening the patient's immune system by supplying it with more of these messenger molecules.

Initial studies with one messenger molecule called interleukin 2 (IL-2) indicated that it was particularly effective in facilitating the immune system's ability to destroy cancer. The response rate to the administration of IL-2 to terminally ill patients with melanoma (a type of skin cancer) and kidney cancer was about 20%. Of these, only 10% enjoyed a complete disappearance of their cancer. More advanced techniques that combined two types of immune system killer cells (lymphokine-activated killer cells and tumor-infiltrating lymphocytes) with IL-2 raised the recovery rate to 40%. This research continues with ever more sophisticated genetic approaches, most of which involve messenger molecules.

We cannot help but notice that these recovery rates are within the same statistical range found for the placebo response in the previous section. These statistical similarities do not account for criticism of Rosenberg's immunological approach (Anderson, 1992), but in association with the previous cases cited here they raise the obvious question about the possibility that the placebo response may be operating with similar mechanisms. Could the mind-body healing effects of the placebo response be mediated through messenger molecules, such as IL-2 that Rosenberg is using, for a purely medical-biological approach to cancer? Can the body's messenger molecules be accessed and facilitated by the mind methods of psychology as well as the biological methods of medicine? If so, does this mean that messenger molecules are the long-sought bridge between body and mind that could account for the many reports of unexplained holistic healing by faith and imagination? Is Rosenberg's purely biological approach to facilitating the immune system by flooding it with IL-2 messenger molecules on a collaborative course with the new science of *psychoimmunology*?

An affirmative answer to these questions is suggested by the more recent research of Ronald Glaser and Janice Kiecolt-Glaser and their colleagues at the Ohio State University College of Medicine. We have known for some time that psychosocial stress, whatever its source (depression, loss of a loved one, financial problems, etc.), can suppress the immune system but we have not known exactly why. In a series of innovative studies Glaser et al. (1990, in press-a & b) explored the actual mechanisms of this suppression at the molecular-genetic level. They found that when medical students experienced major academic stress during exam week their immune system was suppressed because their IL-2 receptor gene expression was curtailed and consequently the production of their IL-2 messenger molecules was depressed.

Most of these recent developments in Glaser's new approach to psychoimmunology that bridges the gap between mind and gene must be replicated before we can fully appreciate their practical significance for a genuine science of mind-body healing. Once confirmed, however, Glaser's research may provide the first solid molecular-genetic communication link between the purely biological approach of Rosenberg's immunological approach to cancer and the many surprising statistical studies that indicate how positive psychosocial forces such as group psychotherapy can facilitate survival rates with cancer (Spiegel et al., 1989; Spiegel, 1991).

The finding that a messenger molecule such as IL-2 is a common denominator at the molecular-genetic level between biological medicine and psychotherapy has profound theoretical implications. It leads us to *the hypothesis that mind and body are united by messenger molecules, the common communication channel between the emotions, sensations, thoughts, and images of consciousness and the molecular-genetic mechanisms of the body.* If we can fill in all the communication links between words and ideas with the molecular-genetic mechanisms of every cell of the brain and body, then there can be no Cartesian gap between mind and body. We have, for the practical purposes of mind-body healing, found the grand avenue of clinical research that can lead to systematic progress in the borderland between medicine and psychology. For the first time we can make sense of the ancient as well as modern folklore of healing in such apparently diverse circumstances as the naive placebo response of the likeable Mr. Wright, the apparently "spontaneous healing" of Mr. DeAngelo's cancer, the negative expectations of voodoo victims, and the very real healing of stress and traumatic disorders via the positive interpretations of Franz Alexander and Norman Cousins. Each chapter of this book seeks to document another communication pathway between current theory, research, and practice in this newly evolving psychobiological science of mind-body healing.

2

Information Transduction in
Mind-Body Healing and Hypnosis

THE BASIC IDEA of the psychobiology of mind-body healing is that information is the central concept and connecting link between all the sciences, humanities, and clinical arts. Psychology, biology, and physics now have information as their new common denominator. To really understand how this is possible we need to have a clear appreciation of the fact that *all forms of organization on the psychological, physical, and biological levels actually are expressions of information and its transformations* (Stonier, 1990). The atoms in a stone, the genes in every living cell, and the evolving patterns of our personal relationships, families, and governments are all forms of organization in transition and change. The changes we see around us and experiences we sense within can all be understood as the transformations in the organizations of information. The transformations between mind and body are called information transduction.

Transduction refers to the conversion or transformation of matter, energy, and information from one form to another. A windmill transduces wind energy into the mechanical energy of the turning blades. If the mechanical energy of the turning blades is attached to a generator, it is transduced into electrical energy, which can in turn be transduced into light energy by an electric bulb. In the typical clinical application of biofeedback techniques, the biological "energy" of the body's muscle tension can be transduced into the visible "information" of a measuring device that enables the subject to alter his muscle tone. These examples, together with the basic concepts of information, communication and cybernetic theories, have led to a view of all biological life as a system of information transduction.

A history of the evolution of the concept of information transduction

23

TABLE 1 Evolution of the concept of information transduction as the basic problem of psychobiology and mind-body healing

RESEARCHERS	CONCEPT
Bernheim (1886/1957)	Ideosensory and ideomotor reflex converts hypnotic suggestion into body processes.
Selye (1936, 1982)	Transduction of information via the "stress" hormones of the *hypothalamic-pituitary-adrenal axis* is the essential mechanism of psychosomatic problems.
Papez (1937)	Mental experience is transduced into the psychophysiology of emotions by the *limbic-hypothalamic system* and related structures.
Scharrer & Scharrer (1940) Harris (1948)	Central nervous system controls endocrine's hormonal messengers via *hypothalamus*.
Moruzzi & Magoun (1949)	The ascending reticular activating system (ARAS) of the brain stem projects to the *limbic-hypothalamic system* to stimulate wakefulness.
Shannon & Weaver (1949)	Mathematical theory of communication.
Wiener (1948)	Cybernetic view of life as systems of information transduction.
Meyers & Sperry (1953) Sperry (1964)	Consciousness associated with left and right hemispheres which function independently when neural connections are severed between them.
Olds & Milner (1954) Delgado, Roberts, & Miller (1954)	Discovery of reward and punishment centers in the *limbic-hypothalamic system*.
Jouvet (1973, 1975)	"Paradoxical sleep" or dreaming as a process of integrating behavior via cortical and *limbic-hypothalamic system*.
Black (1963, 1969)	Hypnosis can modulate psychophysiological mechanisms of the immune system.
Nauta (1964)	"Fronto-limbic" system integrates "planning" functions of anterior frontal cortex with *limbic-hypothalamic system*.
Delbruck (1970)	Information transduction is the basic problem of psychobiology.
Weiner (1972, 1977)	Psychosomatic problems are a function of mind-body information transduction involving *limbic-hypothalamic*-pituitary system.

(*continued*)

TABLE 1 *Continued*

RESEARCHERS	CONCEPT
Bowers (1977)	An informational approach to hypnosis involves "the transduction of semantic information into a form that is somatically encodable."
Ader (1981)	Psychoneuroimmunological research demonstrates how the *hypothalamus* mediates mind-body communication with immune system.
Mishkin (1982)	Sensory information is stored and integrated with "cross-modal association" areas in the *limbic-hypothalamic system.*
Eigen & Winkler- Oswatitsch (1992) Pribram (1991) Stonier (1990) Wheeler (1990)	Theories of the origin of information in physics, biology, and psychology that are fundamental for mind-body communication.

as the basic problem of psychobiology and hypnosis is summarized in Table 1. For the purposes of this book, it is convenient to begin our survey with the views of Bernheim, who is generally recognized as being one of the "fathers" of therapeutic hypnosis. In the following quotation, Bernheim described his understanding of the essence of hypnotic suggestion as a process of "transforming the idea received into an act" (Bernheim, 1957, pp. 137–138):

> The one thing certain is, that a *peculiar aptitude for transforming the idea received into an act* exists in hypnotized subjects who are susceptible to suggestion. In the normal condition, every formulated idea is questioned by the mind. After being perceived by the cortical centres, the impression extends to the cells of the adjacent convolutions; their peculiar activity is excited; the diverse faculties generated by the gray substance of the brain come into play; the impression is elaborated, registered, and analyzed, by means of a complex mental process, which ends in its acceptance or neutralization; if there is cause, the mind vetoes it. In the hypnotized subject, on the contrary, the transformation of thought into action, sensation, movement, or vision is so quickly and so actively accomplished, that the intellectual inhibition has not time to act. When the mind interposes, it is already an accomplished fact, which is often registered with surprise, and which is confirmed by the fact that it proves to be real, and no intervention can hamper it further. If I

say to the hypnotized subject, "Your hand remains closed," the brain carries out the idea as soon as it is formulated. A reflex is immediately transmitted from the cortical centre, where this idea induced by the auditory nerve is perceived, to the motor centre, corresponding to the central origin of the nerves subserving flexion of the hand;—contracture occurs in flexion. There is, then *exaltation of the ideo-motor reflex excitability, which effects the unconscious transformation of the thought into movement, unknown to the will.*

The same thing occurs when I say to the hypnotized subject, "You have a tickling sensation in your nose." The thought induced through hearing is reflected upon the centre of olfactory sensibility, where it awakens the sensitive memory-image of the nasal itching, as former impressions have created it and left it imprinted and latent. This memory sensation thus resuscitated, may be intense enough to cause the reflex act of sneezing. There is also, then, *exaltation of the ideo-sensorial reflex excitability, which effects the unconscious transformation of the thought into sensation, or into a sensory image.*

In the same way, the visual, acoustic, and gustatory images succeed the suggested idea.

The mechanism of suggestion in general, may then be summed up in the following formula: *increase of the reflex ideo-motor, ideo-sensitive, and ideo-excitability.*

Although Bernheim's words now sound a bit antiquated, he aptly described information transduction as the basic process of therapeutic hypnosis. Indeed, virtually all modern approaches to mind-body communication attempt to facilitate the process of converting words, images, sensations, ideas, beliefs, and expectations into the healing, physiological processes in the body.

After a period of abeyance, modern research in hypnosis was initiated by Hull (1933), Erickson,* and Hilgard (1977), who stimulated a new generation of researchers (Fromm & Shor, 1979; Sheehan & Perry, 1976). These researchers developed methodologies for objective studies that led to an informational approach to understanding hypnotherapeutic phenomena. For example, in his pioneering volume, *Mind and Body* (1969), Stephen Black used a very broad philosophical and experimental approach, guided by information theory, in his investigations of how hypnosis could modulate psychophysiological mechanisms of the immune system. Bowers has summarized the informational view of hypnosis as follows (1977, p. 231);

---

*See all four volumes of *the Collected Papers of Milton H. Erickson on Hypnosis* for a comprehensive presentation of Erickson's hypnosis research spanning five decades (Erickson, 1980).

. . . The tendency to split etiological factors of disease into either psychic or somatic components, though heuristic for many purposes, nevertheless perpetuates, at least implicitly, a mind-body dualism that has defied rational solution for centuries. Perhaps what we need is a new formulation of this ancient problem, one that does not presuppose a formidable gap between the separate "realities" of mind and body.

One way of reformulating the question involves the concept of information. The entire human body can be viewed as an interlocking network of informational systems—genetic, immunological, hormonal, and so on. These systems each have their own codes, and the transmission of information between systems requires some sort of transducer that allows the code of one system, genetic, say, to be translated into the code of another system— for example, immunological.

Now, in mind, with its capacity for symbolizing in linguistic and extra-linguistic forms, can also be regarded as a means for coding processing and transmitting information both intra- and inter-personality. If information processing and transmission is common to both psyche and soma, the mind-body problem might be reformulated as follows: How is information, received and processed at a semantic level, transduced into information that can be received and processed at a somatic level, and vice versa? That sounds like a question that can be more sensibly addressed than the one it is meant to replace. And some knowledgeable people are beginning to ask it. For example, in a discussion section of the New York Academy of Science's Second Conference on Psychophysiological Aspects of Cancer, Jonas Salk commented on a stimulating paper by Shands (1969) as follows: "Human language is a specialized form of communication. You then jumped to the molecular level, and I was glad you did that, because there are parallels in that both express forms of communication. The code needs to be translated . . . "

Unfortunately, we are a long way from being able to understand the complex mechanisms that help to transduce information from a semantic to a somatic level, but some such mechanisms surely exist, since, as we have seen, the selective and specific impact of suggestion on body structure and functioning seems very well supported indeed. And I would like to suggest that the capacity for deep hypnosis is an important variable in this transduction process. We have already shown that the healing potential of suggestions seems to be maximized in persons capable of deep hypnosis.

A great deal of progress has been made in the ten years since these words were written. An approach to answering questions about how hypnosis can facilitate the process of mind-body information transduction will be surveyed in the following sections of this chapter. First we will review evidence for the view that the limbic-hypothalamic system is the major mind-body transducer. Then we will outline how many of the major pathways of brain activity involved with memory, learning, and behavior support the limbic-hypothalamic system in this process of mind-body information transduction.

THE LIMBIC-HYPOTHALAMIC SYSTEM: THE MAJOR MIND-BODY INFORMATION TRANSDUCER

The most significant development in mind-body research began when the young Hans Selye broke through the prejudices of the medical establishment of his day to introduce the psychological idea of *stress* as a factor worthy of study (Selye, 1936, 1976). Selye's lifetime of groundbreaking research culminated in a theory of how mental and/or physical stress is transduced into "psychosomatic problems" by the hormones of the "hypothalamic-pituitary-adrenal axis" of the endocrine system. Selye called this transduction process the "General Adaptation Syndrome." An overview of Selye's General Adaptation Syndrome, updated to emphasize the mind-modulating role of the limbic-hypothalamic system on the autonomic, endocrine, and immune systems, is illustrated in Figure 1. (In addition, Figure 1 provides an overview of the entire process of mind-body information transduction that is presented in greater detail throughout this volume.)

Selye's work was in agreement with the anatomical research of Papez (1937), who demonstrated that mental experience was transduced into the physiological responses characteristic of emotions in a circuit of brain structures that constituted much of what is now called the *limbic-hypothalamic system*. The Scharrers (1940) and Harris (1948) then initiated the exquisitely detailed work which led to the discovery that "secretory cells within the hypothalamus," could function as molecular information transducers by converting the neural impulses that encoded "mind" into the hormonal messenger molecules of the endocrine system that regulated "body." The conversion of these neuronal signals of mind into the messenger molecules of body was called "neuroendocrinal transduction" by Wurtman and Anton-Tay (1969).

The next major breakthrough in understanding the role of the limbic-hypothalamic system in mediating and modulating mind-body communication and behavior came with the discovery of *pleasure (reward) centers* and *pain (punishment) centers*. When miniature electrodes are carefully inserted into certain areas of the hypothalamus (particularly, the medial forebrain bundle and the lateral and ventromedial nuclei*), experimen-

---

*See Figure 5 in Chapter 6.

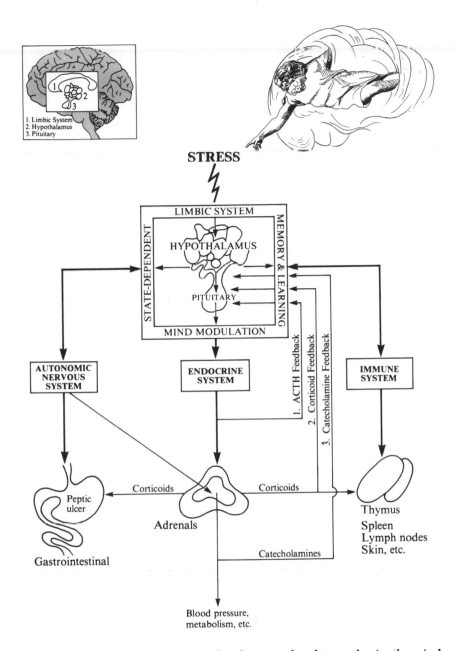

FIGURE 1 Selye's General Adaptation Syndrome updated to emphasize the mind-modulating role of the limbic-hypothalamic system on the autonomic, endocrine, and immune systems. The state-dependent memory and learning theory of therapeutic hypnosis is illustrated by the limbic system "filter" (square box) surrounding the hypothalamus.

tal animals will press a lever up to 15,000 times per hour to give themselves a sense of reward (Olds, 1977; Olds & Milner, 1954). Indeed, the
animals would rather press the lever giving them the good feeling than
eat! On the other hand, placing the electrodes in closely adjacent areas
such as the periventricular structures of the hypothalamus and the thalamus, among others, touches off the centers for pain and punishment
(Delgado, 1969; Delgado, Roberts, & Miller, 1954). To demonstrate the
potency of the punishing and inhibiting centers of pain-controlling behavior, Delgado—with an inimitable élan not seen previously in neuro-
physiologists—actually stood alone in a bull ring with an aggressive
fighting bull. At the moment the bull was about to charge him, Delgado
pushed the button that fired an electrode implanted in the pain centers
of the bull's brain. The bull instantaneously stopped in his tracks, as
the crowd roared its approval of a most dramatic, public demonstration
of mind-body science. These demonstrations of the reward and punishment centers in the limbic-hypothalamic system again suggest why it is
the major center of mind-body information transduction: Pleasure and
pain are the great reinforcers of learning, behavior, and how we experience and express ourselves.

Since it was known that the corticoid hormones from the adrenals
could suppress the immune system, it was supposed that this was the
psychobiological route by which the mental mechanisms of hypnosis
could affect the body's immune system. In a series of incisive studies,
however, Black (1963, 1969; Black & Friedman, 1965) was able to demonstrate that this was not the case. Hypnosis was effective in modulating
the immune system, particularly by inhibiting allergic skin reactions,
but this therapeutic response was mediated by an as yet unknown
mind-body process. This mystery is only now in the process of being
resolved by psychoneuroimmunological research (Ader, 1981), which is
demonstrating how the immune system can communicate directly with
the hypothalamus via its own "messenger molecules," called "immunotransmitters."

By 1970 the physicist Delbruck was able to state that an understanding
of the mechanisms of information transduction was the central problem
of neurobiology. In his monumental survey of psychobiology and human disease, Weiner (1972, 1977) took his inspiration from Delbruck and
explored a number of models of information transduction to determine
which were most appropriate for an understanding of psychosomatic
problems. Weiner recognized the value of therapeutic hypnosis in a
variety of the psychosomatic problems he studied, but concluded that
we still do not know enough about the specific biology of each disease

to determine the exact psychobiological routes of healing. In order to explore what these routes might be, we will review those areas of the brain that funnel their stimuli and information-processing activities into the limbic-hypothalamic system in the next four sections.

THE RETICULAR ACTIVATING SYSTEM: THE AWAKENED, NOVELTY-SEEKING, AND DREAMING MIND

Another line of significant research for understanding mind-body information transduction began with the research of Moruzzi and Magoun (1949). They discovered the ascending reticular activating system (ARAS) in the brain stem, which projects its nerve connections to the limbic-hypothalamic system, thalamus, and widely throughout the cortex to stimulate the brain into wakefulness. The reticular formation has been described as "a state-level structure within the pons and brain stem" (Bloom, Lazerson, & Hofstadter, 1985) that plays an important role in body-mind information transduction: It receives sensory information from all of the body's neural pathways and acts as a "filter," passing on to the brain only the information that is novel or persistent.

It is the brain's ability to wake up, to become alert and attentive to novel patterns of sensory stimuli and information, that enables it to focus its activity on new learning and creativity. The mind's ability to attend to the new has its psychobiological basis in the activity of a cluster of norepinephrine-containing neurons in the locus coeruleus of the pons area of the brain stem. When novel stimuli are received by the locus coeruleus, its neural connections stimulate the onset of brief states of heightened responsiveness in the higher cortical areas of the brain, and in the limbic-hypothalamic center that integrates memory and houses the reward or pleasure mechanisms. In other words, the locus coeruleus transduces novel stimuli into a heightened psychobiological state. Dull, repetitive situations, on the other hand, decrease the activity of the locus coeruleus and lead to relaxation, drowsiness, and sleep. The fact that what is novel and fascinating actually heightens brain activity is a very important, though still generally unappreciated, precondition for all forms of creatively-oriented psychotherapy and mind-body healing experiences. It is one of the fundamental principles used in the language of human facilitation that we will explore in Chapter 5.

The relation between activity in the locus coeruleus and dreaming was discovered by Jouvet (1975). When he destroyed the part of the nucleus locus coeruleus that normally inhibits motor activity during dreaming, he found that cats would act out their dreams in the form of what he called "pseudohallucinatory" behavior. From these observations, he developed an interesting theory of dreaming as a process of integrating genetic or innate behavior (Jouvet, 1973, 1975) that has become the psychobiological basis for more recent theories of dreaming as an experimental theater wherein many patterns of mind-body communication and healing can be explored (Dement, 1965, 1972; LaBerge, 1985; Mindell, 1985a, b; Rossi, 1972/1985).

What is the difference between the activity of the dreaming and the awake mind? One answer to this question is in the voluntary, overall organization of mental activity. There may be creative, very revealing bursts of metaphorical imagery in the dream, but they are not usually under voluntary control. LaBerge (1985) has recently described experiments in which specially trained (and talented) subjects apparently could control the content of some of their dream states, as well as their access to some of their own psychophysiological functions (e.g., sexual arousal, respiration). This relatively rare ability, called *lucid dreaming*, however, may be the exception that proves the rule. The successful lucid dreamer is the individual who can use a certain degree of conscious planning and voluntary control to transduce mind into physiological responses. Let us now turn our attention to the major areas of the brain that are involved in this planning and voluntary control process.

THE FRONTAL CEREBRAL CORTEX: THE ORGANIZING AND PLANNING MIND

The frontal (or prefrontal) cerebral cortex, with its specialized planning functions, has been described as the most recently developed area of the human brain. Proportionately larger than that of any other animal, it occupies one-quarter of the total mass of the cerebral hemisphere and does not attain maturity until the child is about seven years old. The frontal cortex has rich connections with both the reticular formation (ARAS) and the limbic-hypothalamic systems, which we reviewed in the two previous sections. The integration of information transduced in these two areas by the organizing activity of the frontal cortex is the main subject of this section.

The awakening and attention-getting novel stimuli transduced into the brain by the reticular formation and its specialized nuclei (e.g., the locus coeruleus) are organized and expressed as normal human responsiveness by the planning and sequencing functions of the frontal cortex. The frontal cortex also has such rich connections with the limbic-hypothalamic system that some investigators have considered it as a single "fronto-limbic system" (Nauta, 1964, 1972; Nauta & Domesick, 1980; Nauta & Feirtag, 1979). Luria has summarized the overall planning and organizing function of the frontal cortex as follows (1966, p. 233):

> . . . The fact that the frontal region is closely connected with the underlying structures of the limbic lobe, and through them with other nervous apparatuses concerned with interoception, gives reason to suppose that it receives signals of the various changes taking place in the organism and that it is intimately involved in *the regulation of body states*. Evidently, changes in body state occur not merely because of the appearance of new stimuli, evoking arousal reactions, but also because of the body's response activity. It may be postulated that these changing states may lead to corresponding further changes in the activity of the body. There are, therefore, important grounds for believing that *the frontal lobes synthesize the information about the outside world received through the exteroceptors and the information about the internal states of the body* and that *they are the means whereby the behavior of the organism is regulated in conformity with the effect produced by its actions*.

The organization and synthesis of external and internal information for the "*regulation of body states*" are important for our developing understanding of mind-body communication and healing. This regulation of body states takes place when the organized stimuli of the external and internal worlds are funneled through the limbic-hypothalamic system. Psychophysiologists such as Achterberg (1985; Achterberg & Lawlis, 1980, 1984) have assembled evidence for the view that mind-body communication and healing are mediated by the "body image." The body image is an organization of visual imagery that apparently is constructed in the fronto-limbic system, particularly with the help of the right cerebral hemisphere. Recent research at the neurotransmitter level has implicated dopamine in frontal lobe function as a locus of hypnotherapeutic suggestion involving the body image described by Spiegel and King as follows (1992, p. 96):

> The frontal lobes have been implicated in the embedding of perceptual and motor activity into a pattern of perceptual and motor activity into a pattern of meaning, for example, planning for future activity (Goldman-Rakic 1988). This working memory function is impaired by injection of DI dopamine receptor antagonists into the prefrontal cortex (Sawaguchi & Goldman-Rakic 1991). Hypnotic instructions involve altering sensory and motor function. The experience of involuntary movement of the hand, for example, is a consequence of the imagined lightness in the hand. Thus, subjects must link perception to a previously learned image. This would plausibly involve fron-

tal lobe function. This study suggests a role for dopamine activity, possibly involving the frontal lobes, in hypnotic concentration. Future research might involve tests of frontal lobe activity, functional brain imaging, and studies of the effects of dopamine agonists and blockers on hypnotic concentration.

To approach an understanding of this idea, we will now overview the process of information transduction by the right and left cerebral hemispheres and their contributions to the facilitation of mind-body communication and healing.

THE CEREBRAL HEMISPHERES: THE LOGICAL AND METAPHORICAL MINDS

A great area of discovery about information transduction in the brain during the 1950s and 1960s was initiated by Meyers and Sperry (1953), who discovered that when the nerve connections (the corpus callosum) between the left and right cerebral hemispheres in the cat were severed, each hemisphere apparently functioned in part independently. Since this operation did not seem to impair mental faculties, Sperry (1964) and his colleagues resorted to this surgical procedure with carefully selected human subjects who had very severe and uncontrollable *grand mal* epileptic seizures. If the source of the epilepsy was located in one cerebral hemisphere, they reasoned, the operation would at least prevent the seizure activity from spreading to the other half of the brain. The operation was remarkably successful in relieving the epilepsy. When psychologists carefully examined these ''split-brain'' patients, however, they encountered a series of fascinating discoveries about the intrinsic differences in the way information was transduced or processed in left and right hemispheres (Gazzaniga, 1967, 1985). For the purposes of our study of mind-body communication and healing, it is most important to note that the left hemisphere is specialized in the verbal-linguistic transduction of speech and analytical thinking, while the right plays a more predominant role in the holistic, analogical-metaphorical information transduction characteristic of emotions, imagery, and particularly, the body image (Achterberg, 1985). The basic hypothesis that has emerged is that the right hemisphere's modes of information transduction are more closely associated with the limbic-hypothalamic system and mind-body communication in the placebo response and therapeutic hypnosis. Ian Wickramasekera has summarized this idea as follows (1985, pp. 274–275):

> . . . Good placebo responders, like good hypnotic subjects, inhibit the critical, analytic mode of information processing that is characteristic of the domi-

nant verbal hemisphere. Good placebo responders will tend to be individuals who are prone to see conceptual or other relationships between events that seem randomly distributed to others. They will inhibit the interfering signals of doubt and skepticism, which are consequences of the more analytic mode of information processing typical of the dominant (left) hemisphere. Like good hypnotic subjects, good placebo responders are likely to embroider or elaborate on the given stimulus properties of a drug potentiating it, out of their own rich subjective repertoires. Alternatively, they may negate or attenuate the effects of a . . . drug through negative attributions.

Shapiro (1971) describes placebo nonresponders as "rigid and stereotypic and not psychologically minded" (p. 445). There is a striking similarity between this description and that of a poorly hypnotizable subject. There is increasing evidence (Bakan, 1969; Graham & Pernicano, 1976; Gur & Gur, 1974; Lachman & Goode, 1976) that hypnotizability or suggestibility is predominantly a right-hemisphere (nondominant or minor-hemisphere) function for right-handed people. Minor-hemisphere functions include holistic and imaginative mentation with diffuse, relational, and simultaneous processing of information (Ornstein, 1973; Sperry, 1964); the tendency to "see" some relationship or "meaning" in data, however randomly generated (e.g., a Rorschach inkblot), would appear to be an aspect of creative mentation that is posited to be a property of the nondominant hemisphere. This explanation can account for the common features of good placebo responders and good hypnotic subjects.

The intense interest of psychotherapists of all persuasions in learning to facilitate the creative mind-body healing potentials of the right hemisphere has led to many controversial efforts to find observable facial or body language cues about the process. Eye movements associated with characteristic styles of thought or reflection were independently described by Teitlebaum (1954) and Day (1964). Bakan first suggested that right or left cerebral hemispheric dominance or activity could be the basis of the tendency for eyes to move to the right or left, respectively, when involved with the transduction of logical versus analogical information.

In more recent reviews of the many research studies in this area, Bakan (1980) concluded that the right hemisphere does, in fact, have a primary role in the production of *raw imagery*. This raw imagery tends to be facilitated during sleep, dreaming, muscular relaxation, free association, mind wandering, and under the effects of certain drugs that block interhemispheric communication. When the cerebral hemispheres are in good communication, however, the raw imagery of the right hemisphere is "cooked" or transduced by the left hemisphere. This has led to the "paradoxical" finding that subjects who do well in structured tests of imagery and spatial relations tend to move their eyes to the right, indicating a heightened left-hemispheric involvement. Observations of eye movements as a clue to which hemisphere is most activated must therefore take into account the degree to which the imagery is transduced by a primary process (raw) or secondary process (cooked).

This difference between the cerebral transduction of raw and cooked imagery may be characteristic of all the other sensory modalities. It is found, for example, that the right cerebral hemisphere is activated by music in the untrained listener who is simply enjoying it, while the professional musician's left hemisphere is activated while he is analyzing the same music (Mazziotta, Phelps, Carson, & Kuhl, 1982). These differences in information transduction by the left and right cerebral hemispheres (Rossi, 1977) is the basis of many of the approaches to the facilitation of mind-body communication that we will explore in later chapters.

MEMORY AND LEARNING, MIND AND CONSCIOUSNESS

The direction of recent psychobiological research in memory and learning is confirming the importance of mind-body information transduction in the limbic-hypothalamic area of the brain for understanding how sensation and perception are integrated with thought and behavior. In this section we will cover only the two areas that are of greatest significance for our theme. These concern (1) the role of hormones in memory and learning; and (2) the manner in which sensation and perception are integrated with memory and learning in the limbic-hypothalamic system. McGaugh, a physiological psychologist, has summarized the role of hormones in memory and learning as follows (1983, pp. 163–164):

> It is well known that sensory stimulation activates nonspecific brain systems [via the ARAS system, as we have seen above]. Sensory stimulation also results in the release of hormones, including ACTH, epinephrine, vasopressin, and the opioid peptides, enkephalin and endorphin. A great deal of recent research has shown that learning and memory are affected by these hormones. . . . These findings raise two important questions. First, is the release of these stress-related hormones part of the normal . . . processes involved in the endogenous modulation of memory storage? Second, do the effects of treatments known to produce retrograde amnesia and retrograde enhancement of memory involve influences of hormones? If the answer to these questions is yes, as much recent research suggests, then the major question to be addressed is the basis of the effects of endogenous hormones

on brain activity underlying memory storage. . . . Our findings, as well as those of other laboratories, suggest that retention is influenced by epinephrine released from the adrenal medulla (McGaugh et al., 1982). We have for several years also studied the effects on memory of post-training electrical stimulation of the brain. Our recent findings . . . indicate that the effects of amygdala [a part of the limbic system] stimulation on memory may involve the release of peripheral epinephrine. The convergence of these two lines of research has provided evidence strongly supporting the view that *hormones released by experience act to modulate the strength of the memory of the experience and suggest that central modulating influences on memory [in the limbic-hypothalamic system] interact with influences of peripheral hormones.* (Italics added)

McGaugh's research provides us with what may become the basis of many therapeutically useful methods of facilitating mind-body communication and healing. Although our understanding of the incredible intricacies of these processes is still at an elementary level, it is nonetheless sufficient to suggest an important integration of the work of Hans Selye and Milton Erickson in the field of psychosomatic medicine, as we shall see in Chapter 4.

The work of Mortimer Mishkin and his colleagues at the National Institute of Mental Health is tracing the route by which the sensory information in the visual area of the cortex is transmitted to the limbic system where it is stored and integrated with processes of memory and learning. The limbic system (particularly its component structures, the amygdala and hippocampus) is the area where information stored by many different sensory systems can be combined and integrated. This type of "cross-modal association" makes sensory-perceptual information available to the hypothalamus for flexible patterns of information transduction into the body's psychophysiological responses (Murry & Mishkin, 1985).

We may regard this research on cross-modal association as the latest formulation of Bernheim's original concept of the *ideodynamic* as the psychophysiological basis of therapeutic hypnosis. Mishkin's work is thus a new research base for the investigation of mind-body communication and healing in hypnotherapy. His research into the relation between the visual modality and the limbic system must be extended to all other sensory modalities.

In an earlier work (Rossi, 1972/1985), I concluded from a study of the phenomenological content and processes of dreams that inter-modal shifts between sensations, perceptions, emotion, imagery, cognition, identity, and behavior were characteristic of the process of psychological growth and change. Mishkin's work is providing the experimental foundation for such psychological studies of creative development and for the renaissance of new methodologies that are currently being developed in psychotherapy to facilitate these processes (Mills & Crowley, 1986). We will continue the study of the processes of information transduction in the "language of human facilitation" presented in Chapter 5.

Mishkin's work is clarifying the great debate between the *behaviorist* and *cognitive* approaches to understanding how memory and learning take place and the role of thinking, awareness, and consciousness in the process. Mishkin (Mishkin, Malamut, & Bachevalier, 1984; Mishkin & Petri, 1984) has developed a two-level psychobiological theory that has a place for both behaviorist and cognitive frameworks. *Habits,* which have been described by behaviorists as automatic stimulus-response connections that take place whenever there is an adequate reward, are designated by Mishkin as the more basic process that operates at all levels of life, from the most primitive one-celled organisms to man. A cognitive process of self-reflection and thinking is not required for the formation of such habits. The acquisition of information, knowledge, and a self-conscious and self-driven memory system, as described by the cognitive learning theorists, requires the evolution of a "cortico-limbic-thalamic" pathway that is characteristic of all the more advanced life forms, such as mammals and man.

From the broad perspective developed in this chapter, *we could define consciousness or mind as a process of self-reflective information transduction.* This definition may not be satisfying for philosophers, but it is sufficient as a practical guide for our thinking about mind-body communication and how we may go about creating new approaches to mind-body heal-ing. The major processes and pathways of self-reflective information transduction described in this chapter are beginning to emerge as the psychobiological basis of self-driven consciousness and mind-body com-munication. All of these pathways focus on the limbic-hypothalamic system* as the major center of mind-body information transduction.

Mishkin's research and current investigations in the "multichannel integrations of nonverbal behavior" (Siegman & Feldstein, 1985), pro-vide a new experimental research base for studying how information is transmitted, transduced, and sometimes "stuck" in a state-bound form so that it becomes what people ordinarily label as a "problem" or a "symptom."

---

*For the reader sophisticated in anatomical studies, it may be well to point out that we are using the term "limbic-hypothalamic system" in this book in the broadest sense to include the following: amygdala, hippocampus, cingulate gyrus, fornix, septum, and certain nuclei of the thalamus and the Papez circuit.

C. G. Jung was one of the early explorers in depth psychology who used intermodal information transduction as a therapeutic method. He called this process of integrating conscious and unconscious elements the "transcendent function" (Jung, 1960, pp. 67–91). When Jung's patients became overwhelmed with emotions, he sometimes would have them draw a picture of their feelings. Once the feelings were expressed in the form of imagery, the images could be encouraged to speak to one another. As soon as a dialogue could take place, the patient was well embarked on the process of reconciling different aspects of his dissociated psyche, Jung described his approach as follows (Jung, 1960, pp. 81–83).

In the intensity of the emotional disturbance itself lies the value, the energy which he should have at his disposal in order to remedy the state of reduced adaptation. Nothing is achieved by repressing this state or devaluing it rationally.

In order, therefore, to gain possession of the energy that is in the wrong place, he must make the emotional state the basis or starting point of the procedure. He must make himself as conscious as possible of the mood he is in, sinking himself in it without reserve and noting down on paper all the fantasies and other associations that come up. Fantasy must be allowed the freest possible play. . . .

The whole procedure is a kind of enrichment and clarification of the affect, whereby the affect and its content are brought nearer to consciousness, becoming at the same time more impressive and more understandable. This work by itself can have a favourable and vitalizing influence. At all events, it creates a new situation, since the previously unrelated affect has become a more or less clear and articulate idea, thanks to the assistance and cooperation of the conscious mind. *This is the beginning of the transcendent function, i.e., of the collaboration of conscious and unconscious data.*

The emotional disturbance can also be dealt with in another way, not by clarifying it intellectually but by giving it visible shape. Patients who possess some talent for drawing or painting can give expression to their mood by means of a picture. . . . Visual types should concentrate on the expectation that an inner image will be produced. As a rule such a fantasy-picture will actually appear—perhaps hypnogogically—and should be carefully observed and noted down in writing. Audio-verbal types usually hear inner words, perhaps mere fragments of apparently meaningless sentences to begin with, which however should be carefully noted down too. . . . Such persons have little difficulty in procuring the unconscious material and thus laying the foundation of the transcendent function.

There are others, again, who neither see nor hear anything inside themselves, but whose hands have the knack of giving expression to the contents of the unconscious. Such people can profitably work with plastic materials. Those who are able to express the unconscious by means of bodily movements are rather rare. The disadvantage that movements cannot easily be fixed in the mind must be met by making careful drawings of the movements afterwards, so that they shall not be lost to the memory. Still rarer, but equally valuable, is automatic writing, direct or with the planchette. This too, yields useful results.

We now come to the next question: what is to be done with the material obtained in one of the manners described? To this question there is no *a priori* answer; it is only when the conscious mind confronts the products of the unconscious that a provisional reaction will ensue which determines the subsequent procedure. Practical experience alone can give us a clue. So far as my experience goes, there appear to be two main tendencies. One is the way of *creative formulation*, the other the way of *understanding*.

This quotation comes from Jung's paper, "The Transcendent Function," which he worked on for 40 years (between 1916 and 1957) before he consented to its publication. One could say that it represents the essence of his psychotherapeutic methodology. From the psychobiological point of view being formulated in this book, Jung is describing a process of transducing into consciousness the state-bound information that encodes symptoms and problems by "whatever sensory-perceptual-expressive modality is most natural to the patient." His methods can be seen as the generally unrecognized forerunners of the use of similar techniques in gestalt therapy, transactional analysis, cognitive and behavior therapy, psychosynthesis, and all the more recent forms of analogy and metaphor in Ericksonian psychotherapy (Lankton & Lankton, 1983; Mills & Crowley, 1986; Zeig, 1985).

From this point of view we may understand how the entire history of hypnosis (and the many schools of psychotherapy that evolved from it) may be metaphorized as the struggle of the blind men to describe the elephant that experimental psychology currently calls the encoding and decoding of information available to consciousness by state-dependent memory, learning, and behavior (SDMLB). Before we turn to a deeper study of how state-dependent phenomena function as a bridge between mind and body, however, we must gain a fuller comprehension of just what information is.

Three Stages in the Evolution of Information

Up to this point we have sketched how information is transformed within the mind-body and we have assumed in a rather friendly way that we all understand what information is. But do we really? Recently there has been a growing recognition of the need to formulate a general theory of information and its evolution. When and how does information make its appearance in the universe? For our understanding of mind-body communication and healing we will review three major theories.

1. *Information Begins With the Big Bang*

Tom Stonier (1990) has formulated one of the most recent and radical approaches to a general theory of information by identifying it with the structure and organization of the universe. Science began with the study of *matter* and even today that is what most people think the universe is made of. Within the past 200 years, however, the study of *energy* has absorbed our attention, culminating in Einstein's famous equation $E = MC^2$, where energy and matter (times the speed of light squared) are transduceable into each other. Within our generation, Stonier now maintains, *information* has finally been recognized as the organizational principle of the universe that has an equal status with matter and energy. Matter, energy, and information are all ultimately transducable into each other. Stonier outlines the evolution of information from the organization of matter out of basic forces of nature within the first second of the Big Bang to the literature of Shakespeare as follows (1990, pp. 70–72):

> The very large numbers associated with the improbability of advanced information systems causes one to wonder how such systems are possible in the first place. The answer lies in the recursive properties of information systems. Organised systems exhibit resonances. Resonances lead to oscillations. Oscillations represent timed cycles during which changes may be introduced. Such changes may dampen or amplify the existing oscillations. Alternatively, they may create new resonances and excite new sets of oscillations. The more complex the system, the greater the likelihood of introducing changes into the system during any given cycle. Hence the exponential growth of information.
> In the light of the preceding considerations it becomes clear that fig. [1] [see Box 2], which plots the relationship between information and entropy, also plots the evolution of the universe: At the far right—where entropy approaches the infinite and information the zero state—we have the Big Bang. As we move to the left, the information content of the universe begins to increase, first as the forces of nature—gravity, weak and strong nuclear forces, electromagnetism—differentiate out, then as matter appears. As we move further to the left, we see the evolution of matter into increasingly complex forms. By the time we approach the ordinate—the zero entropy

BOX 2 The evolution of the universe from the Big Bang to the Self. This illustration was adapted from Tom Stonier's mathematical formulation in *Information and the Internal Structure of the Universe*.

state—self-organising systems begin to appear, and as we move into the left quadrant we see not only the further development of more advanced self-organising systems, we have now reached the realm of biological systems. We also see the emergence of an entirely new phenomenon—intelligence. From here on in, the curve depicting the growth of information becomes increasingly steeper, reflecting the autocatalytic processes which characterise advanced systems capable not only to organising themselves, but with increasing efficiency, also of ordering their environment. . . .

Early, archaic life forms depended on the prior existence of complex molecules, derived form combinations of simpler molecules, which arose from the forces linking up atoms, which in turn were formed by the intra-atomic forces linking fundamental particles into nucleons and atoms. Complexity utilises pre-existing complexity to achieve higher degrees of complexity, building up the information content of evolving systems *ad infinitum*. It began with the zero information state of the Big Bang: First the fundamental forces, then matter differentiated; the process of evolution had begun. The exponential growth of information was inevitable.

Improbability fed further on existing improbability. One does not start with zero information and have proverbial monkeys typing at random hoping to author "Hamlet." Instead, a highly advanced information system named William Shakespeare was born into an advanced information culture, and in due course added further information as the universe cycled on.

The concept that as the universe evolves, its information content increases, is in opposition to the idea that the increase in entropy will inevitably lead to the "heat death" of the universe.

Stonier traces the development of his mathematically based theory from his predecessors in the study of the relationship between thermodynamics and information: Ludwig Boltzmann, Erwin Schrodinger, and Claude Shannon. His calculations permit him to make an initial estimate about the relationship between energy and information as, "One entropy unit equals approximately 10^{23}/mole, or 1 J/K $= 10^{23}$ bits." It remains one of the most challenging frontiers of mind-body science to integrate Stonier's equation of information and energy with Einstein's equation of energy and mass to obtain an experimentally verifiable formula for all three of these basic concepts: mass, energy, and information. This is the ideal of John Archibald Wheeler's (1990) new vision of an "informational physics" expressed in his phrase, "It from Bit." Wheeler seeks a common denominator between all the sciences by conceptualizing every It (atoms, living cells, societies, or whatever) in terms of the Bit as the basic informational unit capable of describing everything that is in mathematical terms.

2. Information Begins with Genes

The Nobel Prize winning molecular biologist Manfred Eigen has eloquently summarized a lifetime of research tracing the origin of life to the first ensembles of self-replicating nucleic acids that make up the genetic code which he regards as the true beginning of information as follows (Eigen & Winkler-Oswatitsch, 1992, p. 65):

> With the self-replication of nucleic acids, we have arrived at the fundamental step leading from chemistry to biology: the four bases of the nucleic acids begin to play the part of linguistic symbols. The sequence of these symbols can encode a message. There thus arises an attribute that is new to the world of physics and chemistry, one unknown to the science of material interactions, of atoms, molecules, and crystals: that of information.

The definition of information requires, first of all, a restricted set of symbols; secondly, the concatenation of these symbols into chains, or sentences, whose structure is defined by a grammar and whose meaning is realized by semantic agreement; and thirdly—a requirement often tacitly ignored—an apparatus for the reading (and, if necessary, for the translation) of the message contained in the symbol sequence. All of the three requirements for the use of nucleic acids as information stores are fulfilled on the basis of chemistry.

The key step in the evolution of autocatalytic or self-replicating nucleic acids into genes and finally living cells is what Eigen calls the "hypercycle": the cyclic process by which a group of genes will cooperate with each other in facilitating their mutual molecular existence and evolution with positive and negative feedback. Margulis and Sagan have admirably summarized this cooperative process that makes life possible as follows (1991, p. 53):

> From both theoretical calculations and laboratory evidence, it has been suggested that an interaction of two or more autocatalytic cycles could have produced a "hypercycle." Some scientists theorize that such catalyzing compounds "competed" for elements in the environments, thus automatically limiting their existence. But the basic idea of the hypercycle is quite the opposite. Far from destroying each other in a fight for chemical survival, self-organizing compounds complemented each other to produce lifelike, ultimately replicating, structures. These cyclical processes formed the basis not only of the first cells but of all the myriad structures based on cells and their products that followed. Cyclical processes are very important to life. They allow life to preserve key elements of its past despite the fluctuations and tendency toward disorder of the larger environment.

Eigen's research on the cyclic processes of life is the deepest source of what we will call "the wave nature of consciousness and being" in this volume. Admirable as his efforts are to extend the process of information and communication down to the molecular-genetic level, more traditional psychological theorists prefer to limit their conception of information to the human or sentient creature level.

3. Information Really Begins with Creatures Such as Humans

In a seeming complete contradiction to the broadly based theorists summarized above, the psychologist Karl Pribram has recently brought together the experimental data to formulate a mathematically based theory of brain and perception that requires living creatures for the existence of information (1991, p. 40):

> Note that "informative pattern matching" is an active process. . . . "[I]nformation" is a function of a participating processing agency, ordinarily a living creature or its surrogate. Information does not exist per se in the absence of such an agency any more than sound or sight exists without a sentient being equipped with the capability to select and interpret patterns "existing" in the physical environment.

Central to Pribram's theory of the "neurodynamics of image processing," however, is what he calls the "fundamental oscillations in dendritic networks" of the brain. The fundamental operation of the neural networks of the brain are described mathematically by a neural wave equation of which he says (1991, p. 286), "Interestingly, *it is of the same form as the wave equation in quantum theory,* and will be called '*a neural wave equation.*'" But does this not sound as if even Pribram, who is primarily concerned with human information and communication, is returning to the quantum level which is the beginning of information in Stonier's theory?

To account for the sensory-perceptual aspects of information processing in animals and humans, Pribram must return to the molecular level to describe the fundamentals of neural (dendritic) and brain function as follows (1991, p. 281):

> Once the distribution of charge carriers in the ionic bioplasma evolves due to the distribution of dendritic isophase contours, *the pattern of oscillations of the membrane potentials in each location changes.* This is because the amount of charge carriers in each location affects the Ca^{2+} controlled *ATP cyclic process* and so the resulting *oscillations of biomolecules* of high dipole moments. Thus, the fundamental activity of the dendritic network is represented by a reciprocal feedback and feedforward control of the distribution of the dendritic ionic bioplasma due to the *oscillating component of membrane polarizations.* (Italics added)

It is interesting that even while Pribram maintains that the concept of information only makes sense in the context of a perceiving organism, the neural wave equation that he proposes as the fundamental mathematical description of neural action and brain functioning is isomorphic with the quantum level. This, of course, brings us back to Stonier's idea that information begins with the organization of matter in the Big Bang.

It will not have escaped the notice of most readers that to a surprising extent all three levels of information theory outlined above emphasize the role of oscillations, cycles, time, and rhythm in the evolution of life. This recognition of the essential role of cyclic processes will be described in more detail as "the new homeostasis" in Section II of this volume. For now it is enough to recognize that the fundamental processes of life are not static but rhythmic in nature. This rhythmic nature of life is basic to our new understanding of the role of stress in the etiology of psychosomatic problems and a host of new approaches to facilitating mind-body healing which we will illustrate with a variety of case histories in the following chapters.

The essential communication links between the mind-brain level and the cellular-genetic level of the body in health and illness are mediated by a variety of messenger molecules that encode all forms of novel experience. This is particularly true for those life experiences that lead to heightened states of awareness, emotion, and motivation related to the kinds of shock, trauma, and stress that result in mind-body problems. This type of mind-body encoding, SDMLB, accounts for most of the typical clinical phenomena of distress, dissociation and defense that are associated with mind-body problems. State-dependent memory, learning, and behavior is the basic dynamic in mind-body communication that is the hidden common denominator behind most schools of psychotherapy ranging from hypnosis, psychoanalysis, and behavior therapy to the holistic methods of imagery, relaxation, and meditation. Since these state-dependent phenomena are the generally unrecognized scientific basis of psychotherapy as a "talking cure" and the so-called "magical effects of words on the body," we will devote the next chapter to exploring the evolution of their central place in the history of psychotherapy and their possibilities for developing more effective approaches to mind-body healing in the future.

3

State-Dependent Learning in Mind-Body Healing and Hypnosis

IN ORDER TO FULLY appreciate the scope of the state-dependent theory of mind-body healing and hypnosis, it is necessary to review its evolution over 200 years (outlined in Table 2). In Chapter 1 we saw how Bernheim originated the concept of information transduction in mind-body healing and hypnosis. In this chapter, we begin with the words of James Braid (1795–1860), who originated the concept of the altered state or state-dependent theory of mind-body healing and hypnosis. Braid recommended that hypnosis be defined as follows (quoted in Tinterow, 1970, pp. 370–372):

> Let the term *hypnotism* be restricted to those cases alone in which . . . the subject has no remembrance on awakening of what occurred during his sleep, but of which he shall have the most perfect recollection on passing into a similar stage of hypnotism thereafter. In this mode, *hypnotism will comprise those cases only in which what has hitherto been called the double-conscious state occurs.*
>
> And, finally, as a generic term, comprising the whole of these phenomena which result from the reciprocal actions of mind and matter upon each other, I think no term could be more appropriate than *psychophysiology*.

In the first part of this quotation, Braid defines hypnotism as a process of dissociation or reversible amnesia giving rise to the "double-conscious state." Modern researchers call this a process of state-dependent memory and learning: What is learned and remembered is dependent on one's psychophysiological state at the time of the experience. Memories acquired during the state of hypnosis are forgotten in the awake state but are available once more when hypnosis is reinduced. Since

47

TABLE 2 Evolution of the state-dependent memory, learning, and behavior theory of mind-body healing and therapeutic hypnosis

RESEARCHERS	CONCEPT
Braid (1855)	Double-conscious state manifest as "reversible amnesia" is the "psychophysiological" basis of hypnosis.
Janet (1889, 1907)	Dissociation manifest as a block or reversible amnesia between the conscious and unconscious is the source of psychopathology that can be accessed and healed by hypnosis.
Freud (1896) Jung (1910) Rank (1924)	The root of psychoanalysis: Emotional trauma leads to dissociation, repression, complexes, and amnesia as the basis of neurosis and functional psychosis.
Erickson (1932, 1943a, b, c, d, 1948)	Demonstrated how traumatic amnesias and psychosomatic symptoms are psycho-neuro-physiological dissociations that can be resolved with "inner resynthesis" in hypnotherapy.
Cheek (publications from 1957 to 1981)	Hypnosis occurs spontaneously at times of stress, suggesting that this phenomenon is a state-dependent condition.
Overton (1968, 1972, 1973)	Reviewed 40-year literature establishing state-dependent memory and learning as a valid experimental basis of dissociation in many paradigms of drug and psychophysiological research.
Fischer (1971a, b, c)	State-bound information and behavior are conceptualized as the psychophysiological basis of "altered states," dissociations, mood, multiple personality, dreams, trance, religious, psychotic, creative, artistic, and narcoanalytic phenomena.
Rossi (1972, 1973)	Psychological shocks and creative moments occur when habitual patterns of state-dependent memories and associations are interrupted.
Erickson & Rossi (1974)	Research in state-dependent learning lends experimental support to the general view of all amnesias and psychological experiences as state-bound.
Hilgard & Hilgard (1975) Hilgard (1977)	Formulated the *neodissociation theory of hypnosis*, which implies that state-dependent memory and learning are the same class of psychophysiological phenomena as hypnotic dissociation.

(continued)

TABLE 2 *Continued*

RESEARCHERS	CONCEPT
Rossi (1981, 1982)	Formulated *ultradian theory of hypnotherapeutic healing*: (1) The source of psychosomatic problems is stress-induced distortions of state-dependent ultradian psychobiological rhythms in the suprachiasmatic nucleus of the hypothalamus; (2) Erickson's "utilization" hypnotherapy normalizes these ultradian rhythms with autonomic system balance.
Werntz (1981) Werntz et al. (1981)	Correlation of ultradian rhythms in nasal and cerebral hemispheric dominance is centrally controlled by hypothalamus mediating autonomic system balance.
Benson (1983a, b)	The "relaxation response" in yoga and meditation has its psychosomatic healing source in "an integrated hypothalamic response resulting in generalized decreased sympathetic nervous system activity."
Zornetzer (1978) McGaugh (1983) Izquierdo (1984)	The endogenous state dependency hypothesis of memory formation; "stress hormones" of the adrenals modulate memory and learning in the limbic-hypothalamic-pituitary-adrenal system.
Shors, Weiss, & Thompson (1992)	Stress hormones can strongly encode classical Pavlovian associations of traumatic situations while inhibiting the ability to do something about it (instrumental learning).

memory is dependent upon and limited to the state in which it was acquired, we say it is "state-bound information."

In the second part of the quotation, Braid invented the generic term *Psychophysiological* to denote all the phenomena of "the reciprocal actions of mind and matter upon each other." This early use of the term psychophysiological was his way of conceptualizing the process of information transduction between mind and body in healing and hypnosis.

Pierre Janet (1859–1947) was the next major figure in the history of hypnosis to use the phenomenon of reversible amnesia as the basis for building a "dissociation theory" of mind-body problems. A dissociation or "block" between the conscious and unconscious minds was conceptualized as the source of psychopathology that could be accessed and healed by hypnosis. Freud adopted this view and used "free association" rather than the formal induction of hypnosis to access the dissociated or repressed memories that had become the basis of psychological and psychosomatic problems.

The earliest roots of psychoanalysis were concerned with investigating the necessary and sufficient conditions for such reversible amnesias and dissociations. In his pioneering paper on "The Aetiology of Hysteria," Freud (1896) discussed the role of trauma as follows (cited in Freud, 1956, p. 186):

> For let us be quite clear that tracing an hysterical symptom back to a traumatic scene assists our understanding only if the scene in question fulfills two conditions—if it possesses the required *determining quality* and if we can credit it with the necessary *traumatic power*.

Life circumstances that had the requisite "determining quality" and "traumatic power" led to the formation of complexes. The effects of such complexes on memory and behavior were investigated experimentally by C. G. Jung in his association experiments and described as follows (Jung, 1910, p. 363):

> At the end of the [association] experiment, the subject is questioned as to whether he correctly recalls the reaction he gave previously to each single stimulus word; it then becomes apparent that forgetting normally takes place at or immediately after disturbances caused by a complex. We are in fact dealing with a kind of "Freudian forgetting" [that is, repression]. This procedure provides us with complex indicators which have proven to be of practical value.

Otto Rank (1924/1925) later pushed the possible source of complexes and neurosis back to the original trauma of birth. Thus the entire edifice of psychoanalysis could be said to rest upon this effort to explain how trauma gave rise to emotional complexes by initiating dissociation, repressions, and amnesias. Current psychoanalytic theorists are recognizing how *the concepts of dissociation, repression, and amnesia all have state-dependent memory, learning, and behavior as a clinical common denominator* in post-traumatic stress disorder, multiple personality disorder and the dissociative disorders associated with child abuse and sexual molestation (van der Kolk, 1987; van der Kolk & van der Hart, 1991).

Milton H. Erickson (1902–1980) then demonstrated how amnesias caused by psychological shocks and traumatic events are psycho-neuro-physiological dissociations that can be resolved by "inner resynthesis" in hypnotherapy (Erickson, 1948/1980). One of Erickson's early students, David Cheek, M.D., systematized an ideomotor signaling approach for investigating emotional trauma, stress, and psychosomatic symptoms. Over a 25-year period, Cheek's clinical case studies led him to formulate the theory that severe stress invariably causes an altered state, identifiable as a form of spontaneous hypnosis which encodes state-bound problems of symptoms. He recently expressed his view as follows (Cheek, 1981, p. 88):

> Hypnosis occurs spontaneously at times of stress (Cheek, 1960), suggesting that this phenomenon is a state-dependent condition mobilizing information previously conditioned by earlier similar stress (Cheek, 1962b).
> At such times, the individual tends to revert in memory and physiological behavior to an earlier moment of great stress. The formal induction of hypnosis may suddenly release disturbing memories of experiences associated with spontaneous hypnoidal states. This can be helpful in the search for factors responsible for maladaptive behavior but can embarrass an inexperienced hypnotist who may find his subject identifying him with some evil person in past experience. This flashback phenomenon is nonspecific. The trigger mechanism may evoke a totally inappropriate response, as I have frequently found in evaluating anesthesia experiences.

Cheek's many clinical publications comprise the most extensive documentation of the psychobiological approach to mind-body communication and healing currently available in the literature on therapeutic hypnosis. His approach will be described and illustrated in more detail in Chapter 5.

When Erickson and I updated the history of therapeutic hypnosis with basic theory and research in modern psychology, we built upon Fischer's view of the relation between state-dependent learning and amnesia as follows (Erickson & Rossi, 1974/1980, pp. 71–90):

> Taken together these clinical and naturalistic investigations strongly suggest that hypnotic trance is an altered *state* of consciousness and amnesia, in particular, is a natural consequence of this altered state. Recent research in "state-dependent learning" lends experimental support to the general view of all amnesias as being "state-bound." We can now understand hypnotic amnesia as only one of a general class of verifiable phenomenon rather than a special case. Fischer (1971c) has recently summarized the relation between state-dependent learning and amnesia as follows:

Inasmuch as experience arises from the binding or coupling of a particular state or level of arousal with a particular symbolic interpretation of that arousal, experience is state-bound; thus, it can be evoked either by inducing the particular level of arousal, or by presenting some symbol of its interpretation, such as an image, melody, or taste.

Recently, some researchers had 48 subjects memorize nonsense syllables while drunk. When sober, these volunteers had difficulty recalling what they had learned, but they could recall significantly better when they were drunk again. Another scientist also observed amphetamine-induced excitatory, and amobarbital-induced, "inhibitory," state-dependent recall of geometric configurations. His volunteers both memorized and later recalled the configurations under one of the two drugs. However, while remembering from one state to another is usually called "state-dependent learning," extended practice, learning, or conditioning is *not* necessary for producing "state-boundness." On the contrary, a single experience may be sufficient to establish state-boundness.

Déjà vu experiences and the so-called LSD flashbacks are special cases of the general phenomenon of state-boundness. Note that neither focal lesions nor molecules of a hallucinogenic drug are necessary for the induction of a flashback—a symbol evoking a past drug experience may be sufficient to produce an LSD flashback.

It follows from the state-bound nature of experience, and from the fact that amnesia exists between the state of normal daily experience and all other states of hyper- and hypoarousal, that what is called the "subconscious" is but another name for this amnesia. Therefore, instead of postulating *one* subconscious, I recognize as many layers of self-awareness as there are levels of arousal and corresponding symbolic interpretations in the individual's interpretive repertoire. This is how multiple existences become possible: by living from one waking state to another waking state; from one dream to the next; from LSD to LSD; from one creative, artistic, religious, or psychotic inspiration or possession to another; from trance to trance; and from reverie to reverie (p. 904).

We would submit that hypnotic trance itself can be most usefully conceptualized as but one vivid example of *the fundamental nature of all phenomenological experience as "state-bound."* The apparent continuity of consciousness that exists in everyday normal awareness is in fact a precarious illusion that is only made possible by the associative connections that exist between related bits of conversation, task orientation, etc. We have all experienced the instant amnesias that occur when we go too far on some tangent so we "lose the thread of thought" or "forget just what we were going to do," etc. Without the bridging associative connections, consciousness would break down into a series of discrete states with as little contiguity as is apparent in our dream life.

According to this view, what we usually experience as our ordinary everyday state of awareness or consciousness is actually habitual patterns of state-dependent memories, associations, and behaviors. I have conceptualized "creative moments" in dreams, artistic and scientific creativity, and everyday life as breaks in these habitual patterns (1972/ 1985). The new experience that occurs during creative moments is regarded as *"the basic unit of original thought and insight as well as personality change."* I have described the possible psychobiological basis of creative moments as follows (Rossi, 1972/1985, p. 158):

> Experiencing a creative moment may be the phenomenological correlate of a critical change in the molecular structure of proteins within the brain associated with learning (Kimble, 1965) or the creation of new cell assemblies and phase sequences (Hebb, 1963).

Erickson's use of psychological shock (Rossi, 1973/1980) to evoke creative moments during hypnotherapy as a means of breaking out of maladaptive patterns of state-bound learning will be explored in Chapters 4 and 5.

Meanwhile, experimental support for the essential identity between the processes of psychological dissociation and state-dependent learning was forthcoming from the Hilgards' research on the use of hypnosis in the relief of pain (Hilgard & Hilgard, 1975). The Hilgards expressed their view as follows (p. 183):

> Another approach to dissociated experiences is the peculiar action of certain drugs upon the retention and reinstatement of learned experiences, leading to what is called state-dependent learning. If learning takes place under the influence of an appropriate drug, the memory for that learning may be unavailable in the nondrugged state, but return when the person is again under the influence of the drug. This occasionally happens with alcohol: the drinker forgets what he said or did while intoxicated, only to remember it again when next intoxicated. Because the memory is stored, but unavailable except under special circumstances, this phenomenon has some characteristics of hypnotic amnesia. Presumably, when the site and nature of these effects become known, they may have some bearing on the physiological substratum for hypnosis.

In his neodissociation theory of hypnosis, Ernest Hilgard then integrated historical and modern, experimental and clinical data to document how the major classical phenomena of hypnosis can be conceptualized as forms of "divided consciousness" (Hilgard, 1977, pp. 244–245):

> If information acquired in one state, as under the influence of a drug, is forgotten in the nondrugged state, but recalled again in the drug state, that is an experimental illustration of a reversible amnesia. This arrangement is of course the paradigm of *state-dependent learning*. The literature has been reviewed by Overton, who is also one of the leading investigators in the field (Overton, 1972, 1973) . . . According to Overton (1973), drug discrimination . . . may be based "on the dissociative barrier which impairs a transfer of training between the drug and the no-drug condition." *The concept of dissociation employed by Overton is consonant with neodissociation theory. That is, two types of behavior may be isolated from each other because of different available information.* (Italics added)

The next development in my understanding of the relation between hypnosis and state-dependent learning came in the early 1980s, when I experienced the similarities between the psychobiological characteristics of ultradian rhythms and the "common everyday trance" that Erickson utilized for hypnotherapeutic healing (Rossi, 1972/1985, 1981, 1982, 1986a). This led to the formulation of the ultradian theory of hypnotherapeutic healing, which was summarized as follows (Rossi, 1982, p. 23):

> The similarities between the behavioral characteristics of ultradian cycles (a multioscillatory system of psychophysiological processes involving many parasympathetic and right-hemispheric functions which have a 90-minute periodicity throughout the 24-hour day) and those of the "common everyday trance" led the author to propose a new state(s) theory of hypnosis. The background for this proposal developed over eight years of observing the clinical, hypnotherapeutic techniques of Milton H. Erickson, whose work appeared to utilize a similar 90-minute periodicity. The ultradian theory of hypnotherapeutic healing proposes that (1) the source of psychosomatic reactions is in stress-induced distortions of the normal periodicity of ultradian cycles, and (2) the naturalistic approach to hypnotherapy facilitates healing by permitting a normalization of these ultradian processes.

Extensive reviews of the research (Kripke, 1982) indicated that *the suprachiasmatic nucleus of the hypothalamus was probably a major regulator of these rhythms, which were sensitive to learning and conditioning by both psychological and physiological factors.* An independent verification of these findings came when I accidentally stumbled upon the remarkable work of Werntz (1981; Werntz, Bickford, Bloom, & Shannahoff-Khalsa, 1981), who found additional experimental evidence for the role of the hypothalamus as the source and mediator of ultradian rhythms in cerebral dominance, nasal dominance, and autonomic nervous system integration. The exciting theoretical implication of Werntz's work was its provision of an empirical link between Western psychophysiological research on altered states of consciousness and the Eastern yogic practices of ancient times (Rossi, 1986a). This developing rapprochement between Eastern and Western conceptions of the relationship between mind and body is further supported by Benson's independent line of research (1983a, b), which described the "relaxation response" in yoga, meditation, and prayer as having its healing source in an integrated *hypothalamic* response, resulting in a generalized decrease in sympathetic nervous system activity.

The next breakthrough in my understanding came about a year later when I read McGaugh's (1983) review of recent research on the neurobiology of memory and learning. This research reported that hormones released during periods of stress modulated memory and learning in the limbic system (specifically, in the amygdala and hippocampus). I immediately realized that: (1) these were the same hormones of the hypothalamic-pituitary-endocrine system that Selye had found to be the source of stress-related psychosomatic problems; and (2) the new neurobiological research on memory and learning, and Selye's classical psychosomatic research were both essentially state-dependent memory and learning phenomena.

More recently, Izquierdo (1984) has independently reported laboratory research on "endogenous state dependency"; he confirms that memory depends on the relation between neurohormonal and hormonal states. According to Izquierdo, the first explicit statement regarding the endogenous state dependency hypothesis was made by Zornetzer in 1978 (p. 646):

> In normal memory formation the specific pattern of arousal present in the brain at the time of training may become an integral component of the stored information. The neural representation of this specific pattern of arousal might depend on the pattern of activity generated by brainstem acetylcholine, catecholamine, and serotonin systems. It is this idiosyncratic and unique patterned brain state, present at the time of memory formation, that might need to be reproduced, or at least approximated, at the time of retrieval in order for the stored information to be elaborated.

Zornetzer's psychobiological hypothesis appears to be the clearest forerunner of what I am formulating here as the "state-dependent theory of mind-body healing and therapeutic hypnosis."

Although state-dependent memory, learning, and behavior (SDMLB) have been the subject of well-controlled experimental research for the past 40 years (Overton, 1978; Rossi & Ryan, 1986), they are less familiar than classical Pavlovian and Skinnerian operant instrumental conditioning. Therefore, it might appear on first acquaintance that SDMLB is an exotic and highly specialized form of learning that is a minor variant of classical or operant conditioning. Actually, the reverse is true: SDMLB is the broad, generic class of learning that takes place in all complex organisms that have a cerebral cortex and limbic-hypothalamic system; Pavlovian and Skinnerian conditioning are specific varieties of SDMLB. The pioneering investigators and their followers were unaware, for the most part, of the role of limbic-hypothalamic SDMLB factors in their early learning experiments.

Pavlov, for example, was not able to take into account all the subtle *internal* responses of stress in his dogs that were conditioned to salivate with the *external* paired association of powdered meat and a sound. Most current psychobiologically oriented researchers and theorists in memory and learning (Lynch, McGaugh, & Weinberger, 1984) are in general agreement (though with varying vocabularies) that there are at least two classes of *internal* response involved in the memory and learning of all higher organisms: (1) there is a specific locus of a memory trace on a molecular-cellular-synaptic level (Hawkins & Kandel, 1984; Rosenzweig & Bennett, 1984); and (2) there is an involvement of the amygdala and hippocampus of the limbic-hypothalamic system in processing, encoding, and recall of the specific memory trace that may be located elsewhere in the brain (Mishkin & Petri, 1984; Thompson et al., 1984). It is this second factor involving the limbic-hypothalamic system that engages memory, learning, and behavior with the subtle state-dependent factors that encode psychosomatic problems that are resolvable by therapeutic hypnosis and other methods of mind-body healing.

Current research is clarifying the connections between stress, information processing and the different forms of learning. It has long been known that stress can interfere with instrumental learning where it is necessary to process and synthesize new information in tasks such as learning how to do something like solving "puzzle boxes." The impaired performance of animals exposed to the stress of inescapable shock, for example, has been described as "learned helplessness" which is believed to underlie some forms of depression in humans (Seligman, 1975). In sharp contrast to this is the recent finding by Shors et al. (1992) that learning by classical associative Pavlovian conditioning can be *increased* by exposure to stress in the form of unescapable shock in animals. These researchers report, "Apparently, classical conditioning in the freely moving rat is sufficient to strongly activate the hypothalamic-pituitary adrenal axis . . . " They found that corticosterone concentrations (the rat's stress hormone from the adrenals corresponding to the human's stress hormone cortisol) was significantly higher in the stressed animals than controls. This, of course, is precisely the defining condition of state-dependent memory, learning, and behavior where peripheral hormones from the body's adrenal glands are able to encode and modulate information processing in the limbic-hypothalamic-pituitary system.

These recent findings have profound implications for the types of human situations wherein a psychological or physiological shock and stress can lead simultaneously to (1) the immediate state-dependent encoding of a strong classical Pavlovian association to traumatic events due to stress release of adrenal hormones (e.g., civilian accidents and traumatic war situations, sexual seduction of children, etc.) and (2) an impaired ability to do something about it as is typical of learned helplessness due to the inhibition of instrumental learning under the same stressful conditions. I hypothesize that *it is precisely this type of psychobiological double bind wherein shock and stress strongly encode traumatic events and simultaneously impair effective coping behavior that leads to the genesis of many types of mind-body dysfunctions that are typically called "psychosomatic problems."*

A careful comparison of work of Selye and Erickson indicates that they were both dealing with the same basic phenomenon of *state-dependent memory and learning* as the genesis and resolution of psychosomatic problems: Selye from the perspective of physiological research; Erickson from the psychological perspective. Neither, however, was apparently aware of the concept of state-dependent memory and learning, and of how it could serve as the common denominator of their work. I will present the work of Selye and Erickson in more detail in the next chapter. First, however, let us consolidate our understanding of the state-dependent theory of mind-body healing and therapeutic hypnosis with two illustrative clinical problems: traumatic amnesia and multiple personality.

Illustrative Case Examples

Traumatic Amnesia

In a recent doctoral dissertation on "Mood State-Dependent Memory and Lateralization of Emotion," Gage (1983) has described Erickson's pioneering role in developing state-dependent memory approaches to therapeutic hypnosis as follows (pp. 14–15):

> Milton H. Erickson, who investigated memory phenomena such as hypnotic hypermnesia, posthypnotic amnesia and posthypnotic suggestion, was an early pioneer in the area of mood SDM [State-Dependent Memory]. Although in his writings he never labeled his work "state-dependent memory," this was clearly the topic of some of his investigations. He perfected a method which would allow people who were amnesic for clinically relevant events to remember them in every detail. His method was based on a reorienting process which recreated the sights, sounds, sensations, thoughts and feelings surrounding the forgotten event (cf. Erickson, 1937, 1939). His "reorienting' is clearly the same process as that described by mood SDM.

A direct quotation from Erickson's report on the "Development of Apparent Unconsciousness During Hypnotic Reliving of a Traumatic Experience" will serve to illustrate this point. In this case, Erickson utilized age regression as a means of investigating the "psychic development" of a young man who had recently recovered from a psychotic episode (Erickson, 1937/1980, pp. 45–59):

> The experimental procedure consisted of training the patient to enter profound somnambulistic hypnotic trances, during which, by means of a series of hypnotic suggestions, he was disoriented completely and then reoriented to an earlier period of his life. When thus reoriented, by the employment of carefully worded systematic suggestions and questions, he was induced to relive past events in a chronologically progressive fashion, describing them in detail to the experimenter as if they were in the course of actual development in the immediate present. An attending stenographer recorded in full the entire course of the experimental events, including the descriptive material. In every instance for which adequate data were available from sources other than the patient himself, it was found that events of the distant past were relived and recounted by the patient with remarkable vividness and with richness and accuracy of detail.
> Study of the experimental findings disclosed an incident of peculiar interest, illustrative in an unusual fashion of psychosomatic interrelationships. This incident concerned the development of what appeared to be a state of unconsciousness as the patient relived the experience of a homicidal assault which had occurred two years previously, when he was 17 years old. All previous information concerning this assault consisted of the statement by the patient that he had been "taken for a ride" and beaten so badly that hospitalization had been necessary. He seemed to have complete amnesia for all informative details of this experience, including even the name of the hospital. Extensive and persistent questioning in the ordinary deep hypnotic

trance, as well as in the normal waking state, secured only unimportant items, despite the fact that he seemed to be cooperating to the limit of his ability.

When the day of this event was reached in the hypnotic reliving of his past life, the patient expressed his fears over his employment as a police informer, vividly portraying intense anxiety concerning threatened criminal vengeance, and his entire behavior and appearance were suggestive of a most harried state of mind. When the hour of 4 p.m. was reached in his reexperiencing of the events of this day, he relived, with marked intensity of feeling, the scene of his being ordered into an automobile by two men whom he knew to be criminal characters and his fearful behavior during the course of a long drive, during which he pleaded piteously with his abductors in a terrified fashion. Finally, he reenacted his forced acceptance of a bottle of pop from the criminals, fearfully and hesitantly drinking from an imaginary bottle. As he swallowed, he grimaced, mumbled that it tasted bitter, asked if it was poisoned, and dodged and cowered as if evading a blow. His entire appearance continued to denote intense terror. Shortly after completing the act of drinking, he belched and suddenly looked bewildered. His pupils, which previously had been fluctuating constantly in size, became widely dilated, and fine lateral nystagmus developed. He then rubbed his eyes, complained that he could not see plainly, said that everything was getting dark and that he was dizzy, and began shaking his head as if to throw off something or to rouse himself. Questioning by the experimenter elicited the information that the patient felt himself becoming sleepy. It was noted that his speech, previously clear, was now thick and indistinct and that his appearance had changed from that of terror to that of somnolence.

At this time the patient was sitting on a couch, and every few seconds the experimenter had been testing him for the presence of catalepsy as an index of his continuance in the hypnotic state. After about two minutes of decreasing activity, during which the patient shook his head more and more slowly and mumbled with increasing inarticulateness, his eyes closed, despite his apparent effort to keep them open. Suddenly he gave a short, gasping grunt and collapsed, sprawling inanimately over the couch. Immediate examination by the experimenter disclosed complete loss of hypnotic rapport, with absence of the catalepsy which hitherto had been consistently present. Physically, there were sagging of the lower jaw and marked atony of the muscles of the legs and arms. Also, the patellar and pupillary reflexes, which are consistently present during hypnotic states, were absent. The respiration and pulse, which had been greatly increased during the state of terror, had decreased somewhat during that of somnolence. Now they were found to be markedly diminished in rate and so weak and faint as to be barely perceptible. In brief, the patient presented every appearance of being unconscious. However, before the blood pressure and accurate counts of the pulse and respiration could be taken, the patient seemed to be recovering. He stirred slightly and moaned, and catalepsy returned slowly. Shortly he opened his eyes and, after staring vacantly around, weakly closed them again. It was noted that the pupils were still widely dilated, that fine nystagmus was present, and that the eyes were not focused. The patient licked his lips repeatedly, moaned for water, and weakly rubbed his forehead, grimacing with pain as he did so. He paid no attention to the experimenter's insistent questions, "What's the matter? What's happening?" except to say, "It's dark, dark." This was followed by a second collapse, of slower onset than the first but apparently of the same character, with the same physical findings except that the respiration was deep and labored while the pulse was slow and firm. Repeated attempts were made by the experimenter to arouse the patient, but he remained unresponsive for several minutes. Finally, catalepsy returned, and the patient opened his eyes and stared about unseeingly. Nystagmus was absent, and the pupils were somewhat dilated but responsive to light. He twisted his head about, moaned, rubbed his neck as if it were painful, rubbed his forehead gently, grimacing as if with pain, and shivered constantly. Again, he licked his lips repeatedly and kept moaning for water. No response was made to the experimenter's insistent questioning except the monosyllables "light" and "woods." Now and then he put his hands to his ears, rubbed them feebly and mumbled, "buzzing."

Soon the patient seemed to recover to a considerable degree, and he again became fairly responsive to the experimenter's inquiries, which concerned the events he was reliving. There followed a relatively inadequate account, as compared with his initial communicativeness, of lying in a ditch alongside a road through a woods, of being cold, wet, and uncomfortable, and of suffering from intense thirst, roaring in the ears, headache, and a painful, bleeding wound on his forehead, from which he went through the act of wiping blood in a gingerly fashion. He also declared that it seemed to be morning.

From then, he recounted in a fragmentary fashion the experience of being picked up by some men and taken to a hospital. The reliving of the next two days was also disjointed and inadequate, but that of subsequent events was complete, during the course of which the name of the hospital was obtained.

This reexperience of a homicidal assault illustrates how state-bound information is generated by an altered psychophysiological state (particularly the alarm reaction of the autonomic nervous system and the endocrine system, leading to increased respiration, pulse, and blood pressure) that can be accessed via therapeutic hypnosis. Erickson accessed state-bound information by carefully retrieving the contexts and frames of reference in which it was embedded (Erickson & Rossi, 1979). As he said in the above case, "The employment of carefully worded systematic suggestions and questions . . . to relive past events in a chronologically progressive fashion" was an important key to the success of his procedure. These systematic questions and suggestions accessed the memory sets that enabled the patient to relive the traumatically isolated (amnesic) state-bound memories.

Erickson's manner of accessing state-bound memories by reviewing the context and sensory-perceptual cues surrounding their original acquisition was fundamentally different from the manner of traditional authoritarian hypnotism involving direct suggestion. For example, in the traditional procedure of inciting the subject to "Remember!" there was a reliance on the alleged "hypersuggestibility" of the hypnotic state. Erickson (1932/1980) found in his initial investigations, however, that *hypersuggestibility was not a characteristic of hypnosis*. He described it as follows (p. 495):

> In the writer's own experience . . . *hypersuggestibility was not noticed, although the list of individual subjects totals approximately 300 and the number of trances several thousand.* Further, a considerable number were hypnotized from 300 to 500 times over a period of years. Also, several of the subjects were immediate relatives with consequent intimate daily contact, and they were trained to respond, in experimentation, quickly and readily to the slightest suggestion. *Far from making them hypersuggestible, it was found necessary to deal very gingerly with them to keep from losing their cooperation, and it was often felt that they developed a compensatory negativism toward the hypnotist to offset any increased suggestibility. Subjects trained to go into a deep trance instantly at the snap of a finger would successfully resist when unwilling or more interested in other projects.* Even when persuaded to give their consent against their original wishes, the induction of a trance was impossible. Nor were those subjects more suggestible to other people, since, when their services were "loaned" to the author's colleagues, the production of hypnosis in them, despite their extensive training, was just as hard as it had been originally for the author. And the same thing was found true when the author "borrowed" subjects. In brief, *it seems probable that if there is a development of increased suggestibility, it is negligible in extent.* (Italics added)

The clause, "it was found necessary to deal very gingerly with them," is the key to a more adequate interpretation of therapeutic hypnosis as Erickson developed it. Hypnotic subjects are *hypersensitive*, not hypersuggestible (Ellenberger, 1970, p. 115). It could be said that good hypnotic subjects have an easy access to their state-dependent experiences because of their sensitivity. This sensitivity is the quality that makes them amenable to accepting and carrying out suggestions if they are in a cooperative relationship with the hypnotherapist. It is also the quality that enables them to be more receptive to the subtle and often unrecognized nuances of hypnotic communication that have been called the "demand characteristics" (Orne, 1962) or the "minimal cues" (Erickson, 1964/1980, 1980b) of the hypnotic situation. Some particularly talented subjects can utilize their sensitivity to realign their sensory-perceptual and mental processes in a way that allows them to experience the classical phenomena of hypnosis and a variety of unusual and innovative state-dependent patterns of mind-body interactions.

Multiple Personality and State-Dependent Memory

In her Ph.D. dissertation, Jody Lienhart (1983) has formulated a state-dependent theory of multiple personality as exemplified by five well-documented cases (Sybil [Schreiber, 1973]; Chris Sizemore [Thigpen & Cleckley's *The Three Faces of Eve*, 1957; Sizemore, 1977]; Christina Peters [Peters, 1978]; Betsy [Brassfield, 1980, 1983]; and herself, Jody Lienhart [Brassfield, 1983; Putnam, 1982]). Lienhart had the opportunity to present an unusually thorough analysis of both the objective and subjective facts of each case, since she herself is one of them. She described the scope of her study and some of the theoretical assumptions she found support for, as follows (1983, pp. 6–7):

> Implicit in each of the studies of childhood trauma is the pervasive nature of paradoxical communication. Frequently, this double bind communication style appears during the formative, preverbal stages of childhood in which interpretation of these messages is confused. This results in insufficient experiential learning which would allow appropriate translation of the confused messages (Hilgard & Marquis, 1961).
> Characteristically, hypnosis is produced by paradoxical statements in which the messages are incongruent (Haley, 1963). Numerous studies have revealed that the processes of learning and recall differ under the hypnotic state than in normal "forgetting" (Hilgard, 1977).
> This study presents the theoretical assumption that multiple personality is developed through early childhood state-dependent learning. Furthermore, it is hypothesized that this learning occurs as a result of the hypnoidal effects of childhood trauma such as abuse and sexual molestation. The child, unable to translate the paradoxical nature of the messages he receives, fragments into a trance state. Furthermore, it is suggested that memories incorporated during each of these hypnoidal experiences are similar to knowledge acquired during state-dependent learning.

Under hypnosis, Lienhart was able to recall the critical incident of her own traumatic dissociation and the formation of a new personality before her fourth birthday, when she was seduced by her "Uncle Bulen."

She provides an unusually vivid description of her subjective state of being confused and "hypnotically stunned" by this traumatic incident (1983, pp. 74–75):

> The actual incident which triggered the first personality fragmentation was an attempt by Bulen to force the child into an act of fellatio. Jo Ella certainly had no conception of why the erect penis was being shoved into her mouth. She could only respond to his ominous threats and the sensation of choking on this enormous "thing." She could neither cope with the awful fear nor could she flee from it. At this point, Jo Ella's mind simply blanked out the dreaded experience. It was as if she had completely separated from her body and had disappeared.
>
> Moments, or maybe even hours later, the figure of the small child could be seen huddled against the large stucco building. It was late afternoon and the chill of early autumn brushed through her homemade dress. But this was not the same Jo Ella who had earlier struggled against the powerful grasp of her favorite "Uncle Bulen." The new child, Jo Ella II, was later dubbed the Kid. All memory traces of the earlier incident had vanished.
>
> The Kid was a perfect mimic and could ape the original personality very precisely. But this child was a totally new person in almost every way. Her perception of her world had been irretrievably altered. The previous incident had left complete confusion in the child's mind and this "lost time" could not be re-established within its contextual setting. Neither was it possible to cope with the incident because there were no experiential counterparts with which to compare it. Jo Ella II was hypnotically stunned and yet unable to find any of the words which would have allowed her to deal with the experience, either for herself or others.

Lienhart evaluates her own case (1983, pp. 89–90):

> Jody's case history is replete with similar self-contradictions which bind the child into an unresolvable conflictual state. The good, generous and loving uncle becomes a person who is cruel and sexually exploitive. Since the early Jo Ella cannot reconcile these extreme polarities, she enters into a trance state which emotionally removes her from the scene. The emergent personality, Jo Ella II, is amnesic for the incident. Indeed, the only access to the encapsulated experience is through hypnosis or through its reemergence in a situation which may have similar contextual cues.

In this description of the formation of a multiple personality, we find the salient characteristics of the *state-dependent theory of therapeutic hypnosis: a situation of extreme psychophysiological distress results in an amnesia for the stressful incident that is reversible by hypnosis.* Jody's case, as well as others in Lienhart's dissertation, emphasizes another important feature required of an adequate state-dependent theory of therapeutic hypnosis: It illuminates *the process of falling into a spontaneous state of hypnosis under circumstances of traumatic stress* (Cheek, 1960); it also illuminates the role of the double bind or paradoxical communication in precipitating and maintaining the dissociated state. Lienhart's case well illustrates the role of therapeutic hypnosis in accessing the memories encapsulated by the traumatic process of state-bound learning so that they can be therapeutically reintegrated into the total personality.

Lienhart concludes her analysis with a formulation of the role of context and mental sets in making knowledge consciously available in one state and not another. We will quote a portion of her view because it serves as a bridge to the language of "memory cues" as it is used by experimental psychologists in state-dependent memory research. Lienhart's insight that knowledge is separated into intellectual and emotional sets is of particular significance, since it provides support for Erickson's hypnotherapeutic approach of accessing emotional and intellectual memories independent of one another when he felt he was dealing with traumatic processes in his patients (Erickson & Rossi, 1979). Lienhart concludes (1983, pp. 88–89):

> Just as hypnosis requires intense concentration rather than "sleep," the multiple has learned to concentrate totally on certain memories from the past. The underlying problem appears to be one of retrieval from an infinite number of memory sets. It is within the retrieval process that the perceptual distortions occur. This creates a chaotic confusion because the individual memory units are not encapsulated within the proper "sets" in an orderly fashion. Thus, a memory cue from one period of life is stored with the wrong "memory set." Consequently, certain stimulus cues may trigger one of the behavior response sets but within the wrong context or sequence. The process is crudely similar to the distortions, condensations and symbolic connections which occur during the dream state. Knowledge which is accessible in one state is not available during the altered state as it is integrated poorly and distributed more randomly within the range of recall of the dominant personality.
>
> Another interesting feature demonstrated by multiples that is not well understood by researchers is the emotional detachment from the appropriate "intellectual" set. It would appear that some affective experiences are stored independently from their intellectual counterparts. As a result of this, an emotional unit from one set may attach itself to a constellation of cues which make up a totally different cognitive set.

The "infinite number of memory sets," each more or less state-bound, is what makes up the seemingly random patterns of associations that we experience as subjective consciousness in everyday life (Erickson, Rossi, & Rossi, 1976). Therapeutic hypnosis accesses these memory sets in a systematic manner to reactivate precisely those that are required for healing (Erickson & Rossi, 1979).

Recent theory and research on the phenomenon of multiple personality indicate that the subpersonalities can have different cognitive (Silberman, Putnam, Weingartner, Braun, & Post, 1985) and psychophysiological response patterns as well. Braun (1983a, b) has used the concept of state-dependent learning to account for the different memory systems in multiple personalities because "information which is encoded under one psychophysiological condition is best retrieved under the same psychophysiological condition" (1983a, p. 133).

In an objective study of multiple personality, Ludwig et al. (1972) found that "the only dissociated functions among the different states of consciousness pertained to *emotionally laden* information, skills, and activities associated with each specific personality" (Ludwig, 1983, p. 94). Neutral information, skills, and activities unrelated to the emotional issues of any aspects of the multiple personality were not dissociated. This emotionally laden aspect of dissociated or state-bound information in both multiple personality and hypnosis points once again to the functional involvement of the limbic-hypothalamic system as the major mind-body connection (transducer) for emotional processes.

Phobias and State-Dependent Memory, Learning, and Behavior

Since the first edition of this book a number of new papers have documented the value of state-dependent theory and practice in a variety of clinical situations: with psychosomatic states (Ciompi, 1991; Trum & Ritchie, 1992); with sex offenders (Carich & Parwatikar, 1992); and hypnotherapeutic abreactions with all forms of posttraumatic stress disorder (Putnam, 1992). The following cases from Bodden (1991) at the Scott and White Clinic of Texas A & M University are particularly interesting because they suggest how the earlier approaches of psychoanalysis and behaviorism can be understood as subsets of our more inclusive state-dependent memory and learning approach (pp. 24–25):

> Research has consistently shown that systematic desensitization is the treatment of choice for phobias. The current author has used this approach with good results for many years. Although therapeutic failures have been relatively infrequent, two recent cases involving simple phobias have caused this author to revise his thinking about direct symptom removal. The two

cases reported in this paper are important because taken together they seem to suggest a more adequate understanding of the issue of symptom removal and how hypnosis and ideomotor signaling can enhance treatment effectiveness achieved by behavior therapy alone.

The Case of "Ms. H."

After several sessions of systematic desensitization for a phobia of crossing bridges, "Ms. H." improved somewhat but then reached a plateau. Quite by chance the patient saw the movie *Mississippi Burning* before one of our sessions. It proved to be a very emotional experience because the point was a young girl in Mississippi during the period portrayed in the movie. The experience of seeing the movie enabled the patient to recall spontaneously the basis of her fear, what Rossi (1986c) would call a state-bound memory. This ability to recall consciously the origin of her phobia enabled the patient to conquer completely her fear with no further treatment.

The Case of "Dr. S."

"Dr. S." is a college professor who sought help for his intense fear of traveling and remaining overnight in a hotel. Desensitization gave the patient partial relief, but he was unable to rid himself completely of the phobia until we used ideomotor signaling in a hypnotic state (as described by Rossi & Cheek, 1988), enabling the patient to recall consciously the traumatic origins of his fear. It is important to note that as the patient began recalling the earlier traumatic memories he became quite emotional. Recalling the traumatic memories that served as the basis of the phobia enabled the patient to conquer completely his fear.

Theoretical Implications: The two main psychological explanations of phobic behavior are psychodynamic and behavioral. The psychodynamic approach is built upon the early writings of Freud (1956) on the traumatic basis of neurosis. Freud speculated that the intense anxiety (psychic pain) associated with the emotional trauma lead to dissociation, repression, and amnesia. Symptoms represented a dissociated or symbolic vestige of the repressed ("forgotten") trauma.

Behavioral explanations are built upon classical and operant conditioning models of learning. Classical conditioning explains how a neutral stimulus (e.g., a bridge) can acquire reactivity and elicit a fear response. Avoidant behavior, which preserves the phobia, is acquired and maintained by operant conditioning. Treatment apparently involves gradual extinction of the fear response.

These two divergent explanations have spawned quite different therapeutic approaches, with the behavioral approach (systematic desensitization) demonstrating greater empirical support for its effectiveness. The problem is made complex theoretically by the fact that desensitization doesn't always work, even when applied in a competent fashion. The theoretical question is "Why?" Each theory can, to some extent, account for failure of the other approach, but they cannot account for the other's successes.

Freud's early work on the traumatic basis of neurosis pointed to but offered an incorrect explanation of phobias whose origins were unconscious or state bound (i.e., not available to recall during the normal conscious state). The behavioral explanation was a good fit for explaining phobias whose origins were available to conscious recall (and thus not state-bound).

The seemingly opposite explanations offered by behaviorism and psychoanalysis can perhaps be understood as subsets of a broader and more inclusive theoretical construct: state-dependent memory and learning.

A Psychobiological Resolution of the Mind-Body Problem

If we take these views of recent psychobiological research to their logical conclusion, we have a pragmatic solution to the centuries' old mind-body problem—indeed, a resolution of the Cartesian dualism of mind and body. Mind and body are not separate phenomena, one being somehow spirit and the other matter. Mind and body are both aspects of one information system. Life is an information system. Biology is a process of information transduction. *Mind* and *body* are two facets or two ways of conceptualizing this *single information system*.

Most theories of mind-body relationships stop short at this point without saying anything more definite about *how* mind and body are connected and *how* they communicate. Here, we will not avoid this basic issue by omission or vague philosophical nostrums. The state-dependent theory of mind-body communication and healing can be expressed as four integrated hypotheses:

1) The limbic-hypothalamic system is the major anatomical connecting link between mind and body.
2) State-dependent memory, learning, and behavior processes encoded in the limbic-hypothalamic and closely related systems are the major information transducers between mind and body.
3) All methods of mind-body healing and therapeutic hypnosis operate by accessing and reframing the state-dependent memory and learning systems that encode symptoms and problems.
4) The state-dependent encoding of mind-body symptoms and problems can be accessed by psychological as well as physiological (e.g., drugs) approaches—and the placebo response is a synergistic interaction of both.

The major thrust of these hypotheses is that *mind-body information transduction* and *state-dependent memory, learning, and behavior* mediated by the limbic-hypothalamic system, are the two fundamental processes of mind-body communication and healing. Medical science has specialized in all the anatomical, physiological, and pharmacological methods of accessing and facilitating healing; that is, it has focused almost exclusively on the "body side" of the mind-body equation. In this chapter we have developed an experimentally based psychophysiological rationale for understanding how *psychological* factors can facilitate healing as well. State-dependent memory, learning, and behavior phenomena are the "missing link" in all previous theories of mind-body relationships. They bridge the mysterious gap between mind and body; they are the common denominator between traditional Western medicine and all the holistic, shamanistic, and spiritualistic approaches to healing that depend upon highly specialized cultural belief systems, world views, and frames of reference.

We are now in a position to explain the many forms of iatrogenic illness and healing that have been so difficult for Western medicine and psychology to understand. The state-dependent theory of mind-body healing can elucidate, for example, how even in our modern age, researchers (Dunlap, Henderson, & Inch, 1952) could have found that 30 percent of the 17,000 medical prescriptions they studied in England were actually placebos in the sense that the drugs did not have any specific physiological effect on the conditions for which they were prescribed. We can now understand how *any drug that alters any aspect of the body's sensory-perceptual or physiological responsiveness on any level can disrupt the more-or-less fragile state-dependent encoding of symptoms and thereby evoke a "nonspecific" but very real healing effect that we call the "placebo response."*

Let us now turn our attention to a more detailed study of the relationship between mind-body symptoms, state-dependent learning, and therapeutic hypnosis through a comparison of the pioneering research of Hans Selye and Milton Erickson.

4

Stress and Psychosomatic Phenomena

DURING THE PAST HALF century, the study of stress and psychosomatic phenomena has been the major stimulus for investigating mind-body communication and healing. Our approach to this area will be to update and integrate the work of two major pioneers: the physiologist Hans Selye, and the psychiatrist and hypnotherapist Milton Erickson. These two investigators contributed profoundly original observations to our understanding of psychosomatic phenomena: Selye primarily from his innovative physiological experiments on stress; Erickson primarily from his open-ended, naturalistic investigations of spontaneous psychosomatic dysfunctions during hypnosis. Integrating their work leads to a more comprehensive understanding of mind-body problems and the means of facilitating their resolution.

In this chapter we will review Selye's formulation of the *General Adaptation Syndrome* (GAS), which has been described aptly as the foundation of psychosomatic medicine. We will use the concept of *state-dependent memory and learning* and its natural consequent, *state-bound information and behavior*, to update Selye's view of the GAS. Recent research that has deepened our understanding of the functions of the hypothalamus then will be used to integrate Selye's concept of the GAS with Erickson's view of the experiential and psycho-neuro-physiological basis of hypnotherapy.

SELYE'S CONCEPT OF THE GENERAL ADAPTATION SYNDROME (GAS)

Selye acknowledged the influence of the great French physiologist, Claude Bernard, in the evolution of his concept of the GAS (1974). Bernard stated that one of the most characteristic features of all life is its ability to maintain the *constancy of its inner milieu*, the environment within its skin. Walter Cannon (1932, 1953) later called this property

homeostasis: the characteristic of maintaining a steady internal physiological state despite external changes in the environment. Life's response
to any injury or disease could be characterized as an effort to maintain
its homeostatic balance against the intrusion or change from the outside
world. Selye's first original contribution was to show that whatever the
source of *biological stress* intruding upon the organism, it would react
with *the same pattern of response* to restore its internal homeostasis. He
described his process of discovery as follows (Selye, 1974, pp. 24–27):

> In 1926, as a second year medical student, I first came across this problem
> of a stereotyped response to any exacting demand made upon the body. I
> began to wonder why patients suffering from the most diverse diseases that
> threaten homeostasis have so many signs and symptoms in common.
> Whether a man suffers from a severe loss of blood, an infectious disease, or
> advanced cancer, he loses his appetite, his muscular strength, and his ambi-
> tion to accomplish anything; usually, the patient also loses weight, and even
> his facial expression betrays that he is ill. What is the scientific basis of what
> at that time I thought of as the "syndrome of just being sick"?
>   . . . *How could different stimuli produce the same result?* In 1936, this problem
> presented itself again—under conditions more suited to exact laboratory anal-
> ysis. It turned out in the course of my experiments in which rats were injected
> with various impure and toxic gland preparations that, irrespective of the
> tissue from which they were made or their hormone content, the injections
> produced a stereotyped syndrome (a set of simultaneously occurring organ
> changes), characterized by enlargement and hyperactivity of the adrenal cor-
> tex, shrinkage (or atrophy) of the thymus gland and lymph nodes, and the
> appearance of gastrointestinal ulcers.
>   . . . It soon became evident from animal experiments that the same set of
> organ changes caused by the glandular extracts were also produced by cold,
> heat, infection, trauma, hemorrhage, nervous irritation, and many other
> stimuli. . . . This reaction was first described, in 1936, as a "syndrome pro-
> duced by various nocuous agents" and subsequently became known as the
> *General Adaptation Syndrome* (GAS), or the *biological stress syndrome*. Its three
> stages—(1) the alarm reation; (2) the stage of resistance; and (3) the stage of
> exhaustion.

While the basic observations underlying Selye's concept of the GAS
have been confirmed, recent research on the messenger molecule system of stress has led to a broader understanding and reinterpretation of
his three stages. There have been many apparently conflicting results in
research programs designed to determine what actually constitutes the
stress response, the psychobiological processes associated with it, and

the defenses against it (Munck, Guyre, & Holbrook, 1984). It is most puzzling to learn, for example, that even after two generations of research we cannot always predict whether the various psychological shocks and novel experiences will summate to increase the stress response or whether a kind of adaptation and inhibition will occur in a particular situation. The relationships between "psychological meaning" and information transduction at the mind-brain level are obviously complex and nonlinear (Rossi & Cheek, 1988).

Current developments at the Santa Fe Institute in New Mexico suggest that the new mathematics of *complex adaptive systems* may be the most promising approach to a clinical understanding of these constantly evolving and emergent psychobiological dynamics even if we cannot always predict them (Holland, Holyoak, Nisbett, & Thagard, 1986; Kaufmann, 1993). This leads us to a fundamental shift away from the ideal of "prediction and control" that was so typical of the oversimplified "stimulus-response, black-box behaviorism" of past generations that is still lauded so highly in traditional psychology (Lattal, 1992). The new psychotherapeutic approaches to be outlined in this and the following chapters will present an alternative to behavioral programming in clinical work that is more in keeping with the complexities of stress, healing, and creativity as experienced by real people. We will learn how to access each patient's unique repertory of inner resources to facilitate a creative resolution of personal problems that often comes as a *surprise* to both patient and therapist.

Sapolsky (1992a, b) has presented a realistic account of these complexities and clarified how Selye's third stage of *exhaustion*, in particular, is wrong. Chronic stress does not lead to an exhaustion of the arousal (stress) messenger molecules such as adrenaline (epinephrine) and cortisol. The exact reverse is true. It is the chronic excess of these arousal messengers over time, even when an emergency is no longer present, that leads to an eventual collective breakdown of various parts of the mind-body that we call the "stress" or "psychosomatic" response. Stress becomes pathogenic when it persists over time because we lose the capacity to turn off the mind-body's signals that there is or has been a problem. These new psychobiological insights suggest how we may reformulate the time course of Selye's GAS into two stages as illustrated in Figure 2 where there is (1) an initial *complex adaptive response* of alarm and arousal on the left half and (2) the eventual maladaptive consequences of the *prolonged stress response* when arousal becomes chronic, leading to the mind-body problems listed on the right side of Figure 2.

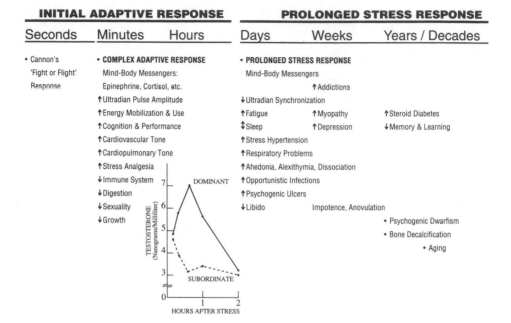

INITIAL ADAPTIVE RESPONSE			PROLONGED STRESS RESPONSE		
Seconds	Minutes	Hours	Days	Weeks	Years / Decades

• Cannon's 'Fight or Flight' Response

• **COMPLEX ADAPTIVE RESPONSE**
Mind-Body Messengers:
Epinephrine, Cortisol, etc.
↑Ultradian Pulse Amplitude
↑Energy Mobilization & Use
↑Cognition & Performance
↑Cardiovascular Tone
↑Cardiopulmonary Tone
↑Stress Analgesia
↓Immune System
↓Digestion
↓Sexuality
↓Growth

• **PROLONGED STRESS RESPONSE**
Mind-Body Messengers
         ↑Addictions
↓Ultradian Synchronization
↑Fatigue   ↑Myopathy   ↑Steroid Diabetes
↕Sleep   ↑Depression   ↓Memory & Learning
↑Stress Hypertension
↑Respiratory Problems
↑Ahedonia, Alexithymia, Dissociation
↑Opportunistic Infections
↑Psychogenic Ulcers
↓Libido   Impotence, Anovulation

                   • Psychogenic Dwarfism
                   • Bone Decalcification
                   • Aging

FIGURE 2 Outline of some of the major mind-body responses to alarm, trauma, and stress. The initial adaptive response ranging from a few seconds to hours is usually positive for survival; the prolonged (chronic) stress response is negative for health. The graph illustrating the contrasting course of testosterone levels to the same stressor in socially dominant versus subordinate male baboons is a striking example of the typical ultradian periodicity of the stress response (adapted from Sapolsky, 1990).

Seconds.   The initial complex adaptive response to a mentally perceived danger (anything from an obstruction on the road while driving to the actual trauma of an accident) requires less than a second and is usually experienced as instantaneous. This first mind-brain-body signaling of the sympathetic nervous system releases the messenger *norepinephrine* from most nerve endings of our sensory-perceptual system (particularly sight and sound) which enhances the possibility of a highly adaptive, rapid activation of our reflex response system (the "fight or flight" response as Cannon called it). In addition, the sympathetic nervous system signals the adrenal medulla to flood the blood stream with the related messenger *epinephrine* (the catecholamine feedback of Figure 1) within a few seconds to evoke adaptive responses in many tissues and cells throughout the body such as the release and utilization of *glucose* as a fuel to energize emergency responses.

These two initial almost instantaneous catecholamine messengers (norepinephrine and epinephrine) together with glucose encode the various sensations, perceptions, images, emotions, and memories of the emergency in a state-dependent manner (McGaugh, 1989). When the mind-body returns to normal within an hour or two and the encoding levels of the messenger molecules drop down to basal levels, the details of the emergency may appear to fade from memory; with emotionally disturbing situations, in particular, an apparent amnesia may already be in progress. As we illustrate with much of the case material of this volume, it may require a subtly activating hypnotherapeutic process to rearouse the level of the messenger molecules to bring the memories back up to awareness (Weinstein & Au, 1991).

Within seconds after a stressor is perceived on the mind-brain level, certain cells within the hypothalamus transduce the neurally encoded information into the emergency messenger molecule corticotropin-releasing hormone (CRH). CRH signals the neighboring pituitary gland to release the "master brain-body messenger molecule" adrenocorticotropin (ACTH) into the blood stream within about 15 seconds where it travels throughout the body evoking many adaptive responses in the heart, lungs, liver, brain, and muscles in 20 to 30 seconds.

This first stage of the complex adaptive response is now recognized as being much more intricate than Selye could have known. CRH is only one of about half a dozen hypothalamic messengers that signals the pituitary to release ACTH. Further, it is now believed that different stressors experienced by the mind-body may release different combinations of these messengers to be sent from the hypothalamus. Thus Selye's GAS is not as nonspecific as he believed. The main direction of the circular (cybrenetic) informational loop between the limbic-hypothalamic-pituitary system of the mind-brain to the adrenals of the body and back again illustrated in Figure 1 remains correct, however.

This recognition of the specificity of many of the relationships between stressors and the mind-body's messenger molecules that mediate adaptation as well as stress and healing is one of the most important insights in psychobiology during the past generation. There has been the gradual realization that ACTH is only one of a complex of many messengers released by the pituitary that may encode state-dependent memory, mood, learning, and behavior (De Wied, 1984, 1990). Many of these mind-body messengers (which will be detailed later in the second half of this book) can signal different patterns of genes to turn on and off to regulate most of the metabolic and healing functions of the body in response to the accidents, traumas, and stressors life is heir to. Our major hypothesis is that psychotherapeutic processes can access the state-dependent encoding of these stressors of the complex adaptation response and mediate healing by the same or similar patterns of mind-body messengers.

Minutes.		Within a few minutes after receiving the ACTH messenger, cells within the cortex of the adrenal glands release cortisol (one of the major glucocorticoids) in the blood stream. Cortisol is recognized as the major activating messenger that signal a multitude of adaptive emergency responses in the various organs, tissues, and cells throughout the body; this is summarized on the left side of Figure 2. There is a mobilization of energy, an increase in cardiovascular and cardiopulmonary tone, as well as a sharpening of perceptions and cognition so that performance is enhanced on a variety of levels from physical strength and speed to intellectual skills. This performance optimization is a *catabolic* (using up) process that requires a tremendous expenditure of psychobiological resources, however. This fast burn of inner resources is bought at the price of temporarily suppressing the natural processes of growth and healing—the *anabolic* (building-up) processes. There is an inhibition of digestive, sexual, and immune systems. A "stress-induced analgesia" is typically evident during the traumatic emergency situations of war and accidents; even in everyday life people report being "numb" with emotional shock or distress.

Evidence for the central role of psychological factors, such as the perception of danger or a frustrating situation, in the expression of the physiological aspects of the stress response has been well described by Sapolsky (1992b, p. 313) in a simple but ingenious experiment as follows:

> Suppose two monkeys are both deprived of food to the point where metabolic homeostasis is disturbed and to an equal extent in both animals. Both should then secrete glucocorticoids; if there are marked differences in the amount of glucocorticoids secreted, the well-trained physiologist should immediately think of explanations such as differences in ACTH half-lives in the blood, differences in adrenal perfusion rates, numbers of glucocorticoid receptors, and so on. This would be the traditional approach of stress physiologists.
>
> One study suffices to show how much more complex the picture really is. In the study cited above, the two monkeys differed in one critical way. While both were deprived on any nutrition, the second was fed a non-nutritive, flavored placebo. That monkey did not secrete glucocorticoids, whereas the first one had a sizeable stress-response. Nothing in the world of Selye and

the physiologists could have predicted this outcome because their homeo-static balance was equally disturbed (they were equally hypoglycemic). The second monkey did not **perceive** things to be as stressful as did the first one.

This study signaled a major change in the study of stress physiology. The prior view held that if you knew how physiologically disruptive the external insult was, you had a good chance of predicting the magnitude of the stress-response. Suddenly, there was a critical intermediary—psychological factors could modulate the stressfulness of a stressor. Psychological factors could even trigger a stress-response in the absence of homeostatic disruption: Animals and humans were shown to have classic stress-responses during bereavement, difficult cognitive tasks, conditioned fear, and so on.

This *perception* of food deprivation that leads to a negative experience of stress requires time. How long does the adaptive phase of the alarm response last? How much time is required before the initial adaptive period of performance optimization during the alarm response is converted to the negative consequences of prolonged stress listed on the right side of Figure 2? How long can we continue to expend energy and resources (catabolism) at the expense of building up and storing energy and resources (anabolism)? This is a complex question, indeed, that takes us to the leading edge of mind-body stress and healing research.

Another way of approaching this question is to ask, how long does a good fight last? From an evolutionary point of view, how long do predator and prey chase, escape and/or fight before the resources of one or the other are exhausted—a few minutes, 5 minutes, or 10 to 20 minutes at a maximum? On a variety of levels, from the molecular-genetic and the neuroendocrinological to the processes of memory and learning, it is now recognized (Lloyd & Rossi, 1992a) that a 20-minute period is needed for important transitions. During the Iraq-Kuwait war the French army engineer Jacques Damen reported that 20 minutes was the optimal performance period of concentration for soldiers probing the sands of Kuwait for land mines armed with little more than a small shovel and their steady nerves. After about 20 minutes their nerves apparently gave out and they began to shake. While there certainly are wide individual differences in stamina between people and their responses to various performance and stress situations, we can safely say that the optimal period of the arousal stage of the alarm response usually peaks within the domain of minutes.

Hours. It is now well-established that the flow of endocrine messenger molecules from the hypothalamic-pituitary system and the adrenals to the body takes place in a pulsate rather than a steady manner

(Veldhuis, 1992). There are, for example, almost hourly pulses of corti-sol activating the mind-body that are followed about twenty minutes later by a pulse of β-endorphin that quiets it down. As we shall review in greater detail later in Chapter 8, these circahoral (about an hour) or ultradian (more than the once a day "circadian" rhythm) divide the typical work day into natural performance periods that are typically punctuated by 15- to 20-minute breaks (Rossi & Nimmons, 1991). A 90-minute "basic rest activity cycle" is apparently associated with the pulsate release of messenger molecules of the neuroendocrine axis in a widely fluctuating, adaptive manner that may be more adequately described by the new mathematics of complex adaptive systems (Wal-drop, 1992) rather than the idea of biological clocks and regular rhythms. Similarly, at night there are approximately 90-minute cycles shifting between 20- to 30-minute dream peaks and deeper troughs of slow-wave sleep.

An exquisite illustration of the intimate relationships between time, the hormonal messenger molecule testosterone, stress, and social be-havior within the ultradian domain is presented by the graph in Figure 2. Sapolsky (1990; Sapolsky & Ray, 1989) found that under the extreme stress of being captured and submitted to chemical anesthesia, wild male baboons showed strikingly different profiles of testosterone re-sponse. Socially dominant males experienced a peak of testosterone within an hour while subordinate male baboons had a trough. Within two hours, a typical basic activity rest cycle, testosterone leveled out to the same level for both social types. Sapolsky believes that a rise in testosterone could lead the dominant males to a more advantageous and aggressive social profile because it is related to an increase in energy availability and glucose consumption. Like many other hormones such as cortisol and β-endorphin, testosterone has a typical ultradian period-icity of about 90 minutes in human males (Veldhuis et al., 1987). It appears as if the emergency stress of Sapolsky's wild baboons adap-tively entrains the natural ultradian periodicity of the arousal response mediated by cortisol as well as the relaxation response by β-endorphin.

Most everyday human activities have a similar 90-minute periodicity plus or minus about 30 minutes: work and study periods, housework and shopping, a good lunch or dinner, music performances, movies, and theater all have a similar ultradian period. The natural ultradian pulses of the neuroendocrine axis marshals our forces for a performance push in the outside world for an hour and a half or so and then we usually experience a need for rest, food, and relaxation that may be associated with actual sleep and daydreaming. The left and right cerebral hemispheres of the brain undergo similar ultradian shifts in dominance that most of us hardly even notice as our mental skills, moods, and personality dynamics subtly shift throughout the day in a wave-like manner (Rossi, 1992d; Rossi & Lippincott, 1992).

The various forms of psychotherapy have varying ultradian periodicities that appear to entrain behaviors associated with different phases of the basic activity rest cycle. We may suppose that the very directive and brief consultation-therapy sessions of 15 to 20 minutes favored by the medical community either shock patients into a peak phase of arousal (e.g., the typical phenomenon of blood pressure increase just when it is measured during an office visit) or, paradoxically, a trough phase of submissive acceptance associated with a mild mental and physical shutdown (perhaps accounting for not quite remembering what the doctor said and the consequent inability to comply with medical recommendations). The typical 50-minute hour of psychoanalysis would obviously entrain the natural 20-minute ultradian trough period when the patient lays down on a couch to "free associate." Freud thought he had given up hypnosis; chronobiological research had not yet documented the proclivity to fantasy and imagery during this ultradian rest phase (Globus, 1972; Globus, Phoebus, & Moore, 1970; Kripke, 1982; Kripke, Mullaney, & Fleck, 1985).

Similarly, most holistic psychotherapists, whatever their method (acupuncture, biofeedback, body-work, meditation, imagery, music, and various forms of hypnosis and the relaxation response) are also entraining the naturally rejuvenating aspects of the ultradian healing response without realizing it (Rossi & Nimmons, 1991). Patients therapeutically reframe emotional problems in a seemingly spontaneous (autocatalytic) manner when they can experience the arousal phase of emotional catharsis (shouting, crying, etc.) and the dramatic uncovering of traumatic memories associated with the release of the stress hormone messengers that encoded the traumatic memories in the first place. Of course they would report feeling "really alive, free, and empowered" during such peak periods of ultradian activation when the cortisol family of messengers is energizing their entire mind-body. It is, then, not at all surprising that when the β-endorphin family of relaxation messengers just naturally slips in about 20 minutes later they feel "so comfortable, good, and really well" with such gratitude and positive "transference" for their wonderful therapist. New insights easily flow at such times because the β-endorphin family of messenger molecules also encodes different aspects of SDMLB, as well as mood and emotions (Izquierdo et al., 1988a, b; Rossi, 1987, 1990b).

Days, Months, and Decades. When the arousal response is prolonged in a chronic manner beyond hours to days, weeks, months, and even decades people will experience to varying degrees the mind-body problems listed on the right side of Figure 2. The common denominator to most of these stress-related dysfunctions is that the hormonal messenger molecules are sent in larger amounts for prolonged periods of time; the initial adaptive alarm response does not shut off. Messenger molecules in the blood stream flood the entire mind-body with an excess stimulation beyond the normal ultradian time domain. Why does the alarm response not shut off? The answer appears to be that when the cell receptors that receive these messengers are overwhelmed with excessive, prolonged stimulation a self-protective process called *downregulation* takes place. Just as you would turn down the annoying volume of a too-loud radio receiver, the individual cells of the brain and body can pull in many of the thousands of receptors they normally have on their surface and destroy them before the excessive signal destroys the cell itself.

The Addictions. These dynamics of the messenger molecule and cell receptor system are the mind-body basis of a similar four-step process that takes place in all the addictions: (1) any prolonged period of exertion will lead to an excess of adrenaline, cortisol, and their associated messengers flooding the mind-body in a state-dependent manner; (2) receptors for these messengers will downregulate to the point where they are below normal; (3) since the receptors are below their usual level the person will now experience *withdrawal*; they will not feel up to their normal energy, mood, and performance level; and (4) the person is now tempted to compulsively overwork to get back their "adrenaline high." Many overachievers—professionals, executives, athletes, perfectionistic housewives, and computer hackers—complain that they just don't feel right unless they are busy. Caught in an ever-accelerating and self-destructive positive feedback cycle that whips them on higher and faster, they eventually get so busy that their mind-body breaks down into varying patterns of the psychosomatic symptoms listed on the right side of Figure 2.

Some people are tempted to use artificial stimulants when faced with the performance decrements, fatigue, anhedonia, alexithymia, and depression of the withdrawal experience. This is particularly true during the period between three and five o'clock in the afternoon when many people experience what some researchers call "breaking point," (Tsuji & Kobayshi, 1988). At this time the day's most prominent energy dip takes place when the low point of the daily circadian cycle and ultradian rhythms coincide. Instead of taking a sensible nap at this time the addictive personality will engage in a desperate effort to hype up the mind-body artificially with excess calories, caffeine, alcohol, and worse (i.e., all the addicting drugs such as amphetamine, cocaine etc.). *From this perspective it is fascinating to realize that virtually all addictions and psychosomatic problems are dysfunctions of mind-body communication in the broad cybernetic loop between the psychosocial pressures of human experience and the messenger molecule-receptor levels of gene expression.* Many addictions that have their source in the prolonged stress of everyday life involve an initial ignoring or active suppression of our normal mind-body signals to enjoy a few comfortable ultradian healing-rest breaks throughout the day (Rossi & Nimmons, 1991); these addictions can often be resolved with psychotherapy oriented toward insight, attitude, and behavior change. When excessive social-community pressures and/or the medical prescription of drugs initiate an addictive cycle of substance abuse, however, more extensive psychosocial support is required on all levels from the twelve-step programs to the rehabilitation of entire neighborhoods.

Stress, Neuronal Death, and Aging.   Without doubt, one of the most surprising and alarming findings of clinical neuroscience in recent years is that chronic stress can lead to the death of the neurons in the hippocampus of the brain that are associated with learning and memory formation. It has been shown in a wide range of animals, from rats and primates to humans, that the hippocampus also plays a central role in the negative feedback loop that in effect tells the adrenals to stop secreting cortisol (the glucocorticoids) during stress (Sapolsky, 1992a). During chronic stress, however, the glucocorticoids can inhibit glucose and oxygen utilization by hippocampal neurons so that memory, learning, and hormonal messenger feedback is impaired in a ever-worsening cycle. Finally, actual neuronal death takes place along with hypersecretion of the glucocorticoids. Diagnostic tests can pick up this loss of feedback sensitivity (the dexamethasone suppression test) in the normal human aging process. About 50% of patients with major depression evidence signs of glucocorticoid hypersecretion during certain times of the day. Hypercortisolism is also associated with psychotic depression in aged patients. Major problems of aging associated with Parkinsonism and Alzheimer's disease are also implicated in the process of excessive neural "excitotoxicity" of stress (Taylor, 1992).

It is probably not coincidental that depression and aging share another commonality: a loss in the normal ultradian and circadian syn-

chronicity of many hormonal messenger molecules of the neuroendocrinal axis. Stress engenders the desynchrony of many mind-body
rhythms associated with optimal performance and healing in a variety
of ways that could be interpreted as contradictory and paradoxical or
perhaps more simply as a sign that complex adaptive systems are involved as described above. Sometimes stress is associated with *low amplitude dysrhythmia* wherein the person reaches neither the peaks of
alertness required for optimal performance in outer world tasks nor the
depths of slow-wave sleep associated with the healing effects of the
release of growth hormone during the first 90-minute period of sleep
(Rossi & Nimmons, 1991; Wever, 1988).

Other stress conditions that are commonly dealt with in psychotherapy can effect the amplitude of cortisol secretion in various ways. The
acute stage of recovery from alcoholism, for example, increases cortisol
amplitude while sustained abstinence leads to a decrease (Iranmanesh
et al., 1989a). Fasting leads to an increase in cortisol amplitude, while
alterations in both ACTH and cortisol have been found in patients with
eating disorders (Vance & Thorner, 1989). All of these changing psychobiological processes that take place in a more or less hidden manner
during the typical course of psychotherapy probably account for much
of the apparent mystery of the patient's constantly shifting state-
dependent, emotional, memory, and defensive processes to which we
will now turn our attention.

Stress and State-Dependent Memory, Mood, and Behavior

The first two stages of Selye's GAS, the alarm reaction and the state
of resistance—which we now prefer to call the complex adaptive response—take on a profoundly new significance in the light of recent
research on state-dependent memory, learning, and behavior. The
alarm reaction is characterized by the activation of the sympathetic nervous system, which stimulates the release of epinephrine and norepinephrine from the adrenal medullae. As we noted earlier, McGaugh's
research (1983, 1989) demonstrated that these are the same hormones
(among others) that modulate the retention of memory. *Learning and
memory acquired during Selye's alarm reaction therefore tend to be state-
dependent!* A person in a traumatic car accident experiences an intense
rush of the alarm reaction hormones. His detailed memories of the accident are intertwined with the complex psychophysiological state associated with these hormones. When he returns to his usual or ''normal''

psychophysiological states of awareness a few hours or days later, the memories of the accident become fuzzy or, in really severe cases, as illustrated in the case of traumatic amnesia of the previous chapter, the victim may be completely amnesic. The memories of the accident have become "state-bound"—that is, they are bound to the precise psycho-physiological state evoked by the alarm reaction, together with its asso-ciated sensory perceptual impressions of the accident.

Gold (1984) recently validated this experimentally when he found that "a single injection of epinephrine results in long-lasting change in brain function. . . . The findings suggest that some hormonal responses may not only regulate neuronal changes responsible for memory storage but may also themselves initiate long-lasting alterations in neuronal func-tion" (p. 379).

Such alterations at the mind-brain neuronal level lead to a period during which psychosomatic symptoms become particularly evident and troublesome. In our car accident example, the psychosomatic re-sponse could be any part of the alarm reaction that was originally experi-enced—anxiety, pain, hysterical paralysis, headaches, ulcers, etc. The victim now is struck with a subtle "problem of adaptation" that tradi-tional physical medicine often does not know how to deal with. This is especially the case when the initial cause of the stress (such as the car accident) has disappeared and yet the mind-body—having learned a new defensive (psychosomatic) mode of adaptation, continues with it. *The psychosomatic mode of adaptation was learned during a special (usually traumatic) state-dependent psychophysiological condition; it continues because it remains state-bound or locked into that special psychophysiological condition even after the patient apparently returns to his normal mode of functioning.*

Selye proposed a number of solutions for the psychosomatic prob-lems manifested during this *stage of resistance*. Most typically, medica-tion could be used to counteract the stressor hormones or, in extreme cases, surgery could remove the adrenals that produce the hormones. Selye frequently described this stage of resistance as being "stuck in a groove." That was his way of describing what we now recognize as state-bound psychophysiological behavior. Selye reasoned that if a shock could get one stuck in a groove, perhaps another shock could get one out again so that the person could "snap out of disease" (Selye, 1976, p. 9). He believed that the various forms of shock (electroconvul-sive and insulin shock treatment for the mentally ill, psychological shock, etc.) were types of *nonspecific therapies* that counteracted many of the *nonspecific aspects* of the GAS. In a following section we will see how this understanding of the relationship between shock and the nonspecific approach to psychosomatic problems has an almost exact, though previously unrecognized, correspondence to Erickson's use of psychological shock as a general (nonspecific) approach to a variety of emotional problems.

State-Dependent Memory, Mood, and the Murder of Robert Kennedy

An unusually clear example of how a traumatic situation involving the heightened state of Selye's alarm reaction can generate state-bound information accessible by hypnosis is provided in the following description of the assassination of Robert Kennedy (Bower, 1981, p. 12):

> [This] illustration involves a talk I had recently with Bernard Diamond, a forensic psychiatrist who lives in the Bay Area, about a famous criminal case he dealt with—the case of Sirhan Sirhan, the man who assassinated Bobby Kennedy in Los Angeles in 1968. . . . Interestingly, Sirhan has absolutely no recollection of the actual murder, which occurred in the small kitchen of the Ambassador Hotel where he pumped several bullets into Kennedy. *Sirhan carried out the deed in a greatly agitated state and was completely amnesiac with regard to the event.* Diamond, called in by Sirhan's attorneys, hypnotized Sirhan and helped him to reconstruct from memory the events of that fateful day. *Under hypnosis, as Sirhan became more worked up and excited, he recalled progressively more, the memories tumbling out while his excitement built to a crescendo leading up to the shooting.* At that point Sirhan would scream out the death curses, "fire" the shots, and then choke as he reexperienced the Secret Service bodyguard nearly throttling him after he was caught. On different occasions, while in trance, Sirhan was able to recall the crucial events, sometimes speaking, other times recording his recollections in automatic writing, but the recall was always accompanied by great excitement.
>
> The curious feature of the case was that material uncovered under hypnosis never became consciously available to Sirhan in his waking state, and he denied that he committed the murder. Moreover, he denied that he had ever been hypnotized by Diamond, denied that it was his own voice on the tape recorder, and denied that it was his handwriting—he alleged that Diamond must have hired an actor or a handwriting specialist to mimic him. Sirhan eventually did accept the theory that he must have killed Bobby Kennedy, rationalizing it as an act of heroism in the cause of Arab nationalism. But his belief was based on "hearsay," much as is my belief that I was born on a Wednesday evening—I must have been there but I sure cannot remember it. (Italics added)

The generation of state-bound information in an extreme psychophysiological state of alarm is clearly evident in this case: "Sirhan carried out the deed in a *greatly agitated state* and was *amnesiac* with regard to the event. . . . Under hypnosis, as Sirhan became more and more worked up and excited, he recalled progressively more, the memories tumbling out while his excitement built to a crescendo leading up to the shooting." The "greatly agitated state" was a heightened state of the psychophysiological alarm response that was so extreme that Sirhan's memories became state-bound: They were *dissociated* from his normal waking consciousness so that they had a complete amnesia for the shooting. Hypnosis enabled Sirhan to reexperience this extremely altered psychophysiological state, and with it, "the memories [came] tumbling out while his excitement built to a crescendo." This well-documented illustration of the intimate association between the endocrine system, the alarm response, and state-bound information in the form of an amnesia that can be reversed under hypnosis is typical of many examples. By accessing the heightened state of emotion in which these memories were state-bound, hypnosis was able to retrieve them.

The objection could be raised that the extreme stress of the Sirhan Sirhan case might be an exception in generating state-bound information; after all, the situation is very different in more typical daily living where emotions and moods are of a milder nature. Bower (1981; Gilligan & Bower, 1984) has undertaken a series of experimental studies investigating this generation of state-bound information by the emotional and mood states typical of daily living. He used "hypnotically induced moods . . . to create an experimental analog of affect-state-dependent learning" to measure memory and recall (Bower, 1981, p. 131). He found that when subjects learned material in a hypnotically-induced happy mood, they recalled it better when they were again in a happy mood. The same affect-state-dependent learning took place when a hypnotically-induced sad mood was the acquisition condition for learning.

Emotional states were also significant for recalling childhood memories: In a happy mood, subjects recalled more happy memories from childhood; in a sad mood, they recalled more sad memories. Bower's work demonstrates how emotions can generate state-bound information that is accessible by hypnotically-induced moods matching the acquisition condition in which the information was first encoded. Bowers formulated an "associative network theory of memory and emotion" to explain the "mood-state-dependent retrieval" that can be activated by physiological or symbolic verbal processes. Gazzaniga (1985) has discussed recent research in left and right cerebral hemispheric processes supporting the view that these associative "networks of the mind" can act as semiautonomous "modules" with many of the functional characteristics of the "unconscious" and with what we are calling here "statebound information and behavior."

It is precisely in such interactions of the physiological and symbolic, demonstrated in the work of Bower and Gazzaniga, that we recognize the type of mind-body connections most easily accessible by hypnosis. This experimental work, together with that of other investigators (Blum, 1967, 1972; Gage, 1983) thus provides a sound research base for the efficacy of therapeutic hypnosis, in which patients' associative networks and frames of reference are carefully accessed and utilized for resolving mind-body problems (Erickson, 1985; Erickson & Rossi, 1979).

ERICKSON'S HYPNOTIC INVESTIGATIONS OF PSYCHOSOMATIC PHENOMENA

Erickson's original contributions to the field of psychosomatic medicine are contained in four papers that were published together in the January 1943 issue of the journal *Psychosomatic Medicine* (1943a, b, c, d/ 1980). These papers on the *psychological* components of psychosomatic phenomena summarized the results of a decade of wide-ranging experimental and clinical hypnotic work that took place during the same time period when Selye was making his fundamental discovery of the *physiological* components. In a sense Erickson's and Selye's research was both complementary and reciprocal: Selye discovered the same physiological response to different stressors—the GAS; Erickson discovered psychologically different responses to the same stressor in what he termed "coincidental phenomena." Taken together, their work provides a comprehensive picture of the genesis and methods of resolving psychosomatic problems.

Viewed in isolation, Selye's work would imply that since different stressors all generate the same physiological syndrome (adrenal cortex enlargement, immune system suppression, and gastrointestinal tract ulceration), everyone should manifest the same physiological dysfunctions, whatever the source of stress (mental or physical). The fact that each individual actually manifests different physiological patterns indicates that there is another component to the stress response. This was called the "specific component" by Selye: It included the specifics of the physiological trauma (a knife wound and a burn both arouse the same GAS but each obviously has different physical and physiological features), as well as the psychological variations of those learned conditioned responses accumulated from the individual's life history. Selye, however, was silent on the subject of the dynamics of these conditioned psychological components. It is this unique pattern of psychologically conditioned responses within each individual (which makes up the state-dependent filter of Figure 1, p. 26) that Erickson explored in his studies of psychosomatic phenomena.

Erickson begins one of his early papers on the "Hypnotic Investigation of Psychosomatic Phenomena" with the following description of "coincidental phenomena" (1943c/1980):

The purpose of this paper is to present an account of various psychosomatic interrelationships and interdependencies frequently encountered as *coincidental phenomena* during the course of hypnotic experimentation on normal subjects. . . . These *coincidental phenomena* are not those usual and expected changes in psychological, physiological, and somatic behavior that are essentially common to all hypnotic subjects in profound trances, such as alterations in reaction time, sensory thresholds, muscular tonus, and similar items of behavior. Rather, they are distinct from such psychosomatic manifestations of the hypnotic trance, and *they are in all probability expressive, not of the state of hypnosis itself, but of the interrelationships of hypnotically induced behavior and conditions* within the trance state. That is, after a profound trance state has first been secured, specific hypnotic instructions can then be given to the subject to elicit responses of a particular sort and in a chosen modality of behavior. *However, in addition to the behavior that is suggested, there may also be elicited, seemingly as coincidental manifestations,* marked changes in one or another apparently unrelated modality of behavior. (pp. 145–146)
. . . Thus, for example, one subject rendered hypnotically deaf might show many changes in visual, motor, and other forms of behavior . . . while another subject rendered hypnotically color blind might show many disturbances of motor behavior but no changes in the auditory sphere. . . . Subjective feelings of nausea and vertigo invariably developed in one subject whenever a state of hypnotic deafness became well established for her. . . . Additionally she showed nystagmoid movements and pupillary dilation. . . . Another subject . . . with the onset of hypnotic deafness [experienced] an extensive anesthesia. Until this anesthesia was corrected he could not recover his hearing. . . . Several other subjects have shown a comparable inability to recover from induced behavior changes until the *coincidental developments* were first corrected. (pp. 148–149; Italics added)
. . . They [the coincidental developments] constitute essentially individual manifestations which occur under a wide variety of circumstances and many different associations. Furthermore they are not constant in their appearance for all subjects in the same situation. . . . However, the findings do tend to remain constant for the specific modality of behavior under investigation

in the individual subject, although *repeated hypnotic experiences tend to lessen progressively the extent and duration of the phenomena likely to cause the subject discomfort*. (p. 146; italics added)

From the point of view developed in this section, we would characterize Erickson's "coincidental phenomena" as manifestations of the uniquely individual state-bound patterns of information and behavior that each person acquires as a result of his or her particular life history of experiential learning. These individual patterns are the basis of each person's unique repertory of hypnotic responsiveness, which can be utilized therapeutically. (These individual patterns may also be conceptualized as manifestations of the "creative unconscious" of each person.) When the person is subjected to undue stress over a period of time, these "coincidental phenomena" become the basis of the psychosomatic symptoms that express the experiential learnings encoded in the memory filters of the limbic system.

Erickson's finding that "repeated hypnotic experience tend to lessen progressively the extent and duration of the [coincidental] phenomena likely to cause the subject [psychosomatic] discomfort" is the basis of one of his hypnotherapeutic approaches to mind/body dysfunctions. An example of Erickson's early use of this approach was presented in his paper called the "Hypnotic Investigation of Psychosomatic Phenomena: A Controlled Experimental Use of Hypnotic Regression in the Therapy of an Acquired Food Intolerance." A review of this case provides us with a clear example of how the state-dependent learning of a psychosomatic symptom and a phobic response (perhaps involving the autonomic nervous system, and especially the gastrointestinal component of Selye's GAS) can be resolved hypnotherapeutically (Erickson, 1943b/1980, p. 170):

A subject in her early twenties was inordinately fond of orange juice and drank it at every opportunity. One day, because of gastrointestinal distress, she decided to try self-medication and proceeded to take castor oil, first mixing it with orange juice to disguise its taste. Unfortunately this concoction caused acute gastric distress: she became violently nauseated and she vomited repeatedly. Following this she went to bed. The next morning she felt much better and very hungry. She went to the kitchen to get her customary glass of orange juice. Quite unexpectedly she found that the sight, smell, and taste of orange juice caused immediate nausea and vomiting and she could not drink it.

Instead of making a spontaneous recovery from this acute violent distaste for oranges, she continued to manifest it until it became almost phobic in character. She could not endure the thought of oranges in the refrigerator, and her family had to cease using them. Even the sight of oranges in fruit markets caused her to develop feelings of nausea.

Erickson reported that the origins of this conditioned gastrointestinal problem had another, highly emotionally charged determinant which resolved itself within a few days, and which he did not detail in his paper. The subject's conditioned distaste for orange juice persisted, however. This is very typical of psychosomatic problems and goes to the heart of the dilemma they present. The problem origins of a state-dependent pattern of memory and learning are often easily resolved, but the psychosomatic symptoms that they give rise to persist! The new dysfunctional pattern has become "functionally autonomous": It endures as a form of state-bound information and behavior that expresses itself independently and indeed frequently in seeming defiance of the conscious will/ego.

Because of the now-isolated character of the symptom, Erickson refused to treat it with direct hypnotic suggestion, even though the subject pleaded with him to do so. Instead he chose an indirect approach. At a social gathering one evening, the subject was persuaded by the guests to act as a hypnotic subject. Erickson then used her to demonstrate age regression, wherein she was reoriented to a period two years before she experienced her unfortunate association between orange juice, castor oil, and the highly charged emotional problem. After being in this age-regressed state for 20 minutes (a typical time period Erickson used to "set" a deeply somnambulistic hypnotic trance), she was able to join the guests in drinking orange juice without any adverse reaction. At no time was she given any direct suggestions to ameliorate or resolve her symptom. She was merely provided with an opportunity to drink orange juice, and she did so with pleasure. She was then awakened from trance with an amnesia for all that had taken place. During the remainder of the evening, "her facial expression was frequently puzzled and reflective, and she kept rolling her tongue about her mouth and passing it gently over her lips as if she were trying to sense some elusive taste." Several days later the subject reported that she had somehow "spontaneous unconditioned" herself and had regained her original liking for orange juice.

The salient feature of this case is how Erickson's indirect approach enabled the subject to reexperience her original liking for orange juice in an age-regressed state without interference from her learned negative gastrointestinal response. From the state-dependent memory and learning point of view, we would say that her age-regressed state-of-being bypassed the gastrointestinal symptom that was learned in a later state-of-being. When she was to once more experience her original liking for orange juice, the symptom was depotentiated or unconditioned (Rossi, 1973/1980; Erickson & Rossi, 1976/1980) without any interference from her conscious mind's negative expectation.

This form of hypnotherapy is very different from the classical approach of using direct suggestion to "command away" or inhibit a symptom. Erickson's indirect approach utilizes the mind's own naturalistic means of self-healing, without the intrusion of direct suggestions that could only be expressive of the therapist's limited view of how the cure "should" take place. The therapy takes place not by a hypnotic command imprinted on the subject's mind, but by circumventing what Erickson called "learned limitations" and accessing therapeutic response potentials that already exist within the subject. In this case, the learned limitation was a clear example of "a state-bound pattern of information and behavior" that encoded a distressing symptom which interfered with the subject's original response of enjoying orange juice. Erickson's indirect approach via age regression accessed her state-bound symptom in a permissive manner that allowed her own creative resources to do the actual healing. Later, I will provide additional case examples of how this type of therapeutic hypnosis can be more adequately conceptualized from our psychobiological perspective rather than from the traditional but misleading perspective of hypnosis as a programming of mind and behavior. Indeed, Erickson characterized programming as a "very uninformed way" of attempting to do hypnotherapy (Erickson & Rossi, 1979, p. 288).

In a little known or appreciated paper on the nature of hypnotic psychotherapy, Erickson (1958/1980) outlined his rationale for a radically new concept of "trance" as a period of creative reorganization. He states it as follows (p. 38):

> The induction and maintenance of a trance serve to provide a *special psychological state in which the patient can reassociate and reorganize his inner psychological complexities* and utilize his own capacities in a manner in accord with his own experiential life. . . . Therapy results from an *inner resynthesis* of the patient's behavior achieved by the patient himself. It's true that direct suggestion can effect an alteration in the patient's behavior and result in a symptomatic cure, at least temporarily. However, such a "cure" is simply a response to suggestion and does not entail that reassociation and reorganization of ideas, understandings and memories so essential for actual cure. *It is this experience of reassociating and reorganizing his own experiential life that eventu-*

ates in a cure, not the manifestation of responsive behavior which can, at best, satisfy only the observer.

Let us now turn our attention to a more detailed exposition of this creative approach to the reassociation and reorganization of mind-body problems, which I have described as a new language of mind-body communication and therapeutic hypnosis (Rossi, 1987a).

5

The New Language of
Mind-Body Communication:
Ten Teaching Tutorials

IN THIS CHAPTER WE will focus on effective approaches for facilitating mind-body communication. We will learn how words, phrases, questions, and a variety of search strategies can access the problems encoded in state-bound memory and make information available for self-help. These approaches are all explorations of how we can best actualize human potential rather than manipulate and control behavior. Our work does *not* involve overt or covert conditioning, "influence communication," or programming. We do not even use "suggestion" in the conventional sense of putting an idea into another person's mind. Rather, we simply access state-dependent memory, learning, and behavior (SDMLB) systems and make their encoded information available for problem-solving. The locus for control of the healing process remains within the patient at all times. The therapist is a faciliator, guide, and consultant.

Insofar as it is possible, we will always use the patient's own words, attitudes, and world view as the most desired route to accessing the problem areas. Our approaches are usually problem-centered because "problems" are paths to the person's "growing edge." Symptoms are often signals of the need for personal development. All of our therapeutic approaches actively involve the patients in taking action, even in the first session, that will move them quickly to better coping skills and a position of self-efficacy.

EVERY ACCESS IS A REFRAME

The basic premise for all the approaches outlined in this book is, "*Every access is a reframe.*" Each time we access the SDMLB processes that encode a problem, we have an opportunity to "reassociate and reorganize" or *reframe* that problem in a manner that resolves it. This premise is based upon the recent research in memory, learning, and cognition that was examined previously (Chapter 3; Lynch, McGaugh, & Weinberger, 1984). Memory does not operate like a tape recorder in which we simply play back exactly what we learned. Memory is always a constructive process whereby we actually synthesize a new subjective experience every time we recall a past event. Pribram (1986) expresses this active process of memory as follows:

> Images and other mental contents as such are not stored, nor are they "localized" in the brain. Rather, by virtue of the operation of the local brain circuitry, usually with the aid of sensory input from the environment, images and mental events emerge and are *constructed*. A similar mechanism involving the motor mechanisms of the brain can account for intentional, planned behavior. The evidence that such a mechanism exists is presented in *Languages of the Brain* and elsewhere (Pribram, 1971, 1976; Pribram et al., 1981). Much of my laboratory research has been involved in demonstrating that *brain function is active, not passive*, in its interactions with environment and elucidating the processes operative in this active aspect of mind. This research has shown that the *intrinsic cortex and limbic formations of the forebrain actively organize sensory input*, etc. (see review by Pribram, 1980). (Italics added)

Mind and nature are in constant change and creative flux. It is irritating to us when our memories of the same event are different from those of another person, and when even our memories change over time. These entirely natural differences and changes are the despair of our courts of law, which are based upon the rather naive view of a constant, unchanging, objective reality where "facts are facts" rather than the subjective constructions of our own minds. The law requires that a witness repeat the same story in the same way every time. The natural mind, by contrast, tends to repeat the same story with variations, seemingly seeking to constantly update and reframe "reality" in keeping with the new information and views it is spontaneously generating.

What is the despair of the law, however, is the opportunity of the psychologist! When the mind naturally reviews memories from slightly different perspectives, for example, it is spontaneously engaged in constructing alternate realities. This spontaneous construction of alternate realities has survival value in a constantly changing environment. People who do not recognize, welcome, and integrate these spontaneous changes are condemned to living an uncreative existence in an outmoded past (Rossi, 1972/1985). Most of us are unaware of how strongly we have been programmed to live in this way. We struggle in vain to preserve our past way of thinking, feeling, and doing until a symptom or problem becomes manifest evidence of our lack of adaptation to the current and ongoing changes that are taking place. Our symptom or problem is then our best guide to where "inner work" needs to be done to readapt and recreate ourselves. Each time we mentally review (access) what our problem is about, we can depend upon our mind to spontaneously reframe it in a slightly different way as it seeks an answer.

Recent psychoimmunological research documents how even the simple process of writing about personal traumatic experiences is associated with improvements in physical health (Kiecolt-Glaser & Glaser, 1988; Pennebaker, Kiecolt-Glaser, & Glaser, 1988a, b). We utilize this natural tendency as the basic dynamic for facilitating healing by accessing and reframing problems with our new language of mind-body communication in two ways: we are constantly striving to help patients *(1) recognize their symptoms as important mind-body signals and (2) utilize their psychological problems as opportunities to explore and actualize their creative resources.* A epigrammatic way of saying this is that *symptoms are converted into signals* and *problems are reframed into creative resources.* This is illustrated in our first tutorial, "Going with the Flow," wherein the therapist sets up and facilitates the optimal conditions whereby each patient can learn to recognize and go with their unique, natural flow of psychobiological healing from initial expression of symptoms or problems to their final resolution almost as easily as they would in everyday life if given an opportunity.

TUTORIAL ONE: GOING WITH THE FLOW: CONVERTING SYMPTOMS INTO SIGNALS AND PROBLEMS INTO RESOURCES

All symptoms are signals. Everyone acknowledges the truth of this basic psychobiological fact, yet most of us try to "kill the messenger" rather than respectfully heed the message. Many billions of dollars each year are spent on "pain killers" and palliative, rather than genuine, therapeutic agents. Rather than try to "control the symptom" or "eliminate the pain," we need to ask, "What is the mind-body trying to tell us with a fleeting mood of depression, a chronic fatigue, a headache, an ulcer, or a recurring neurodermatitis under stress? Classical Freudian psychoanalysis seeks to resolve physical symptoms by analysis; classical behaviorism deals with them by conditioning and extinction; authoritarian forms of hypnosis try a mixed bag of relaxation and programming.

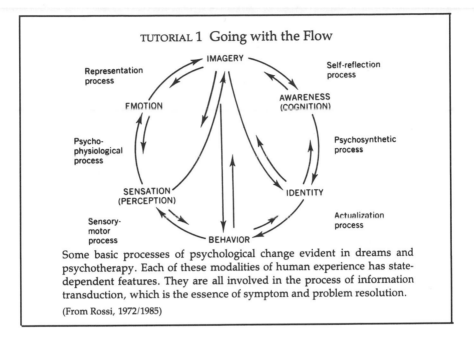

TUTORIAL 1　Going with the Flow

Some basic processes of psychological change evident in dreams and psychotherapy. Each of these modalities of human experience has state-dependent features. They are all involved in the process of information transduction, which is the essence of symptom and problem resolution.

(From Rossi, 1972/1985)

Our psychobiological approach, by contrast, seeks to carefully receive the symptom-signal and then facilitate creative processes of information transduction that may transform the negative aspects of the symptom into therapeutic responses.

Tutorial 1 illustrates some of the major modalities of mind-body communication and healing. Each modality has its own genius. *Emotions*, for example, can express profound depths in ways that *imagery* and *thoughts* cannot, and vice versa. Ideally, however, each modality can be transformed, at least in part, into the others for optimal information processing and problem solving in novel and challenging life situations. People usually report being "stuck" or "blocked" when they feel something but cannot put it into words. They may be obsessively intellectualized and rigid when they really know something conceptually and can talk about it, but they cannot feel it or translate it into appropriate changes in their behavior. People have symptoms and problems when their experience is *stuck or state-bound* in one modality or another so they cannot use the natural genius of other aspects of their nature.

The arrows in Tutorial 1 show only a few of the pathways of information flow between some of the various modalities of human experience.

There are infinite possibilities for the autocatalytic evolution and transformation of information between them. *Sensations, perceptions,* and *emotions* are frequently the initial mind-body modalities signaling that something is coming up to consciousness. Sometimes we may feel embarrassed or depressed even before we know why. Some people may then experience *imagery* that presents a meaningful metaphor about our emotions on the way to a more *cognitive* pattern of *awareness* about what is being experienced. These cognitive or thought processes are usually a record of our personal history and *identity*. Ideally new experience leads to an appropriate updating of our old records and identity along with innovative patterns of *behavior*. A clinical illustration of how symptoms are converted into meaningful signals and problem solving by the process of information transduction is illustrated in Tutorial 1. The state-bound symptoms and the important transition moments of information transduction and mind-body communication are italicized.

A woman graduate in her middle twenties complains that for the past few years she has had *"a series of mysterious gynecological problems."* She has seen many physicians, taken many medical tests, and even had an exploratory operation "down there." Several excellent internists she greatly respects have now told her that there is nothing medically wrong with her. "One wonderful woman medical doctor," she says, "finally told me that I do not need another exploratory operation with a surgical knife, I just need to be nicer to myself, so here I am."

On the very first therapy session she enters the consulting room announcing that she has given herself a *"migraine headache today."* With a sympathetic manner I ask her, **"Tell me what you are actually experiencing with that headache at this moment."** She responds with a wrinkled face of pained distress and speaks of *"A terrible, tight band all around my head* that won't leave me alone—*it has been pounding all day* since I have been worried about my boyfriend. *I couldn't sleep at all last night* since I can't get it out of my mind. I just don't know what to do to get rid of this migraine! I can't even think straight right now, *my mind is all fuzzy-like.* How am I supposed to study?"

With continuing sympathetic interest I again ask her, **"What are you actually experiencing now?"** The supportive tone of my voice and my optimistically eager, exploratory manner imply that her symptoms are of great interest and may already be changing. She responds with *a moment of puzzlement* as she apparently tunes into herself, she then wrinkles her brow with even greater distress and loudly says, *"The migraine is coming on even worse! Oh, gosh, it's flashing on and off in the worst way! And now it even seems to be spreading down the back of my head and I'm starting to get a stiff neck! Oh, I just hate this, it* *is like a burning sensation is spreading from my head and neck to my right shoulder. My whole body is just a mess!''*

I respond to this worsening crisis with, **"Well, it really seems as if your whole mind and body are trying to tell us something, especially about your relationship with your boyfriend, so let yourself receive whatever comes all by itself right now."** She tentatively *speaks about her difficulties* with him for a few moments and then seems to breakdown with *loud sobs, shaking, and crying* that momentarily threaten to get out of control so I respond with *a therapeutic dissociation:* **"That's fine, you can continue to let yourself really feel that as strongly as you need to because there is another part of you that can watch wisely and keep you safe so you can understand what these feelings are telling you."** She then lapses into quieter sobs and finally a silence for two or three minutes, apparently deeply engrossed within herself. I remain absolutely still not daring to move a muscle least I disturb her excellent self-absorption. She then softly notes, *''Oh, my cheeks are hot, so hot now, why is that? It's almost as if I'm embarrassed about something. Why am I so embarrassed?''*

She looks at me with wide open eyes in apparent expectation and puzzlement looking to me for an answer. I note that *the pupils of her eyes seem dilated* and I wistfully respond, **"Yes, I wonder what it is? I don't know if you need to** *keep some of that private.* **Just continue to receive whatever comes to you all by itself now—only telling me what I really need to know to help you further."** She remains silent for a few minutes and then *with rapidly fluttering eyelids says with some surprise, ''Oh, my whole body is hot and full of energy—it's like my whole body is shaking and vibrating. Why am I so nervous? What is happening to me, what is this vibrating all over my skin, I don't know if I itch or what? What is this burning energy I feel all over?''*

With quiet eagerness I whisper, **"Yes, I wonder what it is? What is coming to you? Let's see just what it is?"** (Of course, this was a technical error; I made an error by mentioning the word "see" and thereby unwittingly suggested the visual modality to her.) She remains silent for a few moments and then with *a slow tear rolling down her cheek she whispers, ''I see myself writing him a 'Dear John' letter. I'm not blaming him or myself. I've always known this, I've always known it could not really work between us,* but it was such fun for both of us in the beginning that I wanted it to just go on. I realize now that we really are such different people. I so much enjoyed his parties and social friends at first, but *I now know I am different than they are, I need my solitude— that's when my poems come, like little children tugging at my skirt, and then I write.* The poems have all vanished from my head since we have been going out together, but I cannot live without my poems, they are me. It's just the dynamics, you know, its just the dynamics that don't work between my boyfriend and me. I just hate these dynamics but its true, you know? I hate it, but it's good to know what I have to do.''

She *closes her eyes, rolls her head about slowly and takes a few deep breaths. With a wry smile she says, ''See, I told you I just gave myself that migraine—its completely gone now! I feel so much better, oh, I feel so good now*, thank you. Oh, *the whole world suddenly seems brighter, like I can actually see this room more clearly.*'' She remains rapt in silence for a few minutes and then her eyes and lips move slowly as if she is in communion with herself. She finally says, ''Umm, *just the wisp of a phrase*, it is the beginning of a poem coming on, *I can really feel it.* Oh, thank heavens, its like an epiphany of clear crystal ice at the moment of melting with spring in the north sea.''

She seems to have found her own solution but I tentatively test it by humorously playing the devil's advocate, **"Oh, you're really going to write him a "Dear John" and tell him all the dynamics!?"** She *playfully* responds, ''Oh, no, you silly! I'm just going to write him a nice letter—who knows— maybe even a poem! He knows, he knows the truth already and I'm going to deliver the letter to him myself tonight and get this thing done with *so I can really sleep tonight*. Oh, what time is it? Oh, I'm sorry, I have to go! I'm committed to going to my women's group this afternoon; they will really understand. Then I will write the letter and deliver it personally. Thank you so much, you really have been a help, even though you don't seem to say much!''

Our psychotherapeutic ideal is to facilitate the normally creative pro-cesses of everyday-life to help people like this young woman recognize and receive their natural patterns of mind-body communication and healing. In this illustration, that is so similar to what people normally experience in everyday life that one might hesitate to call it ''psycho-therapy,'' it is easy to recognize how her presenting symptom of a migraine headache underwent a highly unique and personally creative pattern of intermodal information transduction on her way to a thera-peutic resolution. When this process of mind-body communication is ''blocked'' or incomplete so that the person remains ''stuck'' in a vi-cious cycle of apparently unending fatigue, depression, symptoms, or emotional crisis, it can be stigmatized as emotional hysteria (Ellen-berger, 1970) and mental illness (Rossi, 1972/1985). When this mind-body communication is successful we usually can recognize three dis-tinct phases of converting symptoms into signals and reframing a problem into creative resources.

Phase 1: Experiencing Symptoms and Psychological Problems.   Most pa-tients come to therapy because they are ''stuck'' with debilitating symp-toms or problems they ''don't know'' how to resolve. They expect the therapist will cure the symptom or provide the answer to the problem. The therapist does not do either of these two things. Instead the thera-pist offers the patient an open field of exploration, an opportunity to play with many possible approaches to accessing the state-bound sources of the problem and exposing it to the patient's uniquely personal repertory of inner resources for problem solving. In this case I initiated an open field of mind-body exploration by casually asking her to **"tell me what you are actually experiencing with that headache at this moment."** Note how specific and exactly focused this question is on her symptom of a *painful sensory modality* of experience—I am helping her focus and perhaps even amplify this sensory experience to access its state-bound sources. Notice how this sharply focused question contrasts with the classical psychoanalytic directive of asking the patient to "free associate," or, the more typical garden variety psychotherapeutic inquiry, "tell me about it." These more general directives obviously are useful in many cases, but they miss the sharp precision of accessing exactly those unique *sensory-perceptual modalities* of the patient's mind-body experience that may be a more direct path to problem solving.

Phase 2: Mind-Body Communication, Resistance, Crisis, and Therapeutic Dissociation. In response to the sharply focused accessing question, her headache went through a series of *sensory-perceptual transductions* from a *tight band* and *pounding*, to *fuzzy awareness and cognition.* Her deepening *puzzlement* and focusing apparently made these symptoms worst for a moment or two and then transduced them into a *stiff neck and burning sensations* that spread to her shoulder. This momentary worsening or crisis point is not always present, but I emphasize it here because of its historical significance. Modern patients rarely go through the kinds of florid hysterical crisis that have been described in the past (Ellenberger, 1970), particularly in the era of animal magnetism between 1780 and 1834 (Tinterow, 1970). The diminutive type of momentary crisis described above is much more typical of our current psychosocial climate, but I believe it is homologous with the more bizarre hysterias of the past.

Apparently therapists of the past did not know how to modulate an emotional crisis with a *therapeutic dissociation* as illustrated above, so many of their patients did fall into self-destructive hysterias of ever-worsening intensities that were labeled as "mental illness." Today's therapists need to know that an emotional crisis can be a valid and valuable part of the therapeutic process of breaking through traumatic amnesias and accessing state-bound memories that are at the source of mind-body symptoms and problems. This crisis point of therapeutic accessing need not be shut off prematurely by the therapist who may be afraid that emotions will get out of control. If the therapist does have such fears, the patient's crisis can be safely modulated and attenuated with any variation of the therapeutic dissociation that reassures the patient while permitting their emotional accessing to work its way through to the recovery of important memories and the achievement of healing and new insights.

She responds to the therapeutic dissociation with concentrated inner work that leads to the heat of embarrassment. She looks at me with puzzlement and expectation for an answer. For many years I would respond to this bait and offer the poor helpless patient a brilliant answer, a wonderful psychodynamic reconstruction of the patient's experience that would in one stroke clarify a pathetic life of neuroticism and confusion. Of course, I was thereby robbing patients of their own potentially *creative moments* (Rossi, 1972/1985). In this case I try to do something a bit better: I present her with a paradoxical inquiry when I say, **"Yes, I wonder what it is? I don't know if you need to keep some of that private . . . only [tell] me what I really need to know to help you further."** I am telling her that she needs to continue to receive her most embarrassing experiences, but she need not tell me anything she does not want to. This is an important means of avoiding, discharging, or *depotentiating the so-called resistance* (Erickson & Rossi, 1979) she is probably feeling. She can review those embarrassing experiences *privately* for all the therapeutic values they may have, but she need not fear what I will make of them; she need tell me only what I have to know to help her further. She maintains the locus of control within herself; she is thereby empowered to receive, monitor, and facilitate her own therapeutic process in a more adequate manner than any outside therapist could possibly hope to.

Phase 3: Healing, Insight, Symptom and Problem Resolution.   She then experiences a number of spontaneous shifts between *cognitive-emotional-identity modalities* with a slow tear as she accesses her own way of dealing with her boyfriend; this is the rapid culmination of a profoundly significant shift from a series of *physical symptoms* to *emotions*, and the *cognitive* understanding of a *relationship problem* that she is now able to process in an optimal manner, independent of the therapist who simply supports and allows her creative work to take place within herself. She achieves her own problem solving by spontaneously accessing her *inner creative resource* of writing a letter. Simultaneously with this *she recognized and recovers her lost poetic identity*. With this successful recovery and self-reinforcement of a deep aspect of her *personal identity* she finally experiences a therapeutic shift so that the headache symptoms and the sensory signals of heat, vibration, and "energy" are transduced into *genuine comfort and relaxation as a natural mind-body signal of a job well done*—rather than a programmed comfort and relaxation suggested by the therapist in the beginning of the session that may abort the natural phase of arousal and crisis in problem solving.

From this point of view we can understand how the typical psychotherapist's habitual and mindless application of suggestions for relaxation and comfort in the beginning of the therapeutic work actually may distort the patient's own natural mind-body signals. Anxiety, stress, tension, and symptoms at the beginning are natural readiness signals to do important psychotherapeutic work; this "readiness energy" needs to be utilized with appropriate accessing questions to motivate the therapeutic work—not frittered away with spurious placating and reassurances by the therapist.

All of these therapeutic approaches are designed to help people side-step their learned limitations (that is, being state-bound in a way that is usually described as being "blocked," "stuck," or "*not knowing*") so they can learn to experience when and how their natural intermodal shifts of information flow and healing are taking place. Occasionally the therapist may facilitate the kind of creative experience that allows new patterns of mind-body communication to take place as illustrated above. For the most part, however, both therapist and patient simply need to get out of the way of the emergent patterns of healing. How does the therapist learn to facilitate, but not get in the way of the patient's own unique, emergent patterns of healing? It is an art that requires careful observation, sensitivity, skill, humility, and restraint by the therapist. It is best taught in graduate study programs and professional workshops where three-step tutorials and learning routines such as the following are demonstrated and practiced.

Three-Step Tutorials: Learning Routines for the Psychotherapist

At the Evolution of Psychotherapy Congress in Phoenix, Arizona, it was estimated that there are now over 300 different forms of psychotherapy (Rossi, 1987a). All these therapies facilitate mind-body communication and healing to some degree. One could get lost in their bewildering complexities by trying to focus on all the nuances of difference between them. On the other hand, they all share the same three-step routine for problem-solving:

1) Therapist and patient initiate communication;
2) They engage in some sort of therapeutic work; and
3) They hopefully have some criteria for problem resolution so they know when to discontinue the interaction.

In traditional hypnotherapy the three steps are:

1) Establish trust and rapport;
2) Initiate a formal ritual of hypnotic induction; and
3) "Wake up" the patient and ratify the resolution of the problem (Erickson & Rossi, 1979).

If the problem is not resolved, then carry out the same three steps again in another way, perhaps using different suggestions and patterns of inner work based upon what was learned from the first effort. The process is iterative: You do the three steps over and over, each time learning more about the patient's inner condition and resources, which then can be facilitated with greater effectiveness the next time around.

The three-step routines presented in this chapter range from the simple to the complex. They are easy to learn in the order in which they are presented, since experience with each builds the therapeutic skills needed. These three-step tutorials are reminiscent of the simple sets of rules that the new science of complex adaptive systems uses to generate creative, emergent behavior that emulates the evolution of living systems and novel behavior within the computer (Levy, 1992; Reynolds, 1987). All of these tutorials are variations of *the basic accessing question* to which we will now turn our attention.

Tutorial Two: The Basic Accessing Question

The basic accessing question initiates an open field of mind-body exploration that (1) accesses the source of the patient's problem; (2) facilitates information transduction and healing; and (3) gives the patient and therapist an observable behavioral signal indicating when the job is done. The basic accessing question is "fail-safe" because the therapist is only asking the patient a question—the worst that can happen is that nothing happens—which only means that another accessing question needs to be tried, as one might search for the right key for a lock. The therapist is never in a position of directing the patient to do something that the patient cannot do. The therapist is simply initiating an exploratory process for problem solving.

TUTORIAL 2 The Basic Accessing Question

1. *Time-binding introduction initiating inner search*
   As soon as your inner mind [creative unconsicous, spiritual guide, etc.] knows

2. *Accessing state-bound sources of problem*
   that you can review some important memories related to the source of that problem,

3. *Observable behavioral signal of problem-solving*
   will your eyes close?

The basic accessing question may be expressed in many different ways, but it always has three standard parts:

1) A time-binding introduction that initiates an inner search of state-dependent memory, learning, and behavior systems;
2) Accessing and transduction of the state-bound problems and symptoms;
3) An observable behavioral response signaling when the process of accessing and therapeutic transduction is completed.

While some patients will respond to this basic accessing question with a mild therapeutic emotional crisis as illustrated in Tutorial 1, many patients respond by quieting down and closing their eyes. These are entirely natural and observable behaviors indicating that inner work is taking place. This is an entirely natural and easily accepted approach to inner problem solving, because it utilizes the typical everyday process we all experience when we turn inward momentarily to figure out how to deal with an issue. This expression of the accessing question introduces and facilitates a process of reviewing memories associated with the problem.

The simplest expression of the basic accessing question is outlined in Tutorial 2. Whenever patients openly acknowledge that they are "stuck" or "don't know" the answer to a significant question it is very simple for the therapist to ask, "Well, since you feel you do not know how to answer that question will it be okay for us to ask your unconscious?'' Of course the therapist needs to use whatever term for the ''unconscious'' the patient finds acceptable. For some it might be better to call it one of the following: *your inner mind, the back part of your mind, the part of you that really knows the answer, what your heart really feels, your mind-body, your symptom, your intuition, your spiritual guide, etc.* These are all metaphors that the therapist may select for facilitating mind-body communication within a frame of reference that is familiar to the patient.

Research on creative thinking (Rossi, 1972/1985) has demonstrated that the essence of *the new* is usually generated within us on an unconscious level. The conscious mind simply receives the new idea and subjects it to validation and integration with previous patterns of understanding. The basic accessing question structures an opportunity for something new to happen on an unconscious level at the source of creativity. It is a way of focusing a patient's mental resources (e.g., state-dependent memories, sensory-perceptual associations, emotions, habits, and various patterns of learning, etc.) and directing them toward a creative state of problem solving. Recent research in the neurobiology of learning (Rosenzweig & Bennett, 1984) suggests that new proteins are synthesized in appropriate brain cells during learning. We may speculate that the various forms of the accessing question outlined in this and the following tutorials actually ''facilitate the internal synthesis of new protein structures that could function as the biological basis of new behavior and phenomenal experience'' (Erickson, Rossi, & Rossi, 1976). Let us now examine some of the variations of the basic accessing question that are particularly useful for clinical problems.

TUTORIAL THREE: ACCESSING CREATIVE RESOURCES

This general three-stage approach to problem-solving by accessing the patient's inner resources was originally described by Erickson and Rossi (1979, pp. 1–14) as a basic model for therapeutic hypnosis. It is being generalized here into a procedure that is useful for a wide range of problems that patients can resolve for themselves during a problem of ''inner work.''

Stage 1: Readiness Signal for Inner Work.   In this first stage of the approach, the therapist asks the patient to review the history and nature of the problem. This review begins *the activity of accessing and spontaneous reframing* that is characteristic of all memory processes. This review thus initiates the actual process of therapy, even though the patient may believe the problem is ''only being talked about.'' In the positive atmosphere generated by the empathic therapeutic transaction, the patient will often experience a spontaneous partial remission of the symptom, or may gain some insights into how the problem might be resolved. These initial therapeutic explorations are, of course, supported by the therapist, who helps the patient recognize how the "inner mind" or "creative unconscious" is in a constant state of inner work, during which it is attempting, and even now succeeding with, various parts of the total problem-solving process. The patient is encouraged further, for example, by reviewing earlier life situations in which the patient or an acquaintance may have solved a similar problem.

The first stage of this approach reaches its climax when a positive therapeutic framework has been established and the patient now looks expectantly to the therapist for an "answer." The answer is supplied by introducing the patient to an internal problem-solving process, somewhat as follows:

> **"Now that you are ready to continue therapy on an even deeper level, you can begin by simply becoming more sensitive to yourself. [Pause]**
>
> **"When a deep part of your inner mind knows it can resolve that problem** [pause] *will you find yourself getting more and more comfortable, as your eyes close all by themselves?*

In the typical therapy situation, the patient already has sufficient cultural frames to support this expectation that creative problem-solving can be initiated by a relaxed process of inner work and reflection. When the patient does, in fact, make a few bodily adjustments to get comfortable, and the eyes close, the therapist has the observable behavioral responses indicating that the internal psychobiological conditions for inner healing are being set in motion.

The phrase "getting more and more comfortable" is more than just a cliché—it initiates a shift in autonomic system balance from sympathetic toward parasympathetic dominance. It lowers the patient's overall psychobiological level of arousal, as the proprioceptive and kinesthetic input from all of the body muscles diminish. This tends to shift attention away from irrelevant external stimuli toward the internal state-dependent memory, learning, and behavioral systems that need to be engaged for problem-solving. Closing the eyes immediately enhances alpha wave (and eventually theta wave) generation in the brain, which is associated with creative sensing, feeling, and imagistic experience. This, in turn, means we have facilitated a shift from the rational and linear processes of left-hemispheric thinking toward the more primary, holistic

---

TUTORIAL 3 Accessing Creative Resources

1. *Readiness signal for inner work*
   When a deep part of your inner mind knows it can resolve that problem [pause], will you feel yourself getting more and more comfortable, as your eyes close?

2. *Accessing and transducing state-bound resources*
   Now your inner mind can continue working all by itself to solve that problem in a manner that fully meets all your needs.
   [Pause]
   Are there are memories, life experiences, and abilities that your inner mind can use in many ways you may not have realized before?

3. *Ratifying problem-solving*
   When your inner mind knows that it can continue to deal effectively with that problem, will you find yourself wanting to move a bit [pause], and will you open your eyes and come fully alert?

---

processing characteristic of the right hemisphere, with its closer associations to the mind-body, limbic-hypothalamic information transduction system.

The Therapeutic Double Bind.   There are many possible variations in the patient's response to this *readiness signal for inner work*, however. Instead of relaxing, closing the eyes, and turning inward, for example, a patient may occasionally become more restless or distressed and alert. This indicates that the ideal therapeutic conditions for the first stage have not been met yet, suggesting that there may be another issue the patient needs to deal with before the creative process of problem resolution can begin. The therapist needs to reengage the patient with therapeutically double binding exploratory questions, somewhat as follows:

> **But if those eyes don't close, will you wonder if there are other questions or problems you need to deal with first—before you access your inner resources?**

This carefully worded exploratory question contains an important *implication*: The patient *will do* the inner work after first dealing with whatever other issue remains (Erickson & Rossi, 1979, 1980; Erickson, Rossi,

& Rossi, 1976). This implication is also an instruction that facilitates the planning function of the prefrontal cortex. The creative inner work is being carefully organized and sequenced to follow whatever other issue remains. Once this has been accomplished, the therapist can again offer the readiness signal for inner work.

The first stage of establishing the readiness signal for inner work is thus an iterative therapeutic procedure: It is done over and over again, so as to immediately resolve any issue that interrupts the process of turning inward for a comfortable period of problem-solving.

Stage 2: Accessing State-Bound Resources. After the patient's eyes close, the therapist can allow a quiet period of inner work to proceed entirely on its own. It is valuable to carefully observe the patient during this brief period of time. Many different patterns of responsiveness may be evident. Sometimes the patient's eyelids flutter a bit just as they close, as is characteristic of a classical hypnotic induction. Occasionally the eyeballs will roll upward and/or squint toward the nose as the eyelids close. These movements have been cited by some (Spiegel & Spiegel, 1978) as an indication of a capacity for deep trance. After the eyes are closed, the eyelids may undergo momentary bursts of rapid, fine, vertical vibratory movements that may indicate the accessing of state-bound inner processes. Sometimes there are rapid left and right horizontal movements that suggest an inner landscape is being actively observed. Occasionally there may be large, slow, rolling movements of the eyeballs under the closed eyelids (Weitzenhoffer, 1971), which are again suggestive of deep states of altered experience. These eyelid movements all indicate that the patient is engaged in a search process which is ideal for this stage of inner work.

The therapist may occasionally question patients about their inner experience when they manifest these different patterns of behavior. So little experimental research has been done in this area that we do not always know what individual patterns of response provide useful information about the therapeutic process. In any case, when the patient has been engaged in an inner process of self-involvement for a few minutes, we are ready for the second stage of *accessing and transducing state-bound resources*, that is supported somewhat as follows:

"Now your inner mind can continue working all by itself to solve that problem in a manner that fully meets all of your needs. [Pause]

"Are there memories, life experiences, and abilities that your inner mind can use in many ways you may not have realized before?"

These apparently casual statements contain implications that facilitate the problem-solving process in subtle ways. The clause, "Your inner mind can continue working all by itself," implies that there is a developing *dissociation* between the consciously driven activity of typical left-hemispheric thinking, in which one is engaged in willfully directing one's thoughts, and the self-organizing and autonomous primary process of the right cerebral hemisphere. There is a subtle depotentiation of the conscious mind's typical frames of reference and habitual patterns of activity (that may be reinforcing the problem), and a reinforcement of the more autonomous primary processing that holds the promise of creative problem-solving.

The second question, "Are there are memories, life experiences, and abilities that your inner mind can use in many ways you may not have realized before," is a means of accessing and transducing state-dependent memory, learning, and behavior systems that now need to be engaged for problem-solving. Ideally, patients should receive this most important facilitation in their own words, and in terms that are congruent with their personal belief systems.

Table 3 lists a variety of cognitive, emotional, sensory-perceptual, and

TABLE 3 A partial listing of cognitive, emotional, sensory-perceptual, and behavioral signs of significant involvement with inner work and state-dependent phenomena

Blushing or blanching of face	Sensory-perceptual distortions
Comfort, relaxation	Sleep stages
Emotional responses	Spontaneous altered state phenomena
Economy of movement	Age regression
Eyeball changes	Amnesia
Eyelid changes and closure	Anesthesia
Facial features relaxed	Catalepsy
Feeling distant (dissociated)	Hallucinations
Literalism	Illusions
Movements slow or absent	Time distortion
Retardation of blinking, startle, and	Speech minimal or absent
swallowing reflexes	Stretching
Pulse slowing	Tears
Pupillary changes	Time lag in motor and conceptual
Respiration slowing	behavior
Response attentiveness	Vocal changes
Sensory, muscular, and body changes	Yawning

This table is an adaptation of the "Indicators of Trance Development" in Erickson, Rossi, and Rossi, 1976.

behavioral signs that are indicative of significant involvement in the inner work of accessing and reframing the state-dependent memory and learning systems that encode problems. It is valuable to recognize these signs because they indicate when patients may be more available for therapeutic change. When patients are in tears, for example, they are experiencing particular emotional states that will enable them to respond to questions and therapeutic approaches in a certain, often healing manner. A deeper state of relaxation or therapeutic catalepsy (outer body immobility with correspondingly intense inner work) can obviously enable some patients to be more receptive to those state-bound feelings, impulses, images, and ideas that can be of therapeutic value in helping them reframe their dominant but problem-plagued ways of thinking and being.

Stage 3: Ratifying Problem-Solving.   The third stage of ratifying problem-solving and ending the therapeutic session is, like the first two stages, made dependent upon the patient's inner responsiveness to the therapist's "implied directives." When the therapist senses that a satisfactory amount of therapeutic work has been accomplished, this third stage may be initiated somewhat as follows:

> **"When your inner mind knows that you have resolved that problem to the fullest extent at this time, and that you can deal effectively with it, will you find yourself wanting to move a bit?** [Pause]
> **"Will you open your eyes and come fully alert?"**

The patient usually stretches and readjusts his posture when the eyes open. This spontaneous body reorientation is in part a response to the therapist's words ("You will find yourself wanting to move"), and in part an entirely natural and spontaneous orientation to state-dependent modes of "normal" social relatedness in the world. Patients who have a talent for experiencing deeper altered states traditionally associated with therapeutic hypnosis will often comment how they have been "out," "far away," "really into it," "in a trance," or "felt drugged or hypnotized." The world may seem brighter for a moment or two. There may even be a sense of a loss or enhancement of the third dimension: The world seems flatter or deeper for a few minutes. All these spontaneous reports of altered states are accepted as an entirely natural and positive indication of effective inner work; they are, as noted above, all indications of a deep accessing of state-dependent phenomena that may be reframed for therapeutic change.

The patient usually makes some spontaneous remarks about the inner experience and the constructive symptom/problem changes that have taken place. This is entirely in keeping with the manner in which this third stage of ratifying the therapeutic work was initiated with the words, "When your inner mind knows that it can continue to deal effectively with that problem, *will you find yourself wanting to move a bit?* [Pause] And will you open your eyes and come fully alert?"

These words imply that there will be no impulse to move until an increased ability to cope with the problem has been experienced. This implication, like all the other implications, gives the patient's unconscious processes free choice—in this case, the freedom to complete the inner work in its own way and make its own choice about when movement and awakening will take place (Rossi & Ryan, 1992).

The phrase, "When your inner mind knows that it can continue to deal effectively with that problem," contains a creative ambiguity that again allows the patient's unconscious to make the most suitable choice in line with its own best ways of functioning: It may have been able to completely resolve the problem "here and now" in the therapy session, or it may have to continue active inner therapeutic work after the session has ended. Creative ambiguity facilitates free choice! We all function on many levels; while apparently living our normal lives on one level and playing out certain roles, we can be engaged in intense inner creative work and self-reorganization on levels that are preparing for new roles and activities in the future.

TUTORIAL FOUR: INCUBATING MIND-BODY HEALING

This variation of the basic accessing question derives from a number of different sources. Philosophers such as Vaihinger (1911) and the constructivists (Watzlawick, 1984) discuss the use of imagination via the "as-if" phenomena and self-fulfilling prophecies in the formation of our experiential reality and "fate." We are the victims of fate when we allow our unconscious, via its own autonomous creative process, to construct our future. If we have little or no relationship to these unconscious processes, we have no say in the construction of our future. We can take a hand in the construction of our future with inner work, however. Erickson, for example, developed what he called "pseudo-orientation in time" as a method whereby patients could generate their own futures by accessing and facilitating inner possibilities that existed only in embryonic form. Some clinicians are currently exploring the use of imaging as a major modality for facilitating the realization of positive, self-fulfilling prophecies (Achterberg, 1985; Shorr, Sobel, Robin,

---

TUTORIAL 4 Incubating Mind-Body Healing

1. *Readiness signal for present problem review*
   When your inner mind is ready to review all aspects of that problem as you are currently experiencing it, [pause]
   will your eyes close as you review all aspects of the problem you don't know how to deal with yet?

2. *Incubating current and future healing*
   Now explore the future healing possibilities. How do you see yourself? How do you feel? What are you doing now that the problem is completely healed? [Pause]
   Now let your inner mind review how you are going to get from the present problem [pause]
   to the future when you are healed. [Pause]
   What are some of the steps you will take to facilitate your healing? [Pause]

3. *Ratifying mind-body healing*
   When your inner mind knows it can continue the healing process entirely on its own, and when your conscious mind knows it can cooperate with this healing, [pause]
   will you find yourself stretching, opening your eyes, and feeling refreshed as you come fully alert?

& Connella, 1980) in mind-body healing. Other investigators are using other modalities, such as the "felt sense," which Gendlin (1978) describes as the essence of psychotherapeutic change.

Our approach is to utilize as many modalities of mind-body information transduction as are available to the individual. The accessing questions for *incubating mind-body healing* is an adaptation of Mills and Crowley's "Inner Resource Drawings" (1986), a drawing strategy they use with children. In their approach, the child is asked to draw (1) the problem as it is currently experienced; (2) the problem when it is resolved; and (3) how to get from the first to the second drawing. In work with adults, I have modified this approach by utilizing the basic accessing question to facilitate an inner search in these three areas.

In later chapters of this book we will explore some of the psychobiological pathways by which these mind-body healing processes take place. From a psychobiological point of view, we may suppose that this accessing formula draws upon the imaginative and planning functions of the prefrontal cortex, as well as visually stored images of inner resources and problem-solving routines that may be encoded in previously inaccessible state-bound patterns. The frequent experience of emotional release that accompanies the insights and forgotten memories that come "spontaneously" to consciousness during this three-step routine are the typical signs of having accessed and therapeutically reframed state-bound patterns of memory, learning, and behavior. The psychological reorientation to a future when the problem is solved apparently adds a novel stimulus and therapeutic frame of reference that enables patients to break out of the "present problem frame" that has limited their access to their own inner resources.

TUTORIAL FIVE: SYMPTOM SCALING AND HEALING

This variation of the basic accessing question introduces symptom scaling as a psychobiological approach to coordinating the languages and activities of the left and right cerebral hemispheres in accessing and healing mind-body symptoms. The right hemisphere may encode a symptom or problem in the analogical-metaphorical processes typical of emotions, body language, and dreams. In this form the problem may not be available to the more linear, logical and rational resolution routines of the left hemisphere. These left hemispheric processes may be accessed and associated with the problem by scaling it, since the left hemisphere is more facile with both numbers and words such as "more or less intense, better and worse."

By asking patients to *experience* the problem, we are presumably turning on right-hemispheric processes that have a readier access to the state-dependent encoding of the problem. By simultaneously asking patients to *scale* the problem, we are presumably activating and focusing more consciously directed left-hemispheric skills on the problem. By then asking patients to experience the spontaneous shifts and qualitative changes that naturally take place in many symptoms over time, we are presumably asking them to coordinate left and right cerebral hemispheric activity in getting more and more experience in accessing and reframing the problem's experiential and behavioral manifestations.

A currently evolving principle of mind-body healing is that some functions that are apparently indigenous in beginning their development in the right hemisphere gradually acquire supraordinate controls in the left hemisphere. The average person who simply enjoys listening

---

TUTORIAL 5 Symptom Scaling and Healing

1. *Symptom scaling*
   On a scale of one to 100, where 100 is the worst, what number expresses how much you are feeling your symptom right now at this moment?

2. *Spontaneous symptom variations*
   As you continue tuning into that symptom notice what changes take place all by themselves. [Pause]
   Does it get momentarily stronger and weaker?
   Does it spread or change its quality?

3. *Ratifying the therapeutic response*
   And what number from one to 100 expresses how you feel now?
   [This therapeutic experience ends when the patient has made some obvious therapeutic gain by lowering the original scaling score.]

---

to music, for example, utilizes predominately the right hemisphere in this activity. A professional musician, however, has left-hemispheric dominance when occupied with music (Mazziotta, Phelps, Carson, & Kuhl, 1982; Phelps & Mazziotta, 1985). We could hypothesize that a patient who scales and rehearses a symptom that was originally encoded in the right hemisphere could be developing left-hemispheric control as he develops expertise in turning the symptom on and off. This would lead to the prediction that Positron Emission Tomography would find a shift from right- to left-hemispheric dominance as patients rehearsed and gradually gained control over problematic behavior. We would expect to find the same right-left hemispheric shift in subjects who learned to reframe symptoms via biofeedback.

Paradoxical Therapy.   The so-called paradoxical aspects of this approach of problem and/or symptom prescription deserve further comment since paradox has generated so much interest recently as a new form of therapy (Seltzer, 1985; Weeks & L'Abate, 1982; Zeig, 1980a, b). From our psychobiological point of view, paradoxical therapy is not paradoxical at all: As we have seen, to prescribe a problem or symptom is actually the most direct path to accessing its psychobiological sources encoded within the state-dependent memory, learning, and behavior systems of the brain. Paradoxical therapy only seems paradoxical from a logical point of view wherein patients try to avoid the experience and expression of a problem in the hope that it will thereby "go away." Avoiding, resisting, or blocking a problem, however, only prevents one from accessing and therapeutically reframing it. When a problem or symptom "haunts" a patient, it is only because mind and nature are attempting to bring it up to consciousness so it can be resolved.

As was indicated earlier, research in the neurobiology of memory and learning indicates that the process of accessing and recall is not simply that—accessing and recall are always a synthetic process of reconstruction. As such, prescribing the symptom is actually a process of reconstructing it. When we ask a person to experience a symptom voluntarily rather than resisting it, we are drastically altering the internal dynamics and state-dependent memory and learning systems that allow the symptom to flourish. We have changed it from a dissociated and involuntary action to a voluntary action; we are undoing its state-bound character. When we ask a person to scale the intensity of the symptom, we are changing it further by adding a *novel, conscious, evaluative orientation* to it. This new evaluative orientation immediately potentiates problem-solving processes; it facilitates coping skills and self-efficacy; and the patient's ego is strengthened in its relationship to the formerly dissociated symptom.

The clinical effectiveness of these paradoxical approaches is supported by the fact that they are now used by so many different schools of psychotherapy (wherein they have been given different names). Most theorists in these different schools have expressed a sense of puzzlement as to why these approaches work, however. Since the paradoxical approaches make such exquisite sense from our psychobiological perspective, it may be worthwhile to review the many names and formulations that have been given to them. Our psychobiological approach may be seen as a common denominator underlying all the following (Seltzer, 1985, p. 20):

> From the psychoanalytic perspective, which includes the work of paradigmatic psychotherapists, we have inherited the descriptors "antisuggestion," "going with the resistance," "joining the resistance," "reflecting (or 'mirroring') the resistance," "siding with the resistance," "paradigmatic exaggeration," "supporting the defenses," "reductio ad absurdum," "reenacting an aspect of the psychosis," "mirroring the patient's distortions," "participating in the patient's fantasies," "out-crazying the patient," and "the use of the patient as consultant." From the vantage point of behavior therapy, we may appreciate paradoxical elements in such procedures as

"blowup," "implosion," "flooding," "instructed helplessness," "massed practice," "negative practice," "paradoxical intention," "stimulus satiation," and "symptom scheduling." In gestalt therapy, an approach where the actual term "paradox" is rarely employed, the attempt to foster change paradoxically may be recognized in the therapist's cruel-to-be-kind suggestions to "stay with the [negative] experience," or to "exaggerate the feeling" (sensation, experience, speech, movement, etc.). Lastly, in the communication-systems school of therapy—by far the most vocal in endorsing and elucidating paradoxical strategies—we have the following miscellany of terms and titles: "the confusion technique," "declaring hopelessness," "exaggerating the position," "paradoxical injunction," "paradoxical instructions," "paradoxical rituals and tasks," "paradoxical written messages," "restraining (or 'inhibiting') change," "predicting a relapse," "prescribing a relapse," "positive connotation" (or "interpretation"), "reframing," "redefinition," and "relabeling," "symptom prescription" (or "prescribing the resistance, symptom or system"), "therapeutic paradox," and the "therapeutic double bind." R. P. Greenberg, in an article intriguingly subtitled, "The Power of Negative Thinking" (1973), refers generally to several of the above methods as "anti-expectation techniques," which should serve as a reminder of the point made earlier that the paradoxical essence of all these methods is in their apparent irrationality *from the perspective of the client*.

Our simplified approach to "scaling and problem prescription" may be enriched by the special points of view and vocabulary of all these ways of accessing and therapeutically reframing symptoms and problems.

Tutorial Six: Utilizing the Patient's Behavior

Many typical therapeutic encounters begin with the patient in tension, distress, and perhaps even negative expectations about the possibility of getting any help. Right here in the beginning most therapists have been trained to do exactly the wrong thing: they try to calm, reassure, and relax the patient. The cart is being placed before the horse. The patient's high charge of emotional energy for therapeutic change is immediately lost because of the therapist's insecurity and misunderstanding of the value of what is being presented. The therapist rarely needs to distort the patient's natural mind-body signals of the typical signs of high performance energy associated with the anticipation of problem solving by telling the patient to relax in the beginning of the therapy session.

One very anxious, stressed, and inhibited patient, for example, continually opened and closed her hands in an absent-minded manner

---

TUTORIAL 6 Utilizing the Patient's Behavior

1. *Recognizing the current experiential situation*
   You are dealing with many issues that are difficult to express.
   [Pause]

2. *Accessing and transducing state-bound information*
   So when you feel yourself closing in on an important issue,
   [Pause for a minute]
   will those hands close all by themselves as you get a hold of it?
   [Pause for a few minutes as hands close]
   Will you review it privately in your own mind first?

3. *Expressing and ratifying problem resolution*
   When you have the words and ideas that can help you resolve that issue, will you find those hands opening? [Pause]
   Will you tell me just enough about it so I can help you further with the next issue?

---

while giving a halting account of her problem. It was difficult to get a clear account, but it was obvious that she was attempting to integrate many complex inner and outer issues about whether or not she should have a child. I utilized her spontaneous hand movements to facilitate the exploration, transduction, and integration of her issues, as is indicated in Tutorial 6.

This apparently simple example illustrates a number of significant points about the inner accessing and resolution of problems that patients have difficulty expressing. In traditional psychoanalytic theory, this patient's behavior would be called "resistance." From a psychobiological perspective, however, so-called resistance is a problem in accessing state-bound information and transducing it into a form in which it can be utilized for problem-solving. The first statement, "You are dealing with many issues that are difficult to express," is an obvious truth that the patient found easy to accept. As such, it initiated a cooperative therapeutic framework by recognizing her current experiential reality. I then utilized an ongoing portion of her experiential reality by noticing her spontaneous body language—the opening and closing of her hands (the proprioceptive-kinesthetic modality) as she struggled to express herself in words (the linguistic-verbal modality). This body language was a channel of self-expression already well associated with the state-bound information that was having difficulty reaching the verbal modality.

I therefore utilized this strong body language when I initiated an exploration with "So when you feel yourself closing in on an important issue, let your hands close as you get a hold of it." This metaphor of "closing in" and "getting a hold of" transforms her body language into verbal terms. As such, this simple statement tends to facilitate an intermodal transduction from the kinesthetic to the verbal modality.

The third stage of expressing and ratifying problem resolution was initiated with another form of accessing formula, "When you have the words and ideas that can help you resolve that issue, will you find those hands opening?" The patient is allowed to do her inner work of accessing and problem resolution entirely on her own; she is learning and rehearsing more effective ways of working with herself.

The next question, "Will you tell me just enough about it so I can help you further with the next issues?" directs her to a more focused form of self-expression in order to advise the therapist about the next issue needing resolution. Thus, the entire procedure is patient-centered and iterative: There is an absolute minimum of analysis and interpretation by the therapist; the patient generates, step by step, whatever conscious insights are needed to facilitate further problem-solving.

Even though I never did understand what her problem was, I was able to help her utilize her anxiety as a highly motivational energy for exploring and resolving her issues privately within herself. By the time she came to the end of this experience she felt a natural sense of honest relaxation and well-being from a job well-done.

Tutorial Seven: The Ultradian Healing Response

The most recent psychobiological approach to mind-body communication and healing utilizes ultradian rhythms. Elsewhere I have presented data detailing the similarities between many of the cognitive and behavioral characteristics of these rhythms and the "common everyday trance" (Rossi, 1982, 1986a, 1992a, b, d; Rossi & Cheek, 1988; Rossi & Nimmons, 1991). Since much of the theory and practice of using these psychobiological rhythms for healing has been covered in these papers, we will simply outline an accessing formula utilizing the rhythms in this section.

Since ultradian rhythms occur at 90-minute intervals, plus or minus about 30 minutes, their subtle behavioral manifestations will be appar-

---

TUTORIAL 7 The Ultradian Healing Response

1. *Recognizing and facilitating natural ultradian rhythms*
   I notice your body seems to be getting quieter in these last few moments, and you're not saying much as you look out the window
   [or whatever withdrawal behavior the patient is manifesting]. I
   wonder if that means your unconscious is ready to enter a comfortable period of therapeutic healing? [Pause]
   If it is, will you find yourself getting even more comfortable, with
   your eyes closing?

2. *Accessing and utilizing ultradian healing*
   You can continue allowing that comfort to deepen, just as you do
   when you enjoy taking a break or a much needed nap.
   [Pause]
   You may or may not be aware of just how your unconscious is doing exactly what it needs to do to deal with the issues that can be
   best resolved at this time. [Allow a 5- to 20-minute period of quiet
   inner work.]

3. *Ratifying continuing ultradian healing and coping*
   When your unconscious knows it has dealt with that issue to the
   fullest extent possible at this time, [pause]
   and when your conscious mind knows it can recognize and allow
   you to continue this inner healing a few times a day when it feels
   natural,
   [pause]
   Will you find yourself wanting to stretch and open your eyes, coming fully awake, alert, and refreshed?

---

ent to the observant therapist during most therapy sessions. For example, when it is observed that the patient is spontaneously entering a
quiet or inner-directed mood, one can be fairly certain that an ultradian
resting phase is being experienced. The therapist can facilitate and utilize the healing potentials of this "ultradian break" by simply comment-
ing on it in an approving manner, and by allowing the patient's unconscious to do some quiet inner work for five to 20 minutes without
attempting to sustain the outer dialogue. If the ultradian resting phase
is unrecognized and ignored, then this is the period of the therapy

session during which the patient typically manifests "resistance" in the form of many otherwise unaccountable symptoms (moodiness, partial withdrawal, irritability, tongue slips, memory gaps, and the types of "mistakes" we all make when we are tired and need to rest). While it is always of value to understand the psychodynamic implications of these "resistances," it is also wise to recognize them as the behavioral signs of the need to allow the unconscious to do its own inner healing work.

Practical, clinical illustrations of this ultradian approach will be presented in the second half of this book. Meanwhile, it is important to note that, because the cognitive, emotional, and behavioral manifestations of ultradian rhythms are so similar to manifestations of altered states and hypnosis, there will be a natural temptation for therapists to "suggest" or evoke these behaviors even when they are not present. Indeed, this is what most hypnotherapists do: they "suggest" or "condition" the patient to go into hypnosis when *they* are ready, rather than when the patient's unconscious (and physiology) is ready. This highly directive approach is often successful because ultradian rhythms are very flexible in their manifestation; they can be "skipped" and their cycle lengths easily changed in most individuals. This more direct hypnotherapeutic approach apparently works well enough much of the time. I believe, however, that when the hypnotherapist is too arbitrary in imposing his own, rather than the patient's, timing for hypnotic work, it can set off resistance and paranoid reactions. It is now a question for empirical research to determine whether patients have a better overall clinical response to therapeutic hypnosis when their natural ultradian rest rhythms are utilized rather than ignored (Rossi, 1992e).

It is important to know some of the spontaneous and entirely autonomous types of mind-body healing that can take place within patients during their natural 20-minute ultradian healing response in everyday life as well as psychotherapy (Rossi & Nimmons, 1991). Many of these natural healing responses that are associated with the central nervous system, the autonomic, endocrine, and immune systems will be dealt with in more detail in the following chapters.

The natural healing of stress-related mind-body problems and the optimizing of many life activities (work, play, creativity, etc.) can be facilitated by learning to recognize our natural ultradian mind-body signals for healing. While there are common patterns we all share, each of us is unique in the way we experience them. This typically involves learning to recognize our personal signals of the ultradian stress response so we can correct the stress conditions of our life that cause our problems. We can then learn to use the ultradian healing response to maximize our natural potentials for health and well-being (see Rossi & Nimmons, 1991, for the practical details of how everyone can learn to do this in everyday-life).

I speculate that most of the currently existing holistic methods of mind-body healing such as the relaxation response, therapeutic hypnosis, imagery, meditation, prayer, etc., all utilize the ultradian healing response without realizing it. Since most people chronically experience an ultradian rest deficit, I believe that most of the natural therapeutic benefits of the ultradian healing response immediately take place silently and autonomously just as soon as the patient is given a moment to relax while the therapist performs a healing ritual that supposedly heals them. Indirect evidence for this view is implied by the fact that most of the published research that attempts to document these holistic approaches invariably reports that a 20-minute (plus or minus about 10 minutes) experimental healing period was used to assess whatever approach being tested (e.g., Feher, Berger, Johnson, & Wilde, 1989; Green & Green, 1987). These papers rarely, if ever, present any rational for using this 20-minute period, however. It appears as if the ordinary everyday 20-minute healing-rest period is so common that no one even feels it's worthy of comment.

Research is needed to assess the degree to which many religious healing rituals activate the ultradian healing response simply by providing an opportunity for patients to give up their stress by letting ''god take care of it.'' Twelve-step programs that emphasize that the individual is powerless to deal with their addiction may be setting in motion similar patterns of relaxation that enable healing to take place so that everyone ''feels better'' by the end of the meeting. It is the ''relaxation opportunity,'' and occasional emotional catharsis, however, that actually initiates the real healing factor on the psychobiological level; it allows patients who believe in the ritual to experience their own natural ultradian healing response which then facilitates their healing right down to the molecular-genetic level. On the other hand, the more dramatic forms of healing rituals that activate people with music, dancing, and even painful acts of endurance may be activating, entraining, and extending the high end of the 90-minute basic rest-activity cycle that is associated with the release of many hormones of the neuroendocrinal axis that may be responsible for healing. One of the most practical and easy ways of entraining and utilizing both the high and low end of the basic rest activity cycle in psychotherapy is illustrated in the next tutorial.

TUTORIAL EIGHT: THREE-STEP PROBLEM SOLVING

This three-step problem solving approach enables the therapist to introduce patients to a "healing ritual" that accesses whatever phase of the basic rest activity cycle they may be in to facilitate whatever problem they may be dealing with. This approach is currently being standardized into a general *ideo-dynamic exploratory accessing scale* (IDEAS-1) suitable for administration to individuals or groups for clinical-experimental research in mind-body healing. It is presented here in an abbreviated form as Tutorial 8 to illustrate how it can be used as an easily learned, fail-safe approach to problem solving in general.

As in the case with all the other applications of the basic accessing question, this three-step approach to problem solving works best when the patient is genuinely motivated by an important problem they really don't know how to solve. I do not use it unless I am convinced, after exploring several lines of questioning, that a patient really does not know the answer and admits it. I use this three-step problem-solving approach very sparingly because I don't want its effectiveness to "wear out" for any particular patient. I believe much of its effectiveness is due to the fact that many patients experience the so-called "involuntary responses" it evokes (when their hands apparently "move all by themselves") as something a little strange or even bizarre, something quite beyond their normal range of experience. I speculate that this novelty or numinous effect may be responsible for releasing unique combinations of the stress hormones that encode state-dependent memories and creative resources so that they may be accessed for problem solving in a slightly altered state that some people may experience as "hypnosis."

The wide range of application of this three-step problem-solving approach is well illustrated by two strikingly different cases that I saw for only one session each.

Accessing Memory in Organic Brain Damage.   A mature woman with little education and peculiar speech (that turns out to be due to organic brain damage from a recent auto accident) telephones to request "some of the hypnosis thing" to help her remember where she hid $3,000 worth of rock concert tickets that were delivered to her home during the day when no one else was there. When she comes to the office I initially have her review several times exactly what she remembered on the day the tickets were delivered: from the moment she woke up, to the delivery of the tickets (which she remembered well), to the time when other members of the family returned home after their workday

TUTORIAL 8   Three-Step Problem Solving

1. *An involuntary mind-body signal for problem solving*
   **Place your hands up with the palms facing each other about six to
   eight inches apart and tune into them with great sensitivity** [thera-
   pist demonstrates]. **We know the human body has a magnetic
   field. We don't know if you can actually sense this magnetic field
   or if this is an exercise in the use of imagination. Can you let yourself begin to experience a magnetic field developing between your
   hands right now?**
   **We know that a magnetic field can attract or repel—move things
   together or push them apart.**
   **This is interesting because we believe the inner you can also
   bring people or things together if it feels positive and wants to say
   "Yes." The inner mind can say "No" by pushing things apart.**
   **So let's see if the inner mind-body agrees that the problem you
   have chosen is really the problem that can be explored and resolved right here and now today to the fullest extent that is possible.**
   **If your inner mind agrees and wants to say "Yes," will those
   hands now move together slowly all by themselves as if a magnetic force were pulling them together?"** [Pause for a minute or
   so. If hands do not show any inclination to move together then use
   a therapeutic double bind as follows.]
   **Or will they move apart all by themselves for a moment because
   there is something else that is more important that you need to focus on first?** [If hands do move apart then either allow the patient
   to explore it privately or engage patient in a normal conversation
   about what it is.]

2. *Accessing state-dependent memories*
   **Will just one of those hands now begin to move down slowly all
   by itself to signal that your inner mind and body can now access
   and explore all the emotional sources and memories associated
   with the beginning of that problem?**
   **Only one hand goes down very slowly to signal that your inner
   mind is reviewing all the feelings and memories you need for
   problem solving.**

(continued)

TUTORIAL 8 Continued

3. *Accessing creative resources for problem solving*
   Will the other hand now go down slowly all by itself as your inner mind explores all the possibilities of solving that problem in
   as satisfactory manner as possible at this time?
   Will that hand go down slowly by itself as you really begin to experience some of the positive feelings of well-being and self-confidence that come naturally when you find you can deal with a
   problem successfully? [Pause until the hand comes to rest on lap]
   And when your inner mind knows that it can continue this inner
   work whenever it is appropriate throughout the day or night—
   And when your conscious mind knows it can cooperate by helping you recognize when you need to take "time out" for healing
   rest—
   Will you then come normally alert, stretch, and be ready to cope?

---

to frantically turn the house upside down trying to find where she put
the tickets for "safekeeping."

She was able to visualize herself going from room to room trying to
decide where she should put the tickets; she knows she found a "wonderful place" to hide them in the house, but she simply could not
remember where. After about a half hour of tedious memory review
she seemed tired and weakly pleaded, "But docta, when you doin the
hypnosis?" I demonstrated heroic restraint to myself by resisting the
temptation to give her an earful of the typical academic explanation of
how "hypnosis is nothing but relaxation, visualization and going along
with the therapist's words" and, without much hope, initiated "The
Magical Magnetic Hands Hypnosis," the name I decided to give her for
the procedure of Tutorial 8. She stared in wide-eyed fascination as her
hands slowly moved together "all by themselves" in the first stage to
indicate that her inner mind knew where she hid the tickets. Her mouth
then literally dropped open in silent amazement as one of her hands
began drifting down "all by itself" when I asked it to as a signal that
she now could see exactly how she moved from room to room looking
for a safe place to hide the tickets. When that hand was about halfway
down she closed her eyes momentarily and then suddenly opened them
in obvious astonishment.

With a guileful whisper I intoned deeply, "And now you really know where those tickets are, don't you?!" She slowly nodded her head "yes," while holding her breath and closing her eyes. I confidently whispered, "And you are going to keep remembering until after you wake up and tell me, won't you?!" She nodded "yes" with a tear beginning to flow down her cheek. Quick as a wink I asked her to wake up with a full memory as soon as her hand went all the way down to her lap "real soon." Her hand dropped to her lap like a stone. She opened her eyes and told me how she hid the tickets on the top shelf of the linen closet where, of course, nobody in the family looked because their tradition was that the fine linen was sacred and that closet could be opened only when company came calling. She left the office filled with tearful enthusiasm and forgot to pay me, and I forgot to ask.

Accessing Memory of Sexual Molestation.   A prestigious lawyer, high up in city politics and nearing retirement age, had his executive secretary telephone for an appointment for an "urgent personal matter." The florid man himself came at the appointed hour to confess that his grown daughter, now married with small children of her own, was planning to sue him because she claimed he sexually molested her when she was young. "The thing is," he said, "I remember nothing of what she is talking about, but how can I be sure?" I somehow felt very remote from this man, but I assured him there was one way he could find the truth if he was really sincere about knowing it. We really didn't need any truth serum or lie detectors because, of course, there was a clear record of it in his brain and the truth could become available with a special kind of hypnosis: "a very powerful form of hypnosis where you can learn the truth privately within yourself and you don't even have to tell even me about it if you don't want to."

The idea of learning the truth and being able to keep it secret greatly appealed to this man and he readily agreed to the "special hypnosis for private memory accessing." I administered the three-step problem-solving approach of Tutorial 8 with a somewhat more direct style to fit his authoritarian personality. He spontaneously closed his eyes as his hands came together slowly but surely in Stage 1 to indicate that his inner mind really knew the truth "about this urgent personal matter." With much frowning, sweating, and then an embarrassed, reddening face one hand began drifting down "all by itself" in small spasmodic jerks and apparently involuntary vibration as he "reviewed the history of the matter." After a few minutes the hand softly came to rest in his lap as he slowly shook his head "no" with a flood of tears.

I assumed that he was finding out that his daughter's claim of sexual molestation was untrue and that he was crying with relief. I impassively asked if his other hand would now "go down all by itself" to signal that he now realized the truth and would learn what he could do about it. The second hand went down with more tears, but he managed to pull himself together with some calmness by the time I asked him to "awaken with a full and private memory of the entire matter." Although I evidenced no interest in finding out what he learned, he quickly and matter-of-factly admitted that he had indeed molested his daughter. He vividly recalled pulling down her pajamas and pressing his penis between her legs but insisted that he never penetrated her because he was "just playing, like." He then wondered if he could have at least one more session with his daughter present so they could clear it all up.

TUTORIAL NINE: IDEODYNAMIC MOVEMENTS SIGNALING HEALING

One of the most popular methods of accessing and resolving problems in therapeutic hypnosis today is via ideomotor signaling (Rossi & Ryan, 1992). There are two basic approaches: (1) the original naturalistic or utilization approach of Milton H. Erickson (1961/1980), and (2) the more highly structured approach of Cheek and LeCron (Cheek & LeCron, 1968; LeCron, 1954). Erickson's naturalistic style was to utilize whatever form of ideomotor mannerisms were already being expressed by a patient. If a patient tended to nod or shake his head spontaneously in a seemingly unconscious manner during the therapy session, for example, Erickson would recognize the movement as an ideomotor signal from a nonverbal level of mind-body responsiveness. Other natural ideomotor mannerisms might be expressed through the eyes (blinking or squinting during stress) and movements of the arms, legs, or hands. In Tutorial 6 I utilized a patient's absentminded opening and closing of her hands as a naturalistic approach to ideomotor signaling that was particularly suitable for her.

The more highly structured approach of Cheek and LeCron, by contrast, uses a standard form of ideomotor finger signaling for all patients. Responses of "yes," "no," "I don't know," and "I don't want to answer," are assigned to the different fingers of the patient's hand. This is followed by a series of questions that can be answered with the finger signals. The questions are designed to access the source of the problem and find a resolution of it. A typical approach involves patients in a structured form of age regression in which they are asked to reorient themselves to a time before the problem became manifest. The therapist then asks a series of questions that can be answered by the finger signals to facilitate a careful, detailed review of all the sensory-perceptual learnings, attitudes, and frames of reference that contributed to the source of the problem and to its current maintenance (Rossi & Cheek, 1988).

Tutorial 9 illustrates a way of introducing ideomotor *finger* signaling that is acceptable to most patient. As indicated, all questions are phrased so they can be answered with a simple yes or no finger signal. Cheek and LeCron (1968) give more examples of how a series of questions can be phrased to deal with a variety of clinical problems. Ideomotor *head* or *hand* signaling can be introduced as interesting variations.

TUTORIAL 9 Ideodynamic Movements for Signaling Healing

1. *Identify yes/no finger signal*
   Review a happy or deeply satisfying memory and let's see which finger lifts, lifts up, sort of by itself, to signal yes.
   [Pause as patient identifies the yes finger by lifting it.]
   Now review an unhappy experience and discover which finger lifts to signal no. [Pause until patient identifies the no finger.]

2. *Access source and maintenance of problem*
   Let your inner mind take you back to a time before your experience of the problem, and then let that yes finger signal just so I'll know you're there. Will it be okay to go over it all, step by step, start to finish, just what's happening as you experienced the problem the first time?
   [This is followed by a series of questions that can be answered with yes or no finger signals to identify the state-bound experiences and feelings associated with the original acquisition of the problem. This is then followed by yes or no questions to identify current attitudes and circumstances that maintain the problem.]

3. *Ratify conditions for problem resolution*
   Will it now be okay for you to be completely free of that problem?
   [Pause for one minute; if there is no response continue with:] **Or is there a date in the future when you can see yourself free of it?**
   [If necessary, this is followed by a series of questions to ascertain all the conditions the total personality needs to realize for problem resolution.]

Again, all questions are phrased so that a simple nod or shake of the head is sufficient to answer the question.

In a series of richly documented clinical papers, Cheek (1957–1981) has responded to the criticism that his ideomotor approach encourages patients to confabulate answers that please the therapist. He has formulated a three-point criteria for evaluating the psychobiological validity of the patient's therapeutic involvement with this procedure, which he discussed as follows (Cheek, 1981, pp. 89–90):

> With newer hypnotic techniques using repetitive subconscious review below conscious, verbal levels of awareness, it is possible to reveal cause and effect relationships between sensory input and resulting responses. My conclusions have been drawn in consultation with more than 3,000 surgical patients and 15 men and women who have been unconscious due to head injury. . . .
>
> Can we trust the information offered with ideomotor investigative methods? We know that hypnotized people are peculiarly apt to fabricate information, either to please a hypnotist or to permit their escape from having to relive a very traumatic experience. This ability seems to rest at higher, more conscious levels of thought. It does not seem to occur at deeper horizons of awareness. We can trust the information when its eventual conversion to verbal reporting has followed this sequence:
>
> 1) We witness physiological signs of distress. Frowning, accelerated breathing, and pulsation of neck vessels tell us that something is stressful, but the hypnotized subject does not "know" what is happening when we ask.
>
> 2) An ideomotor signal identifies the beginning of the experience *after* we see the physiological changes. If asked about the event, the subject will continue his verbal level ignorance of the event.
>
> 3) Verbal reporting is possible after a variable number of subconscious scanning of the event. If the event is relatively nonthreatening, it may be quickly reported. [On one occasion] it took 13 reviews of the entire operation before my first success in retrieving a memory.
>
> If there is any question about the validity of a report, we have found we can ask for an answer to the question, "Does the inner part of your mind agree with what you have just told me?" I would not place any weight on evidence offered by a confirmed alcoholic, drug addict, or pathological liar using ideomotor methods, nor would I trust evidence offered by a criminal suspect. My studies of anesthetic experiences have not included people in these categories.

From the point of view developed in this book, I would say that Cheek's physiological, ideomotor, and verbal levels are examples of state-bound patterns of information that had become dissociated from

each other. Psychosomatic symptoms are expressions of these dissociations; therapy is achieved by facilitating information transduction between them. It is evident from Cheek's above statement that his repetitive questioning evokes recursive inner searches on the "deeper,"
state-dependent psychobiological levels until the sought-for material is
transduced into the verbal level. Because this method specializes in the
facilitation of recursive processes, it is most ideally suited for treatment
of traumatic situations.

As we have seen, trauma induces an altered state wherein memories
are encoded in a state-bound form that is frequently not available to
ordinary ego consciousness. Cheek has investigated a variety of traumatic or altered-state situations that produce such state-bound effects:
critical illness (1969), childbirth (1975, 1976), general anesthesia (1981),
accidents (1960), dream states (1965), frightening sexual experiences
such as rape (1960), and the death or serious injury of a loved one
(1960). Cheek's approach is particularly applicable in situations where
highly directive, short-term, and exploratory efforts are needed to
quickly access symptoms and the effects of trauma that reach deeply
into the psychophysiological levels of memory storage, imprinting, and
learning. The highly emotional responses that are frequently obtained
when traumatic material is uncovered with this approach require careful
clinical management by well-trained therapists. In Chapter 7 an example
of Cheek's work will be presented to illustrate its highly variable and
creative characteristics in accessing and transducing mind-body problems associated with the effects of stress on the autonomic and endocrine systems.

In professional workshops where I have taught finger signaling it has
become apparent how it can be very responsive to subtle and nonverbal
psychosocial influences. In one workshop with professionals who had
no previous training in clinical hypnosis, the first volunteer from the
audience to serve as a demonstration subject had an experience that
was entirely new to me. After a satisfactory introduction by identifying
a yes or no finger as illustrated in Tutorial 9, she spontaneously described how one of her fingers felt like it was her mother's personality
while another finger felt it was her father. A very interesting pattern of
psychodynamic experiences then took place when I directed questions
to the mother and father fingers to uncover many of the subject's long
forgotten childhood memories, traumas, etc. Flushed with success I
asked for another volunteer from the professional audience. A second
subject came up, identified a yes and no finger and, without any suggestion from me and with apparent involuntariness, this subject proceeded

to find various personalities of her fingers, portraying mother, father, sister, and brother; again a very moving and meaningful "finger psychodrama" was experienced.

From then on there was no stopping it! Everyone who volunteered to be a demonstration subject was amazed to find their fingers spontaneously jumping about in what we began to call "Finger Family Therapy." Therapists sitting in the audience began to report that their fingers were beginning to twitch "all by themselves" in a family way even while they were watching the demonstration on stage. When the audience broke into small groups of four or five professionals to practice finger signaling among themselves, they too found to their growing amusement that there could be no denying of the new wave of apparently autonomous Finger Family Therapy. We recognized we were all in the grip of "The Madness of Crowds" but no one could stop it. Even those who always felt themselves immune to hypnotic suggestion found their fingers spontaneously playing about in most astonishing ways. By the end of the workshop we all felt we should then and there establish a new Society of Finger Family Therapy but no one was willing to be president, treasurer, or chairperson for the next international congress so nothing came of it.

TUTORIAL TEN: FACILITATING AUTOCATALYTIC HEALING

This is a variation of the basic accessing question that utilizes involuntary hand, arm, finger, and body signaling of all sorts in a more unstructured manner to facilitate autocatalytic healing in more creative, freeform experiences that rapidly lead to insight along with symptom and conflict resolution in people that have a talent for this approach. Just as the experience of feeling "blocked" or "not knowing" is an indication to use the three-step solving approach of Tutorial 8, the experience of being "caught in conflict" between two or more alternatives of behavior or options of personality expression is an indication for the use of the approach outlined in this approach to autocatalytic healing.

People have "conflicts" because of the natural but peculiar psychological property of spontaneously dissociating different sides of their personality so that they are expressed at different times. It's apparently difficult for most people to experience their loving and hateful feelings at the same moment. Its usually "fight or flight" but rarely both at the same time. Such conflicts can be resolved with insight by structuring a mind-body psychodrama that allows the patient to experience both sides together in a therapeutic encounter (Lightfoot, 1992). The thera-

---

TUTORIAL 10 Facilitating Autocatalytic Healing

1. *The simultaneous experience of both sides of a conflict*
   You have been struggling between the spiritual side of yourself and the glutton that overeats. Place your hands in front of yourself with the palms up and let me know which hand feels more like the spiritual and which the glutton?

2. *Engaging and externalizing the inner conflict*
   Now let yourself simply experience what begins to happen between those two sides of yourself that are now active together. [Whatever the patient's experience, the therapist simply encourages the inner drama of active imagination as it is externalized into somewhat involuntary and surprising experience taking place in and between the hands in all the modalities illustrated in Tutorial 1.]

3. *Facilitating conflict resolution and self-empowerment*
   That's right, let those two sides continue until. . . ? Wonderful, now notice what happens next all by itself. . . ? And what is most interesting as this continues. . . ? And how does it all come together?

---

pist's initial task is to formulate an appropriate basic accessing question that facilitates a simultaneous experience of both sides of the contending forces of the personality so they may be engaged in autocatalytic healing.

An ideal way of learning when and how to use this approach is with the typical dreams of a conflict. The therapist asks the patient to extend their hands with palms up to feel what they are experiencing in their dream. Depending on what presenting figures or forces are in conflict in the dream, the therapist might ask the patient which hand seems to feel like the dreamer and which hand seems to feel like the monster chasing the dreamer, for example. This is somewhat analogous to the first step of asking the patient to identify a yes or no finger in the finger signaling approach of Tutorial 9. Typical accessing questions might be:

> Which hand feels like you in the dream and which hand feels more like your supervisor who was criticizing you in the dream?

Which hand experiences the coldness you felt in the first part of the dream and which hand feels the heat of the volcano that suddenly appeared?

Which hand feels some of the pain you experienced in your dream and which feels like the magical elixir you drank to heal it?

Which hand feels more like the angry you and which feels like the fearful you?

Which side of your body feels more like your mother (or any significant figure the patient is in conflict with) and which feels more like you?

Which hand feels more like the adult and which feels more like the child in you?

Notice what sensations you feel in the sexy side and what sensations you feel in the fearful side, and tell me which side is which

You want to deal with that headache [or whatever]. . . . Let yourself really tune into each of those hands to see which one experiences that headache in some way . . . and what comes up within you as that hand experiences more and more of that headache *just for a moment or two*? . . . [Often the patient will report that the headache has spontaneously displaced itself from its original locus to one of the hands.] And you can wonder why your hand now feels that headache and your head does not?! And yet the other hand feels fine? And will one hand be able to help the other? You can now wonder how that good-feeling "healing hand" will help the other . . .

When the patient has identified which hand is which in whatever conflict is being explored, the therapist continues with the second stage by proposing, "Now let yourself simply experience what begins to happen between those two sides that are now active together—let's see [pause] what begins to happen with those hands." When a really essential and motivating issue is being engaged the patient usually stares at the hands with some fascination. The hands will usually begin to move up, down, or about in idiosyncratic ways that begin to express some ideodynamic sensory-perceptual or kinesthetic-proprioceptive behaviors ("going with the flow" of Tutorial 1) expressive of the conflict that seem to take place on an involuntary level. To epigram the process, "The psychodynamics of the unconscious are being entrained and expressed in observable behavior." The fleeting and often incomprehensible "free associations" of Freud, the private "active imagination" of Jung, and the externalized gestalt dialogues of Fritz Perls are being expressed in a new and more comprehensive self-generative process of "autocatalytic healing" (See Rossi 1972/1985 for many examples of "creation de novo" in dream work). The patient feels self-empowered because this approach usually completes itself in an insightful and therapeutic manner with very little interpretation needed from the therapist. Patient and therapist are both participant-observers in a genuine process of autocatalytic healing and discovery.

The therapist simply joins the fun by watching and supporting the self-generative process with an appropriate sense of wonder and surprise. Particularly in the third stage, wherein patients often come to their own spontaneous self-insights and problem resolutions, the therapist does well to maintain a tone of hopeful, tentative inquiry with many dangling phrases and incomplete sentences that cues the patients' inner process to "fill in the blanks." Sometimes the therapist's usual vocal tone of uplift may be mixed with a mildly skeptical attitude that enables the therapist to express doubts in a way that may free the skeptical patient from the burden of having to express them. A creative something or other is happening even if therapist and patient don't know what it is initially. In fact, *this therapeutic process can only be defined as autocatalytic and creative if there is a genuine aspect of surprise, a certain degree of involuntariness (outside the person's typical sense of directing or controlling their thoughts, feeling, or behavior) and unpredictability about the experience.* Otherwise it is merely another form of traditional "talking therapy" with the therapist playing the role of "expert" directing or programming the patient just like they do in the movies with a rather outmoded ideology of authority and stimulus-response psychology.

SECTION II

The Psychobiology of Mind-Body Healing

6

An Overview of Mind-Body Communication and Healing

SINCE ANCIENT TIMES SAVANTS have debated whether mind can move mountains. In this volume we explore the more humble question of whether mind can move molecules. However complex this question may become, we can always turn to the simple picture in Figure 3 to reorient ourselves. We are exploring mind-body relationships between three levels of the metaphorical tree of life: (1) Certainly we are interested in mind, mood, memory, and behavior illustrated as the leaves of the tree; (2) we are learning how the trunk of the tree consists of messenger molecules (hormones, growth factors, information substances, etc.) that communicate between mind and body; and (3) many of these messenger molecules ultimately tell our genes, the roots of the tree of life, to express themselves by using their blueprints to promote growth and healing within every cell of brain and body.

These three levels are illustrated once again in Figure 4 where the focus is on the major pathways of (1) mind-brain communication, (2) brain-body communication; and (3) cell-gene communication. At first glance there seems to be something missing from these pictures. Where are all those complex patterns of nerves that are supposed to be the connecting link between mind and body? The nerves are there, to be sure, and we will illustrate them in the more detailed diagrams of later chapters, but the nervous system is only the "Johnny-come-lately" in the evolution of mind-body communication. Before life invented nerves to specialize in rapid communication between brain and body in large-size organisms, messenger molecules were the original form of communication. Even today the activity of every single nerve in our body and brain is modulated by messenger molecules. This is the new and profoundly deep insight that makes a modern science of mind-body

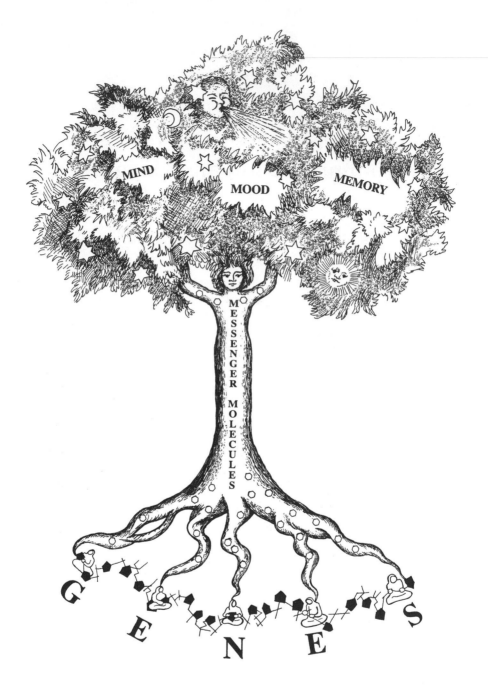

FIGURE 3 The metaphorical tree of mind-body healing

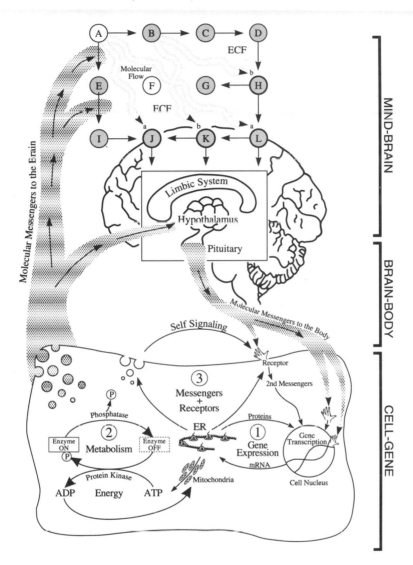

FIGURE 4 The cybernetic communication loop between the mind-brain and the cell-gene levels via the ultradian pulses of molecular messengers that encode state-dependent memory, learning, and behavior. The three basic processes of information transduction at the cellular-genetic level—(1) gene expression, (2) metabolism and energy dynamics, and (3) self-signaling on all levels from cell to body, brain, and mind—are all mediated by the production of proteins on the endoplasmic reticulum (ER).

communication possible: *Messenger molecules are the ultimate common denominator or "bottom line" of psychosomatic communication between mind, emotions, behavior, and the expression of genes in health and illness* (Pert et al., 1985; Kandel, 1989; Rossi, 1987b, 1990a, b).

This new insight into the molecular basis of mind-body communication resolves many of the so-called "mysteries and miracles of the faith healing." The traditional medical textbook diagrams of the neural networks between brain and body (e.g., the central and peripheral nervous system), for example, could not account for the odd, apparently idiosyncratic patterns of hysterical sensations and paralyses typical of psychosomatic problems. Neither can they account for the peculiarities of memory, amnesia, and behavior found in traumatic, stressful, and psychoneurotic conditions. The highly individualized patterns of the state-dependent encoding of memory, learning, and behavior by messenger molecules during the complex contingencies of real life, however, can account for these "apparently idiosyncratic patterns" that do not fit the traditional textbook maps of neural circuits.

From this fresh perspective we can now understand how the mysteries of mind-body healing actually were due to the limitations of nineteenth-century philosophy and anatomy that regarded the "nerves" as the only pathways of communication between brain and body. We now know that this is not true; messenger molecules are the original and more pervasive (holistic) means of communication between all cells of the mind and body. Messenger molecules can encode our memory, emotions, learning, and behavior in the highly personal and individualized patterns of our real everyday life experience and, to some extent, use these learned patterns to modulate all the so-called "self-regulatory" systems of mind and body.

We now know that all the major regulatory systems of mind-body communication such as the *autonomic nervous system,* as well as the *endocrine, immune,* and *neuropeptide systems* are really not as independent, autonomous, or "self-regulatory" as has been thought. They all communicate with one another by many of the same messenger molecules that encode state-dependent memory, learning, and behavior (SDMLB). The following chapters will document the research and current clinical practice of each of these four major systems for mind-body communication and healing.

Our deepening recognition of messenger molecules as an essential link in the general process of psychosocial communication places us in a better position to chart scientific strategies for facilitating mind-body communication and healing. In this important chapter we will briefly overview the three major levels of the psychosomatic loop shown in Figures 3 and 4 from mind to gene. In the following chapters we will provide more detail about each level together with many innovative clinical approaches for facilitating mind-body healing.

MIND-BRAIN COMMUNICATION

Mind-brain communication, illustrated on the top level of Figure 4, is the basic stumbling block for most theorists, clinicians, and researchers who are concerned about "The Problem of Consciousness." Many informed people continue to maintain that we still haven't a ghost of an understanding of what consciousness is, much less do we really know anything about the profound mystery of how mind and brain are related. Rather than fight this attitude, let us simply acknowledge its general truth: the ultimate mystery of the nature of consciousness remains intact. Science, however, usually proceeds by a series of small but verifiable steps. In this section we will review recent research about a few small steps toward and understanding of how the natural languages of mind (words, emotions, images, sensations, etc.) and the molecular languages of the brain and body (molecular messengers such as hormones, molecular codes such as genes, etc.) communicate with each other. We will focus only on ideas and research that will be useful in formulating practical psychotherapeutic approaches to mind-brain communication and healing.

In previous chapters we reviewed the types of clinical and experimental data that enable us to evaluate *the hypothesis that SDMLB encoded with messenger molecules from all cells of the body is the common denominator that bridges the mind-brain gap, the so-called Cartesian dichotomy between mind and body* (Rossi, 1987, 1990a, b; Rossi & Cheek, 1988; Rossi & Ryan, 1986; Lloyd & Rossi, 1992b). Francis Crick, who received the Nobel Prize with James Watson for discovering the informational basis of life by reading the DNA code of our genes, has recently turned his attention to the problem of consciousness (Crick & Koch, 1990) in a manner that is consistent with the SDMLB hypothesis.

Crick and Koch address the question of how it is possible for the "spotlight of attention" to pull together a recognizable picture of the world out of the booming and buzzing confusion of stimuli from the environment that are bombarding the brain at the same time. In a recent interview Koch (1992, p. 98) summarizes the situation:

Now let's say we're outside and having lunch, and there are other people talking behind you. They also move their heads, and so their images will also strike my retina and will also fire neurons. . . . So I have to combine all the neuronal activity corresponding to your face and voice; plus, I have to segregate that from all the other neurons that are also responding at the same time to everything that's going on around you. . . . One way to do this is *oscillation*. Think of a Christmas tree with a billion lights on it; each light flashes only occasionally. Now there's a subset of lights—a very small one, let's say there are only 10,000—and they flash all together. If you just visualize that, you'll see that it will stand out very readily . . .

In other words, all the neurons that currently attend to some aspect of you and your face and your voice all fire in a semisynchronous manner, roughly all at the same time. All the other neurons that respond to anything else found on my retina also fire, but they fire randomly. *This synchronized activity releases some substance, some chemical substance, that sticks around, say for ten seconds or two seconds or five seconds—that constitutes short-term memory.* Whenever I'm aware of something, whenever I attend to something, I put it in short-term memory. It's a very tight link. (Italics added)

The essence of the Crick and Koch model is that consciousness, attention, memory, and the creation of a picture of the world are mediated by two processes: (1) synchronized neural oscillations that coordinate the relevant parts of a conscious experience into a recognizable whole; and (2) this synchronized neural activity releases "some chemical substance" that encodes the recognizable experiences of mind into memory. Let us outline the correspondence between these two processes and the SDMLB theory that was proposed in earlier chapters as the essential link in mind-body communication and healing.

1) The idea that synchronized neural oscillations could coordinate all the components of a conscious perception into a recognizable whole has its scientific documentation in the research of Wolf Singer and his colleagues at the Max Plank Institute for Brain Research (Gray, Engel, Konig, & Singer, 1992). They found a 40-cycle-per-second oscillation in the firing rate of neurons throughout the cortex of the cat that respond to the many different components of a perceptual scene. Analogous research in the owl and monkey visual systems suggests that these coordinating neural oscillations may be a direct neural correlate of awareness. These observations are consistent with the author's "Unification Hypothesis of Chronobiology" that integrates SDMLB with a wide range of mind-body oscillations that coordinates communication

in the wave nature of consciousness and being from mind to gene (Rossi, 1992d; Rossi & Lippincott, 1992; Lloyd & Rossi, 1992b).

2) Crick and Koch are not yet able to specify exactly what "chemical substance" is released by the synchronized neural oscillations, but this substance is certainly what by definition is called a messenger molecule. This second feature of the Crick and Koch model is entirely consistent with our view of how state-dependent memory encoded by messenger molecules from all parts of the brain and body could modulate the coordinated oscillatory activity of the 10,000 neurons of a bit of the brain basis of "mind." Francis Schmitt (1984, 1986) of the Massachusetts Institute of Technology has outlined how such messenger molecules

> can diffuse as much as 15 mm from the cerebrospinal fluid . . . to any site in the cerebral cortex of the adult human brain. There would thus be ample intercellular space for the dynamic interplay of many kinds of informational substances to diffuse from release points to receptors on or in the neurons of the cerebral cortex. (Schmitt, 1984, p. 996)

In the simplest case, a 15-mm^2 neuronal network (variously estimated to containing between 10,000 and 1.5 million neurons) could be turned on or off by the presence or absence of a specific messenger molecule. That is, *the activity of this neuronal network would be state-dependent on the presence or absence of that messenger molecule.* In actuality, of course, the situation is much more complex. We already know that there are almost 100 (and there are potentially thousands) of messenger molecules mediating communication between the brain's neurons in ever-changing patterns of adaptation to the contingencies of everyday life. This means that there may be infinitely complex patterns of messenger molecules encoding state-dependent neuronal networks in ever-changing dynamic structures that function as the psychosomatic basis for the phenomenology of mind, emotions, and behavior. The ever-shifting somatotopic maps of the "mind-brain" that are modifiable by life experience provide particularly vivid experimental evidence for these psychobiological dynamics of neuronal networks (Kandel & Schwartz, 1985).

In the top level of Figure 4, a 10,000 + unit of neurons is illustrated as the small set of circles A through L that encode a momentary bit of state-dependent mental experience. Messenger molecules from the body and the brain cells are pictured as coordinating this bit of mind via oscillating waves of integrated neural activity that are eventually transduced back into the messenger molecules of the body via the limbic-hypothalamic-pituitary system that mediates brain-body communication. Above this neuronal network, we note how a wide variety of environmental stimuli such as light, temperature, food, toxins, bacteria, and viruses are all in cybernetic communication with the entire mind-body right down to the genetic level. A variety of human and animal activities such as sports, sexuality, stress, trauma, and communication are in the same communication loop relating environmental cues and the entire mind-body.

To those of us in the senior generation who were taught that "genes were the units of heredity that had nothing to do with our everyday-life," it is utterly fascinating to learn that the song of a canary will turn on the expression of certain genes in another canary who is listening (Clayton, 1992). Even snails with a very primitive nervous system can learn to respond to environmental shocks by turning on and off certain of their genes (Kandel, 1989; Goelet & Kandel, 1986). On the human level we now know that medical students experiencing the stress of exam week turn off the expression of their interleukin 2 (IL-2) receptor gene in their immune system and thus leave themselves vulnerable to opportunistic infections (Glaser et al., 1990). We will review more examples of such mind-gene pathways of communication in health, stress, and illness in the following chapters.

BRAIN-BODY COMMUNICATION

The major locus of brain-body communication is the limbic-hypothalamic-pituitary system that is like a great funnel drawing in information from all the neural networks from the higher brain of the cortex and transducing this neural encoding of information into the messenger molecules of the body. Visualize the limbic system as a neural network that makes up the top part of the funnel in Figure 4; it serves as the borderland between the higher cortical brain and the hypothalamus-pituitary as the bottom stem of the funnel.

There are cells in the hypothalamus that can transduce information encoded in the form of the electrical impulses carried by the nerves of the higher cortex of the brain into the messenger molecules of the body; this is the essence of brain-body communication. This type of *neuroendocrinal* information transduction changes *neural* information of the brain into the pituitary *endocrinal* information of the body. The pituitary gland is recognized as the master gland regulating most of the endocrines (hormones or primary messenger molecules) of the body. Since the limbic-hypothalamic system plays a central role in brain-body communication we will review its anatomy and functions in more detail.

The Limbic-Hypothalamic System in Mind-Body Communication

One seeks in vain for any final answers on the basic anatomy and functions of the hypothalamus. The limbic-hypothalamic-pituitary system and closely associated parts of the brain such as the hippocampus are currently enjoying a renaissance of research because of the central role they play in mediating communication between the phenomenology of mind such as memory, learning, emotions, behavior, and their psychosomatic manifestations in the body. Each medical text seems to picture something different about this major conduit of mind-body communication depending on which functions are being discussed and which methods are being used (Ganong, 1985; Guyon, 1981; Kandel & Schwartz, 1985; Ornstein & Thompson, 1984). The hypothalamus does not appear to be a discrete, easily identifiable organ as are the heart, the lungs, or the cerebral hemispheres. Rather, the hypothalamus is a locus of tissues with seemingly vague boundaries at the base of the forebrain. It is made up of many important nuclei or centers of mind-body transduction and regulation. The functions of many of these nuclei, as depicted in Figure 5, are so different from one another that they seem to be entirely independent processes, accidentally thrown together in close proximity. What appears on first view to be "accident," however, is assuredly only a sign of our ignorance of nature's significant design. In fact, a careful study of the functions of these nuclei indicates that they are all concerned with the regulation of our internal environment via the autonomic, endocrine, immune, and neuropeptide systems.

The hypothalamus is an incredibly small area of the brain for such an important set of functions: It is about the size of a pea and weighs but a few grams! Figures 5, 6A, and 6B illustrate how the hypothalamus is the central focus of the limbic system in the brain. The word *limbic* means *border*; it was originally used to describe the border between the "higher" mind functions of the cerebral cortex and the "lower" structures of the brain involved with the regulation of emotions and body physiology. The hypothalamus receives signals from all parts of the nervous system so that it functions as a central information exchange concerned with the well-being of the entire body.

Guyon has described the central role of the hypothalamus as follows (1981, pp. 700–701):

The hypothalamus lies in the very middle of the limbic system. It also has communication pathways with all levels of this system. In turn, it and its closely allied structures, the septum and mammillary bodies send output signals in two directions, (1) downward through the brain stem mainly into

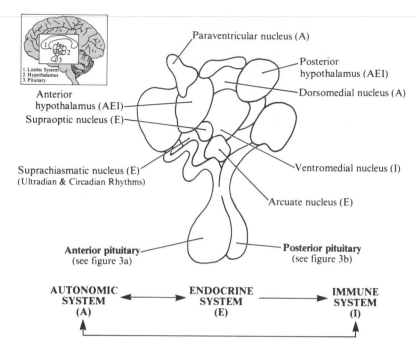

FIGURE 5 Some communication loops of the hypothalamic-pituitary system of mind-body information transduction via the autonomic (A), endocrine (E), and immune (I) systems.

the reticular formation of the mesencephalin, pons, and medulla, and (2) upward toward many areas of the cerebrum, especially the anterior thalamus and limbic cortex. In addition, the hypothalamus indirectly affects cerebral cortical function very dramatically through activation or inhibition of the reticular activating system that originates in the brain stem.

The hypothalamus is thus the major output pathway of the limbic system. It integrates the sensory-perceptual, emotional, and cognitive functions of mind with the biology of the body. *Since the limbic-hypothalamic system is in a process of constantly shifting, psycho-neuro-physiological states, all learning associated with it is, of necessity, state-dependent.*

The Hypothalamus and the Autonomic Nervous System.   The hypothalamus has been called the "head ganglion" of the autonomic nervous system because it is the major integrator of the body's basic regulatory systems (hunger, thirst, sex, temperature, heart rate, blood pressure, etc.). This is of central significance for our concepts because the autonomic nervous system has been regarded traditionally as the major means by which therapeutic hypnosis achieved its biological effects. The autonomic system is itself made up of two branches: (1) the *sympathetic system* that is involved in the energizing or alarm response whereby heart rate, blood pressure, respiration, etc., are stimulated; and (2) the *parasympathetic system* whereby the same functions are relaxed. Recently some researchers (Bulloch, 1985) have included the *entric system* (which is primarily concerned with the internal regulation of the stomach, intestines, etc.) as a third branch of the autonomic nervous system. The entric system usually carries out its functions semi-independently of the autonomic system, however. Since it is primarily regulated by the newly recognized messenger molecules of the *neuropeptide system*, we will discuss it under that heading.

The Hypothalamus and the Endocrine System.   Most of us are familiar with the pituitary as the "master gland" of the endocrine system that regulates all the other hormones of the body. The hypothalamus mediates the information that governs even the pituitary, however. When a person encounters pain, for example, the thalamus serves as a sensory relay station that transmits a portion of the signal directly to the hypothalamus even before the pain is experienced consciously. This is true for all other sensations as well, with the exception of olfactory signals, which are transmitted to the hypothalamus through the amygdala. Even the concentrations of nutrients, electrolytes, water, neurotransmitters, and hormones in the blood and cerebrospinal fluid can excite or inhibit the various feedback control centers in the hypothalamus that regulate the internal environment of the body either directly or via the pituitary. From the other side of the limbic border, the realm of "mind" can influence the hypothalamus by the excitatory or inhibitory neural impulses of the cerebral cortex that are converted into pituitary regulation by the specialized neurons of the hypothalamus.

How much is really known today about these specialized neurons of the hypothalamus—about how mind and body actually communicate on a cellular and molecular level? We all know that the philosophically inclined have debated this problem for centuries, but do we have any real facts about it today? Surprisingly, the answer is a definite *yes*. Figure 6A and 6B are illustrations of the mind-body transducers that function on the cellular level between the hypothalamus and the pituitary.

Whatever mind may be, most of us have a fairly reliable hunch that it

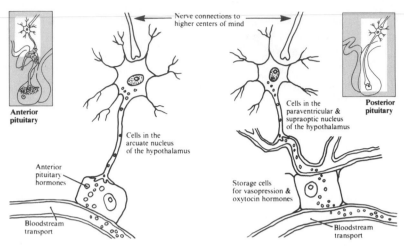

FIGURE 6A Mind-body information transduction between the cortex (higher centers of mind), the hypothalamus, the anterior pituitary, and the body.

FIGURE 6B Mind-body information transduction between the cortex (higher centers of mind), the hypothalamus, the anterior pituitary, and the body.

is intimately associated with the activity of the $2^{100,000,000,000,000}$* connections among the nerve cells of the brain. Whatever the body may be, most of us recognize it at base as flesh, blood, glands, bone, and the way all of these tissues are regulated by hormones, and so forth. Figures 6A and 6B illustrate two types of nerve cells in the hypothalamus that have become specialized into mind/body transducers. They receive electrical impulses of mind (the cerebral cortex) on one end just like any conventional nerve cell of the brain; on the other end, however, they discharge a "releasing factor" or hormone to regulate some tissues of the body.

For example, Figure 6A illustrates how nerve cells in the *arcuate nucleus* of the hypothalamus produce hormone-releasing factors that are released into a local bloodstream to the anterior pituitary. From the anterior pituitary an endocrine hormone *prolactin* is then secreted to turn on milk secretion in a woman's breasts. Figure 6B illustrates how

---

*This is the number two multiplied by itself a hundred million times. According to Carl Sagan (1977), this means that *there are more possible mental states in each person's brain than there are atoms in the known universe!*

cells from the *paraventricular* and *supraoptic nuclei* of the hypothalamus transduce nerve impulses from higher cortical sources into mind-modulating effects on the production of the hormones *vasopressin* and *oxytocin*. These are stored in the posterior pituitary cells until they are released into the general bloodstream to regulate the kidneys and other organs during stress. *Many such cells from the different nuclei of the hypothalamus transduce the neural information of mind into the somatic processes of the body via the pituitary and endocrine system.*

This understanding of how these neurons in the hypothalamus transduce neural information of mind into hormonal messenger molecules of the body is called *neurosecretion*; it is the central concept of modern *neuroendocrinology*. The existence of such *neuroendocrinal information transducers* is the basic reason for conceptualizing the new field of psychobiology as a branch of information theory. It is the key insight that unites biology and psychology within the single framework of information theory in a manner that makes mind-body communication and healing an empirical science rather than a pious hope.

The Hypothalamus and the Immune System.   The most recently recognized regulatory function of the hypothalamus is its influence on the immune system. Our understanding of this central modulation of the immune system is still so new that it has not yet been incorporated into the standard texts of psychophysiology and medicine. The pioneering work of Ader (1981) and Stein, Schleifer, and Keller (1981), among others, however, has begun to uncover the actual psychophysiological mechanisms whereby the hypothalamus can alter both cellular and humoral immune activity in its anterior and posterior nuclei. We will explore some current views on the mind modulation of these processes in a later section on cancer, rheumatoid arthritis, and asthma.

The Hypothalamus and the Neuropeptide System.   Neuropeptides are the messenger molecules that are formed when information is transduced from neural impulses of mind into hormones of the body (described earlier as *neuroendocrinal information transduction*). The concept of the neuropeptide system of mind-body communication is so new that much of its anatomy and functioning is a matter of speculation among a relatively small vanguard of researchers. It is well-known, however, that the hypothalamus is a central hub of neuropeptide activity. This system appears to overlap the autonomic, endocrine, and immune systems, in that they all apparently utilize neuropeptides as "messenger molecules" to communicate within themselves and with each other.

Because these "messenger molecules" travel throughout the body in so many different ways, the neuropeptide system has incredibly pervasive and flexible patterns of communication. *The neuropeptide system may thus be the most multifaceted channel for information transduction and the expression of state-dependent memory and learning.* We will explore a number of speculations about its possible role in the "body image," sexuality, emotions, and the mediation of some of the so-called mysterious phenomena of hypnosis that remain unexplained even today.

CELL-GENE COMMUNICATION

The third level of the mind-body communication loop is illustrated on the bottom of Figure 4 as cell-gene communication. Herein, most people would concede, the true genius of our age is becoming manifest. We are now on the threshold of understanding the molecular informational systems at the cellular-genetic level that are the ultimate basis of life itself. Please note that we are not pursuing a philosophy of reductionism here. We are not simply reducing the processes of life, mind, and communication to the molecular level! That is the most common misconception to be found within the psychological community today. Remember molecular messengers were the first form of communication developed by life on the single cell level; nerves, brains, words, radio, television, and psychotherapy came later, about four billion years later!

Our current and future understanding of life can no longer make do with the purely reductionist and mechanistic concepts of biology as has been the case in the past. Our major leading textbooks in biochemistry, biology, and genetics are now using essentially *mentalistic or communication* concepts such as "messenger molecules, signaling, signal recognition particles, communication, information, sentient molecules, symbolic systems, and metabolic codes" to conceptualize the life process on the molecular level (Alberts et al., 1989; Darnell, Lodish, & Baltimore, 1990). The idea of understanding psychology and life by reducing them to the mechanistic physics, chemistry, and biology of the past has reached a point of diminishing returns.

To the contrary, to understand current advances in physics, chemistry, and biology, particularly on the quantum level (Davies, 1989), we need to introduce the essentially psychological concepts of information and communication. *We may now regard physics, chemistry, and biology as branches of psychology!* Or, to express it more accurately, all the arts and sciences are aspects of a more comprehensive future philosophy of information and communication as the essence of everything of comprehension and special interest to the human mind (Stonier, 1990). In this section we will focus on how information and communication take place on the cellular-genetic-molecular portion of the cybrenetic loop between environment, mind, behavior, and body.

Some of the major pathways of information transduction and communication at the cellular level that are involved in mind-body healing are illustrated on the bottom of Figure 4. These are the most general pathways of communication that are operative in virtually all cells of brain and body. We can discern at least three major loops of communication within the cell: (1) the receptor "receiving stations" of the cell first pick up the "primary messengers" (e.g., hormones from the hypothalamic-pituitary system of the brain) to turn on the gene expression of the blueprints of life; (2) the energy and metabolism loop that involves enzymes and the mitochondria "energy generators" that power all the basic life functions of metabolism within the cell; and (3) the "protein factories" of the cell that make more receptors and messenger molecules that will communicate back to the brain as well as other cells of the body. In this introductory survey we only touch upon the more generalized pathways of molecular communication within and between cells that are involved in memory, learning, sensation, perception, emotions, and behavioral responses to trauma and stress. Introductory though our approach may be, we are actually laying the foundation of a new science of *infokinetics—all those life processes that transduce information (info), energy (kinetics), and matter into each other.* If information and communication are manifestations of the mind, then we may say that infokinetics is the science of how mind interacts with energy and matter—how mind and molecules move each other.

1. From Receptors to Gene Expression

Receptors and Primary Messenger Molecules as a Psychosomatic Network. The first link in the communication pathways of the cell are the receptors symbolized as hands in the bottom of Figure 4. Each cell of the brain and the body actually has hundreds, thousands, or hundreds of thousands of receptors of one family or another. For over 100 years pharmacologists postulated that for drugs to be effective they must somehow gain entry to cells to carry out their therapeutic action (Langley, 1878). There must be some sort of receptor on the cell walls of the nerve and tissues of the body that permit the drugs to enter the cell or at least signal a response within the cell (Bolander, 1989).

Finally, in the 1970s a series of investigators isolated and demonstrated the physical reality of the insulin receptor, the opiate receptor, and others. They also began to uncover the signaling molecules (the hormonal primary messengers, neuropeptides, etc.) that normally bind to these receptors in the normal operation of the body. It was then understood that many drugs have therapeutic actions because their molecular structure is similar to the normal signaling molecules of the brain and the body. These signaling molecules fit like keys into the locks of the cell receptors to turn on certain processes within the cell.

Years later, Candace Pert, who is now Chief of the Section on Brain Biochemistry at the Clinical Neuroscience Branch at the National Institute of Mental Health, generalized these findings into a new theory of how primary messenger molecules and their receptors formed a "psychosomatic network" that was the ultimate basis of all forms of mind-body healing (Pert et al., 1985; Pert, Ruff, Spencer, & Rossi, 1989; Rossi & Cheek, 1988). The details of this story will be presented later in Chapter 10. There we will learn how the endorphins (internal opiates) are just one family of primary messenger molecules that integrate the central nervous system of the brain with the autonomic, endocrine, and immune systems.

It was later learned that other primary messenger molecules could pass right through the cell wall and match up with receptors inside the cell and even within the nucleus to turn on certain genes without the mediation of secondary messengers (note the hand receptor symbol at these locations in Figure 4). It is interesting that many of the most important mind-body functions dealt with in psychotherapy are mediated primary messenger molecules that have such direct links. The steroid hormones that are messenger molecules mediating *stress* (cortisol), *sexuality and aggression* (sexual hormones such as testosterone and the estrogens), as well as *growth* (thyroxine), for example, all have such direct access to the genes.

Secondary Messengers and the Evolution of Communication.   What was the origin of communication? Was it perhaps when a mother first made meaningful eye contact with her newborn child? Or was it even earlier when the mother felt the first kick of her developing fetus in the second trimester of pregnancy? Or was it four billion years earlier when some of the first living cells invented *cyclic adenosine monophosphate* (cAMP) to signal each other when it was time to get together because their puddle was drying up and they needed to form a tough skin and spores to survive during the coming dry spell? The significance of this evolutionary role of cAMP was discussed by Stryer (1988) in his highly regarded text on biochemistry (p. 983):

> Cyclic AMP has a regulatory role in bacteria, too, where it stimulates the transcription of certain genes. *It is evident that cyclic AMP has a long evolutionary history as a regulatory molecule.* In bacteria, cyclic AMP is a hunger signal. It signifies an absence of glucose and leads to the synthesis of enzymes that can exploit other energy sources. In some mammalian cells, such as liver and muscle, cyclic AMP retains its ancient role as a hunger signal. However, it acts by stimulating a protein kinase rather than by enhancing the transcription of certain genes. Another difference is that *cyclic AMP in higher organisms mediates intercellular signaling rather than intracellular signaling* [which has been taken up by the primary messenger molecules]. The role of cyclic AMP in the life cycle of the slime mold *Dictyostelium discoideum,* a simple eucaryote, is especially interesting. When food is abundant, *Dictyostelium* exists as independent cells. When food becomes scarce, cyclic AMP is secreted by the free-living amoebae. Cyclic AMP serves as a chemoattractant that leads to the aggregation of *Dictyostelium* into a slug and to major changes in gene expression [italics added].

Let us explore some implications of these words. When food is abundant, this slime mold exists as a free-living, single-celled amoeba. When food is scarce, each amoeba sends out cAMP as a stress signal into the environment. When other free-living amoebae receive this signal, they are attracted to its source. In this way, these amoebae communicate, find each other, and form a community of beings. They then clump together to form a multicellular organism—the slug—which can then survive in the changed environment to eventually produce spores that can resist even complete drying out and survive until it rains again. Each spore then becomes a free-living single-cell amoeba again until the environment dries out, forcing the development of a multicellular slug for survival. *What we are seeing here is a critical evolutionary step between single and multicellular life; the invention of communication during the stress of a changing environment was necessary for adaptation and the evolution of all the higher forms of life.* As a stress-signaling molecule, cAMP became the communication link that made the evolution of the higher multicellular forms of life with their large bodies and brains possible. It is fascinating to realize that this same cAMP molecule is still active as a "secondary messenger" within every cell of our brain and body. Further, it becomes especially active when we are under stress; cAMP still retains its original evolutionary function of signaling that there is a danger, a stress, in the surrounding environment. Here now is George Engel, a pioneer in mind/body theory with over 300 publications to his credit, speculating about the role of cAMP in human psychology and social relationships (1985, pp. 16–17; quoted in Foss & Rothenberg, 1987, pp. 272–273):

> . . . not only were the "supplies" that I lost upon my father's death multiplex and peculiar for me but also their internal representatives derived not just from my father-relationship but from the whole history of my social relationships since birth. But note that my social relationships actually had their beginnings in a biological context, in the transition at birth from the biologic mutuality of transplacental nutrition to the social mutuality of oral feeding at my mother's breasts. In that process the recurring cycles of hunger-feeding-satiation that I experienced as a neonate not only were regulators of my earliest social relations, they also established a permanent linkage between processes implicated in maintaining cellular nutrition and processes implicated in sustaining human relationship, literally linking cAMP and feelings that reflect human ties. . . .
>
> The very fact that my apprehending of my father's death includes use of symbolic processes historically connected since my birth with regulation of biological supplies in itself predetermines that connections could exist even at the level of molecular symbols. Obviously our inner world of symbols is not a separate world unto itself, as Cartesian dualism would have us believe, it is an integral part of a complex multi-layered network intimately involved in biological regulation even at the cellular level.

Speculative though these prescient ruminations by a biologist may have been, their implications were confirmed five years later when Glaser and his colleagues (Glaser et al., 1990) reported the first firm experimental evidence of how the mental stress of exam week in medical students utilizes this cAMP communication link to alter the gene expression of their IL-2 receptors in their immune system (detailed later in Chapter 9).

Gene Expression, Memory, Learning, and Behavior.   Understanding the loops of information transduction at the cellular-genetic level (at the bottom of Figure 4) requires a clear appreciation of the fundamental difference between the *mutation of genes* and the *expression of genes*. The successful *mutation of genes* is a relatively rare evolutionary event based upon chance errors in copying the informational structure of the gene from one generation to another. When such chance errors have survival value they lead to a permanent change in the heredity of the organism so that, for example, future generations of rabbit hair color will be black instead of white if the gene(s) controlling hair color have mutated to produce that change. Western science maintains that mind has absolutely nothing to do with such changes in the hereditary structure of genes; no mind-body healing here.

The modulation of the *expression of genes*, however, is something very different. It involves *gene transcription*, the process of making copies of certain genes or groups of genes every second of our lives. These copies act like blueprints which are sent out in the form of messenger ribonucleic acid (mRNA) to the "protein factories" (the endoplastic reticulum) of the cell where they serve as templates for the manufacture or "translation" of the mRNA into new proteins. Some of these proteins, called "transcription regulators," return back to modulate the expression of other genes as illustrated in the first loop of information transduction labeled "gene expression" on the bottom of Figure 4. Other proteins serve as enzymes that facilitate all the major functions of the cell, such as energy production in the mitochondria and the basic processes of growth, respiration, healing, etc. (labeled "energy & metabolism" in Figure 4). A third major group of proteins serve as the building blocks for the continual remodeling and replacement of the informational network of the cell (labeled "messengers and receptors" in Figure 4) as it communicates back with itself ("autocrine messengers") and the rest of the body ("neurotransmitter and neuromodulators" for nerve cells and hormones or messenger molecules for most other cells of the brain and body).

Western science is currently exploring the pathways of mind-gene communication by these three major routes of information transduction and communication. One of the most articulate descriptions of the possibilities of mind-body healing comes from Eric Kandel who has done some of the most innovative research on the molecular basis of mind, memory and learning at the genetic level (Kandel, 1989, pp. 122–123):

> The genetic data on schizophrenia and on depression indicate that these diseases involve alteration *in the structure of genes*. By contrast, the data now emerging on learning suggest that neurotic illnesses acquired by learning, which can often respond to psychotherapy, might involve alterations *in the regulation of gene expression*. In this context, it is important to realize, as I have emphasized earlier, that genes have two regions: a regulatory region and a coding region. The *regulatory region* usually lies upstream of the coding region and consists of two types of DNA elements. One type of DNA element is called the promoter. This is the site where the enzyme RNA polymerase binds before it reads and transcribes the gene into messenger RNA. The second type of DNA region is called the *enhancer region*. It recognizes protein signals that determine in which cells, and when, the coding region will be

transcribed by the polymerase. Whether the RNA polymerase binds and transcribes the gene and how often it does so in any given period of time is determined by a small number of proteins, *transcriptional regulators*, that bind to different segments of the upstream enhancer region. *Development, hormones, stress, and learning are all factors that can alter the binding of the transcriptional regulator proteins to the regulatory regions of genes.* I suggest that at least certain neurotic illnesses (or components of them) represent a reversible defect in gene regulation, which is produced by learning and which may be due to altered binding of specific proteins to certain upstream regions that control the expression of certain genes.

According to this view, schizophrenia and depression would be due primarily to heritable genetic changes in neuronal and synaptic function in a population carrying one or more mutations. By contrast, *neurotic illnesses might represent alterations in neuronal and synaptic function produced by environmentally induced modulation of gene expression. Insofar as psychotherapy works and produces long-term learned changes in behavior, it may do so by producing alterations in gene expression.* Needless to say, psychotic illness, although primarily caused by inherited alterations in gene structure, may also involve a secondary disturbance in environmentally acquired gene expression. (Italics added)

Humans have about 100,000 genes. About 30,000 of these are called "housekeeping genes" because their expression is regulated every moment of our lives by the continuous messages they receive from the mind and the brain via the primary and secondary molecular messenger signaling system. We could therefore speculate that about one third of our gene expression is available for modulation by mind methods. Many of these genes are involved in the process of encoding life experience in the form of new memories and learning via the transcriptional regulators described by Kandel.

Kandel and his colleagues have described some of the important ultradian time parameters in the "gene expression" loop of Figure 4 that are involved in the process of learning and memory within neurons as follows (Kandel, 1989, p. 119):

> As we have seen in the intact animal, long-term memory for sensitization is accompanied by neuronal growth. Some of the newly synthesized proteins induced during the training for long-term sensitization presumably not only lead to functional changes but must contribute as well to these structural changes—the growth of new synaptic contacts—that occur in the sensory neurons.
>
> In an attempt to delineate the specific gene products underlying the acquisition phase of long-term memory, Barzilai, Sweatt, Kennedy, and I focused

on *the 1.5 hour period of training* and studied the incorporation of labeled amino acids . . . into proteins in the sensory neurons. . . . The evidence for a gene cascade [in the "gene expression" loop of Figure 4] also derives from the finding that serotonin and cAMP lead rapidly to the altered expression of 15 proteins that have three characteristic features; (1) the alteration in the expression of these proteins is rapid—it occurs within 30 minutes; (2) the alteration is transient—the proteins only remain altered in expression for about 30 to 60 minutes; and (3) the proteins are dependent for their increase on active transcription. These three features resemble those first described for a class of proteins now called *immediate early* or *competence* proteins. These early proteins first were encountered in the course of examining the response of quiescent mammalian cells in tissue culture to stimulation by serum or peptide growth factors [another class of messenger molecules], such as nerve growth factor (NGF). Some of these early proteins, e.g., c-*jun* and c-*fos*, are known to be regulatory proteins that act on later effector genes in a cascade of gene activation for cell growth.

. . . The expression of these early proteins is followed by an increase in the synthesis of still different proteins. The induction of these later proteins is also dependent on transcription. Some of these proteins remain increased in their synthesis for more than a day. This observation suggests that there are distinct rounds of specific protein synthesis and that the later rounds might require the expression of the earlier round.

. . . These several observations suggest that learning and memory involve a flow of information from membrane receptors to the genome, as is seen in other processes of cellular differentiation and growth. (Italics added)

The ultradian time relationships between short- and long-term memory in the "gene expression" loop has been described by Montgomery (1989, p. 54) as follows:

Repeatedly tail shocking a slug leads to several waves of gene expression that result in the production of a number of new proteins that, among other things, seems to keep the kinase [an enzyme we will discuss in the next section] in a long-term active state. Somehow during this *90-minute period*, a command has been sent to the neuron's nucleus to switch on long-term memory genes.

The precise nature of this command and the details of how it's transmitted is [sic] not yet known. But Karen Wagner-Smith is one of several graduate students in Kandel's lab who suspect that the "commander" may be one of ten recently discovered proteins. According to her favorite scenario, the commander protein drifts through the cell until it meets up with the kinase. Then, in effect, it asks the kinase a question: Are you still active? If so switch me on, and I'll go back to the cell nucleus and turn on a wave of long-term memory genes—genes that will help you, the kinase, store memory of this

tail shock by keeping you permanently excited. If you're not active, however—if the shocks from the scientists ended *20 minutes ago* and we have
nothing more to worry about—then you won't switch me on, and I won't do
anything to excite you. We'll just let this short-term memory fizz out.

While this is still only a hypothesis it is intriguing that the ultradian
time relationships described for the conversion of short- to long-term
memory are exactly those described by Kleitman (1969, 1970; Kleitman,
1992) as the basic rest-activity cycle (BRAC). In the BRAC a 90-minute
period of optimal performance, wherein attention is focused on the
outside world, naturally alternates with a 20-minute period of rest (the
author's ultradian healing response, Rossi & Nimmons, 1991). During
the nighttime period of sleep this ultradian rhythm continues with a
90-minute alternation between deep sleep and dream (REM) sleep (usually lasting 20 to 30 minutes). The fact that most research and clinical
practice with holistic methods of mind-body healing, such as self-hypnosis, meditation, imagery, the relaxation response, biofeedback, etc.,
usually take place within the same 20- to 30-minute time frame (Rossi,
1993; Rossi & Lippincott, 1992), suggests that the wave nature of gene
expression in the dynamics of short- and long-term memory described
by Kandel et al. may also be involved as a common denominator in
many forms of "naturalistic healing."

2. The Energy-Metabolic Communication Loop

The second major loop of information transduction at the cellular
level is the double cycle labeled "energy" and "metabolism" on the
bottom of Figure 4. Much of the recently expressed mRNA from the
genes is translated into proteins that function as structural elements of
the cell as well as *enzymes* that facilitate the metabolism and energy
dynamics of life. Some of these proteins are transported to the mitochondria ("energy factories") of the cell which convert glucose, the
basic fuel of the cell, into the energy-rich adenosine triphosphate (ATP)
that is the basic coin of energy exchange in most metabolic processes of
life and virtually all responses to stress. One reason physical exercise is
recommended for general health and "more energy" is that muscle
activity actually increases the number of mitochondria in the cells.

As illustrated in Figure 4, ATP is reduced to its lower energy form of
adenosine diphosphate (ADP) when it gives up a phosphate group to
turn on enzymes that power the fundamental life processes of metabolism, such as growth, respiration, and the manufacture of the special-

ized products that are sent out to other parts of the body. ADP is then brought back up to full strength as ATP when it cycles back through the mitochondria.

In 1992 Edmond Fischer and Edwin Krebs shared the Nobel prize for their early research in the 1950s, when they isolated a key enzyme of energy metabolism within muscle cells. This enzyme turned out to be phosphorylase kinase, one of a general class of proteins called *protein kinases* that were later found to be present in all cells of the brain and body. Fischer and Krebs found that their protein kinase transferred the phosphate group from the energy-rich ATP to enzymes to convert them from their resting state to an active state so they could power all the processes of metabolism.

This reversible on/off switch of protein phosphorylation, whereby enzymes are activated and deactivated, is now recognized as the fundamental mechanism for regulating all the basic functions of life at the cellular level. Although Figure 4 identifies this energetic protein kinase switch within the second loop of information transduction ("energy and metabolism") where it was originally discovered, it is now recognized that it is a universal mechanism that drives important molecular transformations in the first loop ("gene expression") and the third loop (messengers and receptors) as well.

The energetics and molecular transformations of how protein kinases turn enzymes on and how phosphatases turn them off is the bottom line of how life works as described by current textbooks of molecular biology. For a new informational view of this same fundamental life process, Tony Hunter, of the Salk Institute, recently described how protein kinases act as "information processors" of the cell (1987, pp. 823–827):

> Ten years ago there were less than a dozen well-characterized protein kinases. With the advent of molecular cloning and the discovery that many oncogenes encode protein kinases, the number of proven or putative protein kinases has risen to nearly a hundred. I am going to argue that the mammalian genome may encode as many as a thousand different protein kinases, and that protein kinases may be used in cellular regulatory circuits in a fashion analogous to transistors or chips in computers. (p. 823)
>
> . . . A reasonable answer to the question of why there are so many protein kinases would be that they serve as major components of the essential regulatory circuitry of the cell. To draw an electronic analogy, one might term them the transistors of the cell. In electronic circuits transistors are used either as simple on/off switches or as amplifiers for an electric current. Transistors commonly have two inputs, which regulate current flow and gain, and a

single output. Protein kinases share many properties with transistors that make them ideal components of biological feedback and amplification pathways, as well as switching or signaling systems. (p. 826)

What types of circuits are regulated by protein phosphorylation? Several of the well-characterized protein-serine kinases are involved in regulation of metabolic pathways such as glycogen metabolism. Transmembrane signal transduction [the hand receptor in Figure 4] is another system using phosphorylation. A surprisingly large fraction of known protein kinases either span the plasma membrane or are associated with the inner face, and are therefore in an ideal position to transduce signals from external stimuli [ultimately from the outer psychosocial environment]. . . .

To account for the plethora of protein kinases in the brain, one might speculate that protein phosphorylation plays an essential role in neurotransmission. Indeed there are models of memory based on protein phosphorylation (Crick, 1984). A more mundane hypothesis is that protein phosphorylation regulates ion channel opening or desensitization, or neurotransmitter release.

Since these prescient words were written half a dozen years ago, more recent research has honed in on more specific protein kinase involved in memory and learning. Decades of research on the molecular basis of memory by Daniel Alkon (1992, p. 113) and his colleagues, for example, have documented how secondary messenger molecules such as calcium and diacylglycerol (DAG) in association with protein kinase C (PKC) can regulate the flow of potassium ions in neural transmission in learning experiments. Alkon believes that the experience of mind—whether it's the hypothesis of a scientist or the hallucinations of a schizophrenic—are all based on the molecular patterns of information transduction in the neuronal networks of the brain which he describes as follows (1992, p. 139):

> The integrative processes performed by the networks must be different, but the basic storage principles, like chemical-electrical switches on a computer chip, could be the same. That sameness—for example, the protein kinase switch we found in the snail, the rabbit, and the rat—might be tagged in living humans. . . . A camera with enough power might see these tags wherever and whenever a memory was being stored or recalled, revealing new pictures of what memory looks like.

Alkon has found evidence for the hypothesis that malfunctioning of these memory mechanisms may be responsible for Alzheimer's and other dysfunctions of aging. A common denominator of such signaling or informational problems of communication at the cellular level is that they all involve the messenger molecule-receptor system that Pert et al. (1985) regards as the essence of psychosomatic illness. Let us now turn to this messenger-receptor network illustrated in Figure 4 as the third loop of information transduction within and between all cells of the brain and body.

3. Continuous Creation of the Messenger Molecule–Receptor Communication System

The wave nature of memory and learning is a vivid reminder that there is nothing static about life. Most theorists who use computers as crude metaphors of life usually forget to mention that life would have to be described as a sort of transcendent computer that is continually reprogramming itself as a function of ongoing life experience. This is particularly evident in the third loop of information transduction within the cell in Figure 4 that is labeled "messengers and receptors." Most of the proteins within the cell that have key regulatory roles in information transduction, particularly the receptors (the hands of Figure 6.2), have an ultradian half-life of two hours or less (Alberts et al., 1989, p. 715).

The concentration of the cell surface receptors is continually changing; much of this change is modulated by information from the environment as part of the general process of adaptation. Most addicting drugs, for example, achieve their potent mind-body effects by mimicking our natural molecular messengers. When confounded by the unusual flooding of the entire system by such drugs, the receptors that receive them are rapidly withdrawn from the cell surface (called down regulation) in an effort to interfere with the spurious signal of the addicting drug. Very powerfully addicting drugs can down regulate the number of cell surface receptors to the level where they can no longer support the normal signaling processes they were meant to serve; this leads to the uncomfortable feelings of so-called "drug withdrawal." The person feels a craving for comfort that can be re-established only with another even more potent dose of the drug to turn on the now very sparse distribution of cell receptors. The only cure is to endure the symptoms of withdrawal for a long enough period of time for the mind-body to re-establish the normal number of cellular receptors that are needed to facilitate mind-body communication in an optimal manner; this optimal communication is experienced as health, healing, and comfort.

We emphasized earlier that in contrast with the traditional view that neurons are the connecting link between mind and body, we now know that the messenger molecule and cell receptor system is the more fundamental, ultimate bottom line of mind-body communication. While neurons are like wires that do, indeed, carry very rapid messages between mind and body, messenger molecules from all cells of the brain and body can key into the receptors of neurons and thereby influence the activity of neurons and how they express the messages they carry. This is particularly true in emotional states of trauma, stress, and most physical and mental illnesses. When we are sick, for example, we just don't feel like running about and following our usual daily routine. Why not? After all, our brain and nerves are still there. We now know that when we are ill the cells of the immune system, for example, send out messenger molecules that modulate brain and neural activity to turn on fever and lethargy while turning off our usual emotional motivations so that we are more inclined to rest. This "rest" is not laziness, of course, it's actually a heightened state of activity that presumably enables the mind-body to focus its resources more adaptively on the healing process.

As emphasized in Figure 4, all cells of the brain and body send and receive messenger molecules. Traditional textbooks of medicine, however, are usually organized around anatomical and physiological functions in such a way that the signaling and communication processes of central significance in mind-body healing are usually obscured, lost, or just thrown in as a sort of metaphor afterthought about how things work at the molecular level. Because of this and the surprising isolation of specialists in the various medical and psychological disciplines, messenger molecules and their receptors have been given different names in the major systems of the mind-body that deal with adaptation, self-regulation, and communication. It is therefore important to develop an overview of the many different names used to describe the most common communication pathways throughout the brain and body. The successive chapters of this book will be devoted to an exploration of what is currently known about the communication dynamics of each of these four major systems of self-regulation in mind-body healing.

1) The *autonomic nervous system* uses *neurotransmitters* as molecular messengers between one nerve and the next for facilitating states of optimal performance and activity (the *sympathetic nervous system*) as well as relaxation, creativity, and healing (the *parasympathetic nervous system*).

2) The *endocrine system* uses *hormones* ("primary messengers") to regulate all the basic processes of metabolism, such as growth, matu-

ration, digestion, energy, sexuality, etc., with emotions, memory, learning, and behavior.

3) The *immune system* uses *cytokines* as messenger molecules to signal white blood cells (leukocytes) that are involved in the defence against disease, viruses, and cancer, as well as psychological mood and motivation.

4) The *neuropeptide system* uses *neuropeptides* as messenger molecules to modulate the *central nervous system* of the brain and the *peripheral nervous system* of the body as well as our *sense organs*. The neuropeptides are literally "neuromodulators"; they modulate neural communication in mental and behavioral states of emotion, pleasure, pain, stress, trauma, memory, learning, and behavior that are of central interest in virtually all approaches to mind-body healing.

By whatever name they are called, the most salient fact for our evolving understanding of mind-body healing is that messenger molecules and their receptors simultaneously serve two major interlocking functions that enable them to bridge the so-called "gap" between mind and body. Messenger molecules are (1) the major pathways of communication between and within all the regulatory systems of mind and body and, at the same time, (2) they serve as the ultimate keys for the state-dependent encoding of the types of personal emotional experience and behavior that have always been of relevance for psychotherapy and mind-body healing.

The following chapters will document this dual mind-body role for the messenger molecule–cell receptor system in each of the four major systems of mind-body self-regulation and communication outlined above. We will focus, in particular, on the time parameters of the messenger molecule–cell receptor system in order to explore the hypothesis that it is the basis of the fundamental circadian and ultradian time frames of most ordinary human activities. This is one reason why the slower rhythms of the messenger molecule–cell receptor system are more suitable as the basic units for understanding mental and emotional experience rather than the extremely rapid stimulus-response, neurally based activities of brain, and the nervous system that take place in milliseconds. The ultradian rhythms between 20 and 90 minutes, for example, are the typical time periods within which most significant human psychosocial activities and mind-body healing processes take place (e.g., the basic rest-activity cycle underlying optimal performance in everyday life, psychotherapy, and meditation sessions of all sorts, religious rituals, a sexual encounter, a movie or theater production, a good talk, a good cry, a good nap, a good meal, a bad mood, etc. [Lloyd & Rossi, 1992a]). We will explore the view that the chronic abuse of these natural mind-body rhythms can be a major source of stress by distorting many natural healing processes of the mind-body that are mediated by the messenger molecule–cell receptor system.

7

Mind Modulation of the Autonomic Nervous System

HYPNOSIS HAS LONG BEEN recognized as an effective means of modulating the autonomic nervous system (Braun, 1983b; Crasilneck & Hall, 1959, 1985; Gorton, 1957, 1958). Most investigators, however, have had little to say about the actual psychobiological processes involved. An initial approach to exploring these processes is diagrammed in Figure 7, which illustrates some of the major anatomical and functional relationships between mind, hypothalamus, and the autonomic nervous system.

In general, mind influences of the cerebral cortex reach the hypothalamus via its associated limbic system structures, the hippocampus, amygdala, and thalamus. The hypothalamus then mediates these mind influences to the autonomic nervous system via the lower brain stem control centers, which serve as relay stations of the sympathetic and parasympathetic nervous systems. Stimulation in appropriate areas of the hypothalamus, for example, can activate the sympathetic system control centers of the heart strongly enough to increase the arterial blood pressure by more than 100 percent. Other hypothalamic centers can control body temperature by regulating blood flow to or from the surface of the skin, increase or decrease salivation and gastrointestinal activity, and cause bladder emptying.

The vital processes of all the organs regulated by the autonomic nervous system are subject to the influences of state-dependent learning via their association with the hypothalamic-limbic system, which feeds our life histories of experiential learnings into them. In other words, *all the organs illustrated in Figure 7 can respond psychosomatically*. During times of stress, state-bound patterns of information may be generated in the regulation of any individual organ or combination of them. These pat-

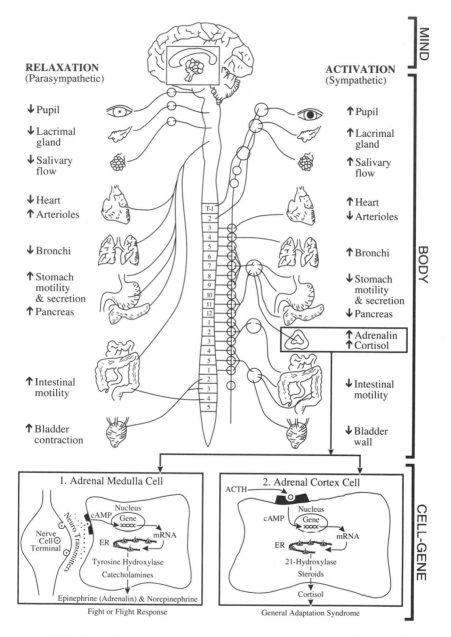

FIGURE 7 Mind modulation of the autonomic nervous system and its two branches, the sympathetic (activating) and the parasympathetic (relaxing), down to the cellulargenetic level.

terns may then become manifest as the unfortunate responses that we call "psychosomatic problems." To understand how this is possible, it will be necessary to look at how mind modulates communication within the individual cells of each organ regulated by the autonomic nervous system.

MIND MODULATION OF CELLULAR ACTIVITY
VIA THE AUTONOMIC NERVOUS SYSTEM

Weiner (1977) has commented on the general state of disbelief and apathy regarding what we now know about how the mind and central nervous system actually modulate the complex chemical machinery of each living cell in the body. It took more than a few centuries for humanity to believe and utilize the implications of Copernicus's finding that the earth revolves around the sun and not vice versa. Likewise, it seems as if it will take more than a few decades, if not centuries, for most people to understand and learn to use the mind's ability to facilitate healing at the cellular and biochemical levels.

Figure 7 is an overview of the three-stage process whereby mind modulates the activities of the cells via the autonomic nervous system. *Stage one* consists of mind-generated thoughts and imagery (neural impulses) in the frontal cortex (Achterberg, 1985). In *stage two* these mind-generated impulses are filtered through the state-dependent memory, learning and emotional areas of the limbic-hypothalamic system, and transduced into the neurotransmitters that regulate the organs of the autonomic nervous system. The autonomic nervous system finally branches into the sympathetic (activating) and parasympathetic (relaxing) systems. The sympathetic system terminal nerve endings secrete the neurotransmitter *norepinephrine* (usually) to activate receptors on the cells of the organs they modulate (the heart, lungs, pancreas, intestines, etc.), while the parasympathetic system terminal nerve endings secrete *acetylcholine*. These neurotransmitters initiate the *third stage* in the process of information transduction from the thoughts, images, and emotions of mind to the biochemical responses within the individual cells of the tissues and organs of the body. This final stage of the process runs somewhat as follows:

1) The neurotransmitters are messenger molecules that signal the tissues of each of the body's vital organs by first binding with receptors in their cell walls. This process is illustrated in the lower portion of Figure 7, where neurotransmitters can be seen crossing

the "nerve-cell junctional gap" and fitting into the receptors of the cell wall. This changes the molecular structure of the receptor.

2) Since the receptor is a part of the cell wall, the change in its molecular structure can alter the permeability of the cell wall to various ions (sodium, potassium, calcium, etc.). These ionic changes alter the electrical properties of the cells to promote activities characteristic of each cell.

3) Another way the receptor can transmit information is by activating an enzyme in the cell membrane such as *adenylcyclase*. This enzyme, in turn, initiates the formation of *adenosine triphosphate* (ATP) and *cyclic adenosine monophosphate* (cAMP)—the so-called second messenger system—which then initiates and energizes the characteristic metabolism of each cell.

Although this outline of the three stages provides only the barest sketch of hundreds of incredibly complex biochemical reactions, it is sufficient to illustrate our major point: *Mind modulates the biochemical functions within the cells of all the major organ systems and tissues of the body via the autonomic nervous system.* Later we will trace the analogous routes by which the endocrine, immune, and neuropeptide systems can also transduce information from mind to molecules in the appropriate cells of the body.

STRESS, TIME, AND MIND-GENE COMMUNICATION VIA THE AUTONOMIC SYSTEM

Black (1991) has made a pioneering effort to outline the entire loop of information transduction between the experience of environmental stress to the mind-brain, the peripheral and autonomic nervous systems, and the cellular-genetic levels. He uses his original research (1975, 1982) on the rate-limiting enzyme *tyrosine hydroxylase* (TH), which plays a central role in regulating the production of the *catecholamines* (dopamine, norepinephrine, and epinephrine) that mediate the *fight or flight behavioral pattern*, to speculate about what may be a typical pattern of mind-gene communication. A summary of his views about "TH as a prototypical transducer molecule" will help us appreciate many of the surprising relationships that are currently emerging between the molecular-genetic level and the practical issues of time and psychotherapy in stress and posttraumatic stress syndromes (1991, pp. 58–59):

These results, viewed with those already cited, suggest that a sequence of events involving (1) environmental stress, (2) increased nerve impulse activity, (3) increased transmembrane sodium ion influx, (4) increased transcription of TH mRNA from DNA [on the genetic level]; and (5) increased synthesis of TH protein underlie induction of TH.

Stated somewhat differently, it appears that environmental events may alter gene readout by altering nerve impulse activity. In turn, alteration of gene readout changes neural and behavioral function. This is not a particularly modest claim. Experience alters the function of neurons at the most fundamental level, the genome. How long do these neuronal changes last?

The kinetics of TH induction are particularly intriguing since brief environmental events are transduced into long-term neuronal changes. Environmental stress and increased sympathoadrenal impulse activity evoke a two- to three-fold increase in TH within two days and enzyme remains elevated for at least three days after increased impulse activity has ceased. In fact, direct nerve electrical stimulation for 30 to 90 minutes increases enzyme molecule number for at least three days. Consequently a brief environmental stimulus is transduced into a long-term neuronal molecular change, providing striking **temporal amplification** by the nervous system.

The temporal amplification exhibited by TH displays a number of properties with notable implications for mind-brain molecules. For example, repetitive stimuli cause a far greater induction of TH than does a single stimulus.

Black also traces in some detail the communication loop whereby TH plays a similar role in the generation of attention and alertness via the *locus coeruleus* of the brain. It is well known that *somatosensory body stimulation* such as touch (e.g., massage and the body therapies), pain, and the sense of position, enhances neural activity in the locus coeruleus that leads, in turn to TH activation and the catecholamine cascade within many parts of the brain. Black's (1975, 1991) research with rats cannot be generalized uncritically to the human situation, but it is suggestive of how trauma and stress have a varying time course at different loci within the brain that are associated with different mind-behavioral states. He reports, for example, that drugs that emulate the effects of stress lead to a peak TH activity in the pons (mediating behavioral states such as sleeping, waking, and attention) in 4 days; in the cerebellum (movement initiation and control) in 8 days; in the frontal cortex (higher planning and foresight, self-image, etc.) only after 12 days. If research can establish similar patterns in humans, it will help us understand why it sometimes takes a few weeks for an individual to grasp the full significance of a physical accident, behavioral or psychological trauma, and stress so that emotions can be integrated. Black (1991, pp. 65–66) then asks a series of significant questions about mind, behavior, and memory that are critical for an understanding of the time course of stress and posttraumatic stress syndromes that are not yet answered today.

> A brief environmental stimulus sets in motion a series of events that results in long-term changes, lasting weeks in locus cortical terminals. On the basis of TH induction and the geometry of proximo-distal axonal transport, the brain remains poised for attention and vigilance for **weeks**. Is this memory? If so, it certainly is an unconventional form. We usually think of memory for information or even for procedures such as bike riding or piano playing. However, the present "memory" is that of a brain state. This phenomenon does have many of the characteristics of traditional memory, however. For example, it is subject to rehearsal effects and does decay. The decay, which we may term forgetting, can be quantitatively described in terms of the progressive fall in TH activity in cortical terminals. Clearly we may have to alter our conception of memory, based on elementary considerations of molecular mechanism and cell biology in the brain. At the very least, TH appears to function as a communicative symbol—a molecule that receives, encodes, stores, and transmits information over time.

From the point of view developed in earlier chapters we can view Black's conception of psychobiological memory on multiple levels as a form of *state-dependent memory, learning, and behavior (SDMLB)*. Black's work helps us understand why recovery from any stress will have a varying and highly individualized course that requires individual psychotherapy as well as broad educational programs for public understanding. We do not know the extent to which these stress dynamics apply to what appear to be purely biological illnesses, but the following section dealing with cancer and the autonomic system is suggestive.

The Psychobiology of Healing at the Cellular Level: Tissue Regeneration and Cancer

At a recent conference on neuroimmunology Melnechuk outlined how the autonomic nervous system plays an important role in the psychobiology of healing as it operates at the cellular level (1985, pp. 57–58):

> It should also be recalled that nerves, the immediate source of neurotransmitters, play a trophic (growth) role in the emergence of at least some organs during embryonic growth and development. In later life, nerves are also known to play a role in the continuous development of taste buds and in

the regeneration of the adrenal gland and other tissues. Since nerves go everywhere in the body, the neurotransmitters they release may play a life-long role in the metabolism, biosynthetic activity, and division of all cells. Neurotransmitters would do this either as trophic factors in themselves, as some evidence suggests, or additionally, as I propose, by modulating the activity of the growth factors effective in the tissues they innervate.

In the latter case, they would affect either the growth factors themselves, or their receptors, or the second messengers triggered by the growth factors in their target cells. It is worth sketching this elaboration because oncogenes, the genes whose expression can cause cancer, seem to code for variants of growth factors, growth-factor receptors, and their second messengers. Accordingly, psychoneural modulation of oncogenic growth factor activity may help explain so-called spontaneous and miraculous cancer remissions. . . .

Positive emotions appear to have specific biochemical correlates, which in turn have specific effects on tissues and diseases. Since the autonomic nervous system, which is affected by emotions, appears to secrete not only the long-familiar catecholamine neurotransmitters [e.g., epinephrine, norepinephrine, dopamine] but also the newly recognized peptide neurotransmitters, it can in principle deliver quite specific profiles of messengers to individual tissues. Recently, sensory nerves have been found to secrete peptide neurotransmitters at their peripheral ends, so they too could affect tissue growth.

From this perspective, then, in which the nervous system releases neurotransmitters that modulate growth factors, the brain, as the organ of emotions and attitudes, seems to be in a position to dispatch appropriate mixtures and amounts of growth-modulating neurotransmitters and hormones to particular sites.

It is evident from this quotation that psychobiologists are finally beginning to discover the actual biochemical steps by which mind can modulate molecules at the cellular and genetic levels, thereby explaining the mysteries of spontaneous healing, the placebo response, and so-called miracle cures. The challenge for hypnotherapists is to determine how to facilitate healing at these specific biochemical stages within the cells, as they are illuminated by basic research. While we are still very far from being able to do this, the following sections touch upon some pioneering studies in this area.

MIND MODULATION OF BLOOD FLOW AND
THE AUTONOMIC NERVOUS SYSTEM

Barber (1978, 1984) has brought together a fascinating overview that demonstrates how therapeutic hypnosis can be effective in healing a wide variety of apparently unrelated mind-body problems. This suggests that the phenomena of focused attention, imagery, biofeedback, and therapeutic hypnosis all operate by altering the direction of blood flow. Altering blood flow by directed thinking, imagining, and feeling is one of the basic, common factors in the resolution of most, if not all, mind-body problems. The following well-documented list expands upon Barber's work by detailing the healing processes that can be facilitated by the mind modulation of blood flow to the various tissues and cells of the body:

1) Warming and cooling different parts of the body to deal with headaches (Barabasz & McGeorge, 1978; Barber, 1978, 1984; Erickson, 1943c/1980);

2) Controlling blushing and blanching of the skin (Barber, 1978, 1984; Erickson, 1980c);

3) Stimulating the enlargement and apparent growth of breasts in women (Barber, 1984; Erickson, 1960a/1980; Williams, 1974);

4) Stimulation of sexual excitation and penile erection (Barber, 1978, 1984; Crasilneck, 1982);

5) The amelioration of bruises (Barber, 1984; Cheek, 1962a);

6) Controlling bleeding in surgery (Banks, 1985; Cheek, 1969);

7) Minimizing and healing burns (Barber, 1984; Cheek, 1962a; Crasilneck & Hall, 1985; Ewin, 1979, 1986a, b; Moore & Kaplan, 1983; Rossi & Cheek, 1990; Schafer, 1975; Wakeman & Kaplan, 1978);

8) Producing localized skin inflammations similar to previously experienced burns (Barber, 1984);

9) Curing warts (Ewin, 1974, 1992; Johnson & Barber, 1978; Spanos et al., 1988, 1990; Ullman, 1959);

10) Producing and curing diverse forms of dermatitis (Barber, 1984; Ikemi & Nakagawa, 1962);

11) Ameliorating congenital ichthyosis (Barber, 1984; Mason, 1952, 1955);

12) Aiding coagulation of blood in hemophiliacs (Banks, 1985; Barber, 1984);

13) Ameliorating the alarm response (Cheek, 1960, 1969; Rossi, 1973/1980);

14) Ameliorating hypertension and cardiac problems (Benson, 1983a, b; Gruen, 1972; Hornig-Rohan & Locke, 1985; Schneck, 1948; Wain, Amen, & Oetgen, 1984; Yanovski, 1962);

15) Ameliorating Raynaud's disease (Conn & Mott, 1984; Jacobson et al., 1973);

16) Enhancing the immune response (Black, 1969; Glaser et al., 1990, in press-a, b; Hall, 1982–83; Hall et al., 1992a, b; Lewis, 1927; Mason, 1963).

The next step is to identify the actual psychobiological mechanisms that govern the processes of blood flow hypothesized to underlie this diverse array of healing. Here, however, we rapidly reach the limits of our current understanding. To comprehend even these limits, we first need to review what is definitely known about the control of blood flow. The regulation of blood flow is usually considered under three headings: (1) autonomic nervous system, (2) humoral systems, and (3) local tissue controls. We will consider each in turn.

1) *Autonomic Nervous System.*   With its branches in the sympathetic and parasympathetic systems, the autonomic nervous system regulates blood flow by dilating or constricting blood vessels. This regulation takes place primarily via the action of neurotransmitters at sympathetic nerve endings located on the arteries, arterioles, metarterioles, veins, and venules (but not on capillaries and their sphincters). The parasympathetic system, by contrast, has only a minor role in the regulation of blood flow: Its only important effect takes place via the vagus nerve, which can decrease heart rate and contractility.

There are important characteristics of this autonomic nervous system control: It can occur quite rapidly (it begins within one second and reaches full development in five to 30 seconds), and it can regulate large parts of the body simultaneously. The entire system usually acts automatically on an unconscious level under control of the vasomotor center in the brain stem. This automatic control center, however, is subject to mind modulation via the limbic-hypothalamic system, which can send excitatory or inhibitory information to it. Many parts of the cerebral cortex can modulate the controls of the vasomotor center, usually via the limbic-hypothalamic system. These parts include the motor cortex, the anterior temporal lobe, and especially the frontal cortex with its capacity for utilizing and directing the psychobiological expression of learning encoded within the limbic system. Many parts of the cerebral cortex dealing with a variety of sensory-perceptual processes (imagery, kinesthesia, audition) can initiate the routes by which state-dependent memory and learning can be funneled through the limbic-hypothalamic system to modulate blood flow by the autonomic nervous system.

One of the major effects of the autonomic nervous system on blood flow that is mediated by the hypothalamus is the alarm response. When suddenly exposed to a personal danger, strong patterns of stimulation to the hypothalamus are transduced into powerful vasodilation and/or constriction of blood supply to muscles and glands. Arterial blood pressure rises, heart output increases, and the blood system becomes ready to supply oxygen and nutrients to the tissues that need them. This alarm response is one of the "mass action" effects of the autonomic nervous system on blood flow. It is of great value in preparing the body to meet emergencies, but it leads to stress and associated psychosomatic problems if continued for an unreasonably long period.

2) *Humoral Control of Blood.*   Humoral control refers to the substances such as hormones, ions, and other factors in the body fluids that can regulate blood flow. A number of hormones that are part of the endocrine system (to be outlined later) can be turned on by the autonomic nervous system. The sympathetic branch of the autonomic nervous system, for example, can stimulate the adrenal medulla (center of the adrenal glands) to secrete two such hormonal agents, epinephrine and norepinephrine, that are distributed throughout the body to regulate blood flow by constricting or dilating blood vessels. Norepinephrine constricts most of the vascular systems of the body. Epinephrine has a similar effect on most tissues, except for its mild vasodilation of skeletal and cardiac muscles when blood is needed (particularly during the alarm response).

This humoral control over blood flow lasts longer than the faster but shorter-acting direct stimulation by the release of neurotransmitters at the sympathetic system nerve endings, which act on the major endocrine organs illustrated in Figure 7. When this longer-acting, humoral mechanism gets out of control, however, it leads to excess and continued stress, eventually resulting in the psychosomatic problems associated with Selye's General Adaptation Syndrome.

3) *Local Tissue Controls of Blood Flow.*   As we get closer to the local control systems which determine how much blood reaches the individual cells of tissues via the arterioles and capillaries, our knowledge of the possibilities of mind modulation grow even dimmer. It has been mentioned that arterioles are innervated directly by the sympathetic nervous system and indirectly by epinephrine and norepinephrine released into the blood by the adrenal medulla. Arterioles are thus subject to mind modulation via the hypothalamic-autonomic route. Capillaries, on the other hand, are more closely regulated by the local tissue needs for oxygen and nutrients. The mechanism of this control is the

small muscular *precapillary sphincter* that surrounds the origin of the capillary.

There are two major theories regarding the regulation of these precapillary sphincters: the vasodilation theory, and the oxygen demand theory (Guyon, 1981). The vasodilation theory proposes that the greater the rate of metabolism, the greater the release of local vasodilators (such as carbon dioxide, lactic acid, and adenosine phosphate) that open the precapillary sphincters, metarterioles, and arterioles. Adenosine is a particularly important dilator at this level because it is released by heart cell muscles when coronary blood flow becomes too little; thus, insufficient release of adenosine could be related to the incidence of cardiac problems. The fundamental role of ATP as the "second messenger system" within the cells of the body that transduces mind information from the cortical-limbic-hypothalamic-autonomic pathway is diagrammed in Figure 7.

The oxygen demand theory is also known as the "nutrient demand" theory since many nutrients are also involved. The locus of action in this theory is on the precapillary sphincters, which are continually in vasomotion and whose openings are approximately proportional to the metabolic needs of the tissues. I am not aware of any proposed mind-modulating effects at this level, although one could speculate that the appetite and thirst control centers of the hypothalamus could be involved through processes not yet well understood.

A pioneering research effort in the voluntary and hypnotic control of oxygen in the tissues was recently performed by Olness and Conroy (1985). They found that children (ages 7 through 17) who were experienced in self-hypnosis were able to increase oxygen in their tissues (as measured continuously by a Novamatrix transcutaneous monitoring system). One child even voluntarily *decreased* the oxygen level. The authors of this study do not discuss the psychophysiological mechanisms involved, but they conclude that their study documents voluntary control over this aspect of autonomic nervous system functioning.

HYPNOTHERAPEUTIC APPROACHES TO THE AUTONOMIC SYSTEM

An important example of the mind modulation of cellular activity via the autonomic nervous system occurs when its sympathetic branch signals the adrenal medullae (center of the adrenal glands) to secrete epinephrine and norepinephrine into the bloodstream to activate the alarm response throughout the body. Coping with this alarm response is of great importance during accidents, life emergencies, and medical interventions (such as surgery) in which the victim's or patient's fear could contribute to excess blood loss, hypertension, cardiac problems, and even physiological shock. Reassurance from any responsible person (doctor, nurse, medical aide, helpful bystander) can greatly mitigate the stress-induced aspects of the emergency by attenuating the sympathetic alarm reaction and substituting the calming effects of the parasympathetic system. In this section we will review a number of hypnotherapeutic approaches that have been used successfully in a wide variety of clinical practice dealing with the alarm response.

1) *Controlling Bleeding During Surgery and Hemophilia.*   Banks (1985) has recently reported how hypnotic suggestion can be used to control bleeding during acute gastrointestinal hemorrhage, angiography (X-ray studies of blood vessels), and embolization (intentional injection of vessel blocks into arteries feeding an abnormality). Banks recognizes that stress and confusion during these medical procedures are in themselves sufficient to induce a state of heightened sensitivity wherein the patient is receptive to suggestions without the formal induction of hypnotic trance. During the angiography procedure, for example, excess bleeding can be stopped or turned on again with the following suggestions (Banks, 1985, p. 80):

> "This may seem strange, but has anyone asked you to stop bleeding yet?"
> The patient's quizzical look and verbal response of "no" elicited the following short verbalization:
> "Then why don't you stop bleeding? *Now!* I know it *sounds* like an unusual request, but it really would help us to help you; and after all, you really have been controlling bleeding—all of your life—probably without knowing consciously what you have been doing. You get cut or scratched and you *stop bleeding*, just like you increase your heart rate when you get frightened, and you slow it down when you relax—you *do it* but you don't know how. So you don't need to *consciously* know how you stop your bleeding but it will help us if you just *let it happen . . . now!*"
> If it is later required to turn bleeding back on, the doctor suggests the following:
> "So far you have really done well. You have stopped your bleeding completely. But in order to show what *was* bleeding, you now need to *undo* whatever it was that you have done. You don't need to know how, but just let it go ahead and bleed, *now*, so we can see if we have found the correct spot."

These simple but well-formulated requests take advantage of a number of indirect hypnotic suggestions summarized by Erickson and Rossi (1980). The reader can recognize how these requests are actually a variation of our basic accessing formula: (1) There is a time-binding introduction of "Why don't you stop bleeding? *Now!*"; (2) there is an accessing of state-dependent unconscious processes that can control bleeding "if you just let it happen"; and (3) there is a recognizable behavioral response that ratifies the inner process when the bleeding actually stops.

Banks asks why a hemophiliac patient can stop bleeding from a tumor that should not respond to normal physiological controls, as follows (1985, p. 85):

> Does he produce a spasm in normal feeding arteries? . . . Activate clotting factors? Neither hemophiliacs nor physicians who work with them have a logical explanation of *how* they achieve their dramatic results without demonstrable circulating factor VIII [a blood factor needed for normal blood coagulation but absent in hemophiliacs]: we can do no better.

From the theoretical perspective of this book, one could infer that the limbic-hypothalamic-autonomic system is the route by which hemophiliacs achieve their results: The sympathetic branch of the autonomic system could constrict blood vessels and thus shut off the blood flow.

2) *Ideomotor Signaling for Accessing Problems Associated with Surgical Anesthesia, Accidents, Critical Illness.*   David Cheek (1959) made a number of original discoveries on the "Unconscious Perception of Meaningful Sounds During Anesthesia as Revealed Under Hypnosis." A typical example of his work was reported as follows (Cheek, 1957, p. 109):

> This 27-year-old dentist volunteered for investigation of his appendectomy at the age of 15. He stated that he had always wondered if a "ghost" surgeon had done the operation but had never known just why he felt this. He was curious to find out if his impression was correct, and it was the impression of the writer that the curiosity was free of malevolence.
>
> During the induction the subject related his sensation of light trance to that experienced after he had been knocked unconscious during a football scrimmage at the age of 16. Asked if there were another experience which felt similar, he indicated a "yes" with his finger and regressed back to the induction of anesthesia for his appendectomy one year earlier. This equating of the hypnotized state with previous experiences of delirium or with unconsciousness from diabetic coma or chemical anesthesia has been frequent in the writer's experience.
>
> Q: "Where are you now?"
> A: "I think I'm in the O.R. [operating room]—I'm not going down very well." (Respiratory rate jumps from 14–28.)

Q: "Are you scared?"
A: Finger: "No."
Q: "Do you hear any sounds?"
A: "The fan is going—they are talking back and forth—not to me."
Q: "Is there anything that worries you?"
A: Finger: "Yes." Verbal: "No."
Q: "Would it be all right to hear it consciously?"
A: Finger: "Yes." Verbal after a pause: "You better cut here."
Q: "Where does it come from?"
A: "It seems to be coming from Sobie" (the family physician). The subject
    is now urged to go back over this and give the exact words as though
    he were replaying the record.
A: "I think we better cut here."
Q: "Is there anything after that that disturbs you?"
A: "Yes" (with finger after pause of ten seconds.) Verbal: "It seems like
    they can't find it. 'It's tucked under'—that comes from the doctor on
    the left side of the table" (Sobie). After another pause (25 seconds),
    "Come on, we got to get this out of here."
Q: "Whose voice is that?"
A: "It doesn't seem to be Sobie. He seems to be on the left and somebody
    else is on the right, and somebody is down at the foot."
Q: "Does this statement frighten the deep part of your brain?"
A: Finger: "No."
Q: "Does the deep part of your brain feel anything?"
A: Finger: "No." Verbal: "Just a little hyper-awareness of the lower right
    quadrant." (Note the later-orientation choice of words.)
Q: "Do you feel any discomfort while they are looking?"
A: Verbal: "No."

When now asked to indicate the next thing, he states that nothing is being
said, but he senses a feeling of relief and he knows they have found the
appendix.

A little later the subject says, "Now the light is right over my head. It
didn't use to be over my head. It's brighter. I guess they must have taken
the mask off or something."

Q: "Are they finished?"
A: Finger: "No."

He now seems disturbed because, although they have talked as though
finished with the surgery, they decide to put another clamp on the skin.

This illustration of the ideomotor finger signaling method of accessing
state-bound information encapsulated from normal waking consciousness by chemical anesthesia reveals a number of interesting features.

The first is that the patient's respiratory rate jumped from 14 to 28. This indicates that an important psychobiological shift was taking place as the traumatic memories of the operation were beginning to be accessed under hypnosis. Another significant feature of this finger signaling example was the conflict between the ideomotor and verbal levels. Thus in response to Cheek's question, "Is there anything that worries you?" the finger signaled "yes" while the patient answered "no." Such conflicting responses are the reason why Cheek uses three levels of psychobiological responsiveness to assess the degree of therapeutic involvement and validity of his clinical investigations. Let us review these three levels again in the context of the above illustration.

1) The first level typically involves increased perspiration, respiration, and heart rate. These are all indications of *autonomic system arousal* and, together with McGaugh's (1983, 1989) work cited earlier on the hormonal and neuroendocrinal encoding of life experience, would be the basis of this first level of psychobiological responsiveness. Responses on this level can be regarded as involuntary.
2) The second level is the *ideomotor finger signal* itself, which is usually experienced by subjects as moving in an autonomous and involuntary manner. Some subjects, however, experience the movement as partially voluntary; others simply do not know whether or not it is completely involuntary.
3) The third level is that of *verbal report*. Many subjects experience this as completely voluntary; others are less sure; and for some, it even seems to be involuntary.

I would describe these three levels as interacting patterns of state-bound information. Because of the traumatic acquisition conditions under which the limbic-hypothalamic autonomic nervous system encoded this information, it is not available to the person's usual associative networks of consciousness. The normal processes of information transduction have broken down. Cheek's finger signaling approach to accessing this state-bound information is a unique way of reestablishing the process of information transduction between the physiological, ideomotor, and verbal levels.

Cheek has his subjects review the state-bound memories at the ideomotor level a number of times before attempting to obtain a verbal report. It is tempting to speculate that this need to "review" is actually a procedure for accessing and reactivating Hebb's (1949) "cell assemblies and phase sequences'' (1949) and Gazzaniga's "mind modules" (1985) that encode the state-bound information in neural associative networks. Repeating the accessing and reactivating process increases the probability that transduction between the physiological and verbal levels will be reconnected. Confirmation of Cheek's general ideomotor approach to accessing and reframing traumatic memories is currently appearing in numerous research programs. Barnett (1984), for example, has recently reported the results of a ten-year study of "the role of prenatal trauma in the development of the negative birth experience." In this study he has used the finger signaling method to access memories that could be implicated in a wide range of functional disorders, including alcoholism, anxiety, depression, asthma, phobias, nail-biting, sexual dysfunction, and marital problems.

From the area of laboratory research, Cheek's work on the unconscious perception of meaningful sounds during surgical anesthesia was confirmed in animal research by psychobiologists Weinberger, Gold, and Sternberg (1984). They found that anesthetized experimental animals could learn the conditioning of an auditory signal when they received a dose of epinephrine to put them in a state of heightened psychophysiological arousal. These researchers suggested that since epinephrine is an important neurotransmitter, it functions to consolidate memory storage. This is a striking confirmation of McGaugh's work quoted earlier on the psychobiological encoding of state-bound information.

In human research Henry Bennett (1985), a psychologist at the University of California at Davis, is confirming that unconscious learning during surgery can influence its outcome and the rate of recovery. Clearly, more work with humans under controlled conditions is needed to explore the parameters, limitations, and further possibilities in this area (Liu, Standen, & Altkenhead, 1992).

The Psychobiology of Coping: Converting Negative Threat into Positive Challenge

The ability to cope with stress is currently emerging as one of the most significant factors in the psychobiology of health and illness (Gentry, 1984). Most schools of psychotherapy consider enhanced coping skills as a goal and criterion of the effectiveness of the therapeutic work. Selye's pioneering work on the psychobiology of stress, of course, is the source of this current recognition of the significance of coping. In the later stages of his work, Selye (1974) differentiated between the type of stress that caused illness, and the type of stress—"eustress"—that was life-enhancing. This distinction corresponds nicely with the views of humanistic psychologist Abraham Maslow (1962), who divided human motivation into two branches: (1) *deprivation motivation* that engendered negative feelings and illness because of a lack of the basic necessities of life, and (2) *being motivation* that enhanced life with positive feelings of love, joy, hope, and happiness.

The psychobiological basis of this distinction between negative and positive emotions in response to stress has recently been investigated by a number of researchers (Holroyd & Lazarus, 1982; Lazarus & Folkman, 1984). They found a significant difference in the body's response to "threat" (stress) and "challenge" (eustress). Threat is associated with two factors: (1) an increase in the blood level of catecholamines (epinephrine and norepinephrine, secreted from the adrenal *medulla* in response to sympathetic stimulation described earlier as the alarm response of the autonomic nervous system); and (2) the release of cortisol into the bloodstream by the adrenal *cortex* (signaled by the pituitary gland sending ACTH to the adrenal cortex, as illustrated in Figure 1). Challenge, on the other hand, is associated only with an elevation in catecholamine levels.

In a study on the biochemistry of self-efficacy (or coping), Bandura (1985) found that there was an elevation in catecholamine levels in patients who were experiencing a phobia. He then found that the greater their sense of being able to cope with their phobia, the lower their catecholamine levels. The greater the sense of self-efficacy, the less stress is experienced and the lower the catecholamine levels remain. This suggests a basic principle of psychobiological therapy: *Convert the negative stress of threat into a positive coping experience of challenge.* This novel way of conceptualizing the therapeutic aim of the various forms of the basic accessing formula is illustrated in Tutorial 11.

A hypnotherapeutic approach to phobias based on a variation of our basic accessing formula (originally described as the "three-stage utilization approach to hypnotherapy" in Erickson & Rossi, 1979) was utilized by Nugent, Carden, and Montgomery (1984) "in an effort to validate both the approach and the supposition that creative unconscious processes can thus be accessed and utilized therapeutically." The purpose of their "standard suggestion form" was to "access and direct creative unconscious processes toward the creation and implementation of satisfactory solutions to recurrent problem behaviors" (p. 201). In three experimental cases, they found that a single hypnotherapeutic session was sufficient to resolve sleep disturbance problems and phobias for

---

TUTORIAL 11 Converting Negative Threat to Positive Challenge

1. *Readiness signal for inner work*
   **You will know when you are ready to explore how you can deal
   more effectively with that problem** [pause]
   **when you find yourself getting more comfortable with each
   breath you take** [pause]
   and will your eyes close as you focus on it?

2. *Reframing threat into challenge*
   **Will you review all aspects of your problem that are most threaten-
   ing** [pause], **that's right, having the courage to really feel the truth
   of it all** [pause],
   **and wonder how you will successfully resolve each as a worth-
   while challenge?**

3. *Ratifying problem-solving*
   **And when you know that you can continue that constructive ap-
   proach** [pause],
   **Will you find yourself ready to stretch, awaken, and share just
   one or two effective ways you will enjoy using to meet those challenges?**

---

hypodermic needles. Their therapeutic approach to a phobia for needles
in one college subject they call "B" was described as follows (Nugent,
Carden, & Montgomery, 1984; pp. 202–203):

> Following our pre-induction talk a trance induction was initiated. B re-
> sponded to the internal visualization induction by rapidly developing a deep
> trance. She was then given the creative task of finding a way she could
> remain awake and alert during future procedures involving needles. We gave
> this task via a "standard" suggestion form used in all applications of our
> procedure: "Now your unconscious mind can do what is necessary, in a
> manner fully meeting all your needs as a person, to insure that (*desired thera-
> peutic outcome*), and as soon as your unconscious knows that you will (*desired
> therapeutic outcome*), it can signal by (*appropriate ideomotor signal*)." The specific
> suggestion given B was: "Now your unconscious mind can do what is neces-
> sary, in a manner fully meeting all your needs as a person, to insure that *you
> remain comfortably awake and alert anytime you receive an injection in the future*,
> and as soon as your unconscious knows you will *remain comfortably awake and*

alert when receiving an injection, it can signal by *lifting your right hand into the air off the chair.''* This suggestion was our communicative effort to access and direct unconscious processes to the creation and implementation of altered behavioral responses to injection. Three minutes after this suggestion was given, B's right hand lifted jerkily into the air. She was then awakened and experienced a complete amnesia for the trance period.

It would now be desirable to determine the relative effectiveness of using this hypnotherapeutic formula to lower catecholamine levels in comparison with the behavioral approach described by Bandura.

THE WAVE NATURE OF CONSCIOUSNESS AND BEING: PSYCHOBIOLOGICAL RHYTHMS AND THE AUTONOMIC SYSTEM

The wave nature of consciousness and being refers to the fact that every aspect of our consciousness and psychobiology that can be measured is periodic. Throughout the day we have alternating periods of relatively high alertness and performance that alternate with pauses in our efficiency as the mind-body turns inward to focus on its own healing. The 24-hour *circadian* (once-a-day) rhythm of alternation between sleep and awake is obvious to everyone. The more recent discovery that *ultradian* (more than once-a-day) rhythms of activity, performance, memory, and reaction time by chronobiologists (the biology of time) in government laboratories investigating the source of ''human error'' in accidents has taken most psychotherapists by surprise (Brown & Graeber, 1982; Lloyd & Rossi, 1992a). The discovery of the ultradian rhythms that regulate many functions of the autonomic and endocrine systems is a recent research milestone that has important implications for the development of new approaches to therapeutic hypnosis (see Rossi, 1982, 1986a). In this section we will outline some implications of the ultradian-autonomic link; in the next chapter we will deal with the ultradian-endocrine relationships.

The concept of dominance in the functioning of the cerebral hemispheres has a long tradition in physiology and medicine (Gazzaniga, 1985). Until the present time it was presumed that hemispheric functioning was not only specialized in function but also fixed in time. A series of studies during sleep (Goldstein, Stoltzfus, & Gardocki, 1972; Gordon, Frooman, & Lavie, 1982), however, indicated that there were natural, 90-minute ultradian rhythms in hemispheric dominance that might affect psychological functioning. Every 90 minutes during sleep, for example, most people experience a period of dreaming (REM sleep).

Klein and Armitage (1979) then found that there were natural, 90-minute oscillations of ultradian rhythms in the mental activity and cognitive style of normal subjects when they were awake: Left- and right-hemispheric dominance tended to alternate with this ultradian periodicity.

The next experimental step was taken by Debra Werntz (1981), who found that these ultradian rhythms in cerebral hemispheric dominance were contralaterally associated with similar alternations in the nasal breathing cycle. That is, when the left nostril was open and taking in air, the right cerebral hemisphere had an EEG pattern indicative of greater activity, and vice versa. In a subsequent study (Werntz et al., 1981), she found that changing nasal breathing from one side to the other also changed cerebral hemispheric dominance! Not only was the nasal breathing rhythm a natural, non-invasive window on cerebral hemispheric activity, but voluntarily induced changes in airflow between the left and right nostrils could be used to change the locus of activity in the left and right cerebral hemispheres in the highest levels of brain and mind! She and her colleagues outlined a theory of these relationships with the autonomic nervous system as follows (Werntz et al., 1981, pp. 4–6):

> We feel that the correlation of the nasal cycle with the alternation of cerebral hemispheric activity is consistent with a model for a single ultradian oscillator system and imposes a new conceptual understanding for the nervous system. . . . We propose an even more complete and integrated theoretical framework which incorporates an organization for all ultradian rhythms and their regulation by the autonomic nervous system, most specifically the integration of autonomic and cerebral hemispheric activity. It could be suggested at this point that there might be some basis to believe that the "separate forms of intelligence" localized in each hemisphere require an increased metabolic support of the contralateral side of the body in terms of the overall bias they might serve. *In this context, the nasal cycle can be viewed as an easily measurable indicator or "window" for this framework.*
>
> . . . Thus the whole body goes through the Rest/Activity or Parasympathetic/Sympathetic oscillation while simultaneously going through the "Left Body-Right Brain/Right Body-Left Brain" shift. This then produces ultradian rhythms at all levels of organization from pupil size to higher cortical functions and behavior. . . . It is important to note that this represents an extensive integration of autonomic and cerebral cortical activity, a relationship not previously defined or studied. We propose that as the nasal cycle probably is regulated via a centrally controlled mechanism, possibly the hypothalamus, altering the sympathetic/parasympathetic balance, this occurs throughout the body including the brain and is the mechanism by which vasomotor

tone regulates the control of blood flow through the cerebral vessels thereby altering cerebral hemispheric activity.

For thousands of years the Eastern yogis have claimed they could regulate their states of consciousness by regulating their breathing in the practice they called *pranayama* (Rossi, 1985, 1986a). They have also claimed that their supposedly miraculous control over their body physiology was related to the conscious regulation of their breathing rhythms. Since these feats of mind-body control deal primarily with the autonomic nervous system, Werntz's work may provide a theoretical and empirical bridge to the ancient yogic traditions.

Two particularly dramatic cases of what we would today call multiple personality disorder that were apparently related to the alternation of the nasal cycle were reported by Ischolondsky (1955, pp. 8–9). Both cases evidenced an amnesia between an active and passive personality that provided a vivid indication of how lateralized oscillation of the autonomic nervous system between sympathetic and parasympathetic dominance was associated with the nasal cycle and striking alternations of personality as follows:

> . . . two diametrically-opposed personality types. One was an impulsive, irresponsible, mischievous and vindictive personality, full of rebellion against authority and of hate towards the people around her, the patient in this phase was extremely aggressive, using abusive language and scaring other patients with lurid tales of state hospitals, sex relations, etc.; in the opposed behavioral pattern to which the first personality would suddenly switch, the patient appeared dependent, submissive, shy, self-effacing, affectionate, and obedient. In a very timid way she expressed friendliness, sought affection, acceptance, and approval from the same personnel she had reviled and abused. There was no trace left of any inappropriate word or expression, no manifestation of hostility to her surroundings, and not the slightest reference to sex. In fact, any sex thought or word would induce in her extreme fears of perdition, feelings of guilt and anxiety, depression, and shame. . . . examination revealed that the left and right sides of her body responded differently to sensory stimulus: while the right side was hypo-sensitive the left side displayed hyper-sensitivity. Thus, vision and hearing were unclear and far away on the right side but very clear and close on the left side. Her response to touch and pain showed a high threshold on the right, and a low threshold on the left side. Characteristically, with regard to the olfactory sense the patient in this mental state manifested a diametrically opposed attitude: she was hyper-sensitive to smell on the right side and her right nostril was clear, while on the left side her sense of smell was absent and the nostril congested and closed. With regard to the other neurological signs such as the size of

pupils, reflexes, salivation, sweating, there was a similar difference in the response of the two sides of the body: the aggressive personality type displayed on the right side, a small pupil, a hypo-secretion of saliva, absence of sweating on sole and palm and lack of abdominal reflexes, while on the left side there was a large pupil, hypersecretion of saliva, very strong sweating on palm and sole and extremely strong abdominal reflexes. (It is difficult to account for the observation of pupil size etc. inconsistent with nasal congestion.) And just as fast as the psyche switched to the shy, passive, and permissive personality all neurological manifestations also switched to reverse dominance, where the olfactory sense proved now to be very sharp on the left side while completely absent and with nostril congested and closed on the right side.

David Shannahoff-Khalsa (1991) of the Jonas Salk Institute of La Jolla, California, suggested that an exploration of any mind-body state or problem involving the autonomic nervous system could be undertaken safely and easily by shifting cerebral hemispheric dominance via the nasal breathing rhythm. I have detailed several methods for shifting hemispheric dominance in this way previously (Rossi, 1986a, b). My favorite method is to simply lie down comfortably on one side of my body or the other. Lying on the right side, for example, causes the right nostril to become congested, while the left nostril opens within a few minutes. This, in turn, reflexively tends to activate the right cerebral hemisphere. By lying on the left side, the left cerebral hemisphere is activated.

One of the most intriguing areas of recent research exploring the association between hypnosis and psychobiological rhythms is the so-called nasal breath-brain connection. The German rhinologist Kayser (1895) is credited with recognizing and measuring the widely varying ultradian shifts in the degree to which air is inhaled in the left or right chamber of the nose. In humans the left and right chambers of the nose alternate in their size and shape to change the degree of air flow through each every few hours. Recently Debra Werntz (1981) reported a contralateral relationship between cerebral hemispheric activity (EEG) and the ultradian rhythm of the nasal cycle. She found that relatively greater integrated EEG values in the right hemisphere are positively correlated with a predominant airflow in the left nostril and vice versa. In a wide-ranging series of studies Werntz et al. (1982a, b) found that subjects could voluntarily shift their nasal dominance by forced uninostril breathing through the closed nostril. Further, this shift in nasal dominance was associated with an accompanying shift in cerebral dominance to the contralateral hemisphere and autonomic nervous system balance throughout the body (Shannahoff-Khalsa, 1991). The ultradian nasal cycle is not only a marker for cerebral hemispheric activity, but it also could be used to voluntarily change the loci of activity in the highest centers of the brain and autonomic system that are involved in cybrenetic loops of communication with most organ systems, tissues, and cells of the body. Some of these investigators hypothesize that this nasal-brain-mind link may be the essential path by which the ancient practice of breath regulation in yoga led to the voluntary control of many autonomic nervous system functions for which the Eastern adepts are noted (Brown, 1991a, b; Rossi, 1990b, 1991).

These relationships inspired a recent Ph.D. dissertation by Darlene Osowiec (1992) who assessed hypothesized associations between the nasal ultradian rhythm, anxiety, symptoms of stress, and their personality process of self-actualization. She found that "(1) there is a significant positive correlation between self-actualizing individuals having low trait anxiety and stress related symptoms and a regular nasal cycle . . . and (2) non-self-actualizing individuals with high levels of trait anxiety and stress-related symptoms exhibit significantly greater irregularity in the nasal cycle." These results are reminiscent of the ancient texts that emphasize that an irregular nasal cycle, particularly one in which the person remains dominant in one nostril or the other for an excessively long period of time are associated with illness and mental disorder (Rama, Ballentine, & Ajaya, 1976).

In a more recent 12-week follow-up study, Osowiec (personal communication, 1993) is finding that highly hypnotizable subjects evidence more regularity in their ultradian nasal rhythms when they practice self-hypnosis but low hypnotizable subjects do not. Osowiec tentatively concludes that her findings with the ultradian nasal rhythm are similar to the general types of association that are found between stress, symptoms, personality, and responsiveness to therapeutic hypnosis.

To further assess the hypothesis of an association between hypnosis and the nasal breath-brain link, Lippincott (1992c) studied the effect of two forms of hypnotic induction: (1) a traditional form of hypnosis via the Harvard Group Scale of Hypnotic Susceptibility, and (2) a naturalistic form of hypnosis via Rossi's Ultradian Accessing Formula on the nasal rhythm. He hypothesized that since hypnosis has been associated with shifts in cerebral hemispheric dominance (Erickson & Rossi, 1979) one would expect that hypnotic induction would be associated with a shift in nasal dominance. He found that both groups of subjects experienced more nasal dominance shifts than a resting control group and, further, the group that experienced a naturalistic hypnotic induction exhibited significantly more nasal shifts than the traditional hypnotic induction group.

Preliminary exploration with this simple method as outlined in Tutorial 12 have yielded fascinating experiential results. A functional headache due to simple stress or overwork, for example, often can be made to change its intensity and location relatively quickly simply by shifting the nasal rhythm from one side to the other. Some patients have reported that pain can be shifted ideodynamically into a feeling of pleasant warmth, coolness, or whatever, by shifting sides. Moods, negative affects, and body discomfort can be imaged and reflected upon with more meaningful insight after five or six minutes of playing with one's sensory transformations in this manner. Elsewhere I have published some of my personal experiences of accessing profound, autohypnotic states of "lucid somnambulism" by shifting to right-hemispheric dominance during ultradian rest periods (Rossi, 1972/1985).

In his book, *Meditation and the Art of Dying* (1979), Dr. Usharbudh Arya has described an interesting relationship between the nasal cycle, sexual orgasm, and the highest states of bliss in *samadhi*. According to

---

TUTORIAL 12 Shifting Cerebral Hemispheric Dominance
and Mind-Body States

1. *Identifying nasal dominance and mind-body state*
   When you are experiencing a mind-body state you would like to explore and transform, first determine which nostril is clear.

2. *Shifting nasal and hemispheric dominance*
   Lie on your side, with the clear nostril downward. This will shift reflexively your cerebral dominance within a few minutes to the hemisphere on the downward side. Simply receive and wonder about the sensory, perceptual, emotional, cognitive, or symptomatic shifts taking place all by themselves within the next five to 20 minutes.

3. *Ratify hemispheric and mind-body shifts*
   In an upright position, notice that the formerly blocked nostril is now clear, and vice versa. Record the mind-body changes that accompanied this nasal-cerebral hemispheric shift and study the characteristic patterns of your responses to guide yourself further.

ancient yogic literature, both nostrils are open during sexual orgasm, and during the deepest meditative states of *samadhi*. The ecstasy of this form of meditation he describes is due to "upward implosions . . . of kundalini . . . so that celibacy becomes easier and more enjoyable than sex." It remains for Western science to assess these observations.

These preliminary observations on the relationships between the autonomic nervous system, cerebral hemispheric dominance, and behavior open an extremely wide range of interesting possibilities for developing new psychobiological approaches to therapeutic hypnosis, mind-body healing, and the facilitation of human potentials. Another look at Figure 7 at this point will provide the reader with an overview of the profound scope of many of the approaches touched upon in this chapter: Figure 7 illustrates a complete path of information transduction, mediated by the autonomic nervous system, that exists between mind, body, and molecular processes within each cell of the body. This path of information transduction is being modulated constantly and automatically on an involuntary, unconscious level by the state-dependent encoding of memory, learning and behavior from our experiences of everyday life. Continuing research and clinical practice will reveal the avenues by which we can learn to facilitate these mind-body processes of communication in a more voluntary manner. In the next chapter we will extend these possibilities by exploring what we already know about the mind modulation of the endocrine system.

8

Mind Modulation of the Endocrine System

THE ENDOCRINE SYSTEM is comprised of many organs located throughout the body that secrete hormones into the bloodstream to regulate cellular metabolic functions, such as the rates of chemical reactions for metabolism, growth, activity level, sexuality, etc. Figure 8 illustrates how some of the major organs and functions of the endocrine system can be influenced by mind modulation processes via the limbic-hypothalamic system. Virtually all these organs of the endocrine system can either mediate or be the loci of psychosomatic problems.

The pituitary gland at the base of the brain is the "master gland" of the endocrine system: It sends out hormones as "messenger molecules" to regulate all the other hormone-producing organs of the body (see Figure 8). The pituitary, in turn, is modulated by the limbic-hypothalamic system. As indicated earlier, the hypothalamus is comprised of many nuclei or nerve centers that act as receiving stations to pick up information about the *internal environment* from the blood and cerebrospinal fluid, and about the *external environment* from the sense organs. The limbic-hypothalamic system is the major center for integrating this information with the processes of mind, and then transducing this newly integrated information to the pituitary, which in turn regulates all the other organs of the endocrine system. The actual cells of the hypothalamus that transduce the nerve impulses of mind into the secretions (hormonal-releasing factors) that regulate the pituitary were illustrated earlier in Figures 6A and 6B (p. 144).

Within the past decade a revolutionary series of discoveries about the multiple roles of many endocrine hormones has transformed our understanding of memory, learning, and behavior (Guillemin, 1978; Henry, 1982; Snyder, 1980). The traditional role of hormones in regulat-

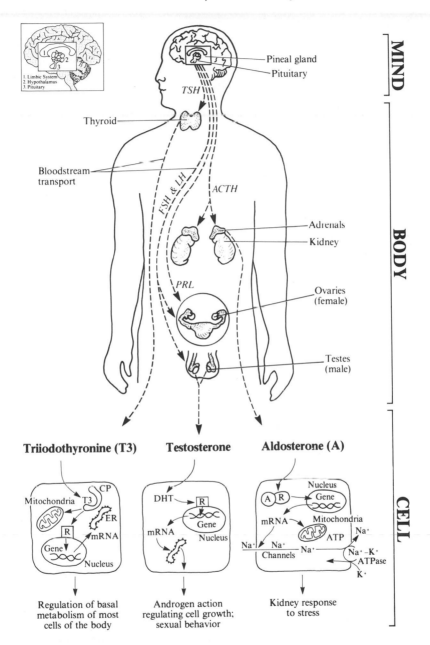

FIGURE 8 Mind-body communication via the endocrine system with three examples of the ''mind-gene'' loop of information transduction.

ing metabolic functions of the body is currently being supplemented by a growing realization of how they also may function as neurotransmitters and neuromodulators that facilitate mind-body communication at many levels within the brain itself. This is possible because the cell receptors that are activated by these hormones are present in brain tissues as well as in body tissues. Table 4 lists a number of endocrinal hormones that operate on cell receptors in both brain and body.

The most extraordinary development that has taken place recently in the field of endocrinology involves the discovery of the new class of pituitary hormones called the *endorphins* and *enkephalins*. These hormones have many regulatory functions of psychological interest, including the modulation of stress, pain, moods, sexuality, appetite, addictions and substance abuse, work and sports performance, as well as the basic processes of learning and memory (Davis, 1984).

The discovery of the endorphins is so new that there is still no general agreement about their physiological classification. Margules (1979), for example, has postulated that the endorphin system represents a new division of the autonomic nervous system that is basically concerned with the "conservation and expenditure of bodily resources and energy in anticipation of famine or feast" (p. 155). This view is supported by many lines of evidence, including the distribution of endorphins throughout the body and many brain areas (hypothalamus, pituitary, nucleus raphe magnus, periaquaductal grey), as well as in the spinal cord and gastrointestinal tract.

Since a major biosynthetic source of one of the major endorphins (β-endorphin) and enkephalins (meta-enkephalin) comes from the same mother molecule as the adrenocorticotropic hormone (ACTH) in the anterior pituitary, however, many authorities now consider this entire system to be part of neuroendocrinology. β-endorphin has the same secretory release dynamics from the pituitary as ACTH: It is basically released into the bloodstream in response to stress (physical, emotional, cognitive, and imaginative), as well as in response to natural daily (circadian) biorhythms. It is important to recall the psychobiological source of the endorphin hormones when evaluating the meaning and implications of the many still contradictory claims concerning the functions of the endorphin system.

Since many of the multiple functions of hormones are mediated either directly or indirectly by the limbic-hypothalamic-pituitary system, they are accessible to mind modulation and hypnotherapeutic intervention. That is, although hormones usually function autonomously, we now know that their activity is modulated by significant life experiences and

TABLE 4 The multiple functions of some hormones that have related functions in mind and body

1) As described earlier, Selye discovered that *corticotropin releasing factor (CRF)* is a hypothalamic hormone which mediates the release of ACTH by the pituitary, which in turn tells the adrenal cortex of the body to release cortisol into the bloodstream. This is the traditional role of hormones acting on receptors in cells of the body's organs as described by classical endocrinology. Recently, however, it has been discovered that there are receptors for CRF and ACTH in brain cells which can mediate stress-like behavior and psychological variables such as attentiveness, memory, and learning (Izquierdo, 1984; McGaugh, 1983; Rigter & Crabbe, 1979).

2) *Cholecystokinin (CCK)* is a hormone that is active from the esophagus in the throat to the small intestine. It modulates gall bladder contraction, pancreatic enzyme, and motility of the gastrointestinal tract. Receptors for CCK also exist in brain cells, however, where it controls satiety (probably by its action on the hypothalamic control centers). Thus, it may become important in future treatment of obesity (Kissilef et al., 1981). This, of course, also suggests a psychobiological route by which mind may modulate appetite. Candace Pert (1986), Chief of Brain Biochemistry for the National Institute of Mental Health, speculates that CCK also may mediate what people mean when they speak of "gut feelings."

3) *Insulin* was first known to be a hormonal secretion of the pancreas involved in carbohydrate metabolism by increasing the uptake of glucose by cardiac, muscle, liver, and adipose tissue, etc. Recent physiological studies of its receptors in the brain, as well as behavioral studies, indicate that it modulates eating behavior by direct effects on cerebral capillaries (Pert et al., 1985).

4) *Gonadotrophin-releasing hormone (GnRH)* from the hypothalamus stimulates the release of pituitary hormones such as gonadotrophins, lutenizing hormone (LH), and follicle-stimulating hormone (FSH), that in turn stimulate growth and regulate the physiology of sexual processes. When receptors in the brain of rats are activated by GnRH, they show sexual behavior and posturing.

5) *Vasopressin or antidiuretic hormone (ADH)* is released from the posterior pituitary when it receives appropriate posterior signals from the hypothalamus. In classical endocrinology, vasopressin was studied for its regulation of kidney action, water balance, and urine flow. Now it is also being recognized for its effects as a vasoconstrictor in regulating blood flow. When cell receptors in the brain are activated, however, vasopressin has been found to enhance memory and learning (McGaugh, 1983). There is also a relationship between circadian rhythms and ADH levels in the cerebrospinal fluid. All of this research suggests that the different levels of learning and memory that occur throughout the 24-hour cycle may be related to ADH fluctuations in its access to many different brain tissues.

encoded in the form of state-dependent memory, learning, and behavior. Rosenblatt (1983) has pointed out that whenever a receptor for a drug is present in the brain or elsewhere in the body, that means there are *endogenous substances* (usually hormones) which are intended by nature to interact with these receptors. This was the important lesson taught by the discovery of the endorphins, which were discovered only when researchers looked for them after the receptors for the opiate drugs (heroin, morphine, etc.) had been identified in the brain.

The autonomic, endocrine, immune, and neuropeptide systems all operate by activating receptors on the surfaces of the individual cells of the tissues of the body. These receptors are like locks that must be opened to turn on the internal activities of the cells' cytoplasm (and even their genes). The neurotransmitters of the autonomic nervous system, the hormones of the endocrine system, and, as we shall see later, the immunotransmitters of the immune system, all function as "messenger molecules" or keys that open the receptor locks on the surface of the cells. *This messenger molecule and cell-receptor communication system is the psychobiological basis of mind-body healing, therapeutic hypnosis, and holistic medicine in general.* If each cell of the body is like a miniature factory, its receptors are locks on the doors. The autonomic, endocrine, immune and neuropeptide systems are communication channels whereby mind may activate genes and the internal cellular machinery. The genes, of course, are the ultimate blueprints for building, organizing, and regulating how the cellular machinery works.

Incredible as this may seem, we already have some understanding of a number of the psychobiological routes by which mind modulates gene action. We touched upon Melnechuk's (1985) view of how mind could modulate gene action via the limbic-hypothalamic-*autonomic* system route in the last chapter. In the next section we will outline a more well-documented route by which mind can modulate gene activity via the limbic-hypothalamic-*endocrine* system.

The Mind-Gene Communication via the Endocrine System

When I first began to discuss the *mind-gene connection* (Rossi, 1985) as a means by which hypnotherapeutic approaches could be developed to modulate gene activity, my conjectures were greeted as a novel form of science fiction. Genes seem so inviolate, with 100,000 or so of them apparently carefully guarded within the microscopic nucleus of each living cell of the body. We usually think of genes as resting quietly until the chromosomes suddenly spring into action in the process of cell division. The actual facts are quite different: Many genes are in a process of continuous, dynamic equilibrium with cellular metabolism. This genetic-cellular equilibrium is, in turn, modulated by neurotransmitters and hormones that ultimately come as messengers from the central nervous system.

To understand how the mind-gene connection could possibly work we need to understand the fundamental difference between *alterations in the structure of genes* and the *modulation of gene expression*. Alterations in the structure of genes is an evolutional event based upon mutations that are errors in copying the chemical structure of the gene; Western science maintains that mind has absolutely nothing to do with such mutations in the structure of genes. The modulation of gene expression, however, involves the turning on and off of certain genes by many environmental stimuli such as light, temperature, food, and *psychosocial cues such as stressful life situations* (Lloyd & Rossi, 1992a, b). These environmental stimuli and psychosocial cues are mediated by the same hormones and secondary messengers which encode the state-dependent processes of mind and behavior as illustrated in Figure 8.

A general model of the mind-gene connection requires a survey of the entire series of transduction processes that take place from mind and neural events, to blood, tissue, and cellular processes, and finally to the molecular activity of genes within the nucleus of each cell. In Figure 8 this transduction process is divided into three stages.

Stage one consists of mind operating in the area of the anterior frontal cortex (Achterberg, 1985) as the generative locus for organizing imagery in healing and health. These frontal lobe processes are then filtered through the individual's repertory of experiential life learnings encoded in state-dependent memory, learning, and behavior processes of the limbic-hypothalamic system.

Stage two is the transduction of these learnings by the hypothalamus into the hormone-releasing factors that regulate the endocrine's pituitary gland (see Figures 6A and 6B, p. 144). The pituitary in turn releases a host of hormones which regulate the entire endocrine system of the body, as illustrated in Figure 8.

Stage three takes place on the cellular level when these hormones turn on the secondary messenger cAMP system or pass directly to the nucleus of the cell to activate gene processes. Genes are involved in providing the information for building new proteins, which in turn serve as (1) structural elements of the cell, (2) enzymes that facilitate the basic biochemical process of each cell, and (3) messenger molecules and new cell receptors. Some of these messenger molecules are released from cells into the blood stream where they may find their way to the brain to encode state-dependent memory, learning, and behavior (SDMLB).

This is the three-stage process which I term the *mind-gene connection*. Let us now review an example of this process at the cellular level to illustrate how thyroid and steroid hormones, modulated by mental stress, actually regulate gene action.

Mind modulates gene activity via the cortical-limbic-hypothalamic-pituitary axis, which, as we have seen, is a basic information transduction route for psychosomatic processes. The pituitary sends hormones to glands such as the adrenal cortex and the ovaries and testes, which in turn secrete steroid hormones that penetrate into the cells and direct the genes to synthesize proteins. These proteins then function as structural elements, enzymes, or vehicles that activate other cellular functions. The sequence of information transfer within the cell runs somewhat as follows.

1) While most hormones require a special receptor mechanism on the cell wall to initiate the process of transfer into the cell, the steroid hormones have a special ability to pass directly into the cytoplasm within the cells.
2) Once within the cell, the steroid hormone enters the cytoplasm (the basic matrix of the living substance of the cell) where it binds with a *specific receptor protein*.
3) This hormone-receptor protein complex is then able to move into the nucleus of the cell where the genes reside.
4) The hormone-receptor complex undergoes transformations that activate a specific set of structural genes on the DNA strand to form "messenger RNA."
5) The messenger RNA then diffuses through the nucleus back into the cytoplasm, where it serves as an information template that tells the ribosomes ("factories" of the cells) how to sequence a series of amino acids into new peptides and proteins. Many of the peptides formed in this manner facilitate communication within the cell as well as between cells, tissues, and the autonomic, endocrine, and immune systems.

Figure 8 illustrates how hormones modulated by mind ultimately influence gene activity in a way that is significant for three levels of behavior: (1) thyroid hormone regulation of our basal metabolism and general level of activity; (2) androgen (testosterone) hormonal regulation of sexual and aggressive behavior; and (3) the stress-mediating effects of adrenal cortical hormones (e.g., aldosterone) on kidney function. Each follows the type of five-stage sequence outlined above, with significant variations as illustrated in Figure 8.

Thyroid hormones play a vital role in regulating the metabolic processes of practically all the tissues of the body. General levels of body activity, emotional tension, and health are all a function of how the thyroid regulates the metabolic machinery of the cells. It is now known that the thyroid operates by acting directly upon the genetic material within the nucleus of each cell. One of the proposed mechanisms by which its hormones enter the cell is illustrated in Figure 8. After entering the cell, one of the thyroid hormones (triiodothyronine, or T3) binds to a cytoplasmic protein (CP) that concentrates it. T3 then binds directly to receptors on the nuclear membrane to gain entry to the genetic material. Messenger RNA (mRNA) is then generated and transported out to the cytoplasm, where it is used as a template by the ribosome "factories" located on the endoplasmic reticulum (ER) to produce the proteins and enzymes characteristic of the cell's functions. T3 can also bind to receptors on the mitochondria of the cell to mediate energy, oxygen, and other metabolic functions.

Androgens. Testosterone is an example of an androgen hormone from the endocrine system that regulates sexual libido. It has been implicated in a wide range of behaviors ranging from normal assertiveness to criminal aggression. It enters the cells and operates directly upon the genetic material by following the general five-stage paradigm described above, with the variations illustrated in Figure 8. After testosterone enters the cells, it is converted into dihydrotestosterone (DHT), which is accepted by the receptor on the nuclear membrane and transported to the genetic site of action. Again, mRNA is produced and enters the cytoplasm to guide the formation of new proteins for the androgen actions of cell growth, and so forth.

The sexual hormones that facilitate information transduction from mind to gene comprise some of the most complete cybernetic psychobiological systems known to date. Since psychotherapy and hypnosis are well-known for their use as modulators of sexual behavior, we would expect that the crucial experiments relating sexual imagery to molecular responses at the cellular level could be explored in this area. The dramatic effects of the sexual hormones on the state-dependent encoding of cognition and behavior are not generally recognized. However, Ben Johnson, for example, was caught using male steroids illegally to enhance his athletic performance in the 100-yard dash in the Olympics at Seoul, Korea. Of the hundreds of articles published about this incident and the bizarre patterns of behavior associated with steroid use by athletes around the globe, however, not one referred to this as an example of state-dependent memory, learning, and behavior. But a moment's reflection will confirm this: When the male steroids are injected into the body, not only is athletic performance temporarily enhanced, but there are also significant changes in mood, memory, and behavior—more aggression, sexuality, and all sorts of high and low moods, and patterns of personality change. When the steroids are metabolized out of the body, the mood, personality, and performance changes return to normal; all the changes were reversible because they were state-dependent on the presence or absence of excess steroids.

Another significant report on sexual steroids is the finding of Hampson and Kimura (1992) that women's mental skills are modulated by the monthly shifts in their estrogen levels. It was found that when women experience low estrogen levels—during and immediately after menstruation—they excel at tasks involving spatial relationships but perform poorly at complex motor tasks, including some involving speech. In contrast, peak estrogen levels are associated with improved performance of motor and verbal tasks but difficulty with problems involving spatial relations. Peak estrogen levels occur briefly just before ovulation and again in the last 7 to 10 days before menstruation. These experimental findings come as striking confirmations of the role of state-dependent memory, learning, and behavior on consciousness and behavior (Rossi & Cheek, 1988). As in the case of Ben Johnson's lost gold medals, none of the published reports by Hampson and Kimura mention how these significant gender issues are examples of SDMLB in everyday-life.

Adrenal Hormones. Aldosterone is a hormone secreted by the adrenal cortex under the influence of stress. Aldosterone has many sites of action throughout the body. The effect of aldosterone on the renal tubular cells of the kidney are illustrated in Figure 8. The cytoplasm of the renal tubular cells contain a *specific receptor protein* that binds the aldosterone hormone and carries it to the genes to produce the new proteins. Within 45 minutes, the new proteins within the renal cells promote sodium reabsorption from the tubules and potassium secretion. This is an example of the vital "sodium-potassium pump" that is basic to many different systems of the body. A chronic excess of aldosterone and other hormones secreted by the adrenal cortex (e.g., cortisol), however, has been implicated in many forms of hypertension and in Selye's "Diseases of Adaptation."

Selye (1976, pp. 170–171) has listed the following "Diseases of Adaptation" due to stress: "high blood pressure, diseases of the heart and of the blood vessels, diseases of the kidney, eclampsia, rheumatic and rheumatoid arthritis, inflammatory diseases of the skin and eyes, infections, allergic and hypersensitivity diseases, nervous and mental diseases, sexual derangements, digestive diseases, metabolic diseases, cancer, and diseases of resistance in general."

It is beyond the scope of this volume to provide further detail about the incredibly complex psychobiological processes involved in each of these mind/body dysfunctions. Medical and psychological specialists are needed to focus on the details of each illness to elucidate the actual psychobiological processes involved. Once these are clarified, we can proceed to create the new hypnotherapeutic approaches of the future that will access and utilize the specific mind-body processes needed to facilitate healing. Current hypnotic approaches do not yet make use of what is outlined here regarding the mind-gene connection. As we learn to use these incredible advances in psychobiological understanding, a great renaissance of hypnotherapeutic suggestion and mind-body healing can take place.

THE WAVE NATURE OF CONSCIOUSNESS AND BEING

As indicated earlier, a salient though still generally unrecognized feature of the regulation of the endocrine system by the hypothalamic-pituitary-adrenal axis is the periodic nature of this regulatory process. We are all familiar with some of the basic rhythms of life: the monthly reproductive rhythm in women, the circadian (24-hour) rhythm of sleep and wakefulness, and the ultradian rhythms (1.5-hour) we began to explore in the last chapter. It is now recognized that all these rhythms are ultimately regulated by neuroendocrinal sources in the brain—primarily in the hypothalamus, the pituitary, and the pineal gland. There is also much to suggest that the entire life cycle of life and death is regulated by hormonal messengers. Since these life rhythms are regulated by the same hormones that modulate memory and learning, we can expect to find state-dependent memory and learning phenomena associated with all the interesting aspects of life we touch upon.

The endocrine system is mediated in a rhythmical manner by nerve centers in the hypothalamus. These "suprachiasmiatic nuclei" of the hypothalamus (Figure 5) function as biological "clocks" (Poirel, 1982) that regulate both the circadian and ultradian rhythms governing a variety of biological processes mediated by the autonomic and endocrine systems. In Chapter 7, I described how ultradian rhythms modulate autonomic nervous system activity. Here I describe how ultradian and circadian rhythms regulate endocrine system activity. Because there are many mind-body functions that are modulated by both the autonomic and endocrine systems (such as stress reactions and activity levels), some of the material of this chapter will overlap with and extend the concepts presented earlier.

Dement and Kleitman (1957) found that a 90- to 120-minute ultradian rhythm was a "basic-rest-activity-cycle" (the BRAC hypothesis) which ran continuously throughout the 24-hour day. In his monumental work on sleep and wakefulness, Kleitman (1963) concluded that this BRAC was due to an endogenous oscillation that had profound implications for physiology and behavior. One implication can be found in the typical pattern of our work-day activity, which appears to fall into 90-minute ultradian rhythms: Begin work at 9:00 a.m.; take a break midmorning, around 10:30 a.m.; have lunch 90 minutes later at noon; return to work at 1:00 p.m. and have mid-afternoon break at 2:30 or 3:00 p.m.; then cocktail time, dinner time, and so forth. Even during sleep, a prominent ultradian rhythm is found in the 90- to 120-minute periodicity of dream (REM) sleep. In a recent summary of ultradian cycle research, Kripke noted how many of these behavioral and psychological processes are associated with endocrine metabolism as follows (1982, p. 336):

> The wealth of phenomenology which has been uncovered in pursuit of the BRAC hypothesis should console any investigator troubled that the hypothesis remains controversial. Dramatic behavioral cycles have been discovered, both in man and lower primates, and perhaps these cycles have important ethologic functions. Cycles in fantasy, hemispheric dominance, and perceptual processing have been described. The significance of these cycles in both normal and pathologic psychologic functioning deserves our attention. *Episodic hormone secretion seems to be a fundamental property of endocrine metabolism, and it is somehow related to the REM cycles.* The suggestion that the pituitary is only responsive to intermittent releasing hormone stimulation is particularly exciting, for it suggests one way in which ultradian cycles may be a functional necessity. (Italics added)

Figure 9 illustrates some of the noteworthy phases of the wave nature of consciousness and being. We tend to have optimal *performance peaks* every hour and a half or so as the BRAC reaches its maximum. These performance peaks alternate with brief 15- to 20-minute periods of "rest" that I call "the ultradian healing response." That period in mid-afternoon around 3:00 or 4:00 p.m. when most people feel a more noticeable slow-down in their mental and physical activity level has been called "breaking point" (Tsuji & Kobayashi, 1988). Throughout the en-

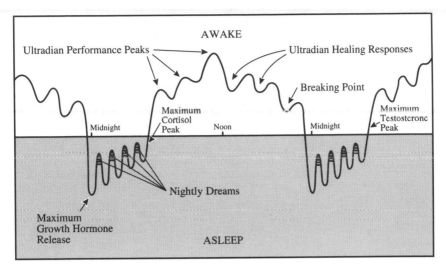

FIGURE 9 The wave nature of consciousness and being. An idealized illustration of the alternating character of our natural ultradian performance peaks, healing responses, and dreams.

tire circadian cycle there are a series of synchronized ultradian rhythms of varying periodicities in the release of many hormones of the endocrine system as indicated in the partial listing of Table 5 (Brandenberger, 1992; Veldhuis, 1992). As illustrated in Figure 9, growth hormone has a circadian peak about an hour and a half after going to sleep; cortisol has its peak just before awakening; and testosterone, right after awakening.

The entire neuroendocrine system is now well-recognized as having prominent ultradian and circadian components related to a variety of psychobiological behaviors associated with mental and physical activity, nutrition, metabolism, and reproduction. There are experimentally verifiable 20-minute couplings between peaks of associated hormones that are released in approximately 90- to 120-minute ultradian rhythms: Luteinizing hormone peaks lead prolactin and testosterone peaks by 10 to 20 minutes (Veldhuis et al., 1987; Veldhuis & Johnson, 1988; Veldhuis, 1992); insulin leads glucose by 15 to 30 minutes (van Cauter et al., 1989); cortisol leads β-endorphin by 20 to 30 minutes (Iranmanesh et al., 1989b). Aldosterone oscillations appear to follow periodicity in plasma renin activity (PRA) with a 20-minute delay (Brandenberger, 1992). These periodicities do not have the regularity of clocks but appear, rather, to be complex rhythms intimately associated with adaptive re-

TABLE 5 The ultradian release of some of the major hormones of the mind-body messenger molecule system

HORMONE	HALF-DURATION (MIN)	PULSES/DAY	FUNCTION
ACTH	19	40	Activity/stress
β-Endorphin (I)	—	13	Relaxation
Cortisol	16	19	Activity/stress
Follicle stimulating hormone	6	13	Maturation, reproduction
Gonadotropin releasing hormone (K & H)	—	24	Maturation, reproduction
Growth hormone	25	12	Growth, healing
Insulin (S)	~60	~12	Energy, glucose level
Luteinizing hormone	6–10	21	Maturation, reproduction
Melatonin (B)	Variable	~20	Sleep
Prolactin	45	20	Milk production
Parathyroid hormone (P)	~22	~12	Bone formation
Testosterone (V)	—	12	Male sex function
Thyroid stimulating hormone	70	20	Metabolism

These data are summarized from Veldhuis, 1992; with additions from Brandenberger, 1992 (B); Iranmanesh et al., 1989 a, b (I); Knobil & Hotchkiss, 1985 (K & H); Simon, Brandenberger, & Follenius, 1987 (S); Veldhuis et al., 1987 (V). These pulses are averaged data that *do not* function with precision like biological clocks; they appear to be complex mind-body informational systems integrating behavioral adaptation with environmental signals in nonlinear patterns of dynamics (Prank et al., 1991).

sponses to environmental signals. Indeed, as Wever (Rossi, 1992e, p. 330) has noted recently in a summary of his lifetime of pioneering research in this area, "Yes, it is surprising—the extent of the interaction between information, social contact, and even imagination on the rhythms of mind and body."

These associations that extend from the molecular-genetic generation of these hormones at the cellular level to their expression at the neuroendocrine level and their interaction with the mind-brain processes of memory, learning, and behavior interacting with the outer environment can hardly be accidental. It has been hypothesized that they play a significant role in the cybernetic process of information transduction between gene and adaptive behavior in health and illness over the entire range of the wave nature of consciousness and being illustrated in an idealized manner in Figure 9 (Lloyd & Rossi, 1992a; Kaufmann, 1992; Rossi & Lippincott, 1992). A great deal of well-controlled psychobiological research will be needed to verify the hypothesis that the 20-minute ultradian healing response is in fact related to many of the 20-minute couplings between peaks of complementary hormones noted in Table 5. There is as yet no well-controlled research to support the speculation that the entrainment and utilization of these ultradian patterns of hormone release by mind-body approaches to healing can actually modulate their functions.

One of the most interesting recent theories about the genesis of psychosomatic problems is that *they result from the behavioral disruptions of the ultradian rhythms that modulate both autonomic and endocrine system functioning.* Orr, Hoffman, and Hegge (1974), for example, reported that most humans manifest a stable ultradian rhythm when under quiet conditions. When their subjects were overstressed with extended performance tasks (e.g., monitoring complex panel meters), however, their ultradian rhythms underwent major disruptions in amplitude and patterning. In association with earlier experimental work with rhesus monkeys, these investigators concluded that psychosomatic responses (heart rate alterations, gastritis, ulcers, asthma, dermatological problems) were a consequent of the continual disruption of the body's natural ultradian cycles. As is typical of psychosomatic problems arising from real-life stress, they found that there were highly individualized patterns in this disruption process: "The same stressor can produce quite different physiological and behavioral response patterns in different subjects . . . and there appears to be no simple relationship between a physiological response and specific behavioral response" (p. 1000).

Work by Friedman (1972, 1978) on oral drive rhythms in obesity-bulimia and by Friedman, Kantor, Sobel, and Miller (1978) on neurodermatitis provides further confirmation of the genesis of psychosomatic problems in the disruption of ultradian rhythms. This interruption of ultradian rhythms was accomplished by keeping experimental animals in continuous activity on treadmills—which is analogous to humans' disrupting their normal ultradian rhythms by not taking a rest break every 90 minutes or so.

The lack of determinism or specificity in psychosomatic illness has been a basic problem that has puzzled researchers and clinicians alike

(Weiner, 1977). Generally, individual differences in psychosomatic responses to the same stressor are attributed to vague genetic, constitutional, and conditioning factors (Selye, 1976). Our focus on the role of state-dependent learning and memory suggests a more exact answer to this problem of so-called "indeterminacy" in psychosomatic illness. As with all mind-body connections, psychosomatic problems are highly individualized expressions of the learnings and life experiences of each person that have been encoded as state-bound information and behavior. Because the sources of this state-bound information are not easily available to the associations and frames of reference of our habitual patterns of awareness, we tend to be amnesic for the reason underlying the problem.

The research on ultradian rhythms of the endocrine system suggests another nonspecific approach to psychosomatic problems that already may be the common denominator in many of the broadly used and frequently effective psychotherapeutic approaches generally described as hypnosis, autogenic training, meditation, relaxation training and the relaxation response (Benson, 1975, 1983a, b). Elsewhere (Rossi, 1982, 1986a) I have described how many of the behaviors associated with the rest phase of ultradian rhythms are identical with Erickson's behavioral observations of readiness for the "common everyday trance." This led to the hypotheses (1) that Erickson was actually using the rest phase of the ultradian rhythms to achieve deeply therapeutic trances; and (2) that self-hypnosis in particular could be most effective during this period (Rossi & Ryan, 1986).

I have summarized the relationship between the genesis of psychosomatic problems by the stress-induced disruption of the body's natural ultradian rhythms and their resolution via hypnosis as follows (Rossi, 1982, p. 26):

> The implications of this association between disruptions of the ultradian cycle by stress and psychosomatic illness are profound. If the major proposal of this section is correct—that therapeutic hypnosis involving physiological processes is actually a utilization of ultradian cycles—then we can finally understand in psychophysiological terms why hypnosis traditionally has been found to be an effective therapeutic approach to psychosomatic problems: *Individuals who override and disrupt their own ultradian cycles (by ignoring their natural periodic needs for rest in any extended performance situation, for example) are thereby setting in motion the basic physiological mechanisms of psychosomatic illness.* Most of this self-induced stress could be conceptualized as left-hemispheric processes overriding their ideal balance with right-hemispheric pro-

cesses and associated parasympathetic functions. *Naturalistic therapeutic hypnosis provides a comfortable state wherein these ultradian cycles can simply normalize themselves and thus undercut the processes of psychosomatic illnesses at their psychophysiological source.*

There are four basic hypotheses at the heart of this new conception of stress, healing, and the wave nature of consciousness (Rossi, 1992c; Rossi & Lippincott, 1992):

1) The timing and cyclic patterns of genetic processes at the molecular level are the ultimate source of all mind-body rhythms and the wave nature of consciousness.
2) All of the self-regulatory systems of the mind-body (e.g., the central and autonomic nervous systems, the endocrine, immune, and neuropeptide systems) are coordinated by and serve these genetic sources.
3) Stress is engendered when we chronically interfere with these natural mind-body rhythms and is a major etiology for psychosomatic problems.
4) Most of the holistic approaches to mind-body healing (e.g., meditation, hypnosis, biofeedback, imagery, body work, etc.) unwittingly utilize the ultradian healing response to normalize our mind-body rhythms to optimize health.

Simply experiencing a comfortable therapeutic trance can normalize our BRAC and its associated regulation of many endocrinal and autonomic system ultradian rhythms that control our basic metabolism. This normalization process can be regarded as the essence of the nonspecific approach to therapeutic hypnosis. In practical clinical work (Erickson & Rossi, 1979), there is always a balance between specific and nonspecific hypnotherapeutic approaches. As we gain increasing knowledge of each, we can proceed with greater confidence and effectiveness.

Taking a Break and the Common Everyday Trance: A Case Study

The following case reported to me by Connie Crosby, M.S.W., during her internship at the C. G. Jung Institute of Los Angeles, illustrates this point:

A middle-aged, Caucasian woman, whose major source of distress was a feeling of inadequacy in every respect, reported that she had gone to her doctor complaining of a strong, persistent smell of ammonia whenever she urinated. The doctor responded by telling her to cease wearing pantyhose and to wash her genital area more frequently. The patient was outraged because, as she said, the smell of ammonia was coming from an internal, not an external, source. How dare this doctor insinuate that she was not fastidious!

She then discussed a second source of discomfort for her, which centered around her secretarial job. She complained that she worked too hard and was not appreciated for it. She was very faithful about *"never"* leaving her desk. She stated, with evident pride, that she urinated before leaving for work and then not again until she returned home. In the next breath she castigated herself for her tendency to daydream and for her inability to concentrate upon the task at hand. Consequently, much of her time at work was unproductive.

Putting the two issues together, I asked her how much water she drank. She replied, "None! Water has not passed my lips for years. I hate it. Besides, if I drank water, I'd have to leave my desk—and who would answer the phone?"

I then explained that people require a break at least every 90 minutes in order to work efficiently. In addition, I suggested that the strong smell of ammonia might be due to a highly concentrated urine and that to heal her body she needed to drink 64 ounces of water daily. But, knowing the patient, I couched my statement in terms of improving her job performance: In order to eliminate daydreaming and work more effectively, she *had* to leave her desk for a few minutes every 90 minutes. She would then find herself returning to work with full concentration. One way to ensure that she made time for breaks was to drink water from a carafe she was to place on her desk. Her body would then remind her to get up by an urgent need to urinate. *To become a truly conscientious secretary, she had to urinate at least every 90 minutes!*

After objecting for a few minutes, the patient agreed to try my plan. Weeks later she reported that the smell of ammonia had disappeared entirely and that, oddly enough, she was actually enjoying her job. Furthermore, she had received a bonus and a compliment from her boss. To top it off, this lonely woman had also made a friend in the ladies' room at work; they have since gone to the movies together.

Overt hypnosis was not used in this case, nor was the patient told that she was experiencing the "common everyday trance" when she let herself take a break, drink, urinate, and daydream every 90 minutes. The simple reframing of "taking a break" into "increased work efficiency," however, introduced enough change to profoundly influence many levels of her functioning—all the way from the biochemical to the social. We will now review how ultradian rhythms can be used more specifically to enhance self-hypnosis and posthypnotic suggestion.

Self-Hypnosis Utilizing State-Dependent Learning in Ultradian Rhythms

I originally developed the ultradian approach to self-hypnosis by the curious route of trying to maximize the effectiveness of posthypnotic suggestion. One of Erickson's basic views about hypnotherapy was that posthypnotic suggestions were most effective when they were associated with "behavioral inevitabilities." It is inevitable that the patient will "wake up" soon, walk out of the office, go home, eat, sleep, dream, work, etc. Erickson would associate therapeutic posthypnotic suggestions with those inevitable daily behaviors mediated by the endocrine system that he felt were most personally meaningful for the individual patient (Erickson & Rossi, 1979). What could be more inevitable than the fact that everyone exercises his or her own unique pattern of slightly altered states via natural ultradian rhythms throughout the day? I have outlined a number of approaches for utilizing these slightly altered states (that Erickson called the "common everyday trance") to enhance the effectiveness of posthypnotic suggestion and self-hypnosis. All of these approaches depend on the state-dependent learning and memory aspect of giving suggestions and training during a specific period of the patient's natural psychobiological ultradian rhythms.

One of the simplest of these approaches is to notice during a clinical interview when the patient's behavior indicates that the rest phase of an ultradian rhythm is being experienced. As described in Chapter 5, the patient will appear to be in a quiet moment of reflectiveness or inner reverie: the body becomes immobile; reflexes such as eye blinking or swallowing may be slowed or absent; the eyes may manifest a "far away" look and simply close spontaneously for a moment or two; heart beat and respiration are slowed, and so forth. (See Rossi, 1986a, for a detailed discussion of the minimal cues indicating how the experience of this rest phase of the ultradian rhythms is similar to self-hypnosis.)

The essence of Erickson's "naturalistic approach" was to utilize this quiet moment for a hypnotic induction with a therapeutically motivating statement such as, "If it's okay for you to continue to explore that issue [or whatever] just as you are, your unconscious will let those eyes close as you continue comfortably." The therapist then simply observes with quiet expectancy. If the eyes do not close after a moment or two, another therapeutic alternative may be offered, such as, "But if there is another issue that is more important, you'll find yourself getting a little restless for a moment or two until it pops into your conscious mind."

These two statements taken together comprise a naturalistic and therapeutic double bind: Whichever alternative is chosen helps the patient move in a therapeutic direction. When the eye-closing alternative is chosen, one can be fairly certain that conditions conducive for state-dependent learning in hypnotherapy are being facilitated. Posthypnotic suggestions then can be associated with similar periods throughout the patient's normal day, when it is appropriate to "take a break and let your eyes close for a few moments to allow your unconscious to review what you need in order to continue your therapeutic progress."

Many people find that the rest phase of their ultradian rhythm is the best time to meditate or do self-hypnosis. An ultradian approach to self-hypnosis utilizes natural psychobiological rhythms that are more deeply rooted in the state-dependent matrices of personality than the artificially conditioned processes characteristic of all other methods. I recommend that patients simply close their eyes and tune into comfort, wherever it may be in their bodies. During such naturalistic rest periods I find it of value to avoid any form of verbal self-suggestion that might distort the self-healing needs of the total personality. I simply suggest that patients "allow your unconscious to do its own work in its own way."

I do recommend, however, that patients *wonder* how their unconscious will resolve whatever problem they want to deal with. *Wondering* is another of those words such as *comfort, relaxation,* and *sleep* that has a specific ideodynamic significance that goes well beyond the cognitive meaning. When we tune into comfort, relaxation, and sleep, we are facilitating state-dependent parasympathetic responses and the restorative and healing effects associated with them. I would hypothesize that the word *wondering* tends to facilitate a degree of dissociation from the person's habitual ego controls, which in turn may facilitate some of the creative and mythopoetic aspects of right-hemispheric processing. Since the right hemisphere has closer associative ties to the limbic-hypothalamic system, *wondering* may be used as a nonrational and nondirective approach to facilitating a healing relationship with one's unconscious processes. Wondering absent-mindedly about a personal problem during the comfort of a psychobiological ultradian rest period is a natural way of accessing and spontaneously reframing and resolving the state-bound encoding of the problem.

Since so many psychosomatic disorders have been found to be exacerbated by the psychobiological stress of disrupted ultradian rhythms, we can regard this form of naturalistic hypnosis as a general approach that could supplement any other orthodox form of treatment. I have discussed how lucid dreaming (LaBerge, 1985), lucid somnambulism, and profound self-therapeutic states of identity transformation are not uncommon among those who have practiced this naturalistic form of ultra-dian self-hypnosis (Rossi, 1972/1985).

CIRCADIAN RHYTHMS, THE ENDOCRINE SYSTEM, AND AFFECT DISORDERS

While the daily 24-hour sleep-awake rhythm has been studied exten-sively for decades, it is only recently that the human circadian system has been found to consist of at least two oscillating rhythms that are normally in a homeostatic relation to each other. One rhythm controls the daily regulation of temperature, cortisol secretion, and REM sleep. The other rhythm controls sleep and the endocrine hormones released during sleep, such as growth hormones and prolactic. Life conditions that disturb these rhythms lead to the breakdowns in optimal function-ing we associate with jet lag, work-shift alterations, and stress-induced changes in the sleep cycle.

One of the major theories of endogenous depression is that it is re-lated to phase disruptions between the two circadian rhythms. Four classical features of depression that could have their source in disrupted circadian phase sequencing are as follows (Wehr, 1982):

1) *Early morning awakening* in which one of the circadian rhythms is out of phase with the other in the day-night cycle;
2) *Diurnal variations in mood* wherein patients feel worse in the morn-ing after awakening and better in the evening just before bedtime;
3) *The cyclicity of mania and depression* with its associated state-depend-ent memory and learning features;
4) *The seasonality of mania and depression*, with depression usually occurring in the spring and mania occurring commonly in the summer.

Great variations in these characteristics are found in individual pa-tients and careful case studies are required to determine effective treat-ment by altering the timing of the sleep cycle, exposure to extra artificial light in the morning and evening, etc. The relationship between light and endogenous depression is traceable to the fact that there are sepa-rate neural channels linking the retina of each eye directly to these suprachiasmatic nuclei in the hypothalamus (Bloom, Lazerson, & Hof-stadter, 1985). These suprachiasmatic nuclei of the hypothalamus act as pacemakers for the entire endocrine system.

A more definite common denominator between the affect disorders mediated by the limbic-hypothalamic-pituitary-endocrine system and hypnosis is that they both involve state-dependent phenomena. It has been found that the cognitive processes of manic-depressive patients manifest typical state-dependent memory and learning characteristics. These patients were able to recall verbal information learned during their manic state better during their next period of mania; likewise, information learned during depression was recalled better when they were depressed again (Weingartner, Miller, & Murphy, 1977). Similar findings on "affect state dependency" have been found in normal volunteers and in depressed patients who were subjected to therapeutic alterations of their mood and biological rhythms through sleep deprivation (Weingartner & Murphy, 1977). These findings have led clinicians to explore the clinical implications for state-dependent learning in psychotherapy (Reus, Weingartner, & Post, 1979).

A popular hypnotherapeutic method that we can now recognize in retrospect as contingent upon such affect state dependency encoded by endocrine system hormones (McGaugh, 1983; Izquierdo, 1984) is what Watkins has called the "affect bridge." In an exploration of the history of problematic emotions and ego states, Watkins (1978, 1980) had his patients "go back in time to when you last experienced that emotion." When a series of memories is recalled through this affect bridge, one arrives at the forgotten traumatic source of a personality problem that had previously been unavailable to the patient. The affect bridge functions as a state-dependent pathway to the encoded source of a problem that can now be accessed and reframed therapeutically.

RITUAL AND THE BODY THERAPIES IN THE SPECTRUM OF MIND-BODY HEALING

The most widely practiced approach to mind-body healing since ancient times is the use of mysterious rituals, touch, and the various forms of massage. Hypnosis in its early days of "animal magnetism" was associated with touch by making rhythmical "passes" over the patient's body (the therapist's hand would lightly stroke or in some cases not even touch but hover over the patient's body) in one direction for about 15–20 minutes to induce profoundly deep trances and then in the opposite direction to awaken the patient from trance. The English surgeon, James Esdaile (1808–1959), became famous for performing surgical amputations with this form of hypnotic anesthesia on the natives of India who believed in him, but this approach did not work as well back home where people were more skeptical. Sigmund Freud began his neurological practice by placing his hand on his patient's forehead with the authoritative injunction to go into trance.

It would certainly raise an incensed hue and cry among the practitioners of the many present day proprietary schools of ritual, touch, massage, and "body work" to assert that they are simply inventing new circumstances for accessing the idiosyncratic state-dependent encoding of mind-body symptoms and their "release and healing" by the various forms of "letting go." But that may be only because they have not read and really understood our cultural history of pre-scientific mind-body healing (Edmonston, 1986; Ellenberger, 1970; Tinterow, 1970; Zilboorg & Henry, 1941). Throughout human history in most cultures and times there have always been ritualistic practices where the medicine person or spiritual authority has achieved healing effects by touch, a glance (the healing or evil eye), smoke, incense, music, chanting, drums, and movements and rhythms of all sorts that succeed in activating state-dependent expectations of healing. In the carnival atmosphere of some current-day TV evangelists I was amused recently to see how one fellow simply took off his jacket (it was hot that night) and, almost in exasperation, waved it at an audience volunteer; she promptly swooned at this wonderful attention and presumably awakened a bit later with a feeling of spiritual healing. It is easy for charlatanism to enter the unending stream of such bizarre practices, because in any large group of people there are bound to be some whose state-bound symptoms will be accessed and sometimes healed to some degree or other by whatever combination of circumstances and stimuli are presented by the so-called "healing ritual" when there is a sincere expectation of healing.

The popular press regularly produces articles that promise all sorts of healing from backaches to migraines and more based on the purported release of endorphins, etc., with touch and deep tissue or organ massage, but it is difficult to track down believable research in reputable scientific journals. Moll (1898, p. 128) discussed some of the earliest efforts to measure the molecular basis of hypnosis associated with bodily states of stillness (ambiguously termed "catalepsy," which has many forms ranging from muscle rigidity to apparently deep relaxation associated with prolonged mesmerism and massage) with these words:

Some special investigations have been made of the organic changes during hypnosis, but no sort of conclusion can be drawn from them in any case. Brock finds that in a short hypnosis of twenty minutes duration, with partial catalepsy, the sum of the solid constituents and the phosphoric acid decreases [in urine samples]; as Strubing has described in catalepsy. But as Brock forgot to examine his patients under analogous circumstances, sitting quietly without hypnosis, his experiments are not conclusive.

This early recognition of the need for control groups in studies of the apparently quiescent body states of hypnosis is being well heeded by current researchers, but a controlled replication of this particular research with phosphoric acid in the urine is yet to be done a hundred years later!

More recently, Ida Rolf, the founder of the school of body work known as "structural integration," reported the following:

> . . . all basic structural changes induced by Rolfing find immediate expression in the chemistry of the body. Even the difference resulting from a single hour of work show consistent alteration in blood and/or urine constituents. Naturally the ten-session program, which brings about a permanent postural improvement, shows a more predictable and more stable alteration in chemistry. Determinations taken from samples at the beginning, middle and end of the ten-session series have been made in thirty cases. In addition to the routine urine tests, blood counts, stool cultures, etc., many other types of indices have been used: blood cholesterol, blood enzymes, redox potential, protein-bound iodine, and various proteins, including albumin-globulin ratio. All of them told the story of an immediate and lasting shift in the hemostatic equilibrium. (Kogan, 1980, p. 95)

The lack of experimental controls, cross-validation, and replication makes such claims as difficult to understand as the reports of Moll one hundred years ago.

Fortunately the situation may be changing as more molecule-wise researchers design research models of mind-body therapies that can be replicated. A well-controlled recent study by Tiffany Field et al. (1993) with 72 children and adolescents hospitalized with a range of disorders from depression to acting-out behavior found that a half-hour back rub daily led to reductions in depression and anxiety. These subjects had lower levels of the stress messenger cortisol in their saliva and significantly lower levels of urinary cortisol and norepinephrine. In a related study these researchers found that a 20-minute massage during the lunch break led hospital personnel to perform better on math tests than their co-workers. But the stress messenger molecules are only one of many classes of mind-body messengers that need to be explored. It is now known, for example, that cells of the endothelium (lining the blood and lymphatic vessels) as well as fibroblasts (cells of the connective tissue of the body) release messenger molecules of the immune system such as interleukin-2 (see the discussion of Figure 11 in the next chapter). Is it really too far-fetched to hypothesize that some forms of tissue massage could modulate release of such messenger molecules of the immune system to mediate some of the purported therapeutic effects of "body work"? Is it not possible that a mother's comforting touch, stroking, and hugging of a child is associated with the modulation of messenger molecules in the endocrine and immune systems of both of them? But why should therapeutic touch be so limited? Would we not expect similar effects in loving contact between consenting adults or even a warm handshake between strangers? It is only in answering such questions that a true therapeutic science of mind-body healing associated with cultural rituals and touch can emerge in the future.

Transformations in Women's Consciousness: The Role of Hormonal Rhythms

We have seen how hormones from the endocrine system are fundamentally involved in the modulation of memory, learning, and consciousness itself. Since there are so many hormonal changes during a woman's monthly reproductive cycle and during pregnancy, childbirth, and nursing periods, we would expect that some state-dependent phenomena would become manifest. While a recent computer search on the relationship between menstruation and pregnancy, on the one hand, and memory, learning, emotions, attitudes, and behavior changes, on the other, produced hundreds of references, none was focused specifically on state-dependent phenomena. A careful reading of these papers, however, reveals many state-dependent effects that were not recognized as such by the authors (Becker, Breedlove, & Crews, 1992; Hampson & Kimura, 1990a, b). In this section we will review only a few of the hormonal rhythms that are known to produce subtle but significant effects on the creative transformation of women's consciousness.

Progesterone and Endorphin in the Monthly Cycle

One of the first reports of such effects involves the hormone progesterone, which was found to facilitate state-dependent behavior (Stewart, Krebs, & Kaczender, 1971). Large quantities of progesterone are released monthly when it is necessary to increase the blood supply to the uterine wall to prepare for the egg's implantation if pregnancy should occur. Progesterone is also a messenger molecule that normally is involved in feedback to the pituitary, which it signals to inhibit the secretion of luteinizing hormone when the ovulation process is completed. Since progesterone has been shown experimentally to produce state-dependent effects, it is at least theoretically possible that its shifting concentration in a woman's body could modulate memory, learning, attitudes, emotions, and personality.

β-endorphin, which is one of the neuropeptide hormones of the endocrine system most strongly associated with endogenous state-dependent effects (Izquierdo, 1984), has been implicated recently in the regulation of luteinizing hormone in women with normal periods (Blankstein et al., 1981). The investigators hypothesize that stress-related distortions in the central nervous system release of β-endorphin are related to amenorrhea (lack of menstruation), and perhaps other menstrual disorders such as premenstrual syndrome (PMS) and dysmenorrhea (painful menstruation).

Hypnotherapy has a long history of successful intervention in menstrual disorders (Crasilneck & Hall, 1985). Leckie (1964) reported that in 25 cases of dysmenorrhea, 80 percent of the patients were freed of the symptom, usually with the presentation of simple, direct suggestions. Erickson (1960b/1980) employed more complex psychodynamic approaches to resolving many forms of menstrual distress that served important psychological needs in women. He reported that menstruation could be skipped, precipitated, interrupted, or prolonged as a function of emotional stress. Crasilneck and Hall (1985) believe that, quite apart from psychodynamic factors, the effectiveness of therapeutic hypnosis in dealing with a variety of menstrual disorders "may lie in calming the patient and allowing more normal functioning of the usual hypothalamic regulation of the menstrual cycle" (p. 361).

Oxytocin and Memory of Labor

Oxytocin is a hormone that is released from the uterus in massive amounts during labor. It is also secreted by the posterior pituitary to modulate lactation and maternal behavior. It is interesting to note that two basic hormones released by the posterior pituitary apparently have opposite effects on memory: vasopressin, as was outlined earlier, has an enhancing effect on memory and learning; oxytocin has the reverse effect in producing amnesia. This effect of oxytocin is regarded by some researchers (Weingartner, 1986) as responsible for the amnesia that usually cloaks a woman's memory of her experience of giving birth.

Many women feel cheated by this memory loss of one of the most significant experiences of their lives, and have consulted hypnotherapists for help in recovering their memory of the event. One such hypnotherapeutic effort was recorded and published in verbatim detail by the author (Erickson & Rossi, 1979, pp. 282–313). The remarkable feature of this case was that as the woman gradually recovered bits and pieces of her memories of giving birth to her child, she spontaneously reorganized her own personal identity. She recovered many earlier traumatic and amnesic memories that had become associated with the process of giving birth. She experienced a spontaneous personality maturation with the retrieval of the lost memories. This is a clear example of the guiding psychobiological premise of our approach as discussed in Chapter 5: *Every assess is a reframe*. In this case, the reframe involved a profound transformation in the woman's consciousness of herself as a total person.

Postpartum Depression

A recent critical analysis of the scientific literature on postpartum depression (Hopkins, Marcus, & Campbell, 1984) indicates that there are three distinct varieties of it:

1) *Postpartum Maternity Blues.* This is apparently a short-lasting depressive alteration in mood that lasts from 24 to 48 hours. It occurs in 50 to 80 percent of women and is characterized by episodes of tearfulness and crying that may be associated with poor sleep (with its consequent alterations in the circadian rhythms discussed above), stress, irritability, and anger.
2) *Postpartum Depression.* About 20 percent of women experience mild to moderate depressive episodes that can last six to eight weeks after giving birth, though the condition may persist for a year in some.
3) *Postpartum Psychosis.* This is a relatively rare reaction that occurs after one in a thousand births.

Because of the profound neuroendocrinal changes that take place during childbirth and parturition, many researchers have postulated a biological basis for these disorders. The wide prevalence of the maternity blues suggests that it is a "normal" psychobiological response. An association between menstrual problems and postpartum depression, however, suggests that women who have difficulty in physiologically compensating for the relatively minor hormonal changes of the menstrual cycle or who are biologically hypersensitive to subtle endocrinological changes, will have even greater difficulty adjusting to the dramatic decrease in placental steroid output during parturition (Dalton, 1971). The tremendous variability in individual reactions to the life stress of the entire birth process suggests the importance of considering the role of attitude, understanding, and social support in these depressive episodes.

A Psychobiological Hypothesis of Personality Transformation in Women

One of the most peculiar myths among some psychoanalysts of the past generation was that when a woman in analysis became pregnant, the analysis might as well cease. It was believed that during pregnancy women would take an artificial "flight into health" and so be resistant to the hard work of undoing psychodynamic repressions. It took me many years to overcome this pejorative view of the situation. Indeed, women do experience profound emotional and personality shifts during pregnancy, but the shifts can involve a truly valuable and nonresistant process of permanent personality transformation and maturation.

The psychobiological perspective suggests an unexpected and highly controversial hypothesis that could be misunderstood and abused all too easily. I will state it nonetheless: *The pervasive hormonal shifts women experience during their critical periods of psychobiological transformation (puberty, menstruation, pregnancy, childbirth, nursing, menopause) lend a certain flexibility to their state-dependent memory, learning, attitudes, and emotional systems, so that they may be more open and available to personality change and transformation during these periods.* As is always the case with change, it can be for good or ill. When the change is unsupported and misunderstood, it can lead to maladaptation, depression, and illness; when the change is welcomed as an opportunity for personality growth and transformation, a more adequate state of consciousness and development can take place (Rossi, 1972/1985).

There is a vast and interesting literature on the role of traditional customs, rituals, and symbolism as support systems for women during their critical periods of psychobiological transformation (Brown & Graeber, 1982; Harding, 1955; Markowitz, 1985). It remains as a fascinating possibility for future research to explore how this psychobiological perspective can be used for facilitating feminine psychology. Moreover, its counterparts in masculine psychology may be even more subtle.

THE PSYCHOBIOLOGY OF RELATIONSHIP

Interest is developing in the role of psychobiological rhythms in relationships. Some investigators have suggested that the synchronization of biological rhythms in men and women could facilitate relationships. Leonard (1981), for example, has described relationship exercises that have been used to teach couples to synchronize rhythms. Circadian and ultradian research suggests that partners who work, eat, and sleep together find that their biological rhythms are in "sync," so that they are often in the mood to make love together as well. When partners are stressed so that their work, eating, and sleeping rhythms are askew, however, their relationship can suffer greatly (Chiba, Chiba, Halberg, & Cutkomp, 1977).

BIOLOGICAL CLOCKS AND THE AGING PROCESS

Recent theoretical developments in the study of the aging process have emphasized how biological clocks of the hypothalamus operate by modulating the activity of the autonomic, endocrine, and immune systems. Since the hypothalamic-pituitary-endocrine axis plays the predominant role in most of these theories, however, we will supplement our previous discussion of the aging process (Chapter 4) (Sapolsky, 1992a) by focusing on other aspects here.

Walford (1983) has integrated much of the experimental data on aging into a comprehensive three-stage theory that corresponds very closely to the three levels we have used to organize our overviews of mind-body communication in Figures 7 (p. 162) and 8 (p. 187) and will use in Figures 10 (p. 219) and 11 (p. 221) as well. It will be helpful to summarize our three levels of mind-body communication as an introduction to discussion of Walford's theory. Our three levels are as follows:

1) The basic mind-body transducer is the limbic-hypothalamic system of the brain.
2) Messenger molecules (neurotransmitters and hormones) are the vehicles for communicating information between all the major systems of mind-body regulation (the autonomic, endocrine, immune, and neuropeptide systems) and their central integration and control center in the limbic-hypothalamic system.
3) The limbic-hypothalamic system ultimately modulates the biochemical processes at the genetic and molecular levels within each living cell of the body.

Walford's theory of the aging process uses a similar outline as follows (1983, pp. 89–92):

> One theory holds that the "clock" of aging lurks in the hypothalamus, a pea-sized area of brain a bit posterior to a spot mid-way between your ears. It regulates hunger, rage, sleep, sexual desires, and to some extent, development and aging. Dr. Caleb Finch at the University of Southern California has detected significant decreases in neurotransmitter chemicals in the hypothalamus from old compared to young animals. Released at a nerve ending and picked up by receptors on the adjacent nerve cell's surface, the neurotransmitters are a class of brain chemicals which transmit impulses from one nerve to the next. The hypothalamus and its transmitters regulate the pituitary gland hanging nearby from the base of the brain. When instructed to do so by the hypothalamus, the pituitary releases a bevy of important hormones such as growth hormone, ACTH, thyroid-stimulating hormone, and others. Hormonal variations programmed by the hypothalamus and carried out by the pituitary may induce the onset of aging, just as other variations within the same axis bring on puberty. . . .
>
> The endocrine system is altered with age not only in its primary hormone levels but in the numbers of receptors located at the surfaces of cell membranes, and within the fluid space inside the cell. Many hormones must first react with cell receptors in order for their message to influence the program of the cell. . . .
>
> The sequence is: hormone receptor → second messenger → cell nucleus → turning on of the appropriate genes. The loss of many types of receptors from the cells of old animals interferes with this progression.
>
> Notice that we are gradually progressing from a molecular level (like DNA repair) to a systems level. There may well be two kinds of aging clock, one in the brain's hypothalamus orchestrating growth and development, another in each individual cell, the two clocks roughly synchronized and providing what is designed to be a fail-safe system. I shall be outlining experiments at the systems level involving either the endocrine or immune machineries that lead to rejuvenation of many features of aging—but not to extension of maximum life span. A two-clock model might explain the reason for what appears at first sight a stubborn paradox.
>
> At a systems level the neuroendocrine and immune systems have been regarded, not necessarily as clocks, but as pacemakers for aging. The cause of aging is at a deeper, molecular level, but the way the molecular disarray manifests itself in sagging tissues, wrinkled skin, gray hairs, and declines in nearly all bodily functions is via the hormonal or immune systems, and probably both.

The prominent role of all the major hormones of the endocrine system is evident in Walford's theory of the aging process. His discussion of how the aging process can be slowed down in a practical manner emphasizes the biological role of exercise and nutrition in modulating the endocrine "pacemakers" of aging. Walford does not deal with the psychological implications of the fact that the biological clocks of the hypothalamus which regulate the endocrine system are so easily modified by our attitudes, thoughts, and emotions, as we have seen in this chapter. Although he recognizes the same three major levels of information transduction that are illustrated in Figures 7, 8, 10, and 11, Walford's focus is on the biological rather than the *psycho*biological.

As we have seen in previous chapters, research on stress is the principal way in which researchers have been able to measure the effects of psychological factors on the biological. Research on the psychobiology of aging uses this same route. Stress reduction is currently seen as the most practical psychological path to life extension (Groer, Shekleton, & Kant, 1979). Since the biological clocks of the aging process are located in the hypothalamus, it is natural to use the limbic-hypothalamic route as a psychobiological approach to facilitating life extension.

As indicated previously, Benson (1983a, b) has gathered extensive cultural and experimental data to support his view that the "relaxation response" in yoga, meditation, prayer, and hypnosis has its psychosomatic healing source in facilitating an integrated hypothalamic response that reduces stress. While Benson has emphasized the role of the hypothalamus in regulating the sympathetic branch of the autonomic nervous system, the data presented in this book indicate that a well-integrated hypothalamic response will also optimize the functioning of the endocrine, immune, and neuropeptide systems. Because all of these systems of mind-body communication are modulated by the biological clocks of the hypothalamus, the ultradian relaxation response outlined in Tutorial 13 (p. 216) may be the most practical, effective, psychobiological means we have at present for accessing and potentiating healing and rejuvenation of mind-body processes.

A well-integrated limbic-hypothalamic system response at the psychotherapeutic level means that we are marshalling the appropriate state-dependent memory, learning, and behavioral processes encoded by hormones of the endocrine system that are needed to facilitate restoration and healing. This is most simply accomplished by using whatever variation of the basic accessing formula is appropriate for a given clinical situation. The accessing formulas all seek to enhance a healing process of ideodynamic information transduction.

We may suppose that encoded in the limbic-hypothalamic system are experiential modes for optimal functioning, as well as the problematic

---

TUTORIAL 13 Naturalistic Self-Hypnosis:
The Ultradian Healing Response

1. *Recognizing and facilitating the ultradian healing response*
   **When you're tired, irritable, or simply feel the need to take a
   break, recognize it as a moment of opportunity to facilitate your
   natural ultradian healing response.**

2. *Accessing and utilizing inner resources*
   **Explore where the comfort is in your body. [Pause]
   Notice how it spreads and deepens, as you idly wonder about
   how your unconscious can utilize therapeutically your previous
   life experiences of optimal healing and being able to deal with current problems all by itself.**

3. *Ratifying continuing ultradian healing and coping*
   **After a while you'll notice that you're awake and aware of your-
   self, but somehow you were not a moment ago. You look at the
   clock and notice that 10 to 20 minutes have gone by that you cannot account for. Recognize the comforting, healing changes that
   have taken place and resolve to do this again, a few times a day,
   whenever you need to.**

---

patterns we have discussed. These optimal patterns are undoubtedly
associated with happy memories of health, well-being, joyful experiences, creative work, and effective coping. They are the *raw material* or
inner repertory of resources that our accessing formulas seek to utilize in
healing. The fundamental task for each individual is to learn how to
access and utilize his or her own unique inner repertory of psychobiological resources that can ultimately modulate biochemical processes
within the cell. In the following two chapters, we will review how current experimental and therapeutic work with the immune and neuropeptide systems is beginning to demonstrate the exciting possibility of
mind modulation of cellular responses to facilitate healing.

9

Mind Modulation of the Immune System

THE MOST RECENTLY researched, exciting, and complex mind-body relationship concerns the role of the central nervous system, early life experience, emotions, and learning in modulating the immune system.

Medical history has always taken note of the anecdotal evidence for the seemingly anomalous miracle cures and faith healings that have been reported from time to time (Ellenberger, 1970). Anthropologists have collected data on the healing rituals and practices of "natural medicine" that seemed a mixture of herbal and faith healing. Now researchers such as LeShan (1977), Achterberg (1985), and the Glasers (Glaser et al., 1990, in press-a, in press-b) have assembled empirical evidence pointing to the role of mind and belief in achieving these healing effects. Until recently there has been no systematic scientific approach to these issues. The research of Ader and the "new immunologists," however, has created an unprecedented bridge between mind and body: Their experimental research demonstrates how behavioral conditioning can inhibit or enhance immune system response (Ader, 1981, 1983, 1985; Ghanta, Hiramoto, Solvason, & Spector, 1985; Solomon, 1985).

The immune system has been recognized only recently as a third major regulatory system of the body, on equal par with the autonomic nervous system and the endocrine system. In this chapter we will outline just enough of the basic facts about the immune system to give us access to new ways of thinking about how hypnotherapeutic approaches to mind-body healing can be developed to facilitate its optimal functioning.

ANATOMY AND FUNCTIONS OF THE IMMUNE SYSTEM

The anatomy and functions of the immune system are simple to understand in a general way but incredibly complex and still mysterious in their particulars. Most textbooks begin by defining the immune system in terms of its function of resisting almost all types of invading organisms or toxins that could damage the body. There are two basic types of immunity: *innate* and *acquired*.

We are born with *innate immunity*, which provides a general, *nonspecific defense* against all invaders. The skin, along with the acid secretions and digestive enzymes of the stomach, provides a first line of innate immunity. The second line of defense is within the blood, where there are white blood cells and numerous molecules (e.g., lysosomes, basic polypeptides, and certain proteins) that can attack and destroy many types of invading pathogens. There seem to be as many ways of portraying an overview of the different types of white blood cells (also called *leukocytes*) as there are textbooks and research papers that try to do the job. The organization illustrated in Figure 10 is designed to emphasize the tissues and cell types that have been found responsive to psychosocial signals in the currently evolving area of psychoimmunology. One broad class of white blood cells called *phagocytes* (''cell eaters'') consists of cells such as *macrophages* (large eaters), *natural killer cells (NK)*, *neutrophils* that actually devour and remove a wide array of foreign invading organisms, cell debris, and intruding particles like asbestos, silica, and smoke.

Figure 10 illustrates some of the major tissues and cell types of the immune system that are directly or indirectly responsive to stress and psychosocial cues. A full description of the many specialized and overlapping functions of these cells in fighting disease is beyond the scope of this volume and are not shown (a general text of the molecular biology of the cell, such as Alberts et al., 1989, would be the next step for more detailed study). The currently emerging view in psychoimmunology is that apparently all of these tissues and cell types are in communication with each other as well as with the central nervous system, and the autonomic and endocrine systems through a variety of messenger molecules that have been given many general names such as *immunotransmitters, cytokines, lymphokines, interferons,* and *interleukins,* as well as more specific designations such as *interleukin 1 or 2 (IL-1, IL-2), interferon gamma, and tumor necrosis factor.*

The adult human has about 7,000 white blood cells per cubic millimeter of blood. There are many types of white blood cells, with typical percentages as follows: neutrophils, 62%; eosinophils, 2.3%; basophils, 0.4%; monocytes, 5.3%; and lymphocytes, 30%. In innate immunity it is mainly the neutrophils and monocytes that destroy invading bacteria, viruses, and other toxins. The neutrophils are the mature cells that

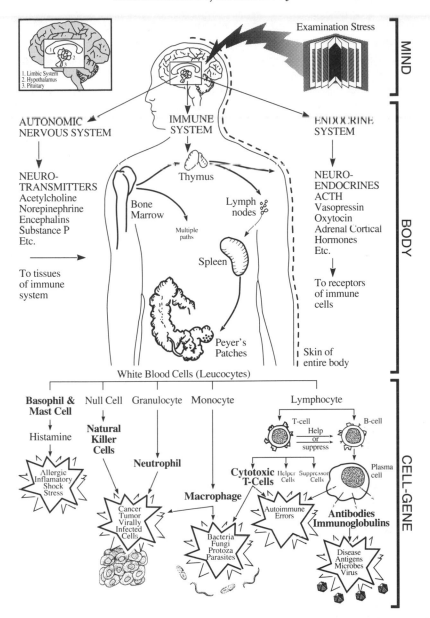

FIGURE 10 Some of the major communication loops between the mind-brain and the interacting networks of the immune system.

attack and destroy bacteria and viruses in the circulating blood. The monocytes are immature cells that initially have very little ability to fight pathogens in the blood. When they enter tissues near areas of injury, however, they increase their size fivefold (to 80 microns, so they can actually be seen with the naked eye): these newly enlarged cells, called macrophages, have a greatly increased capacity for combatting pathogens.

Immunologists acknowledge that all the cells that play an important role in the immune system have not yet been identified so we must regard the illustrations presented in Figures 10 and 11 as only provisional. The complexity of the immune system is heightened by the large number of messenger molecules it uses in the many levels of communication and control of the fast-paced life of its many components. The life span of many of its molecules is in a range between seconds, minutes, and hours while most of its cells have a lifetime of days. It has been estimated that one million lymphocytes are generated per second in humans (Perelson, 1988b). Recent advances in the development of the confocal microscope that uses lasers to image living cells are leading to entirely new perspectives of dynamic life at the level of the highly individualized cell that is very different from the traditional static textbook picture we are used to. Roger Tsien (1993, p. 10), a professor of pharmacology who has done pioneering research on the imaging of the messenger cAMP, for example, describes this new world view as follows:

> Traditional biochemistry, he says, involves "grinding up a couple million cells and running them out on a gel, or doing PCR [polymerase chain reaction] on a whole population," which is useful for ascertaining certain general attributes of that population, but obscures the activities of individual cells.
>
> "When you can see their individual biochemical signals," he says, "you find that different cells are often very individualistic, almost like wild animals, or people.
>
> "Even different parts of the cell have different biochemistry. The cell is not just a featureless bag. It knows which direction it's headed, so its front and its back have to be different, biochemically."

The communication processes engaged in by these "wild animals" is cybernetically balanced in a very delicate manner that is related to the psychosocial messenger molecules of the mind-brain's limbic-hypothalamic-pituitary-adrenal-immune system in ways that we are only now beginning to understand. One of the most important aspects of this communication process, as is typical of all other communication pro-

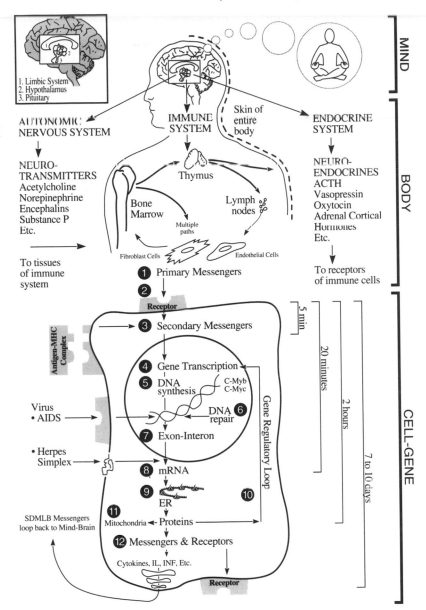

FIGURE 11 The mind-body-gene communication loop of the immune system with some of the major loci and approximate time parameters of information transduction at the cellular-genetic level.

cesses in nature and human devices (radio, TV, radar, etc.), is the relatively narrow bands in which it operates. Too much or too little *antigen* (the foreign molecules on bacteria, viruses, or cancer cells that signal the immune system into attack) can greatly effect how the immune system operates and the outcome of a disease process (Perelson, 1988a, b). The same is true of the concentrations and proportions of how all the messenger molecules of the immune system interact together, as we shall see later, particularly in the case of the interleukins and tumor necrosis factor. If we are to gain a deeper understanding of how the mind-body operates, we now need to learn how the psychoneuroimmune system operates as a communication process rather than a purely mechanical device.

Acquired or *adaptive immunity* is the ability of the body to develop very powerful and *specific defenses* against particular types of lethal bacteria, viruses, and toxins. Acquired immunity does not develop until the first invasion of a foreign substance, the antigen. Acquired immunity develops out of the process of recognizing antigens and creating two broad classes of defense against them: humoral and cellular immunity. Both types of immunity originate in the bone marrow, which produces *stem cells*.

Humoral immunity consists of stem cells from the bone marrow that mature into a type of white blood cell called *B-cell lymphocytes*. These are distributed throughout the lymph system of the body by the blood, as illustrated in Figure 10. The blood is continually filtered through these lymph systems (lymph nodes, spleen and Peyer's patches, etc.). If antigens are present in the blood, they stimulate the B-lymphocytes to evolve into plasma cells which can synthesize *antibodies* (large globulin molecules called *immunoglobulins*) with the specific ability to destroy that antigen. This detection system provides major defenses against viral and bacterial infections and is involved in the allergic reactions. There are five major classes of antibodies which have been named: IgA, IgD, IgE, IgG, and IgM. The *Ig* means immunoglobulin, while the other letters identify the class types. The role of the IgE antibody in producing allergic reactions will be discussed later.

Cellular immunity is developed when stem cells from bone marrow travel to the thymus gland, which matures them into T-cell lymphoctyes (sensitized white blood cells) that destroy the invading antigens directly. Some of these T-cell lymphocytes then travel to the skin via the blood; there the epidermis generates hormones that further facilitate T-cell maturation (Edelson & Fink, 1985). The skin over the entire surface of the body is thus an intrinsic part of the immune system. There are many forms of T-cells that can help or suppress other components of humoral and cellular immunity (Hokama & Nakamura, 1982; Waksman, 1985). At least three classes of T-cells have been found within the mind-cell-gene loop: (1) the *cytotoxic T-cells*, which can kill virus cells directly; (2) The *helper T-cells*, which secrete a variety of local mediators (cytokines or messenger molecules), such as the interleukins that help B-cells make antibodies; they also activate macrophages and other T-cells to proliferate; and (3) the *suppressor T-cells*, which serve the vital function of sending messengers to tell the helper T-cells to turn off when the immune emergency is over. Many of these immune components are open to psychosocial influences (Ader, 1983; Ader, Felten, & Cohen, 1991; Ghanta et al., 1985). Acquired immunity thus has a specific developmental history in each individual; its functions are therefore particularly subject to the influence of state-bound information acquired in early life experience.

EVIDENCE FOR THE MIND MODULATION OF THE IMMUNE SYSTEM

To understand how mind can influence the immune system, we need to view one more special aspect of how the T- and B-lymphocytes operate: They have receptors on their cell surfaces that can turn on, direct, and modify their immune functions. These receptors are the molecular basis of the influence of mind on the lymphocytes. Receptors, as mentioned previously, are like locks that can be opened to turn on the activities of each cell. As also discussed, the keys that open these locks are the messenger molecules of the mind-body: the *neurotransmitters* of the autonomic nervous system, the *hormones* of the endocrine system, and the *immunotransmitters* of the immune system. The form and structure of these messenger and receptor molecules, which must fit each other to turn on cellular activity, give us a profound insight into the essentially architectural nature of life and mind.

As we have seen in the previous chapters, mind regulates both the endocrine and autonomic systems in three stages. Figure 10 illustrates a similar path for the mind modulation of the immune system; however, there are additional complications, since the autonomic, endocrine, and immune systems can also modulate each other's activity. The thrust of the most recent thinking of immunologists is that the immune system can communicate back to the hypothalamus and the autonomic and endocrine systems via immunotransmitters. Nicholas Hall and his colleagues (Hall, McGillis, Spangelo, & Goldstein, 1985) have outlined this conception as follows (p. 806s):

An increasing amount of data supports the hypothesis that there are bidirectional circuits between the central nervous system (CNS) and the immune system. Soluble products that appear to transmit information from the immune compartment to the CNS include thymosins, lymphokines, and certain proteins. Opioid peptides, adrenocorticotropic hormone (ACTH), and thyroid-stimulating hormone (TSH) are additional products of lymphocytes that may function in immunomodulatory neuroendocrine circuits. It is proposed that the term "immunotransmitter" be used to describe molecules that are produced predominantly by cells that comprise the immune system but that transmit specific signals and information to neurons and other types of cells. . . . Certain thymosin peptides can serve as immunotransmitters by modulating the hypothalamic-pituitary-adrenal and gonadal axes. Considerable evidence . . . supports the hypothesis that the nervous system is capable of altering the course of immunity via autonomic and neuroendocrine pathways.

Figure 10 also lists some of the neurotransmitter and neuroendocrinal mechanisms by which other structures of the brain (e.g., sensory ganglia and pineal gland) may modulate immune function. Ader (1983) has summarized six types of experimental data that document mind-modulating influences on the immune system. I have updated his list to include more recent research with humans:

1) Neuronanatomic and neurochemical evidence for the innervation of lymphoid tissue (bone marrow, thymus, spleen, tonsils, Peyer's patches, lymph nodes, etc.) by the central nervous system (Bulloch, 1985). This means that mind (via the central nervous system) has direct neural access for modulating all these organs of the immune system.

2) The observations that inhibiting or stimulating the hypothalamus results in changes in immunologic reactivity, and, conversely, that activation of an immune response in the body results in measurable changes within the hypothalamus (Roszman, Cross, Brooks, & Markesbery, 1985; Stein, Schleifer, & Keller, 1981). Since the hypothalamus is regulated by higher brain centers (via connections with the limbic cortex), these intercommunications between the immune system and hypothalamus may be open to mind modulation.

3) The finding that lymphocytes bear receptors for hormones of the endocrine system and neurotransmitters of the autonomic nervous system (Cohn, 1985; Wybran, 1985). This means that all the mind-modulating effects of the autonomic and endocrine systems may

be communicated to the immune system as well. This conclusion is supported by the next point as well.

4) Evidence that alterations of hormone and neurotransmitter function modify immunologic reactivity and, conversely, that elicitation of an immune response is accompanied by changes in hormonal and neurotransmitter levels (Besedovsky, del Rey, & Sorkin, 1985; Hall & Goldstein, 1985).

5) Data documenting the effect of behavioral interventions, including conditioning, on various parameters of immune function in animals (Ader, 1985; Ader et al., 1991; Gorczynski et al., 1982) and the conscious voluntary immunomodulation of neutrophil adhesiveness in humans (Hall et al., 1992a, b).

6) Experimental and clinical studies in which psychological factors such as stress (Palmblad, 1985; Stein et al., 1985) and depression (Stein et al., 1985) have been found to influence the onset of disease processes.

7) Recent evidence of mind-gene communication in humans by experiments documenting how psychological stress can modulate the expression of IL-2 receptor gene expression and IL-2 messenger RNA in white blood cells (Glaser et al., 1990). Current data on the stress modulation of the protooncogenes *c-myb* and *c-myc* mRNA in human peripheral blood leukocytes (Glaser et al., in press-a).

8) Maclean and Reichlin (1981) and Smith (1991) review many indirect ways in which mind can modulate the immune response through changes in behavior. These include altered diet, circadian rhythms, sleep-wake cycles, body temperature, blood volume, and local vascular reactions.

9) The classical clinical reports by psychotherapists of the efficacy of using hypnosis for the amelioration and apparent disappearance of the recurrent type virus problems (Ewin, 1992; Gould & Tissler, 1984).

The ultimate task of the mind-body therapist is to learn how to access and utilize all these mind-body mechanisms. How far we are from actually doing this! Yet the well-documented research cited by Ader (1983) and Locke et al. (1984) concerning the influence of psychosocial factors, mood, and belief systems on illness, disease, and healing clearly indicates that the mind is continually modulating the immune system. What success mind-body therapy currently achieves in modulating immune function is via the nonspecific approaches that work to a certain degree (even spectacularly well in some cases), even though we usually do not know what the therapeutic mechanisms of action are. We can drive a car quite well without knowing how the engine operates, but when there is a breakdown, the more detailed our knowledge of engine mechanisms, the better we will be able to fix it. The present state of our psychotherapeutic knowledge of these mind-body mechanisms is somewhat akin to the average driver who knows there is an engine somewhere that does something when we turn on a key and push the gas pedal. However, currently there are a number of innovative research programs studying how mind modulation and hypnosis can influence specific features of the immune system. In the following sections we will review some of these programs to learn what they can tell us about developing new mind-body approaches to facilitating immunological functioning.

MIND MODULATION OF INNATE IMMUNITY

It is currently being demonstrated that the immune system can be influenced by mind methods with appropriate education and training. It will be recalled that neutrophils comprise almost two-thirds of the body's innate immunity of white blood cell defenses. Any means of potentiating their function would surely be a significant step in combatting disease. A recent doctoral dissertation study by Barbara Peavey (1982; Peavy, Lawlis, & Govern, 1985) investigated the effect of a training program designed to enhance relaxation by biofeedback (using EMG muscle relaxation and temperature biofeedback). She found that while the number of neutrophils remained the same, they were found to function significantly better with successful relaxation training.

An even more fascinating approach to facilitating neutrophil activity has been reported by Schneider, Smith, and Witcher (1984). They combined belief with imagery training to explore the relationship between imagination and the immune system. Students who *believed* they could consciously control their own immune system were first given information about how white blood cells functioned and shown microscopic slides of actual neutrophils, which were to be incorporated into their imagery training. They then listened to an audiotape with suggestions for relaxation and imagery. They practiced imagining and drawing pictures of their imagery, which were later objectively scored. After six sessions of such training, it was found that subjects could greatly increase or decrease the number of circulating neutrophils in their bloodstream.

Neutrophils could be described as the "wandering Samurai warriors" of the bloodstream. As mentioned earlier, neutrophils are an important part of the immune system's response to bacteria, viruses, and other injurious antigens that attempt to invade the body. They can attack foreign antigens even as they circulate in the blood. Neutrophils have a wide range of activities that enhance their abilities to reach and destroy antigens: They can migrate through the bloodstream to the locus of injury, change their shape, and then squeeze through the pores of the blood vessels to reach areas of tissue damage. This process of movement toward an area of injury is called *diapedesis*. Neutrophils may also adhere to the insides of the blood vessel by the process of *margination*. When tissues are invaded or damaged, they respond by creating an inflammation that tends to physically entrap the injurious agents so that they do not spread any further throughout the body. The inflamed area also diffuses chemical agents through the tissues that attract the neutrophils, thus causing them to stick to the sides of the capillary cell walls (margination) and then squeeze through the walls (diapedesis) to the source of inflammation.

In their analysis of four initial experimental studies, Schneider, Smith, and Witcher (1983, 1984) surmised that their imagery training exercises were influencing the process of margination in neutrophils. That is, the exercises were not increasing or decreasing the number of neutrophils per se in the body but, rather, were changing their movement and the potential loci of their immune system activity. As we shall see later in our discussion of asthma, this finding could have profound implications for using imagery and hypnosis to ameliorate hyperactive responses of the immune system in allergic reactions.

A more recent study by Hall et al. (1992b) confirms the ability of human subjects to voluntarily modulate their innate or nonspecific immunological competence with a "cyberphysiologic strategy" that utilized relaxation and the subjects' personally selected imagery to enhance neutrophil adhesiveness. This study is of particular interest because it found that specific imagery focusing on only one aspect of immune functioning (neutrophil adhesiveness) was able to enhance that function while leaving other immune parameters (such as neutrophil count, monocyte count, while blood cell count, and salivary IgA) unchanged. They describe their procedure for training their subjects as follows.

First, they were given a rudimentary explanation of neutrophils and the process of adherence. Second, during the 30-minute period between sample collections . . . subjects practiced a cyberphysiologic exercise which included concentrating on an image each subject devised to represent an increase in neutrophil adherence. For example, one subject imagined her neutrophils as ping pong balls with honey oozing out onto the surface of the balls causing them to stick to everything they touched. Subjects were requested to focus only on the neutrophil adherence parameter.

Confronted with statistically well-documented examples of the voluntary enhancement of a "nonspecific or innate" aspect of immune competence, both clinicians and researchers must ask, "But how can it be possible; what are the molecular pathways of mind-body communication in such cases?" The authors betray no clue; they simply note in summarizing the implications of their work:

> We recognize that these experiments must be validated by other groups and that subject-specific variables must be further studied. Based on these studies, we do not claim any therapeutic benefit for such brief interventions in healthy subjects. However, it is possible that when more variables have been defined, cyberphysiologic training may prove to be a useful strategy for persons with immune related disorders.

In terms of the theoretical approach being developed in this book, however, we can discern a number of recognizable features of the naturalistic and utilization approach outlined earlier (particular in Chapter 5). First was adherence to the basic principle of utilizing the subject's own personal imagery that presumably has been effectively encoding state-dependent memories and associations that make up the subject's "repertory of inner resources" that can be accessed for healing. Second, the 30-minute period of "cyberphysiologic exercise" falls within the expected parameters of 20 minutes plus or minus about 10 minutes that defines the ultradian healing response. Third, the messenger molecule epinephrine that is released during stress, physical exercise, and psychological trauma is known to produce elevated blood neutrophil counts. Fourth, it is well documented experimentally that epinephrine can encode state-dependent memory, learning, and behavior (SDMLB) in novel or stressful life situations in humans leading to the construction and reconstruction of memory (Izquierdo et al., 1988a, b).

Hall et al. note this connection between epinephrine and neutrophils but, unfortunately, did not measure epinephrine levels in this study. In a preliminary study by Hall et al. (1992a) the role of epinephrine is implicitly recognized in what they call the "paradoxical phenomenon of relaxation-induced anxiety" occasionally caused by increased psychological stress following relaxation and imagery procedures. Further research is now needed to further document how voluntary cyberphys-iological processes of mind-body communication can be utilized to opti-mize immune competence particularly with regard to the s-called "para-doxical phenomena" of activation and relaxation which have already been dealt with earlier in Chapter 5 (Tinterow & Rossi, in press).

Stress and the Mind-Gene Connection in Psychoimmunology

One of the most interesting and productive new paradigms of psycho-immunology is currently being developed by the Glasers at the Ohio State University Medical Center in a series of studies using examination stress in medical students (Kiecolt-Glaser & Glaser, 1991). They de-scribed an initial breakthrough at the genetic level with these words: "While there are ample data demonstrating stress-associated decre-ments in the immune response in humans and animals, these data pro-vide the first evidence that this interaction may be observed at the level of gene expression." (Glaser et al., 1990, p. 707). The scope of their work over the past decade is breathtaking in the boldness of its concep-tion to trace the actual molecular-genetic communication pathways of the mind-gene connection. We gain some insight into the Glaser re-search model with Figure 11 which outlines a dozen of the major loci of information transduction at the cellular-genetic level. Let's take it step by step, utilizing all the sources of the psychoimmunological literature cited in the previous section as well as the major ideas of our general approach to mind-body communication and healing.

1) *Primary Messengers.* Since the many varied cells of the immune system apparently have the receptors necessary to receive signals from the messenger molecules of the central, autonomic, endo-crine and neuropeptide systems (Pert et al., 1985; Besedovsky & del Rey, 1991), we can understand how the highly emotional ex-amination stress of medical students could be transduced via the state-dependent encoding within the limbic-hypothalamic-pitui-tary-adrenal cascade to the surface of the cells of the immune system. Stress-released messengers such as cortisol (glucocorti-coids), the opiates, and the catecholamines signal their specific receptors on the immune cells. Other potential stress-signaling molecules, such as the steroids testosterone and the thyroxines, can pass directly through the cell walls into the interior of the immune cells to signal genes more directly.

2) *Receptors.* The well-formed integrity of the proteins out of which

receptors are made, as well as their number and population dynamics (up and down regulation as described in Chapter 6), are significant factors in the degree to which the primary messengers get their signal into the immune cell. The breakthrough paper by Glaser et al. (1990) provides preliminary evidence on how stress modulates the "down regulation of the IL-2R [Interleukin 2 receptor] expression and IL-2R messenger RNA levels" (p. 707). The actual cell locus of their data collection for this effect is what I have called step 8, mRNA production and duration, in Figure 11, which will be reviewed below.

3) *Secondary Messengers.* Cyclic AMP (cAMP) is only one of the major secondary messengers within the cell that helps transmit the signal from receptors to the genes during stress as outlined earlier in Chapter 6. Since an increase in plasma as well as intracellular cAMP has been associated with psychobiological stress (Engel, 1985; Glaser et al., 1990), one might hypothesize that those mind-body therapies that operate by facilitating relaxation might be operating at this level by lowering cAMP levels. Whether this effect is mediated by lowering the production and circulation of primary messengers (e.g., ACTH, cortisol, etc.) or another mechanism will not be known until the holistic therapists and molecular biologists cooperate on clinical-experimental research programs.

Another secondary messenger, inositol triphosphate (InsP3) may be one of the messengers that signals the genes when foreign invaders such as bacteria betray their presence by yielding antigens that can form the antigen/major histocompatibility complex (MHC) that triggers certain receptors on immune cell surfaces. It is not yet certain whether this is true, however. Crabtree (1989), for example, reports that only five minutes are required for the cytoplasmic events associated with this secondary messenger, but that two hours are required before the T-cell is committed to activation. Recent reports indicate that IL-2 gene expression and proliferation can be initiated in the absence of InsP3. As we have seen, IL-2 gene expression is modulated by psychosocial stress.

4) *Gene Transcription for Metabolic Processes.* Here we come right to the bottom line of what I call "the mind-gene connection" (Rossi, 1987b, 1990a, b, c). Many signals from the environment including light, food, toxins, temperature, and mind-body rhythms, as well as psychosocial stress, have been shown to modulate this stage

of gene expression (Lloyd & Rossi, 1992a). The so-called "house-keeping genes" and "heat shock genes," whose expressions are modulated on a second-by-second basis throughout the day to regulate the metabolism and special functions of each of the approximately 250 different types of cells in the human body, are at this locus of the mind-gene loop. Glaser's research on the stress-modulated expression of the proto-oncogene *c-myc* may be operating at this level (Glaser et al., in press-a). Future research will determine whether this is a fundamental mind-gene communication link in the stress-associated modulation of some forms of cancer.

5) *DNA Synthesis for Cell Division and Replication.* A major finding of Glaser et al. (in press-a) is that "the down-regulation of *c-myc* and *c-myb* mRNA levels by examination stress observed in this study is consistent with our previous studies that demonstrate a stress-induced down-regulation of T-lymphocytes." By blocking the action of these proto-oncogenes that are normally required for the cell to enter into an initial phase of cell division (the so-called "S phase"), examination stress is interfering with the cell division and replication of immune system cells. A psychosocial stress can modulate cell division and growth at the genetic level.

6) *DNA Repair.* Another significant finding by Kiecolt-Glaser et al. (1985) that requires replication is that emotional stress can impair DNA repair mechanisms (as measured by recovery of nucleoid sedimentation following the irradiation of peripheral blood cells with 100 rads of X-irradiation). A significant difference was found in the degree of DNA repair in a small group of 28 newly admitted and nonmedicated, nonpsychotic psychiatric inpatients. The more highly distressed (as measured by the depression scale of the MMPI) had lower levels of DNA repair. It will be of fundamental significance for future research to locate the actual molecular mechanisms of this stress impairment of DNA repair in humans on the genetic level. In animals, Glaser et al. (1985) found that stress impairs the synthesis of the DNA repair enzyme methyltransferase presumably at the locus of its synthesis on the endoplastic reticulum (ER), listed as site 9 below.

7) *Gene Exon-Interon Dynamics Forming mRNA.* When genes are first transcribed in the cell nucleus they are a mixture of coding (exons) and noncoding (interons) molecules. The interons are removed for the formation of purely coding exon mRNA which then moves out into the cytoplasm of the cell interior to the ER

which functions somewhat like protein-manufacturing factories using mRNA as blueprints. There is as yet no direct evidence that stress modulates this cite of information transduction. On a theoretical level (evolutionary theory that proposes that the noncoding regions may be repositories of viral infections, the timing of developmental pathways, and interon size); however, one might predict that this will be found to be a psychobiological stress locus in the future.

8) *mRNA Duration and Degradation.* The measurement of mRNA at this locus is one of the most important for identifying the effects of stress on the cellular-genetic level (Glaser et al., 1985). This could be due more to the fact that the identification and measurement of mDNA is now a standard and popular laboratory procedure than the fact that it is the primary cellular locus of psychobiological stress. This is, however, a major locus for the disruption of cellular-genetic information transduction by viruses whose effects are modulated by psychosocial stress and, by implication, the mind-body psychotherapies. The *herpes simplex* virus, for example, which causes cold sores and some genital infections, like many other viruses, captures the protein-making machinery of infected cells to replicate itself. Researchers have demonstrated how such viruses operate by accelerating the degradation of the cell's normal mRNA's so that the ER will be free to replicate the virus mRNA (Ross, 1989).

Does this purely biological mechanism of viral disruption of mRNA tell us anything about the possible mechanisms by which hypnosis apparently can make the clinical symptoms of *herpes simplex* better (Gould & Tissler, 1984) or worse (Scott, 1960; Ullman, 1947)? Perhaps because of the unfortunate bias in many quarters that hypnotherapy is "merely mental suggestion—merely a bending of subjective perception" that has nothing to do with the body (Rossi, 1989a), modern hypnosis research has fallen far behind our current understanding of psychobiological mechanisms. With but few exceptions (e.g., the Hall and Olness studies cited in the previous section) the field of hypnosis seems very timid about exploring these possibilities. Although there are continuing reports of the clinical efficacy of hypnosis in dealing with viral infections responsible for warts (Ewin, 1992) as well as controlled experimental research (Spanos, Strenstrom, & Johnson, 1988; Spanos, Williams, & Gwynn, 1990), for example, there have been no studies on their possible cellular-genetic mechanisms as proposed here.

There are many interesting temporal synchronies between the production of mRNA and what I have called "the 20-minute ulradian healing response" (Rossi, 1992a, 1993; Rossi & Lippincott, 1992; Rossi & Nimmons, 1991). It is known that the expression of c-myc mRNA can be detected in T-lymphocytes within 30 minutes of stimulation. Crabtree (1989, p. 360) summarizes: "Most primary gene activations in eucaryoats [cells, such as human have, with a nucleus concentrating their genes] require only about 15 or 20 minutes from the time of their initial stimulus to the time that mRNA appears . . . " There is no direct evidence for the hypothesis that the 20-minute healing response is related to these cellular-genetic processes of information transduction; no one has tested this hypothesis yet. The fact that the temporal rhythms of many primary messengers of the endocrine system, as reviewed previously in Chapter 8, are associated with psychosocial cues, demands, and stresses, as well as the production fo mRNA, however, implies that this hypothesized association is now ripe for investigation.

9) *Endoplastic Reticulum and Protein Dynamics.* A recent review of the phenomen of periodicity in protein synthesis covering more than 100 references over the past 30 years summarizes what is currently known with this statement (Brodsky, 1992, p. 23): "The observed periods of oscillations in protein synthesis rates varies from 20 to 120 minutes, thus being different from circadian [daily 24-hour] rhythms, not only in the duration, but also because there is no external pacemaker." These rhythms of protein synthesis are evidently related to many human organ (heart, digestive, and brain) and behavioral systems (REM dream, basic rest-activity cycle, and performance rhythms). I am not aware of any well-controlled research, however, that directly assesses the degree to which human psychosocial stress modulates the process by which the protein factories of the cell translate mRNA into the proteins that make up structural elements of the cell as well as enzymes, growth factors, cytokine messengers of the immune system, and the information system (messenger molecules and receptors) of the cell in general. Figure 11 clearly illustrates how there are known pathways of information transduction between psychosocial stress and the dynamics of protein synthesis at the

locus of the ER, but as is typical, the molecular biologists that have the technical knowledge in this area usually do not interact with psychologists, and vica versa; the theoretical temporal associations between mind and molecule at this level remain to be explored experimentally.

It is well-known, however, that the so-called "heat-shock proteins" and "stress-induced proteins" induced at this level by many forms of biological stress such as heavy metal toxins, ethanol (drinking alcohol), certain amino acid analogues, and viruses can modulate gene transcription at locus 4 above as well as gene translation via mRNA's at this level (Morimoto, Tissières, & Georgopoulos, 1990, p. 2). There is much evidence to support the view that these "stress proteins" as important homeostatic mechanisms to protect cells from the ill effects of trauma and stress as well as the immune system's response to many clinical problems (Pardue, Feramisco, & Lindquist, 1989). An elevation in the expression of stress proteins has been found in many human ills including cancer, fever, inflammation, immune system functions and messengers (IL-1 and tumor necrosis factor), cardiac hypertrophy, metabolic diseases, ischemia, oxidation injury, and tissue damage due to physical trauma (Morimoto et al., 1990). We will have more to say about physical trauma such as burns, heat shock proteins, and the possible relevance of psychosocial factors such as hypnosis in the time cycles of the gene regulatory loop described at locus 10 below.

Todorov (1990) has outlined the cellular-genetic-protein processing dynamics by which life heals itself from the shocks and stresses the flesh is heir to. He details three major "blocks" or stages of gene translation and transcription in response to trauma, shock, and stress. The initial, M (metabolism), block proteins are those that are most quickly mobilized within an hour to produce proteins required for the cell to extract energy from nutrients, the formation of large proteins, and the export of some not needed for survival to other cells. The next, R (ribosomal), block proteins are those involved in the mRNA translation process (rRNA and tRNA) and are produced moderately fast within hours. The third stage produces the N (nuclear) proteins such as DNA polmerases (for making DNA) and histones and is relatively slow, requiring dozens of hours to a day or more.

Is it really too much of a jump of the clinical imagination to hypothesize that these temporal dynamics in the pattern of mRNA transcription and translation in response to trauma and stress at the cellular-genetic level are related to the ultradian and circadian dynamics of the mind-body therapies? Einstein is purported to have said, "It is the theory which decides what can be observed" (Heisenberg, 1989, p. 10). Carefully designed experimental studies are now required to assess whether these common temporal patterns will provide a window into the molecular-genetic processes of the mind-body therapies.

10) *Temporal Order of the Gene Regulation Loop.* The time scale illustrated at the cellular-genetic level of Figure 11 is, of course, only an approximation. The wide range of times required for the expression of certain genes depends upon whether they come early or late in the gene regulatory loop between transcription in the nucleus and translation on the ER. Many of the proteins formed from mRNAs of early genes are "regulatory proteins" in the sense that they cycle back to the nucleus to signal the transcription of later genes. There are over 70 genes that are activated in this informational loop ranging from 15 minutes for the expression of early genes to 14 days for later genes that contribute to the activation and proliferation of immune cells (Crabtree, 1989). Almost nothing is known about the relevance of psychosocial cues in this temporal order of gene transcription and translation. Clearly this is a prime locus of research for assessing the real molecular-genetic basis of any mind-body therapy that claims to influence the time course of healing.

At this point we can only wonder whether the many clinical reports of faster healing and recovery from many forms of trauma, stress, surgical operations (Rossi & Cheek, 1988), and burns (Ewin, 1986a, b; Margolis et al., 1983) with the help of hypnosis is of relevance someplace within the gene regulatory loop initiated by heat-shock proteins (described in the previous section). Therapeutic hypnosis administered within "the golden first two hours" is reported to be particularly valuable in limiting the inflammatory response to a burn (Ewin, 1986b, p. 117). Is this because therapeutic hypnosis can modulate the expression of early genes but not the damaging consequences of the expression of later genes? Margolis et al. (1983) did a small prospective clinical study with matched controls on six patients with burns on 10 to 83% of their body. All these patients were treated with hypnosis within 2.5 to 10 hours after their burn accident and all responded more favorably to standard medical burn treatment on objective criteria (e.g., higher two-day urine output than matched controls). Such clinical studies together with laboratory-oriented research indicating that an inflammatory response can be augmented or turned off in response to an experimental burn (Chapman et al., 1959a, b) now need to be replicated with a documentation of time-associated changes the mRNA's and their heat-shock proteins in order to provide supportive evidence for the hypothesis that hypnosis can modulate healing at the cellular-genetic level.

11) *Mitochondria and the Energy Dynamics of Life.* Stress protein dynamics have also been localized in the mitochondria (the energy factories'' of the cell) in animal cells that have been submitted to heat shock for three hours (Welch, 1990). As we reviewed in Chapter 6, the major molecule of energy dynamics, ATP, takes place at the mitochondria. Heat shock, and by implication stress damage to the cell in general, reduces available ATP. Welch (1990, pp. 238–239) describes the situation with these words: "This reduction in the ATP is most likely correlated with the observed alterations in the integrity of the mitochondria, most notably their "swollen" appearance . . . after heat shock . . . As an aside, it is worth pointing out that these observations regarding changes in cellular energy metabolism may be most relevant for the use of site-directed hyperthermia in the clinical treatment of cancer.''

Human fatigue is a universal accompaniment of all stress syndromes. All forms of mind-body healing purport to "reduce stress and increase energy." I am not aware of any well controlled clinical or experimental studies that relate psychosocial variables to this fundamental level of mitochondrial ATP energy dynamics, however. Until such basic studies are done we simply have no solid scientific evidence at the cellular level for the claims of energy rejuvenation via the many approaches to mind-body healing.

12) *The Messenger Molecule-Receptor Informational Loop.* One of the most remarkably revealing processes of the mind-cell-gene communication loop is at this locus where large "mother proteins" are synthesized as precursors of new messenger molecule-receptor units at the ER. Early in the history of molecular biology it was realized that proteins make up much of the structure, the substance or brute *matter* of the body. It was then realized that many proteins could also function as "catalysts" that facilitated

the biochemical transformations of other molecules that could not otherwise take place; protein catalysts did this by modulating the *energy dynamics* of these molecules of life. Only recently has it been discovered that the immediate destiny of many of the large mother proteins is to split into two parts as they travel to the surface of the cell via the golgi transportation complex. The larger part of the mother molecule becomes a new receptor to receive signals on the cell surface; this is the so-called up-regulation of cell receptors. The smaller part of the mother molecule becomes a new messenger molecule, usually packaged and stored temporarily in little sacks just inside the cell surface awaiting a cue to secrete themselves to signal another part of the body (or even the cell itself in autocrine signaling or neighboring cells in paracrine signaling). This most recent discovery of the role of proteins helps us understand the profound shift that is currently taking place in our understanding of the biology of life from the study of its matter to the study of its energy dynamics to the current study of its *informational* nature.

The messenger molecules of the immune system are called cytokines, interleukins, interferons, tumor necrosis factor, etc. The messenger molecules of the endocrine system are called "hormones." Messenger molecules of the nerve cells that are secreted between one cell and another at synapses are the famous "neurotransmitters." Many cells also secrete messenger molecules known as "neuromodulators" and "growth factors" that are of particular relevance for state-dependent physiology and behavior. During embryological development, tissue development, and growth many cells send out messenger molecules called "trophics" that serve as guiding nourishments for further growth and the pathways of neurons. Most of these messenger molecules ultimately are responsive to environmental stimuli and directly or indirectly to psychosocial cues. They are the "bottom line" of psychobiological science; they are the basic links in the state-dependent dynamics of mind-body communication and healing.

MIND MODULATION OF ACQUIRED IMMUNITY

Smith and McDaniel (1983) began their studies of the mind modulation of the immune response by successfully repeating Black's (1963) initial finding that hypnotized subjects could suppress the so-called

Mantoux reaction (a mild skin test for tuberculosis that is produced by an antigen-antibody reaction of the acquired immune system). Rather than hypnotizing their subjects, however, Smith and McDaniel used a behavioral conditioning paradigm to demonstrate the role of expectation in modulating this particular immune response: The Mantoux reaction took place on the arm of the subjects where it was expected but not on the other arm where subjects did not expect it. This proved that there was nothing intrinsic about hypnosis in the modulation of the immune system; hypnosis was simply a convenient way of focusing the mind's inner resources to activate or inhibit a physiological response.

Smith, McKenzie, Marmer, and Steele (1985) then sought to establish whether the mind modulation of the Mantoux reaction could be replicated using a different type of antigen-antibody response (the body's response to the *varicella zoster* viral antigen) and a different form of mind modulation (meditation rather than hypnosis or conditioning). An advantage of using the *varicella zoster* antigen was that the body's immune response to it could be objectively measured in two ways: (1) in vivo, by measuring the size of the skin test reaction on the subject's arm (just as with the Mantoux reaction), and (2) in vitro, by measuring the degree of lymphocyte stimulation in a blood sample from the subject. Smith and his colleagues (1985) described their elegant, single-case study experimental design, their subject's Eastern meditation method, and the statistically valid results as follows (p. 2110):

> In light of the above findings, we hypothesized that a highly selected subject could use meditation or self-hypnosis to modulate her immune response. The paradigm was a simple, single-case design in which the subject was her own control. She was given a skin test weekly for nine weeks. During the first three weeks (phase 1) she was told to react normally. The second three weeks (phase 2) she was asked to try to inhibit her reaction using any psychologic practice or technique she chose. Finally, for the final three weeks (phase 3) she was again asked to react normally. We hypothesized that the immune response during the second phase would be decreased compared with the first and third phases.
>
> The subject is a 39-year-old woman who has followed an Eastern religious practice for the last nine years. During most of this time, as part of her religious practice, she would usually meditate once or twice daily for about 30 minutes. For the last three years, she has followed a specific tantric generation meditation practice whereby "higher energies" are visualized and she seeks to transform herself into those energies.
>
> During the phase 2 periods of the original and repeat experiment, she

would usually reserve about five minutes of her daily meditation for attention to the study. First she would dedicate her intention concerning the study for universal good instead of self-advancement. She would also tell her body not to violate its wisdom concerning her defense against infection. Finally she would visualize the area of erythema and induration getting smaller and smaller. Soon after each phase 2 injection, she would pass her hand over her arm, sending "healing energy" to the injection site. . . .

The data confirmed the hypothesis that this subject could voluntarily modulate her immune responses by a psychic mechanism. Both a clinical measure, delayed hypersensitivity, and an in vitro measure, lymphocyte stimulation of immune response, were affected. In other words, it appears that the subject, acting with intentions, was able to affect not only her skin test response but also the response of her lymphocytes studied in the laboratory.

Smith et al. concluded their report by noting that their work establishes the intentional direct psychological modulation of the human immune system." Their emphasis on the intentional and voluntary aspect of the psychological situation is of great importance. Previous work on the mind modulation of the immune system via hypnosis, placebos, and behavioral conditioning demonstrated that mind-body healing processes could be activated by outside influences. The work of Smith and his colleagues, however, implies that humans can train themselves to facilitate their own inner mind-body healing processes. The researchers concluded their paper with a note of cautious optimism as follows (1985, p. 2111):

> The results from this study certainly cannot be generalized to all humans; however, perhaps other people have the ability to modulate their immune response or to develop the capacity to do so. Certainly, these data, along with the previously cited results, should allow for many new carefully designed studies to be undertaken.
>
> If it proves to be the case that humans can significantly modulate their immune response, then two important outcomes may occur. The mechanism of infectious or neoplastic disease onset associated with various psychological processes such as hopelessness or depression can possibly be better understood. Perhaps, also, intentional modulation can be used therapeutically to increase or decrease immune response, depending on the particular disease state.

Let us now turn to an overview of how the voluntary modulation of immune system responses could facilitate healing in a variety of illnesses such as cancer, asthma, allergies, and rheumatoid arthritis.

MIND MODULATION OF IMMUNE SYSTEM DYSFUNCTIONS

Bowers and Kelly (1979) have outlined three major ways in which the immune system can become dysfunctional in psychosomatic illness. It can become *underactive, hyperactive,* or *misguided* in its efforts to defend the body. These three errors of the immune system are exemplified by cancer, bronchial asthma, and rheumatoid arthritis, respectively. While this classification is an oversimplification of the facts, it is useful in providing a set of models for organizing our thinking about these issues. In what follows, I will amplify and update Bowers and Kelly's presentation of how the new approaches to therapeutic hypnosis that emphasize patient skills could facilitate healing of these three types of immune dysfunction.

The Underactive Immune System in Cancer

This section will outline how some of the basic elements of the immune system communicate and interact with each other in dealing with the phenomenon of cancer. It is important to understand that the body develops cancer cells as an apparently natural process throughout the entire lifespan without the growth of clinically recognizable cancer tumors. This is illustrated by the fact that one form of cancer cell (neuroblastoma) is much higher even in babies than in the clinical incidence of the disease. On the other end of the scale, postmortem autopsies on practically all males 50 or over show evidence of prostatic cancer cells, yet actual clinical cancer is not evident in most of them.

Since most people do not develop cancer even though cancer cells are continually produced, the body must have a natural immunological surveillance system that seeks out and destroys the single cancer cells before they grow into clinically evident tumors. In general it is found that stress-induced release of adrenocorticosteroids causes a suppression of this natural immunological surveillance system. Amkraut and Solomon (1975), Shavit et al. (1985), and Stein, Keller, and Schleifer (1985) have pointed out that only a slight depression of this system is needed to greatly increase the person's susceptibility to pathogens, particularly those that are constantly present and challenging the body's integrity, such as the spontaneously formed cancer cells.

There are a variety of immune system processes that protect against such tumor formations. These include the previously mentioned macrophages, T-lymphocytes, and B-lymphocytes (Amkraut & Solomon, 1975; Solomon & Amkraut, 1981), as well as K (killer) cells, NK (natural killer) cells, and cytotoxic T cells (see Hokama & Nakamura, 1982, for details). The K cells are of uncertain immunological lineage but are dependent on antibodies for their activity and are therefore also called *antibody-dependent cytotoxic cells*. The NK cells are also of uncertain origin but it is known that their activity against cancer cells is increased by *interferon*. Interferon is a immunological factor that is released by T-cells and macrophages. Recent studies in man indicate that NK cells play a significant role against a variety of viral infections, including those due to herpes and viral oncogenesis (viral-produced cancers). The major theory of oncogenesis is that tumor formation takes place when those components of the immune surveillance system are depressed or underactive (Stein et al., 1985).

Let us now examine a variety of approaches researchers and clinicians are currently developing to fight cancer by enhancing those aspects of the immune system that are depressed. As we found with the autonomic and endocrine systems, it will be necessary to trace the source of the potentially mind-modulating effects on the immune system right down to the genetic and molecular levels.

Cancer as a Communication Disease at the Cellular-Genetic Level. This section will present an overview of current thinking about the genesis of cancer and the lines of natural and acquired defense against it. The cancer story is very much involved with our developing understanding of genes and the messenger molecules that regulate normal cell growth. As we have seen in the two previous chapters, normal cells all have genes that receive messenger molecules from the mind-modulating central control processes in the limbic-hypothalamic system via the autonomic and endocrine systems. Many researchers now believe that cancer begins when these normal growth-regulating genes are damaged and turned into cancer-producing oncogenes. Oncogenes speed up or change the structure of proteins that the cell manufactures so that growth becomes wildly uncontrolled in the form of useless tissues and tumors that eventually take over the entire body and kill it. The normal genes that are turned into oncogenes occupy loci on the chromosomes that are vulnerable to damage. Because of this they are called "proto-oncogenes." They are converted into oncogenes by what have become known as "carcinogens."

Radiation from X-rays, radioactivity, and excess sunlight, *toxins* such as smoke and chemicals foreign to the body, and a variety of *viruses* are among the most well-known carcinogens. Many carcinogens operate by entering the cell nucleus during a vulnerable stage of cell division and transforming a normal proto-oncogene into a cancerous oncogene by causing a genetic mutation (a change in the DNA blueprint for the structure of growth proteins), or breaking the normal arrangement in which genes are recombined into chromosomes.

If the DNA blueprint is not repaired (stage 6 in Figure 11), abnormal mRNA will be sent out into the cell's ER where abnormal protein messenger molecules will be manufactured (stages 8 and 9 in Figure 11). These abnormal protein messengers then enter into the cell's communication system in ways that lead to the uncontrolled growth of cancer via the gene regulatory loop (stage 10) and messengers and receptors (stage 12). It is from this point of view that we can regard cancer as essentially a communication disease at the cellular-genetic level. While there are many types of cancer there now appear to be two fundamental processes that lead to these errors of communication: (1) the generation of *oncogenes* and (2) the malfunctioning of *tumor suppressor genes* (Cooper, 1992).

Oncogenes are like outlaws; they are corrupt forms of normal gene citizens (proto-oncogenes that serve as blueprints for the production of protein messengers that regulate the growth and maturation of the cell) that are out of the normal regulatory loop of information transduction. Oncogenes were originally discovered when it was found that some viruses (called ''acutely transforming retroviruses'') can capture the cell's normal regulatory proto-oncogenes and turn them into outlaws that express themselves at the wrong time and place leading to the excessive proliferation of cells we call cancer. Over 40 such acutely transforming retroviruses have been isolated to date. They are given three- or four-letter names that usually code the species of animal, the tissue invaded, and/or the name of the investigator that discovered them such as *myb* (avian myeloblastosis), *myc* (avian myelocytomatosis), *ras*H (Harvey sarcoma), *ras*K (Kirsten sarcoma) and *src* (Rous sarcoma).

Oncogenes of the *myc* family are commonly involved in many forms of human cancer (breast, lung, neuroblastomas, and Burkitt's lymphoma). C-*myc* is normally turned on by growth factor signals (such as PDGF, blood platelet derived growth factor) to regulate other genes that lead to cell division. Unregulated expression of the *myc* family leads to uncontrolled cell proliferation, which leads to cancer. It is known that in Burkitt's lymphoma, for example, there is an overexpression of antibody (immunoglobulin) genes associated with a translocation of c-*myc* from its normal location on chromosome 8 to chromosomes 2, 14, or 22. We do not know, however, by what communication link a psychosocial stressor, such as examination stress in medical students, can lead to the down regulation of c-*myc* mRNA levels as reported by Glaser (Glaser et al., in press-a). We can speculate that (1) psychological stress can be transduced into (2) the production and release of ACTH from the hypothalamic-pituitary system which signals (3) the release of cortisol and adrenalin from the adrenal glands, and that these primary messenger molecules can in turn (4) signal receptors on cell walls to (5) release secondary messenger molecules (such as cyclic AMP) through the inside of the cell that (6) leads finally to a modulation of gene transcription, and that the remainder of signaling and regulation at the cellular-genetic level (7) eventually produces other messenger molecules that are released back into the blood stream to encode SDMLB in other cells of the body and mind-brain. This possible mind-body-gene loop of information transduction is only an educated guess at this time, however. Tracing out exactly how information in the form of imagery, thoughts, and emotions on a psychological level are transduced into the molecular messengers that regulate *c-myc* family genes will be of essence for a truly scientific mind-body therapy of the future.

Tumor suppressor genes are the second major type of genes whose faulty communications can lead to cancer. While *oncogenes* send signals that stimulate excessive cell growth, *tumor suppressor genes* normally act to inhibit cell growth and tumor development. When these tumor suppressor genes are damaged, inactivated, or lost their mRNA's are no longer sent to the protein factories (ER in stage 9 of Figure 11) and their regulatory proteins (messenger molecules) are no longer available to signal cells to stop dividing. The loss of the *p53* tumor suppressor gene, for example, is believed to be associated with a wide range of human cancers (breast, colon/rectal, liver, bone, nerve cell, immune system, muscle, and lung). Oncogenes and tumor suppressor genes operating separately or together both lead to cancers because of the excess or loss of messenger molecules on the cellular-genetic level. Cancer progression in humans is the result of the accumulation of many errors in communication on the cellular-genetic level that eventually lead to faulty regulation of the normal system of checks and balances of the messenger molecules that regulate the life process. Let us now briefly summarize some of the most well known of these messengers that are currently being explored in cancer therapy.

Messenger Molecules in the Natural and Acquired Defenses Against Cancer. There are a number of well-known ways of defeating the growth and spread of cancer cells once they are formed. This section will review three of the body's natural defenses, and a number of ways by which researchers are enhancing them.

Interferon is a messenger molecule protein that facilitates a process of innate immunity or natural defense against infection. It was originally discovered in 1957 by Alick Isaacs and Jean Lindenmann of the Natural Institute of Medical Research in England. Whenever a virus attacks a cell, the cell produces interferons (alpha and beta are two well-known forms of it) to interfere with the virus's toxic activity. In addition, the interferons can directly attack and kill fully formed cancer cells by (1) interfering with their metabolism or giving T- and B-cells and macrophages messages to destroy cancer cells (Marrack & Kappler, 1986). Early clinical trials with interferon were disappointing because it was only available in small amounts. Researchers have recently learned how to mass-produce interferon in the laboratory, however. When large amounts have been injected into the body, interferon has been successful in enhancing the cancer-fighting potential of T- and B-cells and macrophages against a variety of cancers. In actual practice, it is currently being combined with other forms of anti-cancer processes, such as the following.

Interleukins are also naturally present protein messenger molecules that facilitate immune system communication and defense against pathogens in the body. They operate as hormone or messenger molecules between T- and B-cells and macrophages to facilitate their defense against toxins and even fully formed cancers. A research team lead by Steven Rosenberg (Rosenberg et al., 1985; Rosenberg & Barry, 1992) of the National Cancer Institute has recently succeeded in mass-producing interleukin-2 and using it to activate the body's T-cells to produce cytotoxic T-cells that can directly attack cancer cells. It has been found to be dramatically effective in shrinking tumors by 50 percent or more (including complete cancer remission) in the human trials recently conducted.

Tumor necrosis factor (TNF) is another natural form of innate immunity against pathogens, originally discovered in 1975 by Lloyd Old at the Sloan-Kettering Cancer Center in New York. It has been found that when bacteria infect the body, macrophages increase in number and secrete the protein TNF, which can directly attack cancer cells and tissues as well. Through the processes of genetic engineering in the laboratory, TNF now can be cloned and mass-produced. When injected into the body, it actually attacks and causes cancer cells to blacken and die by some as yet unknown mechanism; when it is used in combination with interferon and other cancer-killing drugs, it is even more effective. In the laboratory, it either destroys or hampers the growth of two-thirds of the cancer cells against which it has been tested. TNF is currently being tested in humans in a variety of major medical centers.

Unfortunately current research indicates that things are not as straightforward as we might wish when efforts are made to facilitate cancer therapy by simply flooding the patient with these and other messenger molecules of the immune system. It is now becoming evident that these molecular messengers are a type of informational therapy that is very different from the "magic bullet" model of chemotherapy initiated by Paul Ehrlich (circa 1910) and continued by Alexander Flemming's discovery of antibiotics (circa 1940) that led to phenomenal success of modern medicine in the first half of this century. The magic bullets were foreign and highly toxic chemicals that were more effective in killing disease organisms when injected into the body than our own cells. As we learned earlier in this chapter, the trillion or so cells of the body are all "individuals" in conversation with one another with a delicate, refined, and highly effective communications that certainly transcends what we have been able to accomplish so far with words and bullets on our human global level of political communication. To simply dump vast quantities of messenger molecules in the body in an indiscriminate manner could be likened to yelling "Fire!" in a crowded theater; certainly that drastic communication will get a lot of people on the move quickly but many may be injured or killed in consequence.

The innocent living cells of the body that are injured or killed in consequence of dumping too many messenger molecules into the mind-body are called "unfortunate side effects." Some of the unfortunate side effects of TNF, for example, include autocrine/paracrine stimulation of further tumor growth, increased tumor motility, and tissue changes that can enhance further tumor invasiveness, increased angiogenesis (increasing blood supply to tumor to nourish its further growth), and cachexia (wasting disease). Current researchers now regard these unfortunately all too real side effects of confused communications within the immune system as "dysregulated cytokine production" as in this recent statement (Balkwill, 1993, p. 207).

> All these arguments make the assumption that TNF treatment would be good for the patients and bad for the tumour. But there is increasing evidence that dysregulated cytokine production may be involved in the malignant process, as it is in infectious and autoimmune disease. The response of a tumour to a cytokine will depend on the context in which the signal is received—sustained local levels of TNF or other soluble mediators, the state of tissue differentiation and the phase of the cell cycle will all influence the

response. In human ovarian cancer TNF is implicated as a paracrine/auto-crine factor that may promote tumour growth and spread . . .

The clinical promise of other cytokines, most notably interleukin-2 (IL-2), is also limited by their toxicity. Indeed, the systemic induction of TNF during IL-2 therapy has been implicated in side effects such as hypotension, fever, rigors and weight gain. There are no data supporting the idea that a mutant IL-2 molecule might have an increased therapeutic index, and although the IL-2 receptor complex has at least three components it does not seem that they regulate different actions. . . .

However that may be, the paper by Van Ostade *et al.* raises important issues. If the complexity and toxicity of cytokine action can be restricted by the use of mutant molecules or specific inhibitors, then the therapeutic potential of these mediators may be greatly increased.

The work of Van Ostade et al. described by Balkwill involves the modification of natural TNF to make a "mutant molecule" that will keep TNF's ability to facilitate the killing of cancer cells while reducing its unfortunate side effects. This strategy attempts to follow the "classical magic bullet philosophy" of chemotherapy by changing the natural messenger function of TNF and turning it into a bullet bent solely on destruction. However unpalatable this may sound, it still may be our best chance for developing a purely *molecular-mechanical* approach to cancer and many related ills with the current philosophy and funding practices of our National Institutes of Health. This is very different from the *molecular-messenger* approach of the psychobiology of mind-body healing we are exploring in this volume. The approach of the alternative methods of holistic medicine would be to learn more about the original communication functions of molecular messengers such as TNF, the interleukins and interferons, and how we can relate to them in a voluntary manner with mind-body communication processes such as words, images, and emotions. This is the essence of the mind-body-gene information transduction process discussed and illustrated throughout this volume. But how far we are from carrying out this program of facilitating mind-body communication in comparison with the "legitimate methods" of current-day orthodox chemotherapy as represented by the magic bullet approach of Ostade! The primitive state of our current psychobiological models for facilitating cancer therapy illustrate just how far behind we are.

Psychobiological Models for Facilitating Cancer Therapy.   A major line of evidence for a mind-body connection in the genesis of cancer is what has come to be known as the *life change stress* studies (Dohrenwend & Dohrenwend, 1974). Any form of stress resulting in a significant life change (e.g., the death of a family member, job change, family relocation) can activate the cortical-hypothalamic-pituitary-adrenal axis described earlier to produce the corticosteroids that suppress the immune surveillance system. Anxiety, depression, and low ego strength are all associated with underactivity of the immune system. The major thrust of current research in this area is that *coping ability* is the significant factor in determining whether stress will have a depressant effect on immunocompetence. Locke et al. (1984), for example, found that experiencing the symptoms of anxiety and depression in response to a stressful life change indicated poor coping ability and resulted in a decrease in the activity of natural killer cells; on the other hand, good coping ability (few symptoms in the face of considerable life change stress) was associated with higher natural killer cell activity.

Well-controlled experimental evidence that hypnosis can effect changes in the immunological surveillance system is gradually accumulating. Hall (1982–1983) has found that highly hypnotizable young subjects can significantly increase their cellular immunity (both T- and B-lymphocyte activity). Frankel (1985) and his colleagues are exploring the use of hypnotic suggestion to either enhance or depress cellular immunity in response to injections of antigens.

A review of the newer approaches to therapeutic hypnosis that have been found effective in enhancing immunocompetence with cancer patients revealed at least five basic applications: relaxation, imagery, reframing, meditation, and reinforcing coping skills. Since stress depresses the immune system by the production of adrenocorticoid hormones, it was an important breakthrough to find that hypnotherapeutic methods emphasizing simple relaxation could lower the plasma level of these hormones (Sachar, 1969).

The popular visualization/relaxation procedure developed by the Simontons (Simonton, Simonton, & Creighton, 1978) contains an interesting *cognitive reframing approach*. While most people who are afraid of cancer typically view it as a powerfully destructive disease, the Simontons reframe this erroneous view: The cancer cells are described as "weak" and "confused" while the immune system's white blood cells are "strong" and "powerful," like sharks attacking meat. Because their cancer program also includes group therapy for resolving underlying problems and developing coping skills, the Simontons have not been able to differentiate which factor of their approach is most effective.

Hall's (1982–83; Hall et al., 1992a, b) work using their imagery and reframing, however, does clarify that this approach can enhance cellular immunity.

An important emphasis on the use of reframing as a way of accessing and increasing sensitivity to our natural modalities of mind-body communication (as illustrated earlier in Tutorial 1, Chapter 5) is described by Temoshok and Dreher (1992, p. 264):

> Cognitive psychotherapists use the term *reframing* for the shift in thinking that brings about a shift in feelings and behavior. Commonly, cognitive therapists show their patients how their false ideas are the cause of depression or anxiety. . . . These methods can be useful for Type C patients, *I used reframing not to reduce depression or anxiety, but rather to increase a feeling of awareness.* This set off a chain of events that, in a rather different way, helped patients to become less depressed, more optimistic, and more in control of their medical care and their lives.

Their research on the Type C melanoma cancer patient suggests that they are pleasant, passive, and self-sacrificing, but their behavior has a "toxic core" of the *"nonexpression of emotions"* as a learned coping style. This is a distinguishing contrast to the Type A behavioral response of *hostility* which has been associated with psychosomatic cardiac problems (Friedman & Ulmer, 1984) and Type B which is a more appropriate emotional response pattern in the middle of the behavioral continuum. Temoshok's research and carefully oriented psychotherapeutic approach is designed to help people recognize and change these learned patterns of thinking, feeling, and behaving "without blaming the victim."

Temoshok (1991, p. 20) summarizes her research on malignant melanoma by reporting that, "the more someone expressed emotion, the lower the mitotic rate of the tumor, the greater the lymphocytic infiltration, and the less the tumor thickness." A change in mitotic rate is often used in psychosocial research as an index of the rate of cell division of cancer cells; a lower mitotic rate is taken to mean that cancer cells are not dividing as rapidly. This in turn implies a lower rate of DNA synthesis at locus 5 in Figure 11. Exactly how an increase in the flow of information via the greater expression of emotions is transduced into a lower mitotic rate is not explained, however. This is the next step for such research. At this point we can hypothesize that emotions are being transduced into hormonal messenger molecules within the limbic-hypothalamic-pituitary system at the mind-brain level. But which messenger molecules in what proportions are entering which cells at what level (locus 2 in Figure 11) to modulate what secondary messengers (locus 3) to modulate what genes (locus 4) to reduce DNA synthesis and presumably cancer cell division in which patients? It is no longer enough to say there are statistically significant relationships between psychosocial and cellular variables in a group of people that may be related to the progression or amelioration of cancer. Because most scientists maintain "statistical correlation is not causation," the interpretation of such research on the correlations between psychosocial variables and cancer will always be open to question. We must now find the actual mechanisms involved in each step of the entire informational loop between the psychosocial level and the gene before we can design a truly effective mind-body therapy.

A seemingly opposite hypnotherapeutic approach has been developed by Ainslie Meares (1982–83) in what he calls "mental ataraxis." He describes this as a form of intensive meditation that evokes an "inner stillness" that is "central in origin." His approach is the opposite of the Simontons' and of all those who seek to increase the patient's comfort, relaxation, or coping skills, because it requires no act of will. As Meares describes it, "An essential feature of this form of meditation is the absence of striving, of trying, and of using one's willpower." He claims his approach leads to a nonverbal understanding of the self and the universe that can effectively lead to a regression of very serious forms of cancer. Meares has had personal, deep experiences in his form of intensive meditation. He believes that this is communicated to patients nonverbally on an unconscious level, thus providing further positive reinforcement of the possibilities awaiting their experiences with "mental ataraxis." Meares obviously accessed and utilized many chronobiological healing processes that are currently described as the ultradian healing response when he described his permissive approach with cancer patients with these words (1990, p. 162):

> The length of time spent in meditation depends on the patient's ability to do it. At the start 10 minutes three times a day may be all the patient can manage. On the other hand, some patients who have been successful in bringing about a regression of their cancer have gotten into the way of meditating for two or three hours a day or more. . . . Those patients who come to like their meditation do best.

Other clinicians have used prolonged hypnotherapeutic states without reporting any awareness of the chronobiological principles they were using. Barabasz and Barabasz (1989) report that after only a few hours of what they call "REST" in an environment of restricted stimulation, patients experience heightened hypnotic susceptibility, reduced pain, and a reduction in symptoms of trichotillomania (Barabasz, 1987). Likewise Kuriyama (1990) reports the effectiveness of two- to three-hour hypnotherapeutic periods as well as "all-night prolonged hypnosis" wherein patients are hypnotized at night and permitted to go into natural sleep until the next morning when they wake up from hypnosis after washing the face. This prolonged hypnotherapeutic approach has been found to be particularly effective for bronchial asthma, anxiety neurosis, angina pectoris, chronic anxiety, and stomach ulcers.

The common denominator between the seemingly opposite approaches of Simonton's (active and highly directive) and the permissive nondirective approaches of Meares and others using hypnosis for prolonged periods is that they all reduce anxiety and increase the patient's sense of self efficacy. It appears as if the active and directive approach is entraining and utilizing the high performance peaks of waking ultradian rhythms while the permissive nondirective approach over long periods may be entraining and extending the lower rest phase of the ultradian healing response. Another hidden connection between these methods is the fact that the tendency toward the experience of imagery and fantasy as well as state-dependent memory, learning, and behavior is itself periodic with an ultradian rhythm throughout the day (Kripke, 1982) as well as at night in the 90-minute REM cycle of dreaming. Is it possible that the facilitation of mind-body healing by the use of vivid imagery and imagination involves the entrainment of certain phases of the ultradian healing response (low points of the basic rest activity cycle while awake) as well as dreaming (the high point of the sleeping wave of being in Figure 9)? It remains a research question for the future to determine whether the associations between these natural mind-body rhythms and so many proprietary mind-body healing methods are real or coincidental.

Most current practitioners use a "garden variety" of all the above approaches with individual (Margolis, 1982–83; Newton, 1982–83) and group psychotherapy (Spiegel, 1991). The work of Finkelstein and Greenleaf (1982–83) is typical: For a prospective three-year study of cancer, they have prepared a ten-minute audiotape containing suggestions that seemingly cover the entire range of hypnotherapeutic methods we have discussed. The advantage of these broadly general methods is that they follow the Ericksonian principle of allowing the patient's own unconscious to select which suggestions are needed to facilitate therapeutic activity (Erickson & Rossi, 1979). This lack of specificity, however, means that we cannot determine scientifically just which therapeutic mechanisms are involved.

Most therapists are in agreement that some sort of special condition, state, or utilization of mind can enhance immunological functioning. From the perspective developed in this chapter, it could be said that human functioning is so complex that there appears to be an almost infinite variety of state-dependent learning and memory mind-body systems utilizable for healing purposes. Because each individual has a unique history of learnings and life experiences, every case is essentially a new therapeutic study in which specific and nonspecific hypnotherapeutic approaches can be explored for their effectiveness.

An overall *psychobiological model for facilitating cancer regression* is presented in Box 3, which is an update and expansion of a similar psychophysiological model presented by Achterberg (1985). The most general and easily accessible route to mind-body healing is through the naturalistic ultradian healing response that can be recognized and utilized every 90 minutes (as described in the previous two chapters). Individuals can learn how to optimize their natural ultradian healing responses by accessing the positive state-dependent psychobiological resources associated with life experiences involving effective coping and feelings of efficacy and hopefulness. For some individuals this approach will be sufficient. Others will do better by using the ultradian healing response to optimize their more active efforts in using the Simonton and Achterberg attack imagery on the weak and hopeless cancer cells. Yet other individuals will engage in the deeper, personal psychodynamic processes of active imagination by psychoanalytic therapists (Hillman, 1983; Jung, 1929/1984; Mindell, 1982, 1985a, b; Woodman, 1984), or the more spiritually oriented approaches of Meares (1982–83). The art and science of these forms of mind-body healing involve essentially a creative and constructive process that individuals must explore in their own way as they learn to maximize their psychobological potentials.

Viruses on the Frontier of Psychoimmunology

It is something of a paradox to realize that some of the most interesting and innovative research in psychoimmunology is currently being done with viruses that are themselves on the borderline between the living and nonliving. It is theorized that viruses were originally bits of the normal genome of an organism that somehow escaped and learned how to propagate independently (Eigen & Winkler-Oswatitsch, 1992;

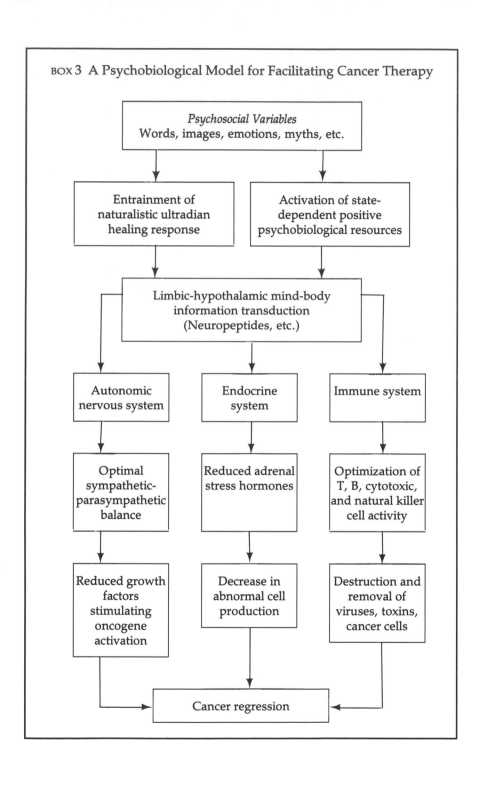

BOX 3 A Psychobiological Model for Facilitating Cancer Therapy

Psychosocial Variables
Words, images, emotions, myths, etc.

Entrainment of naturalistic ultradian healing response

Activation of state-dependent positive psychobiological resources

Limbic-hypothalamic mind-body information transduction (Neuropeptides, etc.)

Autonomic nervous system

Endocrine system

Immune system

Optimal sympathetic-parasympathetic balance

Reduced adrenal stress hormones

Optimization of T, B, cytotoxic, and natural killer cell activity

Reduced growth factors stimulating oncogene activation

Decrease in abnormal cell production

Destruction and removal of viruses, toxins, cancer cells

Cancer regression

Margulis & Schwartz, 1988). Viruses are hardly more than small strings of genes surrounded with a coat of protein. Outside a living organism they may be crystallized and appear to be nonliving. Placed in contact with the appropriate living cells, however, they gain entry by a variety of means (through certain cell receptors or proteins on the cell surface called "viral recognition sites"). They then utilize their genes to redirect the cell's normal metabolism to make more viral genes and their protein coat. In the literature of nonlinear dynamics of mathematical chaos and complex adaptive systems (Langton, 1989; Nadel & Stein, 1992), the way viruses get their foot in the door of life reminds us of the felicitous ideas of Christopher Langton (Lewin, 1992, p. 51):

> I'm saying that the edge of chaos is where information gets its foot in the door in the physical world, where it gets the upper hand over energy. Being at the transition point between order and chaos not only buys you exquisite control—small input/big change—but it also buys you the possibility that information processing can become an important part of the dynamics of the system.

While many viruses eventually destroy the cells they invade, some viruses also have the remarkable (or, rather, reprehensible) ability to insert themselves in the host's genome and replicate themselves without destroying the host when they receive some yet little understood signals from the environment. It is exactly here somewhere within the stress-mind-gene loop that some viruses become "an important part of the dynamics of the system" and seem to signal stress and the distress of the total organism. These viruses remain latent within the genome and become active leading to a variety of problems ranging from warts to cancer only when humans and animals are stressed. These viruses amplify the organisms response to stress even when the total organism tries to ignore it. The provocative implications of much current psycho-immunological research is that this is particularly true with defensive human individuals who do not want to recognize their emotional problems. For people who do not easily recognize their emotional stress, a little friendly virus activity could be a symptom in the process of becoming an important new mind-body signaling system.

Since viruses are basically small gene strings they may be classified as DNA viruses and RNA viruses. The three major DNA virus families clearly associated with psychosocial factors are the papillomavirus (warts and utrine cervix carcinoma), the herpesvirus (simplex type I and II, Epstein-Barr virus) and the hepadnavirus (hepatitis-B associated with some psychosocial risk factors such as alcoholism and smoking). The major RNA virus families with well-known mind-body associations are the retroviruses such as human T-cell leukemia virus type I (HTLV-I, responsible for adult leukemia and lymphoma) and the human immunodeficiency virus (HIV-I responsible for AIDS). We will review only a few of the psychoimmunological studies with these viruses that promise important insights for a mind-body healing of the future.

The Papillomavirus.   The oldest and most popular literature on mind-body healing that extends back in folklore for centuries is certainly the healing of warts by "spells" and coins placed under pillows by generations of children. Even today one finds amiable, white-goateed clinicians who attend psychological and medical conferences with little more to say apart from their practice of giving their children-patients "a dime for every wart" they "buy" from them. Locke (1986) lists 41 papers from 1927 to the present with one-paragraph descriptions of the primarily successful methods of using hypnosis to remove warts attributed to the papillomavirus. Ever more sophisticated studies with sensible controls (Spanos et al., 1988, 1990) are still being published regularly to assure us that psychosocial variables are indeed relevant in all this kid stuff. A recent review (Johnson, 1989, p. 307) assures us that

> the treatment of warts supports the hypotheses that (a) with or without prior administration of a hypnotic induction procedure, suggestions for wart removal are at times effective . . . and (b) that subjects who become vividly involved with suggestion and the imagery of losing warts are more likely to lose warts than those who do not have vivid imagery.

Verruca Vulgaris.   In a recent summary of the clinical literature on hypnotherapy for common warts (Verruca Vulgaris is another papilloma virus) Dabney Ewin (1992), currently the president of The American Society of Clinical Hypnosis, reports "cure rates" of 27 percent to 55 percent for traditional direct suggestion in hypnosis. This percentage jumps to 80 percent when those who failed to respond to direct hypnotic suggestion were helped by a more extended period of hypnoanalysis ("41 consecutive cases with 33 cures"). Hypnotic suggestion can not only cause warts to disappear, but it can also cause them to appear (Gravitz, 1981). That hynotic suggestion involves something more than the magic of words, however, is indicated by Ewin's review of how apparently opposite suggestions can be effective in wart removal: hypnotic suggestions have varied from "stop the blood supply to each wart on your body" (Clawson & Swade, 1975) to "increasing the blood supply to bring in more antibodies and healing substances—make it warm"

(Ewin, 1974; Hartland, 1966) and suggesting tingling in the warts together with images of "killer and guard cells" in the immune system attacking the viruses and destroying them. Although there have been proposals to measure these suggested changes (Noll, 1987), they have not yet appeared in peer reviewed scientific literature.

Condyloma Acuminatum is a venereal wart of the papilloma family that has been found in association with cervical cancer, but the virus is not proven as a causal agent in such cancers (Timbury, 1991). Ewin (1974) has reported four cases of Condyloma Acuminatum treated with a variety of hypnotherapeutic approaches from waking suggestion and direct suggestion to dream and hypnoanalysis. He reports "cures" as a disappearance of the warts for follow-up periods ranging from one to six years. The successful six-year follow-up case was administered a series of suggestions in a light trance that emphasized that the patient's body had the capacity to "overcome the wart virus and heal this infection . . . you will notice a sensation of warmth in the surrounding skin as the blood vessels dilate to bring in more antibodies and white blood cells to fight the infection, and more protein and oxygen to help build the new and normal tissue when the wart has gone away. . . . " There were no controls on these cases and, unfortunately, no measurements as to whether the suggested changes in blood vessels, antibodies, or white blood cells, etc. actually took place. Such clinical successes, however, make it evident that a new experimental clinical model is now needed to document how the papillomavirus operates along the psychosocial-brain-body-cell-gene molecular loop of mind-body communication, somewhat akin to the Glaser team's research on the Epstein-Barr virus which we will now review.

The Herpesvirus.   Five of the six major types of herpesvirus have been implicated with psychosocial factors: Epstein-Barr, Herpes Simplex Types I and II, Varicella-Zoster and Cytomegalovirus. The sixth type, Human Herpes virus 6 (HHV-6), has been discovered only recently as an infection of lymphoid tissue. It is very widespread, it is apparently acquired early in life, its pathogenicity is still unclear, and most infections may be symptomless. all the herpesviruses have the important characteristic of being able to remain latent within the host cells a long time—probably for life—after the primary infection has subsided. It is this ability to remain latent with recurrent infections under conditions of physical (trauma, disease) and psychosocial stress that has attracted the attention of many mind-body therapists. Most therapists claim only to facilitate an amelioration of these recurrent outbreaks though some, as we shall learn, claim apparent cures for some herpesvirus types of infection.

The Epstein-Barr virus (EBV) can be found in 80 percent of the American population, but most of them are probably unaware of its presence because it can insert itself into the human DNA and remain there in an apparently latent form with few if any overt symptoms. Because of the uncertainties about its hidden course within the body and what signals it into symptomatic activity, there has been a great deal of controversy about diseases and mind-body conditions it may be associated with. EBV has been associated with depression and chronic fatigue syndrome (Jones & Straus, 1987; Straus, 1988) and more recently with the development of AIDS (Antoni et al., in press). Many authorities now cite EBV as associated with mononucleosis, Burkitt's lymphoma (cancer of B-Cells), and nasopharyngeal carcinoma. EBV is apparently associated with cancer when an oncogene in the viral DNA is inserted into the host's DNA so that DNA synthesis (in locus 5 on Figure 11) escapes its normal controls and cells replicate in a wild and explosive manner. Here we will touch upon current and still controversial research relating psychosocial variables with EBV.

In a series of studies the Glaser team have used a variety of psychosocial stressors to demonstrate how latent herpesvirus infections such as EBV can be activated. Higher antibody levels to EBV (IgG) in the blood have been found associated with loneliness (Glaser et al., 1985), academic stress (Glaser et al., 1987, in press-b), divorce (Kiecolt-Glaser et al., 1988), and caregiving in Alzheimer's disease family members (Kiecolt-Glaser et al., 1991). In one of their most recent studies, Glaser et al. (in press-b) report how they took a significant new step in identifying the cellular-molecular locus of EBV activity in response to academic stress.

> We explored the relationship between examination stress and a specific immune response to EBV, the memory T-cell response as measured by the ability of peripheral blood T-lymphocytes to respond to EBV specific polypeptides. Significant decreases in memory T-cell proliferation were found during the examination timepoint compared to pre-exam levels for five of the six EBV polypeptides tested. In addition, subjects higher in seeking support had lowered proliferative responses to all of the early EBV polypeptides (i.e., p17, p52/50, p85) as well as higher levels of antibody to EBV-VCA. Subjects higher on seeking support reported more stress and loneliness than their low seeking counterparts, although there was no difference in number of friends or contacts.

This study gains much of its significance from the realization that peptides, polypeptides, and neuropeptides, in particular, comprise the largest class of messenger molecules in living organisms. While this informational function has not been discussed by Glaser et al., it is from their type of research in identifying and localizing the dynamics of the psychosocial-mind-body-molecular messenger communication loops that a psychobiology of mind-body healing of the future will be constructed. The obvious next step is to determine what mind-body healing approaches can either prevent the stress-induced activation of EBV and the polypeptides in the Glaser model to facilitate recovery.

Herpes Simplex Virus Types I & II. Psychosocial factors play an important role in herpes simplex I (HSV-I) (e.g., "cold sores, fever blisters" on tissues of the skin, mouth, and eyes, and brain lesions, and a small proportion of genital herpes) and herpes simplex II (HSV-II), the main cause of genital herpes. After the initial symptoms these herpes viruses can survive for a long time in the host by retreating into the nerve cells and remaining in a latent form where the immune system apparently cannot attack them. When the human host experiences stress of an organic (e.g., menstruation, fever) or psychosocial (depression, emotional problems) source, the virus is somehow signaled into activity (Kiecolt-Glaser & Glaser, 1991). It finds its way back to the original infection site to cause symptoms again. Before the immune system can mount an adequate attack, however, the virus retreats again into the nerve cells. The nature of the messenger molecules that signal this attack-and-retreat strategy are not well understood but the recent research of Bonneau et al. (1993) indicates that stress can induce a modulation of the primary cellular immune response to herpes simplex virus infection that is mediated by the adrenal system cascade as well as other independent mechanisms.

In keeping with previously cited research, we can therefore trace the entire mind-body informational loop ranging from stress hormones of the limbic-hypothalamic-pituitary-adrenal system (primary messengers such as ACTH, cortisol, catecholamines, etc. at loci, 1, 2 of Figure 11)—to the secondary messengers of the cell (locus 3 in Figure 11) like cAMP that pick up signals from the primary messengers—and use them to modulate the dynamics of gene expression (loci 4, 5, 6 in Figure 11) as well as mRNA and peptides associated with viral activity. Like many other viruses, the last stage whereby the herpes virus finally replicates itself is by taking over the cell's ER protein-making factory (locus 9 in Figure 11). Researchers have demonstrated that the virus does this by accelerating the destruction of the cell's normal messenger RNA (mRNA at locus 8) so that only the viral mRNA is present to be translated into viral proteins (Ross, 1989). Viral replication and disease is thus a consequence of nothing less than a series of "informational wars"!

Since we know that negative psychosocial stress can bias the informational war in favor of viral disease at these cellular-genetic levels, can we find evidence that information from more constructively oriented levels of mind-body communication (such as positive images, thoughts, and emotions) access this cellular-genetic level to facilitate healing of viral diseases as well? Alas, the scientific evidence for positive healing is less well-developed than the negative evidence for psychosocial stress abetting viral diseases. As we have seen, the negative evidence has reached sophisticated scientific molecular-genetic levels in the laboratory, but the positive evidence remains for the most part at the anecdotal-clinical level in the consulting room. This unhappy situation will not change until more respect and cooperation develops between the researchers and clinicians mutually engaged in the mind-body enterprise.

Rossi and Cheek (1988) report a series of cases where suggestions for coldness and numbness are effective in ameliorating herpes simplex I (fever blisters), particularly when they are given a posthypnotic suggestion to maintain an anesthesia for 24 hours. As we have seen in the approximate time parameters of the mind-body information transduction loop in Figure 11 this 24-hour period theoretically could be an important factor in insuring that the cellular-genetic portion of the loop has sufficient time for a complete cycle of healing.

Gould and Tissler (1984) reported two successful cases of treating women with herpes simplex II with a variety of hypnotherapeutic suggestions such as "strong cell structure, perfect skin, hormonal balance, cleanliness, and a cooling refreshed feeling in the area of the vagina and perineum" together with Simonton type visualization of "friendly white sharks . . . to devour the virus" and imagery from the patients' personal repertories of appropriate life experiences. Audio tapes of ego-strenthening suggestions were played in daily practice sessions and before bedtime. After a three-year respite from symptoms, one patient was involved in a serious auto accident that apparently traumatized her so that she experienced a minor relapse with herpes lesions reappearing on the labia major. She was once again treated successfully with hypnotherapeutic suggestion. This type of relapse is theoretically very important since it is exactly what one would predict from the state-dependent encoding of mind-body symptoms by the messenger molecules released by trauma and stress as discussed previously in Chapters 3 and 4.

Varicella-Zoster Virus is a complicated condition that appears in two very different conditions: varicella (chickenpox usually in children) and zoster (herpes zoster or "shingles" in adults) are regarded as different diseases but they are due to the same virus. Herpes zoster is responsible for one of the most painful dermatological conditions associated with viruses. Crasilneck and Hall (1985) reported that in some cases this pain persists even after the surface symptoms of the virus infection wanes. They believe that this is evidence that the pain is of central (mind-brain) origin since it seems akin to "phantom limb pain" that sometimes persists after the amputation of a limb. These authors recommend traditional direct hypnotherapeutic suggestion wherein "your discomfort will become much less intense . . . the burning and the stinging will begin to fade . . . you'll be much more relaxed and at ease." They also recommend teaching the patient self-hypnosis so that they can reinforce these suggestions twice a day. This is very similar to the utilization of the ultradian healing response as presented previously in teaching Tutorial 7 to optimize naturalistic rhythms of mind-body healing.

Cytomegalovirus (CMV) associated with mononucleosis syndrome is another of the herpesviruses that has a wide (81% of adults over age 35), if often symptomless, and unrecognized distribution (Crnic, 1991). Like the Epstein-Barr and herpes simplex viruses, CMV is found to be responsive to medical examination stress via the Glaser model (Kiecolt-Glaser & Glaser, 1991). CMV appears to be associated with the same psychosocial factors as AIDS (Solomon, Kemeny, & Temoshok, 1991) and evidence for the activation of CMV precedes the decline in the number of CD4 receptors on the cells of HIV positive people (Munoz et al., 1988), which predicts the eventual development of AIDS to which we will now turn our attention.

AIDS as an Informational Disease of the Mind-Body

There is much to indicate that acquired immune deficiency syndrome (AIDS) is an informational disease on many levels and loci of the mind-body as illustrated in the generic diagram of Figure 11. The HIV infection associated with the development of AIDS gains entry to the cell by attaching itself to the CD4 receptor on lymphocytes; this is a process whereby the virus utilizes the structural information of proteins on its surface to recognize and access the host cell receptors at locus 1 in Figure 11. One of the medical efforts to counter AIDS is to block this entry with peptide T or some other molecular structure (Ruff et al.,

1987). Once attached to the CD4 cell the virus injects its genes in the form of RNA directly into the cell. The virus RNA, a form of pure information, converts itself into DNA and inserts itself in the normal DNA of the host. AIDS is called a "retrovirus" because this process reverses the usual direction of information flow from DNA to RNA in the normal path of gene expression.

When it receives an appropriate signal, the virus DNA is expressed in the typical process of gene expression at locus 4 where it is converted back into RNA and then proceeds to use the host cell's metabolism to make a new virus protein coat at locus 9. The reconstituted virus is now able to break out of the dying host cell to spread to other host cells. Researchers hypothesize that the lethal destructive power of HIV is due to at least four informational levels that the host has difficulty in coping with:

1) The virus is so primitive that it does not have an error-checking apparatus to determine whether it copied itself accurately when it was expressed. This means that it has a high mutation rate; many of the virus's surface proteins, for example, change so rapidly that the organism's immune system cannot keep up with it.

2) Somewhere in its replication process the HIV infection manages to utterly confuse the messenger molecules (produced at locus 12) that normally operate between the different cell types of the immune system. These scrambled signals may, it is currently theorized, lead healthy lymphocytes to self-destruct or attack other healthy cells.

3) The HIV virus may shed fragments of its protein coat so that they unfortunately become attached to the surface of healthy host cells which are then attacked as foreign by the immune system; in this sense AIDS acts a bit like an autoimmune disease.

4) The mind-brain level of informational dysfunction due to AIDS is where many symptoms of memory, learning, emotions, and behavioral deterioration are evident in the terminal stages of the disease.

With so many sites of confusing information it is no wonder that the highly complex AIDS process may be modulated by many psychosocial sources of informational stress and health. While conservative opinion maintains that we do not yet have conclusive evidence about how psychosocial factors can influence AIDS by known informational pathways (Solomon et al., 1991), there is a wide range of studies that implicate many of the same psychosocial factors, such as emotional depression (Irwin et al., 1987; Kemeny et al., 1989, 1990) and psychological coping style (Goodkin et al., 1992; Remien et al., 1992), that we see as cofactors in most mind-body problems. Currently many theoretical and methodological analyses of these issues (Temoshok, 1992) are leading to flow diagrams of potentially therapeutic psychosocial approaches as illustrated in Figure 12.

Current studies of the potentially ameliorative effects of the mind-body therapies on AIDS must be interpreted carefully to determine the degree and locus of the psychosocial intervention. A stress reduction training program, for example, was found effective in changing a psychosocial parameter of AIDS, the number of sexual partners, but no significant changes in immune system parameters (Coates et al., 1989). A well-controlled study (Auerbach, Oleson, & Soloman, 1992) of a number of mind-body approaches (thermal biofeedback, guided imagery, and hypnosis) in an integrated behavioral treatment program with group III and IV HIV subjects found that many negative HIV-related symptoms such as fever, fatigue, pain, headache, nausea, and insomnia decreased, there were no changes in "tension-anxiety or depression," but the desirable coping style of "vigor and hardiness increased." There were no significant changes on the crucial AIDS variable of the number of CD4 cells in these subjects, however.

While the Auerbach study documented therapeutic effects with HIV subjects, there was no way of determining whether these therapeutic effects were specific for HIV or whether they were of the nonspecific ameliorative mind-body effects one finds in many such broadly based behavioral interventions. In a personal communication, however, Auerbach (January 23, 1993) reports the following interesting clinical observations made in this study.

> Individual subjects who reported a particular affinity and enjoyment of the guided imagery practice demonstrated the most significant CD4 cell increases. In the treatment group, the subject who practiced guided imagery and self-hypnosis techniques the most frequently, three times a day for twenty-minute durations each, when he noticed a dip in his ultradian rhythm, had the largest CD4 cell increase after eight weeks of practice.

Such clinical observations provide at least anecdotal support for the use of the ultradian healing response in HIV subjects that will require more extensive clinical-experimental documentation in the future.

The Hyperactive Immune System in Asthma and Allergies

Asthma is currently being recognized as a problem characterized by a hyperactive immune response. From the immunological point of view

(Hokama & Nakamura, 1982), asthma usually involves a hyperirritability of the bronchial mucosa in the lungs with eosinophils (which, as we have seen, comprise two to three percent of the white blood cell count). Specialized cells such as basophils and mast cells release histamine (which leads to dilation of capillaries and constriction of bronchial tissues) as part of the immune system's allergic reaction in hives and hay fever as well as asthma. Asthma can occur at any age and is recognizable by a wheezing and shortness of breath, which can range from mild discomfort to a life-threatening crisis of respiratory failure. There are two broad classes of asthma: *extrinsic* and *intrinsic* (Hokama & Nakamura, 1982).

Extrinsic (also called by the terms *allergic, immunological,* or *atopic*) asthma is mediated by IgE and can be associated with allergic rhinitis (inflammation of the nasal passages) and urticaria (*hives,* a disease characterized by severe itching and slightly elevated white patches of the skin that rarely lasts more than two days). Skin tests are positive to specific antigens and the IgE levels are usually elevated. This is the form of asthma that is common in early infancy, childhood, and about half of the adult population. It tends to be seasonal on exposure to plant allergins, and so forth.

Intrinsic (also called *nonallergic, nonatopic,* or *idiopathic*) asthma occurs primarily in adults, usually after the occurrence of an infectious respiratory illness (which apparently activates the immune system). It tends to be more chronic, with bronchial obstructions occurring unrelated to seasonal exposure to allergins. In addition, the IgE level is generally normal. In spite of these immunological differences, the clinical manifestations of extrinsic and intrinsic asthma are so similar that their psychophysiological mechanisms are believed to follow the same or similar route. The hypothalamus has been demonstrated experimentally to stimulate or attenuate allergic reactions (Frick, 1976; Stein, Schiavi, & Camerino, 1976) in animals. The sympathetic branch of the autonomic nervous system stimulates the allergic reaction by releasing histamine from the tissues, while the parasympathetic (relaxation) branch inhibits it.

Circadian and Ultradian Rhythms in Asthma.   The chronobiological influences of circadian rhythms on the occurrence of asthmatic attacks has been investigated (Reinberg, Gervais, & Ghata, 1977). The peak of dyspenic reactions (shortness of breath) has been shown to coincide in timing with the peak of skin reactions to histamine and allergins over the 24-hour daily cycle, so that most attacks occur between midnight and 3:00 a.m. These daily variations in susceptibility and illness have been traced to circadian rhythms that are apparently initiated in the hypothalamus, which mediates its effects (in association with the pineal gland's responsiveness to the daily light and dark cycle) through the endocrine system. It has been found that circadian rhythms in blood eosinophils depend in part upon the daily rhythms in the release of ACTH from the pituitary and its stimulation of hormones from the adrenal cortex. This is the same hypothalamic-pituitary-adrenal axis described by Selye as the major response to stress in the "Diseases of Adaptation."

There are a number of easily understandable mind-body routes by which the nonspecific hypnotherapeutic approaches (such as Benson's "relaxation response") can ameliorate allergic responses in a variety of psychosomatic illnesses. In my own clinical work, I have found that the form of self-hypnosis described earlier as the ultradian relaxation response is particularly effective when done in combination with symptom scaling so that the patient gradually attains voluntary control over allergic and asthmatic responses. A heightened sensitivity to the minimal cues that signal the beginning of an asthmatic response enable the patient to convert the asthmatic symptom into a signal for facilitating self-healing. Lankton (1987) is currently developing a related Ericksonian approach that combines symptom scaling and metaphor.

The value of hypnotherapeutic approaches to asthma is well documented with children (Alexander et al., 1972; Diamond, 1959) and adults in well controlled clinical trials (Ewer & Stewart, 1986). The obvious and often immediate and dramatic hypnotherapeutic responses are supported by experimental studies that indicate that cognitive suggestions are effective in leading to a worsening of asthma by bronchoconstriction as well as an improvement in symptoms by bronchodilation (Luparello et al., 1970; McFadden et al., 1969).

In working with asthmatics, as well as with any other symptom reaction that might have a life-threatening potential (e.g., *status asthmaticus* wherein the patient literally cannot get his breath), it is always wise to have qualified medical personnel available on the premises. When using the symptom scaling approach in such cases, one never asks the patient to experience anything more than 25 percent, or at most 30 percent, of the worst previous reaction. The symptom scaling should never get above 50 percent of the type of severe response that could cause a medical emergency. Symptom responses scaled in lower and lower ranges are actually the goal, because we are usually attempting to heighten the patient's awareness of only the most minimal cues that are needed to convert the symptom into a signal for healing.

Studies of the effectiveness of hypnotherapy with asthma and its related clinical manifestations have been reviewed by critically minded researchers (Bowers & Kelly, 1979; DePiano & Salzberg, 1979; Edwards, 1960; Wadden & Anderton, 1982). The great variety of methods described as "hypnotic" makes it difficult to assess these studies, which usually are a mixture of what we described earlier as the specific and nonspecific approaches. It seems likely that satisfactory resolution of these issues will be achieved only by isolating and studying the effects of hypnosis on specifically known and easily measurable allergic responses. Pioneering work in this area has been initiated by Ikemi and Nakagawa (1962) for allergic dermatitis and allergic responses to food, and by Kaneko and Takahashi (1963) for chronic urticaria. The largest body of research in the hypnotic alteration of acquired immunological allergic responses (such as the tuberculin skin test by Black, 1969, and Mason, 1963) is ripe for replication in light of the greater knowledge we now have about the mind-body connections involved. One cannot help but wonder, for example, if the movement of neutrophils facilitated by mental imagery discussed earlier (Schneider et al., 1984) could not be adapted to shift the locus of the closely related eosinophils from the bronchial tracts to ameliorate the hyperactive immune response in asthma and its related allergic dysfunctions.

In a recent review of the psychoneuroimmunology of asthma Mrazek and Klinnert (1991, p. 1027) speculate on the path of information transduction in asthma as follows:

> It is interesting to speculate at what level the positive impact of hypnotic suggestions operate. By definition, the effects involve changes in the functional status of the central nervous system. These alterations in consciousness and cerebral metabolism are hypothesized to directly affect the vagal and sympathetic pathways. An alternative mechanism, which could occur simultaneously, is that neurotransmitters released through the process of conducting hypnotherapy could stabilize the IgE-mediated mast cell membrane changes, resulting in decreased mast cell degranulation. Indirect evidence for the operation of this second pathway is the finding that hypnotherapy has been successfully employed to improve related allergic symptoms such as hives or eczema.

The Misguided Immune System in Autoimmune Dysfunctions and Rheumatoid Arthritis

An autoimmune dysfunction is one in which the immune system, in a perilous error of identity, attacks the tissues of the self as well as those of foreign invaders. A fundamental issue in immunology is the means by which the body distinguishes between antigens (or foreign substances) and what is natural: This is the distinction between nonself and self that breaks down during an autoimmune dysfunction. Currently it is believed that this "learning" process takes place during fetal development as a result of the direct contact between the body's own substances and the receptor sites on the surface of the white blood cells. The immune system learns to recognize self by disarming the antigen-antibody reaction in relation to all the natural substances (autoantigens) of the body.

As life goes on, however, there are many pathways for the breakdown of the central mechanisms underlying self-recognition. Usually the breakdown involves a disruption of the normal pathways of interaction between the T- and B-cells with autoantigens. Autoimmune disorders are usually associated with malignancies, immune deficiency syndromes, injuries, and aging. A recent study found that one of the most common types of ulcers of the gums (recurrent aphthous stomatitis), which is thought to be an essentially autoimmune problem, can be ameloriated by a relaxation/imagery treatment program (Andrews & Hall, 1990). In this section we will review recent research on rheumatoid arthritis as an example of how new hypnotherapeutic approaches to autoimmune dysfunctions could be developed.

Rheumatoid arthritis (RA) is a generalized systemic illness that usually has a slow onset manifested by symptoms of fatigue, muscle stiffness, and parathesias (unusual sensations of burning, prickling, numbness). As the disease progresses, the major joints of the body (shoulders, elbows, wrists, fingers, hips, knees, ankles, and toes) are experienced as swollen and stiff. Acute and chronic joint pain develops while moving and even at rest, and there is growing restriction in joint movement. The severity of the problem fluctuates over time with periods of remission occurring; sometimes an apparently complete "spontaneous" recovery takes place.

The physiology of the joint problems in RA is still the subject of research, and the autoimmune aspects of the disease are not yet entirely clear. It is thought, however, that the immediate problem is due to the excess growth of the cells in the synovial membrane, which normally covers the interior of the joint in a thin layer and secretes a lubricating fluid. One hypothesis of the mechanism for this process is that the EBV alters the synovial tissues (or the cartilage or joint tissues themselves) so that the immune system mistakenly marshals an attack that causes the synovial tissues to proliferate excessively (Silberner, 1985). The excess tissue spreads into the joint, causing the swelling that ultimately destroys the cartilage and, in advanced cases, rendering the joint immobile. It is believed that both cellular (T-cell lymphocytes) and humoral (B-cell lymphocytes) immunopathology are involved in the mistaken identity attack that now takes place. Macrophage activity is then greatly increased to remove the debris. Excess enzymes in turn cause more cartilage damage. It is believed that negative emotions increase muscle tension and the resulting excess activation of the sympathetic branch of the autonomic nervous system can further exacerbate this deteriorating condition (Achterberg & Lawlis, 1980; Brewerton, 1992; Weiner, 1977).

The mind-body connection in RA is believed to be mediated via our now familiar *limbic-hypothalamic-pituitary* route. Achterberg and Lawlis (1980) have outlined the possible dynamics of the process, summarized as follows.

1) In the RA patient, the stresses of life that are usually filtered through mind-cortical processes are blunted; the person frequently appears to be devoid of affect, emotionally flat or colorless, and "without soul." This lack of emotion has been described as *alexithymia*—literally, a condition in which one is "without words for feelings." Nemiah, Freyberger, and Sifneos (1976) have proposed that psychosomatic patients have a defective pattern of associative connections between their cortex and their limbic system.

2) Neural activity that is usually associated with emotions is not experienced in the higher cortical pathways of mind but is instead short-circuited through the hypothalamus and its direct associations with the autonomic, endocrine, and immune systems. RA (and perhaps psychosomatic symptoms in general) is thus a form of body language that substitutes for the lack of verbal (left hemisphere) and imagistic-emotional (right hemisphere) language. This condition has also been described as *pensée opératoire*, or the inability to fantasize.

3) The use of body language instead of cognition, fantasy, and emotion may involve an increase in muscle tension in the RA patient which, in turn, increases joint pain and actually accelerates destruction within the joints by increasing intra-articular temperatures (that stimulate lysomal enzymatic activity).

4) There may be an accelerating cycle of interaction between the immune system and the hypothalamus that is characterized by *positive* biofeedback, which worsens the RA condition instead of

correcting it (as would be the case with the normal *negative* bio-feedback processes).

The concept of alexithymia as a structural or genetic defect in the mind-cortical and limbic-hypothalamic areas is still a highly speculative theory regarding the genesis of RA in particular, and psychosomatic disorders in general. A more conventional psychodynamic explanation by Erickson and Rossi (1979) was based on the denial, suppression, and/or repression of right-hemispheric experience so that the left hemisphere lacked the information needed to express the problem in words. While further research will be needed to differentiate between the relative merits of these two views, they are in agreement that *state-bound information* is of essence in psychosomatic dysfunctions. The normal accessing and flow of information in the mind-body system are either blocked, short-circuited, or misguided so that the body is left to process information that would be better dealt with at the level of mind in a symptomatic manner.*

Erickson's approaches to patients who exhibited varying degrees of chronic pain, hopelessness, apathy, or blunted affect involved his usual exploration of their ability to use the classical mechanisms of hypnotic dissociation, displacement, time distortion, and so forth, in combination with his often unusual approach of *emotional provocation* (see Volume 4 of Erickson, 1980). A great deal of the controversy surrounding Erickson's work has centered on his unconventional use of shock, surprise, and embarrassment (Rossi, 1973/1980) to provoke what we now recognize as heightened states of autonomic system arousal. For example, he frequently used bold measures to provoke patients with a variety of organic brain dysfunctions to higher levels of rehabilitative effort (Erickson, 1963/1980, 1980a).

As I mentally review my observation of Erickson's work with a variety of patients during the last eight years of his life, I now realize that this

---

*Videocassettes of the author's live demonstrations with real patients of how to re-frame these personality dynamics into a deeply meaningful psychotherapeutic approaches to arthritis may be obtained from the following training centers (for professionals only):

The Milton H. Erickson Foundation, Inc., 3606 North 24 Street, Phoenix, Arizona, 85016–6500, U.S.A. *Arthritis Demo of 12-4-1992.*

Erickson Institute de Guadalajara, Progreso #271. P.B., Guadalajara, Jalisco, Mexico. *Arthritis Demo of 11-7-1992* with Spanish translation.

factor of emotional arousal and provocation was almost always present. Even when he appeared to be acting in a benign and gentle manner, I frequently would catch a gleam of mischievousness in his eye as he used a seemingly innocent word or phrase with hidden levels of meaning that were designed to arouse the patient's emotional dynamics in unexpected ways. More often than not, however, I would miss these multiple levels of communication that could break through the patterns of state-bound information in the patient's total mind-body system until Erickson patiently explained them to me (Erickson & Rossi, 1979, 1981; Erickson, Rossi, & Rossi, 1976). He always seemed to be having a lot of fun as he engaged patients on these multiple levels, and a positive therapeutic bond would exist even when negative emotions had been aroused. In each case Erickson was careful to access and utilize patients' own unique repertory of life experiences to help them create new mental frameworks and identities that engaged their aroused emotions and personality structures. In this regard Erickson used an integration of both nonspecific (emotional arousal and the alarm response) and specific approaches (the patient's unique life experiences) to facilitate the hypnotherapeutic process. Most of these approaches have never been replicated because they were considered to be manifestations of Erickson's idiosyncratic personality and his flair for the dramatic (Hilgard, 1984) rather than of legitimate therapy. As we have seen in our earlier discussions about the mind modulation of the endocrine and autonomic nervous systems, however, the use of the dramatic to arouse state-bound memories and emotions has a sound psychobiological basis. The blocked or dysfunctional memory, emotion, and fantasy processes of patients with rheumatoid arthritis would seem to be an ideal test category for exploring and extending Erickson's pioneering hypnotherapeutic approaches to the arousal and utilization of each patient's unique mind-body repertory of response abilities.

A case illustration of how state-bound aspects of one's total personality can be encoded in the form of rheumatoid arthritis and released by an accessing process of *active imagination* is provided by a Jungian analyst, Albert Kreinheder (1979). He describes his personal encounter with the disease and his self-healing, as follows (pp. 60–61):

> Two years ago my life seemed to be flowing along beautifully. I had gained some respect in my profession, my health was excellent, and all in all I thought I was doing quite well. At this seemingly high point in my life's achievements I was afflicted with rheumatoid arthritis. I became, by necessity, an anti-hero. I had severe pain in every joint of my body, including

even my jaw bones. After being awake for two or three hours and doing my normal sedentary activities, I would be exhausted and need to go back to bed. My shoulders and elbows were so stiff that unassisted, I couldn't put on my jacket nor without help could I rise from a prone position.

I tried everything, including physicians, chiropractors, nutritionists, masseuses, and tarot cards, but nothing seemed to work. Not knowing what else to do, I decided to talk to my pain. Here is a sample of the dialogues that materialized:

ME: You hold me tight in your grip, and you do not let me go. If you crave my undivided attention, you have received it. Whatever I attend to, I must also attend to you. Even when I write, I feel you in my hand, and always in all parts of my body. I am terribly frightened by you. I have no control over you, no access to you, no power to influence you. You need only go a little further, and then I am utterly helpless. Will you ever stop? Why are you here?

PAIN: I am here to get your attention. I make known my presence. I show you my power. I have a power beyond your power. My will surpasses yours. You cannot prevail over me, but I can easily prevail over you.

ME: But why must you destroy me with your power?

PAIN: I do so because I will no longer let you disregard me. You will bow down before me and humble yourself, for I am He of whom there is no other. I am the first of all things, and all things spring from me, and without me there is nothing. I want to be with you closely in your thoughts at all times. That is why I press you in the grip of my power and make you think only of me. Now, with my presence in you, you can no longer live the same way and do the same things.

These dialogues gave meaning to my disability. Before, my pain was only a curse to be eliminated. Now it is revealed to be "He-of-whom-there-is-no-other." And this great-one desired intimacy with me. Now I knew what before were only words to me: Our wound is the place where the Self finds entry into us. The calamity that strikes may be the election, the call to individuation.

I became aware that my life had to change. When people are in the twenties, thirties, and perhaps through the forties, it is amazing to discover how totally ego-centered people can be and still prosper. But sooner or later, the larger personality asserts itself. "The time is coming," my pain said to me, "when I will put a stop to all those things that come before your love for me." And he said further: "It is so pressing and important that you love me and stay with me that you will be crippled and paralyzed by anything that threatens to be more important than I. Love me first. To ignore me brings death, disease, and destruction."

When a neurosis or a sickness comes to one, it does not mean that he is an inferior person with a defective character. In a way, it is a positive sign showing potentials for growth, as if within there is a greater personality pressing to the surface. When arthritis came to me, I went back into analysis. I did so, I suppose, because I had arthritis. But the intention of the unconscious was probably the other way around. Arthritis came so that I would go back into analysis. We are never fully analyzed. As conditions change, there are new psychic contents to integrate. Once a window is opened to the archetypal world, there is no way to close it again. Either we grow with the individuation urge, or it grows against us.

A recent seven-year follow-up (personal communication) has indicated that Dr. Kreinheder is still symptom-free. This profound view of the deeper possible meaning of illness has been expressed by shamans and healers of all cultures and times. Dr. Kreinheder's experience with arthritis demonstrates how illness can be a call to stop one's habitual activities to seek out the deeper meanings that are evolving in one's existence. This is the basis of the ultradian healing process I call ''converting a symptom into a signal.''

CONVERTING A SYMPTOM INTO A SIGNAL

Tuning into a psychosomatic symptom with an attitude of respectful inquiry rather than the usual patient stance of avoidance, resistance, and rejection is the first step to accessing the state-dependent memories and associations that may be signals from those parts of the personality that are in need of expressive development (individuation). I usually introduce the concept of converting a symptom into a signal of the need for a broader creative development in the patient's inner life somewhat as follows (Rossi, 1986b, p. 20):

> You can use a natural form of self-hypnosis by simply letting yourself really enjoy taking a break whenever you need to throughout the day. You simply close your eyes and tune into the parts of your body that are most comfortable. When you locate the comfort you can simply enjoy it and allow it to deepen and spread throughout your body all by itself. Comfort is more than just a word or a lazy state. Really going deeply into comfort means you have turned on your parasympathetic system—your natural relaxation response. This is the easiest way to maximize the healing benefits of the rest phase of your body's natural ultradian rhythms.
>
> As you explore your inner comfort you can *wonder* how your creative unconscious is going to deal with whatever symptom, problem or issue that you want it to deal with. Your unconscious is the inner regulator of all your

---

TUTORIAL 14 Converting a Symptom into a Signal

1. *Scaling to convert symptoms into signals*
   On a scale of one to 100 where 100 is the worst, what number expresses the degree to which you are experiencing that symptom pain, discomfort, or whatever right now?
   Recognize how that symptom intensity is actually a signal of just how strong another, deeper part of you needs to be recognized and understood right now.

2. *Accessing and inquiry into symptom meaning*
   When your inner mind (creative unconscious, etc.) is ready to help you access the deeper meanings of your symptoms, will you find yourself getting quiet and comfortable with your eyes eventually closing? [Pause]
   You may review the original sources of that symptom [pause], you may ask your symptom what it is saying to you [pause]. Will you discuss with your symptom what changes are needed in your life?

3. *Ratifying the significance and value of new meaning*
   How will you now use your symptom as an important signal?
   [The significance of whatever new meanings come up usually can be recognized intuitively by the subject. New meaning is invariably accompanied by affects (tears, enthusiasm, thankfulness). A rescaling of symptom intensity at this time will usually ratify the value of this form of inner work with a lower number or zero.]

---

biological and mental processes. If you have problems it is probably because some unfortunate programming from the past has interfered with the natural processes of regulation within your unconscious. By accepting and letting yourself enjoy the normal periods of ultradian rest as they occur throughout the day, you are allowing your body/mind's natural self-regulation to heal and resolve your problems.

Your attitude toward your symptom and yourself is very important during this form of healing hypnosis. *Your symptom or problem is actually your friend! Your symptom is a signal that a creative change is needed in your life.* During your periods of comfort in ultradian self-hypnosis, you will often receive quiet insights about your life, what you really want, and how to get it. A new thoughtfulness, joy, greater awareness, and maturity can result from the regular practice of ultradian self-hypnosis.

THE IMMUNE SYSTEM, INFORMATION, AND CONSCIOUSNESS

Stephen Black is an English researcher who pioneered the use of hypnosis in the mind modulation of acquired immunological reactions that previously were thought to be purely biological processes. His research on the use of hypnosis to modulate the immune response of human subjects to the tubercular bacillus (the Mantoux reaction) (Black, Humphrey, & Niven, 1963) and allergic reactions of the skin (Black, 1963; Black & Friedman, 1965) was the inspiration of many researchers described in this chapter (Smith, McKenzie, Marmer, & Steele, 1985; Smith & McDaniel, 1983). Black was guided in his investigation by an ardent philosophical interest in establishing the conceptual unity of mind, body, and life itself. His hypnotic investigations of acquired immunity were for him an empirical means of solving the mind-body problem—the separation of mind and body into two separate conceptual realms since the time of Descartes. Since this is essentially the same mind-body issue we are dealing with in this book, we will review Black's ideas and explore their implications for current thinking.

Black used the newly developing *information theory* of the 1960s as a conceptual base for proposing a common definition of biological life and mind. To understand the significance of his definition it is important to have a basic comprehension of information theory, which we touched upon in Chapter 2. While information theory was originally formulated as a mathematical model (Shannon & Weaver, 1949; Wiener, 1948) for emerging communication technologies, it rapidly was found useful for conceptualizing all processes of change and transformation. In Chapter 2, for example, we summarized the view that all biological and psychological processes could be understood as different forms of information transduction. One way of resolving the mind-body problem is to say that mind and body participate in similar processes of information transduction. We reviewed the work of many theorists and experimental psychologists who used information theory as the conceptual basis for understanding how hypnosis could mediate the mind modulation of the body's physiology (Bowers, 1977).

While information theory is usually formulated in mathematical language, it will be sufficient for our purposes to state its basic idea as follows: *The more improbable an idea or event is, the higher its informational value.* In commonsense terms: Whatever is routine, ordinary, and expected in our lives usually does not contribute any new information to us. What is new, mysterious, and interesting, however, does contribute. Thus whatever is *new* for a person has high informational value.

Chapter 2 described how the ascending reticular activating system (ARAS) and the *locus coeruleus* are the parts of the brain stem that activate consciousness when new and novel stimuli are presented. The *new* can come from the outer environment or be generated within during creative states of thinking and dreaming. Repetitive and routine life situations and habitual patterns of ideation, on the other hand, tend to lower one's level of consciousness and put the mind to sleep. This leads us to the basic insight that consciousness (and mind in general) thrives on information. *Mind is nature's supreme design for receiving, generating, and transducing information.*

In this informational conception of mind, the word *design* has important implications. Design implies form and structure. Information is usually manifest to us as changes in design, form, and structure. The significance of this structural view of information for understanding how the phenomenal aspects of mind and the material aspects of brain and body can be embraced within the same conceptual framework is well described by Karl Pribram (1986, in press):

Maurice Merleau-Ponty, an existentialist philosopher, has authored a book entitled *The Structure of Behavior* (1963), which in both spirit and content shows remarkable resemblances to our own *Plans and the Structure of Behavior* (Miller, Galanter, & Pribram, 1960; see also Pribram, 1965), which tackles the issues from a behavioral and information-processing vantage. I do not mean to convey here that there is no distinction between a behavioristic and an existential-phenomenalistic approach to mind. Elsewhere I detail this distinction in terms of a search for causes by behaviorists and a search for informational structure reasonably (meaningfully) composed by phenomenologists (Pribram, 1979). What I do want to emphasize here is that both approaches lead to conceptualizations that cannot be classified readily as either mental or material. Behaviorists in their search for causes, rely on drives, incentives, reinforcers, and other 'force'-like concepts that deliberately have a Newtonian ring. Existentialists in their quest for understanding mental experience come up with structure much as do anthropologists and linguists when they are tackling other complex organizations. And structural concepts are akin to those of modern physics where particles arise from the interactions and relationships among processes.

Understanding how computer programs are composed helps to tease apart some of the issues involved in the "identity" approach in dealing with the mind/brain relationship: Because our introspections provide no apparent connection to the functions of the neural tissues that comprise the brain, it has not been easy to understand what theorists are talking about when they claim that mental and brain processes are identical. Now, because of the computer/program analogy, we can suggest that what is common to mental operations and the brain "wetware" in which the operation is realized, is some order which remains invariant across transformations. The terms "information" (in the brain and cognitive sciences) and "structure" (in linguistics and in music) are the most commonly used to describe such identities across transformations.

Order invariance across transformations is not limited to computers and computer programming. In music we recognize a Beethoven sonata or a Berlioz symphony irrespective of whether it is presented to us as a score on sheets of paper, in a live concert, over our high fidelity music system, and even in our automobiles when distorted and muffled by noise and poor reproduction. The information (form within), the structure (arrangement) is recognizable in many realizations. The materials which make the realizations possible differ considerably from each other, but these differences are not part of the essential property of the musical form. In this sense, the identity approach to the mind/brain relationship, despite the realism of its embodiments, partakes of Platonic universals, i.e., ideal orderings which are liable to becoming flawed in their realization.

In the construction of computer languages (by humans) we gain insight into how information or structure is realized in a machine. The essence of biological as well as of computational hierarchies is that higher levels of organization take control over, as well as being controlled by, lower levels. Such reciprocal causation is ubiquitous in living systems: thus the level of tissue carbon dioxide not only controls the neural respiratory mechanism but is controlled by it. Discovered originally as a regulatory principle which maintains a constant environment, reciprocal causation is termed "homeostais." Research over the past few decades has established that such *feedback* mechanisms are ubiquitous, involving sensory, motor, and all sorts of central processes. When feedback organizations are hooked up into parallel arrays, they become feedforward control mechanisms which operate much as do the words (of bit and byte length) in computer languages (Miller et al., 1960; Pribram, 1971).

Pribram's use of this structural concept of information enables him to unite mental and physiological relationships in a single framework of reciprocal causation or homeostasis that is characteristic of all our illustrations of mind-body communication (Figures 1, 5–8, 10, 12). With this background of understanding, we can now return to Black's use of information theory to conceptualize how the immune system provides a model of mind-body communication and healing. In the following quotations, Black makes use of the concept of information as structures that are new (improbable) to define life and mind (1969):

It is then the basis of my argument that since the Aristotelian form of *all* matter "contains information" in some degree and since "information in the form of form" is apparently essential to living matter, *it is according to the improbability of the form of matter—as distinct from its energetic substance—that life should be defined.*

I therefore put forward the definition: *that life is a quality of matter which arises from the informational content inherent in the improbability of form.* (p. 46)

I therefore put forward a second hypothesis: *that mind is the informational system derived from the sum improbability of form inherent in the material substance of living things.* (p. 56)

Information, of course, can be transmitted in all sorts of ways—from the modulations in a wireless wave, to the black and white patterns on the pages of this book. And to workers in biology at the molecular level, the concept of both transmitting and recording information "in the form of form" is certainly nothing new.

But the facts here are not generally looked at in this kind of way. Although the difference may even seem trivial—and by some damned as "metaphysical"—it is nevertheless important to my theme. For I hope to show from the clinical and experimental evidence of psychosomatic medicine, that whatever the stability of the genetic substance, much of the information recorded by the body in the form of form can in the course of life make its own contribution both to sickness and to health. (p. 47)

Black's view of *form* as the *inform*ational essence of life and mind sounds very abstract until we remember that it is true at the molecular level. It is, in fact, the form and structure of messenger molecules and their receptors that turn on and modulate the activity of life within all the cells of the body. Black's pioneering research was a step in demonstrating how this is true for mind-body communication via the immune system, as illustrated in Figure 10. As indicated in previous chapters, we now know it is also true for the autonomic (Fig. 7, p. 106) and endocrine (Fig. 8, p. 126) systems. In the next chapter we will learn how it is valid for the neuropeptide system as well.

It was probably because Black was so concerned with the essentially unconscious nature of mind-body information transduction in psychosomatic problems that he did not give any corresponding definitions of consciousness. I believe that the definition of consciousness as "a process of self-reflective information transduction," which I proposed in Chapter 2, fits admirably well with Black's views, however. Some of the major modalities or forms of information transduction that make up the content of consciousness were presented in Tutorial 1 (p. 93). While these mental modalities (emotions, imagery, cognition, etc.) are at a different level of description than body and molecule, they are all united by *our currently emerging view of life, biology, and mind* as being essentially *inform*ational transf*orm*ations of each other.

The practical application of this unitary conception of form in psychobiological phenomena is evident in many of the schools of psychotherapy that developed out of the classical depth psychologies of Freud and Jung. One immediately thinks, for example, of gestalt therapy and all its derivatives. Jung, himself, gave a central place to the significance of form in his basic concept of the archetype as a "psychoid" or psychobiological structure that formed the essence of ideas, symbols, and processes of transformation. He described his views as follows (Jung, 1960, p. 33):

> There is not a single important idea or view that does not possess historical antecedents. Ultimately they are all founded on primordial archetypical forms whose concreteness dates from a time when consciousness did not *think*, but only *perceived*. "Thoughts" were objects of inner perception, not thought at all, but sensed as external phenomena—seen or heard, so to speak. Thought was essentially revelation, not invented but forced upon us or bringing conviction through its immediacy and actuality. Thinking of this kind precedes the primitive ego-consciousness, and the latter is more its object than its subject. But we ourselves have not yet climbed the last peak of consciousness, so we also have a pre-existent thinking, of which we are not aware so long as we are supported by traditional symbols—or, to put it in the language of dreams, so long as the father or the king is not dead.

There are many important associations here. I believe that Black's conception of life and mind as "the informational content inherent in the improbability of form" is the fundamental axiom for an *information theory of image, archetype, symbol, and the mythopoetic dimension of right-hemispheric consciousness in general and mind-body healing in particular*. The profound reach of information theory into our current conceptions of psychotherapy is usually not immediately obvious. When I first formulated the following hypothesis about the significance of original dream experience for the development of identity and consciousness, for example, I had no idea that it was actually a phenomenological expression of an informational theory of mind (Rossi, 1972/1985, p. 25):

HYPOTHESIS 1. *That which is unique, odd, strange or intensely idiosyncratic in a dream is an essence of individuality. It is an expression of original psychological experience and, as such, it is the raw material out of which new patterns of awareness may develop.*

What is "unique, odd, strange or intensely idiosyncratic" is, of course, a subjective experience of what information theory describes as the high informational value of an improbable event. As noted earlier in Chapter 2, we can now better appreciate why the mind-body gives greatest attention to "novel stimuli": Simply put, they have a higher informational value. When we focus patients' attention with what they experience as new or novel, we are maximizing the probability of facilitating therapeutic processes involving information transduction of high value. This can become the basis of many therapeutically stimulating approaches to mind-body healing.

This is probably the reason why patients who have not found help by conventional medicine intuitively turn to the unusual and often seemingly bizarre approaches of other cultures and "holistic medicine." This is how mystery and the *numinosum* (Jung, 1960) of religious practices and strange cults can cure: They all help patients break out of the learned limitations of their familiar thinking and lifestyle that are encoding the adaptive value of their sickness or problem. The unusual practices of the mystery religions and foreign healers break through the constricting and deadening effect of the familiar to access and activate the high informational value of the new within the body-mind of the patient.

This excursion into the byways of an informational theory of psychobiology and mind-body healing has taken us far from the research of Black on the hypnotic modulation of the immune system and the major concerns of this chapter with mind-body healing. However, this integration of previously separate studies in fields as diverse as philosophy, religion, cultural anthropology, psychology, biology, neurology, and molecular genetics is precisely what is most valuable in our developing information theory of mind-body healing. In the next and final chapter, we will witness an even more profound integration of all these areas of inquiry for the creation of consciousness and healing.

10

Mind Modulation of the Neuropeptide System

THE VANGUARD OF neurobiological research today suggests that an entirely new understanding of mind-body communication integrating the autonomic, endocrine, and immune systems is being conceptualized in the *neuropeptide system*. Working in the Brain Biochemistry Division of the National Institute of Mental Health, Pert and her colleagues have proposed that neuropeptides and their receptors function as a previously unrecognized psychosomatic network. They summarized their views as follows (Pert, Ruff, Weber, & Herkenham, 1985, p. 820s):

> A major conceptual shift in neuroscience has been wrought by the realization that brain function is modulated by numerous chemicals in addition to classical neurotransmitters. Many of these informal substances are neuropeptides, originally studied in other contexts as hormones, "gut peptides," or growth factors. Their number presently exceeds 50 and most, if not all, alter behavior and mood states, although only endogenous analogs of psychoactive drugs like morphine, Valium, and phencyclidine have been well appreciated in this context. We now realize that their signal specificity resides in receptors (distinct classes of recognition molecules), rather than the close juxtaposition occurring at classical synapses. Rather precise brain distribution patterns for many neuropeptide receptors have been determined. A number of brain loci, many within emotion-mediating brain areas, are enriched with many types of neuropeptide receptors suggesting a convergence of information at these "nodes." Additionally, neuropeptide receptors occur on mobile cells of the immune systems; monocytes can chemotax to numerous neuropeptides via processes shown by structure-activity analysis to be mediated by distinct receptors indistinguishable from those found in brain. *Neuropeptides and their receptors thus join the brain, glands, and immune system in a network of communication between brain and body, probably representing the biochemical substrate of emotion.* (Italics added)

Pert's use of the term "informational substance" to describe the essential messenger function of the neuropeptide system is a new way of integrating the data and behavior from the previously separated fields of knowledge in psychology, neurology, anatomy, biochemistry, and molecular biology. There is much research suggesting that the central and autonomic nervous systems, and the endocrine and immune systems are all channels, carriers, or vehicles for the messenger molecules of the neuropeptide system (Besedovsky, del Rey, & Sorkin, 1985; Blalock, Harbour-McMenamin, & Smith, 1985; Bloom, 1985; Felton et al., 1985; Pincus et al., 1992). An overview of the neuropeptide system as far as it is currently understood is illustrated in Figure 12. As can be seen, the neuropeptide system adds to, overlaps with, and integrates all the previously discussed systems of mind-body communication.

The outline of branching neurons from the brain to the body on the left side of Figure 12 are meant to illustrate how many of them function as highly elongated communication channels that receive, transduce, and transmit signals very rapidly over large distances between the brain and the body. Some human neurons may be a meter long so only a few may be needed in their typical routes from the brain to important ganglia (nerve centers outside the brain), along the spine, for example, for each other parts of the body. This is important from a mind-body healing perspective because while neurons have been specialized for rapid electrochemical signaling (the action potential or wave of depolarization that carries the signal is measured in milliseconds), nerve cells also transduce many of the signals they receive into new messenger molecules and receptors, as is illustrated on the cell-gene level of Figure 12. Hours, day, weeks, or more (the typical time domain for mind-body healing and recovery from trauma and stress) may be required for this process of information transduction when genes are expressed to make new proteins and then transport them along the neurons to the synapses (connections between nerves). This is particularly true when many neurons are involved together in networks for the encoding, calculation, and transmission of memory and learning.

Some of the basic questions that currently confront us in this process for a general theory of mind-body healing have been well expressed by Ira Black in his quest to understand *Information And The Brain* (1991, p. 95):

> What mechanisms mediate the translation of membrane depolarization into altered gene readout? What is the duration of altered readout with respect to the inciting depolarizing stimuli? Are whole gene families subject

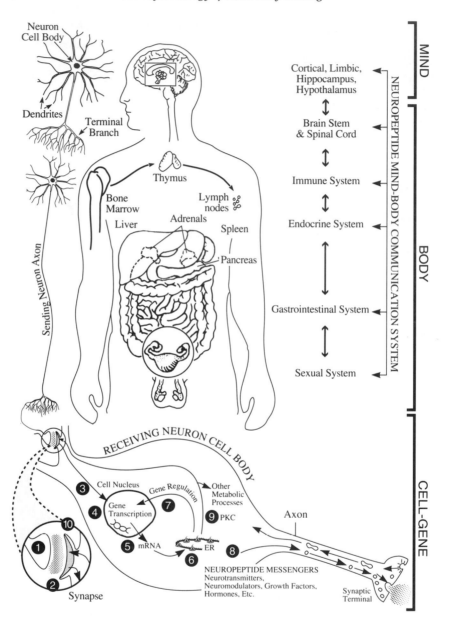

FIGURE 12 The mind-body-gene communication loop of the neuropeptide system with some of the major loci of information transduction at the cellular-genetic level of state-dependent memory, learning, and behavior.

to this regulation, and, if so, will this provide hints regarding the overall orchestration of information in the nervous and endocrine systems?

Thus, peripheral neuroendocrine cells utilize molecular signals as symbols to represent impulse activity. Different combinatorial states transduce different impulse frequencies, evoking different physiologic effects. Hormone and transmitter serve the dual roles of physiologic effector and information encoder. Do virtually all cells use and store extracellular (environmental) information in this manner?

Answers to these questions are the "holy grail" of current research in mind-body communication. While many of the steps outlined in Figure 12 are well-documented in the scientific literature, the overall account presented here can only be regarded as speculative. Communication by neural cells have similarities as well as important differences with the processes of information transduction at the cellular-genetic level in the autonomic, endocrine, and immune systems illustrated in previous chapters. One basic similarity is that when the neural cell is stimulated in an appropriate manner, it goes through the same basic process of information transduction from the cell receptor to the genes and the production of new proteins, messengers, and receptors. Some of these messengers are secreted from the neural cell to signal other neurons and cells of the body. In this sense neurons are secretory cells just as are the cells of the endocrine system that secrete hormones (De Wied, 1990). Neural cells are different in the speed of their signaling and the fact that they keep records of their signaling experience in the form of changed shape and protein structure which leads to greater ease in communicating with each other. The current view is that these changes in shape and function of certain parts of the neuron are the psychobiological basis of memory and learning in what is now called "long-term potentiation" (LTP) (Kimble, 1992).

LTP is the basic psychobiological phenomenon that underlies memory and learning at the neural and cellular-genetic level. Research on the basic process of encoding new patterns of memory and learning has concentrated on the hippocampus and related parts of the brain which, as we have seen (Chapter 4), are particularly sensitive to emotions and the debilitating effects of trauma and stress. Researchers found that after they provided appropriate electrical stimulation to certain cells of the hippocampus, later signals became *potentiated*; a single stimulus from the environment could now evoke a larger response and more readily trigger further signals. This is called *long-term potentiation* because it can last hours, days, weeks, or longer depending upon many state-dependent aspects of the animal's general health, age, and previous experience (Tyler, Perkins, & Harris, 1989). As we have seen in previous chapters, this is the same time-domain for the duration of most traumatic- and stress-related mind-body problems. This leads us to hypothesize that LTP may be the cellular-genetic basis of stress-related problems that are dealt with by the many approaches to mind-body healing.

The actual events leading to LTP *within the neurons* involve the typical route of secondary messengers signaling the nucleus. This in turn signals the expression of genes which leads to the production of mRNA which is sent out to the cytoplasm of the cell where new proteins are made from mRNA blueprints. These proteins then function as enzymes to regulate other chemical functions of the cell including the formation of new messenger molecules, receptors, and proteins that carry out the special functions of the cell. In the case of neurons involved in the LTP and the formation of memory, the proteins are transported to the synapse to "strengthen" the connection between the neurons so that the next signal between them will pass more easily. With increased use the synaptic bond between the two neurons becomes strengthened to form the psychobiological basis of memory and learning in a way first discussed by the psychologist Donald Hebb (1949); these synapses are therefore called "Hebb synapses." Neural networks made up of easily communicating brain cells are presumed to underlie the dynamics of memory, learning, behavior, emotions, and personality (see Chapter 6).

While the details of this process are not well-understood and many different theories are currently being explored (Alkon, 1992; Olds et al., 1989), some researchers believe that the scenario may progress somewhat as illustrated in Figure 12: Long-term potentiation leading to associative learning at Hebb synapses may involve (1) the time-associated release of certain neurotransmitters (e.g., glutamate) by the sending neuron on the presynaptic level (that has picked up a stimulus from the environment) with the appropriate electrochemical state on the receiving neuron (the postsynaptic level); the Specialized NMDA (N-methyl-D-asparate) receptors (2) on the postsynaptic receiving neuron pick up the signal from the neurotransmitter released by the presynaptic sending neuron; secondary messengers (3) such as calcium ions (Ca) help mediate the signal to the nucleus of the cell where (4) genes are transcribed, (5) mRNA sent to the (6) ER where (7) gene regulatory loops are set in motion leading to the synthesis of other proteins that will eventually function as structural elements of the cell, (8) neuropeptide messengers and receptors (Pincus, DiCicco-Bloom, & Black, 1992) as well as enzymes such as protein kinase C (PKC); PKC is then looped (9) to the same loci on the postsynaptic neuron that picked up the original signal from the sending (presynaptic) neuron at (1). Some researchers (Kosslyn & Koenig, 1992) believe that both pre- and postsynaptic neurons are changed in structure and function during this loop of information transduction to make it easier for a signal to be transmitted at this locus the next time. This change in structure and function at the synaptic level may involve changes in the so-called "postsynaptic density structure" (10) (Black, 1991) that facilitates the kind of signal transmission that is the basis of memory, learning, and behavior change.

Although we have introduced protein kinases in this chapter because of their significance for the learning process at the neuronal level, it should be understood that they are produced in all cells of the brain and body where they play many important informational roles in the specialized metabolic processes of each different kind of cell. It has been hypothesized that hundreds and perhaps thousands of different protein kinases operate as "transistors" for the signals regulating cellular processes at the molecular level (Hunter, 1987, p. 226):

> A reasonable answer to the question of why there are so many protein kinases would be that they serve as major components of the essential regulatory circuitry of the cell. To draw an electronic analogy, one might term them the transistors of the cell. In electronic circuits transistors are used either as simple on/off switches or as amplifiers for an electric current. Transistors commonly have two inputs, which regulate current flow and gain, and a single output. Protein kinases share many properties with transistors that make them ideal components of biological feedback and amplification pathways, as well as switching or signalling systems.
>
> To pursue this analogy, the ability of protein kinases to phosphorylate other proteins can be considered the basis for signal (current) transmission, with phosphorylated substrates being the output. This basic transmission activity can be regulated positively or negatively by several types of input such as specific ligands or by phosphorylation of the protein kinases themselves. In this manner the phosphorylation signal (enzymatic activity) can be turned on and off, and the "gain" of amplification of the signal can be regulated as the specific activity of the enzyme is changed. In some ways, however, protein kinases are more sophisticated control units than single transistors, being more akin to integrated chips.

Although 100 protein kinases are known, Hunter predicts that their number will soon reach 1,000. What do therapists know about the protein kinases they are modulating when they attempt to facilitate mind-body healing by use of therapeutic suggestion, cognitions, imagery, symbols, metaphors, and body work? Is it any wonder that their therapeutic results are so notoriously unreliable? No theory of mind-body communication and healing can be considered complete until therapists are able to specify, at least in general outline, the major pathways of communication from what they do on the mental-behavioral level to the cellular-genetic responses that are an inherent part of the mind-body communication loop.

However the details of the cellular-genetic basis of memory, learning, and behavior change may be worked out eventually, *the main point for our current understanding of mind-body communication and healing is that the neuropeptide system of messenger molecules and their receptors that encode memory, learning, and behavior in a state-dependent manner are also the major mediators of cognition, emotion and stress in health, illness, and psychotherapy. Neuropeptides and their receptors are the state-dependent bridge between what we popularly call "mind and body."* By far the largest class of neurotransmitters and neuromodulators are the neuropeptides synthesized on the cellular-genetic level in communication loops with the environment that lead to memory, learning, and behavior. This environment, of course, includes all the psychosocial signals that make up the human enterprise in health, trauma, stress, and illness. These neuropeptides are now generally recognized as the messenger molecules that signal and integrate the basic motivations drives such as hunger, thirst, sexuality, and emotions such as anger and fear, as well as pain and pleasure (Alberts et al., 1989). For clarity we will outline six focal areas of the neuropeptide system that are the subject of intense research at this time. Where possible we will speculate a bit about how some of these areas may be related to our evolving therapeutic approaches to mind-body healing. These speculations are not so much a guide for practical clinical approaches at this time, however, as they are intimations of the psychobiological areas that are now ripe for clinical-experimental research.

1) *The Limbic-Hypothalamic Locus of Neuropeptide Activity.*   Our view of the fundamental role of the limbic-hypothalamic system "filter" in mind-body communication that was illustrated in Fig. 1 (p. 29) is confirmed by recent conceptualizations of the neuropeptide system, as follows (Pert et al., 1985, p. 821s):

A fundamental feature shared by all neuropeptide receptors whose brain distribution has been well studied is profound enrichment at a number of the same brain areas. Many of these neuropeptide receptor-rich areas can be found within an intercommunicating conglomerate of brain structures classically termed "the limbic system," which is considered to mediate emotional behavior; in unanesthetized humans undergoing brain stimulation as a prelude to surgery for epilepsy, far-ranging emotional expression can be elicited by stimulation of cortex near the amygdala, the core of the limbic system. The amygdala, as well as the hypothalamus and other limbic system-associated structures, were found initially to be enriched in opiate receptors in monkey and human brains. Later maps of numerous other neuropeptide receptors in brain [including substance P, bombesin, cholecystokinin, neurotensin, insulin, and transferrin] have continued to implicate the amygdala and other limbic system-associated structures (e.g., the cingulate cortex) as a source of receptor-rich sites where mood presumably is biochemically modified.

Evidence for the central role of the limbic-hypothalamic system and the opiate neuropeptides (the endorphins and enkephalins) in a variety of emotional processes and mood disorders is by now overwhelming. The networks of neurons that mediate these mind-body patterns of communication extend outside the limbic system to other brain areas (olfactory bulb, habenula, interpeduncular nucleus), and to the lower brain stem reticular activating system, to which we will now turn our attention.

2) *The Brain Stem and Spinal Cord Locus of Neuropeptide Activity.*   The new methods of neuropeptide research suggest an extension of limbic system boundaries to include the modulation of sensory information, as follows (Pert et al., 1985, p. 821s):

. . . The dorsal horn of mammalian spinal cord where neurons transmitting information from glands, skin, and other peripheral organs make their first synaptic contact with the central nervous system, is enriched with virtually all neuropeptide receptors. Although it has not previously been considered part of the limbic system, neuropeptide receptors here, as postulated for other sensory way-stations, may filter and prioritize incoming sensory information so that the whole organism's perception is most compatible with survival.

The mind modulation of sensory-perceptual processes is a classical characteristic of hypnotic phenomena (Orne, 1972). The localization of neuropeptide receptors at the major sensory way-stations in the central nervous system strongly suggests that they play an important role in the psychobiological mechanisms of hypnotically generated illusions and hallucinations, as well as in hypnotically induced analgesia and anesthesia.

The periaqueductal grey region of the brain stem and the dorsal horn of the spinal cord are important relay stations for pain transmission; they are rich in their balanced use of the endorphins and the neuropeptide called "substance P." Substance P *facilitates* the transmission of pain; the endorphins *block* pain transmission by inhibiting the release of substance P. There has been a great deal of controversy regarding the possible role of these neuropeptides in mediating hypnotically-induced analgesia. Some early workers (Barber & Meyer, 1977; Goldstein & Hilgard, 1975; Olness, Wain, & Ng, 1980; Spruiell et al., 1983) were unable to demonstrate any effect of hypnosis on their measures of the endorphin neuropeptides, while others (Domangue, Margolis, Lieberman, & Kaji, 1985) continue to find suggestive experimental evidence for it. The many subtle and not easily measurable and controllable variables that influence both hypnosis and neuropeptide activity make these experimental studies doubly difficult to assess. It is probably significant that the one experimental study that found hypnotic anesthesia to be mediated by endorphins was with a subject who was in a deep somnambulistic trance (Stephenson, 1978).

The problem of pain is particularly acute in emergency burns where there have been many reports in the hypnotherapeutic literature of both pain reduction and the facilitation of the healing process. The best results have been obtained if the patient is given therapeutic suggestions within the first two hours of the burn. A typical clinical report is that of Ewin (1986a, p. 7):

> The acutely burned patient arrives in the Emergency Room in a state of frightened anxiety, seeking prompt relief of the burning pain, and in a hypnoidal state that makes him highly susceptible to both good and bad suggestions. The body's response to the thermal injury is inflammation, causing progressive pathologic worsening of the injury. In sunburn, the first degree burn (redness) present on leaving the sun progresses to second degree (blister) in the ensuing 8–12 hours. The "standard" third degree (full-thickness) burn was shown by Brauer and Spira to be only second degree for the first 4 hours. They were able to excise the experimental "full thickness" burn and get 78% of cases to take a skin graft when moved to a non-injured area on the same animal, proving that the deeper dermal layers are not immediately killed by the heat, but rather later by the body's inflammatory response.
>
> Chapman, Goodell and Wolff (1959a, b) showed that inflammation is mediated through the central nervous system by release of a bradykinin-like substance which is released during the first 2 hours after the burn stimulus, but

that the release of this enzyme is held in abeyance by icing the wound. They also showed that hypnotic suggestion can produce a blister (response without a true stimulus), and can prevent blistering when an experimental burn is placed on a hypnotically anesthetized arm (true stimulus without a response). Thus, the damaging inflammatory reaction can be blocked by *early* hypnosis, attenuating the ultimate depth and severity of the burn (Ewin, 1978, 1979) . . .

Hypnotic suggestions of being "cool and comfortable" during the first 2 hours post-burn are valuable in reducing the inflammatory response to the injury. Experimental and clinical evidence shows that this attentuates burn depth. The author's verbalization of the initial encounter in the Emergency Room is included. (p. 12)

Typical protocols of therapeutic suggestions for dealing with emergency burn patients have been presented by Crasilneck and Hall (1985) and Rossi and Cheek (1990). At this time there is no data on the intriguing question of whether the therapeutic importance of administering the patient therapeutic suggestions within the first two hours of a burn accident is related to the neurophysiological dynamics of the BRAC of 90 to 120 minutes and the related ultradian phase release of the major messenger molecules of the neuropeptide system (Tables 5 and 6). There is enough available data (Lloyd & Rossi, 1992a), however, to hypothesize that ultradian dynamics ranging from the psychological-behavioral and neuropeptide levels to the cellular-genetic are all manifestations of *chaotic attractors* of complex adaptive systems (Nadel & Stein, 1992; Rossi, 1989b). Appendix B, from Rossi, 1986c, outlined some new experimental designs and approaches to these mathematical models of nonlinear dynamics in mind-body communication and healing.

What is clear from these studies, however, is that there are at least two, and probably many, mechanisms of anesthesia. In fact, recent experimental research (Shavit et al., 1985) has confirmed that there are at least two forms of analgesia: One is mediated by the endorphins while the other is not. The immune system suppression effects of stress are associated with the endorphin-mediated form of analgesia. This process will be touched upon in the next section.

3, 4) *The Immune and Endocrine System Integration by Neuropeptides.* The immune and endocrine systems that are the third and fourth loci of neuropeptide action are so closely interrelated that we will discuss them together. Most of the hormones, hypothalamic controls, and neuroendocrinal messenger molecules mentioned in this section are neuropeptides. Blalock, Harbour-McMenamin, and Smith (1985) have described this interrelationship between the immune and endocrine systems as follows (p. 858s):

> While numerous studies have demonstrated that the neuroendocrine system can control immune functions, it is only now becoming apparent that the control is reciprocal in that the immune system can control neuroendocrine functions. In this paper, recent studies which seem to provide a molecular basis for this bidirectional communication are reviewed. These studies suggest that the immune and neuroendocrine systems represent a totally integrated circuit by virtue of sharing a common set of hormones, such as corticotropin, thyrotropin, and endorphins, and the receptors. Possible hypothalamic and immunologic controls of this circuitry are discussed.

In a closely related paper, Smith, Harbour-McMenamin, and Blalock (1985) have described the overall significance of this interaction between the immune and neuroendocrine systems for mind-body communication in health and disease, as follows (p. 779s):

> Numerous indirect and anecdotal examples suggest that there is a link between an individual's mental state and his or her susceptibility to or recovery from disease. Although a direct connection has not been proven, it is logical for this to involve an interaction between the brain and immune system. A growing body of evidence has shown that hormones, in particular glucocorticoids [a group of hormones produced by the adrenal cortex] released during stress, can modulate immune system functions. More recent evidence suggests that neuroendocrine polypeptide hormones are also immunomodulatory. This then is fairly good evidence for a mechanism by which the central nervous system might influence the course of a disease. Conversely, the question of how diseases seem to alter mental states and cause apparently unrelated physiologic or homeostatic changes in the host is only beginning to be answered. A possible explanation for this feature of disease is a recent finding in our laboratory that stimulated leukocytes produce molecules apparently identical to pituitary hormones that are capable of signaling the neuroendocrine system. . . . The immune and neuroendocrine systems appear able to communicate with each other by virtue of signal molecules (hormones) and receptors common to both systems.

The endorphin neuropeptides play a central role in the mind-body regulation of all the major systems of the body. If hypnotically induced comfort could be demonstrated to facilitate the activity of any one of these systems, it would be an important link in the growing lines of evidence supporting the therapeutic use of hypnosis as a means of mind-body communication and healing.

5) *Enteric Nervous System: The Gastrointestinal Locus of Neuropeptide Activity.* The enteric nervous system regulates the gastrointestinal organs in semi-independent manner (Bulloch, 1985). This system is estimated to be of comparable complexity with the neural system of the spinal cord (Gerson, Payette, & Rothman, 1985), and it has been used as a model to study the ontogenetic development of the central nervous system. Various hormonal neuropeptides of the enteric-gastrointestinal system are also independently active in the central nervous system: The endorphins, substance P, and somatostatin are among the most prominent (see Table 6, pp. 300–302). The same somatostatin molecule that is used as a messenger substance in neurons of the cerebral cortex, hippocampus, and hypothalamus, for example, is used as a hormone messenger when it is produced in the pancreatic islets to regulate insulin and glucagon secretion.

The use of hypnosis for amelioration of gastrointestinal distress has a long history (Crasilneck & Hall, 1959; Gorton, 1957; Weiner, 1977). The current challenge is to illuminate the actual mind-body communication processes involved in the therapeutic effects. A reassessment of neuropeptide activity in the gastrointestinal areas during hypnosis would seem to be a good approach to this issue (Weiner, 1977).

When our emotional state is optimal, we are hardly ever aware of the enteric system's automatic activity. When we are emotionally upset, however, the entire gastrointestinal tract can express our discomfort. The sensitivity of the gastrointestinal tract to mental stress is one of the most widely recognized manifestations of psychosomatic problems (Alexander, 1950; Weiner, 1977). The way in which the early psychoanalysts such as C. G. Jung described this connection between mind and stomach is typical (1976, p. 88):

> There is hardly a case of neurosis where the entrails are not disturbed. For instance, after a certain dream a diarrhoea happens, or there are spasms in the abdomen. . . . I know of a number of cases of people who did not know what they ought to do, people who got lazy when they should have organized their lives on a somewhat larger scale, who omitted their duty and tried to live like chickens, and they then got frightful spasms in the abdomen.

In another source Jung wrote (1929/1984, pp. 130–131):

> Instinctive powers are released, partly psychological, partly physiological, and through that release the whole disposition of the body can be changed. People in such a state of mind are in a condition for infections and physical disturbances. You know how close the connection is between the stom-

ach and mental states. If a bad psychic state is habitual, you spoil your stomach. . . .

If we update Jung's terminology from "instinctive powers" to "mind-body communication systems," we could hardly have a better description of the far-reaching effects of state-dependent enteric-gastrointestinal distress. It could be speculated that the widespread early practices of "reading" the entrails of sacrificed animals for purposes of divination and healing may have come about because of the easily recognized association between mental and intestinal states. Peoples from many early cultures felt that their thinking actually came from their abdominal area (Jung, 1950). That modern man can learn how to utilize the enteric-gastrointestinal system as a creative feeling function is illustrated by the interesting case of the "third voice of the mind-body" presented below.

A lawyer in his mid-thirties had been accidentally shot in the abdomen a number of years earlier. The bullet had damaged his pancreas and a portion of his small intestine, which had to be removed surgically. The emotionally traumatic aspects of the event, as well as the remaining physical sensitivity in the wounded area, left him with a problem. For many years he had experienced fears, repetitive traumatic dreams, gastrointestinal discomfort, and a haunting lack of self-confidence—even though he had graduated with honors from one of the leading Ivy League universities, had clerked for a well-known senator in Washington, and was acknowledged as a future leader in his special field of international law.

Although he was unaware of the periodic ultradian rhythms of gastrointestinal activity (see Rossi, 1986a), he had learned from his own personal experience that even after recovering from his wound he could no longer subject himself to the abuse of skipping meals and working for extended periods with no rest breaks. In spite of this awareness, he recently had been subjected to a variety of stresses during a critical career shift, which precipitated a severe bout of diverticulitis. This led him to seek psychobiological counseling.

In therapy he was able to learn self-hypnosis well enough to control the pain of his diverticulitis. He also felt reassured to learn that the ultradian rhythms of enteric-gastrointestinal activity were normal, though he recognized that his old bullet wound had awakened him to a special sensitivity to these rhythms. He had always regarded this sensitivity as a "problem" until I inquired about the details of how he experienced it. He reported his "guts" would make loud noises that could be heard by others in the room when he was involved in administrative meetings and discussions with his clients. We soon came to regard this problem as a "third voice" that was present particularly when he was in a tight and "sensitive" professional situation in which he needed "extra wisdom." I suggested that, rather than try to suppress this symptom, he let himself become even more sensitive to it so that he could hear what it had to say when it whispered, rather than putting it off until it had to shout so loud everyone in the room could hear it! In this manner I was helping him convert his symptom into a signal (as discussed in the last chapter).

At this point he experienced a medical emergency which his internist described as a life-threatening attack of diverticulitis. He then had the following dream. (See Rossi, 1972/1985, for a general discussion of healing dreams.)

I dreamed my wife and I were going to the doctor's because I had a cut on my stomach. *I was upset about leaving work for this.* I was also looking at other rehabilitation programs in Philadelphia on the way to the doctor's. I ran into a volunteer nurse from the hospital where I worked. She asked me suspiciously if *I was looking for other work at these hospitals. I told her no—we have visited the hospitals, but did not talk to any administrators about work possibilities.* Then we went outside this other hospital which we were visiting. *I pulled on a swollen part of my stomach and a huge pustular sac came out from my intestine.* The inside of my intestines started to bleed. *I felt good, relieved that I had gotten the infected part out,* but was afraid of the bleeding. I immediately called my internist.

It would be easy to miss the healing processes constellated in this dream by glibly interpreting the events as depicting conflict and mere wish fulfillment. For a professional workaholic, it was naturally upsetting to leave work and all too tempting to seek more work at a hospital. Instead, his dream ego turns away from using the hospital as a work opportunity and facilitates his own healing process by pulling out the infected pustular sac from his intestine. This suggests that he is now rechanneling his excessive and stressful work activity into inner healing in cooperation with his interest. This dream signaled the significant turning point of transforming his problem into a creative function. Indeed, my client gradually succeeded in reframing his problem as he became more and more aware of what the third voice of his mind-body was saying to him. The outside world's voice might threaten him, his own voice might tremble in response, but the third voice within his gut would let him know in no uncertain terms just where and when he had to draw the line. When his conscious voice vascillated in indecision, the third voice of the mind-body would counsel him as follows:

> Be firm, you have to take care of yourself, don't let the world eat you up! Don't let them take up your lunch hour with yet another meeting.
> Don't let anyone step on your guts, be responsible to yourself when no one else is.
> Accepting human limitations is the better part of wisdom. The ego is a madman that has led many excellent men to their destruction.
> It doesn't matter what others think; it's my comfort that gives me life.

The third voice that would no longer permit him to abuse himself physically or emotionally eventually became a creative function that counseled him on many "touchy" international situations in which he had to negotiate with a special sensitivity that only his gut could provide. After many years he eventually recognized that his was essentially the way of the shaman: he was learning to use his former illness to sensitize himself to the hidden ills and ways of healing the societies in collision around him.

This case illustrates the fundamental difference between our psychobiological approach of conceptualizing symptoms as maladaptive forms of information transduction that can become important signals for creative personal development, and the more typical stance of behavioral medicine and classical conditioning therapy which regard symptoms as problems that have to be extinguished (Gentry, 1984). As illustrated in Tutorial 15, our approach is also very different from the traditional psychoanalytic goal of using analysis as a method of resolving problems. The behaviorist and psychoanalytic approaches both throw away valuable information by placing themselves in opposition to the problem network. Our psychobiological approach uses these data by accessing the state-dependent memory, learning, and behavior systems that encode problems and reframing them into creative functions. *Many types of chronic pain and recurrent symptoms and problems are actually information transducers that amplify the minimal stress signals of the mind-body.*

The process of reframing and rechanneling stress signals into appropriate patterns of personal development and meaning resembles the traditional approaches of many forms of cultural and spiritual healing. In these frameworks, sickness is frequently conceptualized as a visitation from God to guide us in our uncertain path through the shadows of life. However, many of these ancient healing practices eventually become limited and dogmatic in their perspective, rather than continu-

---

TUTORIAL 15 Transforming a Problem into a Creative Function

1. *Accessing and amplifying a problem-encoded resource*
   Review the circumstances during which a chronic problem becomes manifest.
   Can you recognize your sensitivity to milder instances of the problem before it causes your usual discomfort?
   Will you wonder how your new sensitivity can become a resource
   for problem-solving?

2. *Transducing a problem into a creative function*
   Use your heightened sensitivity as a radar to scan the minimal
   cues in the situations that are evoking your "problem."
   Can you see, hear, feel, intuit the meanings of your mind-body responses?
   Can you recognize what personal developmental changes are
   needed for a wiser adaptation to life stressors?

3. *Ratifying your new creative function*
   Review and contrast your old, painful and maladaptive way of being with your new understanding. [Pause] Can you now understand your previous life problems in the light of your new relationship to the world? Can you recognize the new self-identity
   that you are actively creating each day?

---

ally experimental and innovative as life is itself. Let us hope that our
psychobiological perspective can integrate the best of the old and new
approaches to mind-body healing by using nature's own messages as
our constant inspiration and guide.

6) *The Sexual System and Neuropeptide Activity.*   In a recent assessment of neuropeptides and their receptors as a psychosomatic network,
Pert et al. (1985) noted that human testes are "as rich a source of messenger RNA for the opiate peptide proopiomelanocortin as the pituitary
gland." Proopiomelanocortin is the celebrated "mother molecule" that
generates ACTH and endorphin, which, as we have seen, are perhaps
the most ubiquitous messengers of the entire neuropeptide system. A
rich research literature is developing around the mind-body connections
between the limbic-hypothalamic system, the process of dreaming, and

sexual activation (Rossi, 1972/1985). This literature emphasizes the ACTH-endorphin pattern of neuropeptide regulation. Indeed, the relationship between sex, stress, and aggression that has been emphasized in the psychoanalytic literature may find its psychobiological basis in this ACTH-endorphin system. Stewart has touched upon recent thinking in this area as follows (1981, p. 774):

> Although there has been considerable speculation about the role of this brain ACTH-End system, only now is it possible to advance a reasoned hypothesis as to what that role may be. We propose that this set of neurons is a major regulator of central nervous system activity, principally through its influence on the midbrain monoamine systems. In certain circumstances it appears that this system can cause the higher cortical centers to be turned off or else disconnected, so that the organism functions under the control of the evolutionarily ancient midbrain centers mediating primarily instinctive behavior. This "turning off" appears to occur during acute stress, and the "disconnection" during paradoxical sleep (PS).

Stewart continues (1981, p. 778):

> Massive peripheral ACTH release occurs in acute stress, and central events can be presumed to mirror this situation. Acute stress, and particularly asphyxiation, which is considered to be a potent "humoral" stress, cause erection and orgasm, the well-known "agonal orgasm." Some persons can evidently achieve orgasm only under such stress, a fact which leads to accidental deaths from choking and perhaps also to much of the interpersonal violence of our times. Stress-induced orgasm is depicted in such works of literature as Samuel Beckett's *Waiting for Godot*, John Hershey's *The War Lover*, and the works of de Sade.
> The diurnal rhythm of ACTH release also contributes confirmatory evidence to the hypothesis. ACTH is secreted principally in bursts during episodes of paradoxical sleep (rapid eye-movement sleep). PS is characterized by sexual stimulation. . . .

Since therapeutic hypnosis has been used to access and modulate this same complex of stress, dreams, aggression, and sexual functioning (Araoz, 1982, 1985), one cannot help but wonder, once again, if neuropeptides are the common denominator.

One of Erickson's most celebrated cases of psychosexual rehabilitation, which took place with a patient who had organic spinal cord damage, dealt with this entire complex of stress and emotions and can serve as a clinical illustration of what is possible in this area. A highly condensed version of this case is excerpted from Erickson and Rossi (1979) as follows (pp. 428–439):

Some years ago a young woman in a wheelchair approached the senior author and declared that she was profoundly distressed—in fact, suicidally depressed. Her reason was that an accidental injury in her early twenties had left her with a transverse myelitis: she was lacking in all sensations from the waist down, and she was incontinent of bladder and bowel. Her purpose in seeing the senior author was that she wanted to secure a philosophy of life by which to live; the incontinence of bladder and bowel and confinement to a wheelchair were more than she felt she could endure. She had heard the senior author lecture on hypnosis and had reached the conclusion that perhaps by hypnosis some miraculous change in her personal attitudes could be affected. She explained further that as a small child she had been extremely interested in cooking, baking, sewing, playing with dolls, and fantasizing about the home, husband, and children she would have when she grew up. At the age of twenty she had fallen in love and made plans to marry upon completion of college. She had set to work filling a hope chest with hand-sewn linens and designing her own wedding dress. All she had ever wanted was a husband, a home, children, and grandchildren. Her love for her own grandmothers was a strong factor in her life, and she shared much emotional identification with them.

The unfortunate accident resulting in the transverse myelitis put an end to all her dreams and expectations. After some ten years of stormy difficulties and complications, she became able to use a wheelchair and to return to her university studies. Even with this improvement in her situation she saw no future for herself in the academic world, and became progressively depressed with increasing suicidal ideation. She had finally reached a point at which she felt some definite decision had to be made. Therefore she wished the author to induce a ''very deep hypnotic trance and discuss possibilities and potentialities for me. . . .''

Her request was abided by and, probably because of her deep motivation, a very deep somnambulistic trance state was elicited. She was tested with great care for her ability to manifest the phenomena of deep hypnosis. Depersonalization, dissociation, time distortion, and hypermnesia of the happy past were either avoided or the suggestions were worded so carefully that there could not be even a seeming attempt to change her views and attitudes. . . .

One suggestion of a therapeutic character that did come to mind was a well-known song of the old variety, which she was asked to hallucinate, visually and auditorily, with an orchestra and singer. The song was the one about the toebone being connected with the footbone, the footbone with the heelbone, the heelbone with the anklebone, and so on. . . . [Erickson continues:]

"I noticed that you were left-thumbed, left-eyed, and left-eared last week, and I made up my mind that you should have free access to what your conscious mind knows about your body but does not know that it knows, and what your body knows freely but that neither your conscious nor your unconscious mind openly knows. *You might as well use well all knowledge that you have, body or mind knowledge, and use all of it well.* What does your body know and know full well, which you know and know full well consciously and unconsciously? Just this little thing! You think that erectile tissue is in the genitals, *just the genitals*. But what does your body know? Just take your finger and thumb and snap your soft nipple and watch it stand right out in protest. It knows that it has erectile tissue. You have had that knowledge without knowing it for a long time. And where else do you have erectile tissue? In New York State you stepped out of doors in thirty degrees below zero and felt your nose harden. Naturally! It has erectile tissue! Why else would it harden? And watch that hot baby slobbering for a kiss from the man she loves and see her upper lip get thick and warm? Erectile tissue in the upper lip!. . . .

"The external genitals are connected to the internal genitals, and the internal genitals are connected to the ovaries, and the ovaries are connected with adrenals, and the adrenals are connected with the chromaffin system, and the chromaffin system is connected with the mammaries, and the mammaries are connected with the parathyroids, and the thyroid is connected with the caratid body, and the carotid body is connected with the pituitary body, and the system of all these endocrine glands is connected with all sexual feelings, and all your sexual feelings are connected with all your other feelings, and if you don't believe it, let some man you like touch your bare breasts and you feel the hot, embarrassed feeling in your face and your sexual feelings. Then you'll know that every word I've said is true, and if you don't so believe, try it out, but the deep red flush on your face right now says you know it's so.

"So continue sleeping deeply, review carefully every word I have said to you, try to dispute it, to argue against it. Try your level best to disagree, but the harder you try the more you will realize that I am right.

"Now put a look of starry-eyed expectation on your face, clothe yourself in an air of happy confidence. Romance for you is just around the corner [a crucial statement], I don't know which corner [a statement that leaves the question undecidable and hence requiring further consideration], *but it's just around the corner!* Don't ever forget there's a Rachel for every Reuben and a Reuben for every Rachel, and every Jean has her Jock and every Jock has his Jean, *and around the corner is your "John Anderson, my Jo."*

"One doubt you will have, but naturally you are wrong! Your body knows, so does your conscious mind, so does your unconscious mind. Only you, the person, don't know.

"Is there anything more ecstatic than the maiden's first sweet kiss of true love? Could there be a better orgasm? Or the first grasping of the little lips of the baby on your nipple! Or the cupping of your bare breasts by the hand of your love? Have you ever felt the chills run up and down your spine when kissed on the back of your neck?

"Man has but one place to have an orgasm—a woman has many.

"Continue your trance, evaluate these ideas, make no error about their validity."

A Ten-Year Follow-up

Within two years she was married. Her husband was a dedicated research man, and his field of interest was the biology and chemistry of the human colon. They have been married happily for over ten years, and there are now four children, all by caesarian operations.

Ten years after the marriage the author happened to be lecturing in the state of her residence. She noted a news story on the author and called him on the telephone, asking him to lunch with her the next day. Before meeting her, three duplicate sets of questions were typed out. The answers were filled in on one set, which was sealed in an envelope. The other two sets were placed in separate envelopes.

The purpose of the duplicate sets of questions was to obtain an objective report from her regarding her sexual experiences and compare them with what Erickson thought they would be. Her responses indicated that she was experiencing sexual orgasms three or four times a week with her husband. She had learned to shift her genital orgasmic response to her breasts, neck, and lips. Erickson quoted her descriptions of her sexual experiences as follows (Haley, 1985, Vol. 1, p. 26):

> I have excellent orgasms. I have plenty of orgasms in my breast, I have a separate one in each nipple. I get a very warm, rosy feeling of engorgement in my thyroid, and my lips swell up quite a bit when I have an orgasm, the lobes of my ears. I have the most peculiar feeling between my shoulder blades. I rock involuntarily, uncontrollably, I get so excited.

Erickson liked to use this case as an illustration of the psychoneurophysiological alterations that were possible with therapeutic hypnosis. There is much to suggest that the neuropeptide system is the psychoneurophysiological basis of this type of hypnotherapeutic response. This hypothesis is based on the mind-body communication system illustrated in Figure 12 and the outline in Table 6, which both suggest how neuropeptide messenger molecules, channeled through the autonomic, endocrine, and immune systems, could mediate the all-encompassing scope of Erickson's seemingly nonsensical hypnotic rhyme about "the footbone connected to the heel bone. . . . the external genitals connected to the . . . ovaries . . . adrenals . . . chromaffin system . . . mammaries . . . parathyroids . . . thyroid . . . cartoid body . . . pituitary body . . . [and the] endocrine glands connected with all sexual feelings.'' It will require the ingenuity of unique teams of psychobiological researchers and hypnotherapists to explore the actual mind-molecule communication systems that mediate such healing responses.

The wide distribution of the neuropeptide system, as well as its seemingly unlimited ability for information transduction between all the channels of mind-body communication, can act as a springboard for a number of new approaches to mind-body communication and healing. This is particularly the case when a life problem is accompanied by feelings of hopelessness and depression, as in the case above. I have previously described how depression can be a signal of the need to break out of an outmoded pattern of adaptation into the actualization of a new identity that is already developing spontaneously within the person on an unconscious level (Rossi, 1972/1985). I frequently describe the process as ''transforming a problem into a creative function.''

MIND-BODY COMMUNICATION AND HEALING: FROM MIND TO MOLECULE

Can we bring together the apparently incredible complexities of our new view of mind-body communication and healing into a simple picture of how it all works? Perhaps only now, at the very end of our journey, we may emerge above the timberline to gain the perspective we need to see the entire forest. As we look around we see three landscapes, each with a neatly painted sign as follows:

1) *Messenger molecules and their receptors* are the informational basis of life itself as well as mind-body communication and healing.
2) *The state-dependent encoding of life experience* via messenger molecules and their receptors is the psychobiological basis of the subjective states of consciousness and behavior in health and illness.
3) *The wave nature of consciousness and being* is the natural psychobiological foundation of the highly adaptive rhythms of optimal performance and healing in everyday life. The chronic disruption of these complex adaptive rhythms leads to stress and its related disorders. All approaches to mind-body healing involve the psychosocial entrainment of various aspects of these complex adaptive and state-dependent rhythms for therapeutic purposes.

Let us look around for one final clarifying overview of these landscapes that were tracked in great detail as we wandered, often lost, among the hidden trails of the mind-body throughout each of the preceding chapters.

Messenger Molecules and Their Receptors

Messenger molecules and their receptors are the bottom line of mind-body communication and healing. They are not only the earliest form of communication to have evolved, they actually make life itself possible at the multicellular level. Without the evolution of messenger molecules and their receptors life would have remained at the single-cell level. One of the major challenges of this book has been to understand them as a part of the natural loop of information transduction from environment to mind to molecule rather than to see them in a purely reductionistic perspective as is typical of the academic science of molecular biology. Messenger molecules are as much a part of the information transduction loop between mind, body, cell, and gene as are words, emotions, images, and sensations. We can bridge the so-called cartesian gap between mind and body only with this broadly inclusive view of the fundamental nature of information and communication.

Table 6 is an abbreviated outline of a few of the significant mind-body messenger molecules we have mentioned in this book together with some of the overlapping systems of mind-body communication in which they appear. A fascinating new class of messenger molecules in the brain are what were previously regarded as being simply highly toxic gases: carbon monoxide, which everyone knows is a "killer gas" from auto exhaust, and nitric oxide, which is a pollutant in cigarette smoke and smog. Both of them are currently being investigated for possible roles in LTP in the hippocampus as well a number of other specialized functions for each (Barinaga, 1993). Nitric oxide was called the "Molecule of the Year" in 1992 because of all the interesting theoretical issues and practical therapeutic significance it may have for the future for a wide-ranging pattern of mind-body communication functions in the immune system, neural action, blood pressure, and penile erection (Culotta & Koshland, 1992; Snyder & Bredt, 1992).

The essential role of all these molecular messengers in the mind-body communication loop leads us to suggest that we must encourage a new *completion criterion* for a more comprehensive description of all research on methods of mind-body healing. The completeness criterion for describing hypnotherapeutic suggestion, for example, requires tracking the entire path of cybrenetic information exchange between society, mind, body, cell, and gene; this is our update of the original vision of

TABLE 6 Information transduction in mind-body communication. Some of the major messenger molecules of the autonomic, endocrine, immune, and neuropeptide systems are listed in the channel column.

SENDER	CHANNEL	RECEIVER	REFERENCES

AUTONOMIC
Limbic-hypothalamic brain stem system; spinal nerves
	VIA NEURON CHANNEL
	NEUROTRANSMITTERS
	Amino Acids:
	  Aspartic
	  Glutamic, etc.
	Monoamines:
	  Acetylcholinie
	  Catecholamines
	  Dopamine
	  Norepinephrine
	  Serotonin
	Neuropeptides
	  Endorphins
	  Somatostatin
	  Substance P
	  Nitric oxide
	  Carbon monoxide
		Receptors
		On neurons to all target organs in ANS, heart, GI tract, lungs, pupils, etc.
			Hypnotic Literature
			Barber, 1984; Black, 1969; Braun, 1983a, b; Crasilneck & Hall, 1985; Dunbar, 1954; Erickson, 1943a, b, 1977; Hudgins, 1933; Lewis & Sarbin, 1943; Olness & Conroy, 1985; Sternbach, 1982

ENDOCRINE Hypothalamus	**VIA BLOOD CHANNEL** *HORMONES* Thyrotropin-Releasing Hormone (TRH) Gonadotropin-Releasing Hormone (GnRH) Somatostatin Corticotropin-Releasing-Factor (CRF) Growth Hormone-Releasing Hormone (GHRH)	**Receptors** Pituitary	**Hypnotic Literature** Crasilneck & Hall, 1985; Delhounge & Hansen, 1927; Dunbar, 1954; Erickson, 1943a, b, c; Gorton, 1958; Kroger & Fezler, 1976; Wolberg, 1947

SENDER	CHANNEL	RECEIVER	REFERENCES
ENDOCRINE Anterior Pituitary	**VIA BLOOD CHANNEL** Adrenocorticotropic Hormone (ACTH) β-Endorphin Melanocyte-Stimulating Hormone Prolactin Growth Hormone (GH) Luteinizing Hormone (LH)	**Receptors** Glands in endocrine system: adrenals, pancreas, testes, ovaries, thyroid, etc.	**Psychobiological Literature** Besedovsky et al., 1985; Bulloch, 1935; Domangue et al., 1985; Pert et al., 1985; Rosenblatt, 1983; Stewart, 1981; Weiner, 1977
Posterior Pituitary	Vasopressin Oxytocin Neurophysins		
Enteric-Gastrointestinal	Vasoactive Intestinal Polypeptide (VIP) Cholecystokinin (CCK) Enkephalins Endorphins Substance P Neurotensin Bombesin Secretin Glucagon Insulin Gastrin		

(continued)

301

TABLE 6 Continued

SENDER	CHANNEL	RECEIVER	REFERENCES
IMMUNE Organs such as bone marrow, lymph, thymus, spleen, tonsils, etc.; lymphocytes, B & T cells, macrophages, natural killer cells, neutrophils, etc.	**VIA BLOOD AND LYMPH CHANNELS** ACTH, TSH Endorphins Thymosins Lymphokines Interleukins Interferon	**Receptors** On neurons in the hypothalamus and other brain areas; leukocytes in blood, spleen, thymus, lymph, skin, GI tract; blood vessels; endocrine glands	**Hypnotic Literature** Achterberg, 1985; Black, 1969; Ewin, 1974, 1992; Gould & Tissler, 1984; Gravitz, 1981; Hall, 1982–83; Ikemi & Nakagawa, 1962; Mason, 1963; Schneider et al., 1983; Spanos et al., 1988, 1990; Ullman, 1947, 1959
NEUROPEPTIDE DNA → RNA → Peptide in limbic-hypothalamic system; GI tract and other nodal centers	**VIA NEURONE, BLOOD, LYMPH CHANNEL** *PEPTIDES* *Hypothalamic Releasing Hormones* e.g., Somatostatin (growth) *Pituitary Peptides* e.g., ACTH (stress) β-endorphin (emotions) Vasopressin (memory) *Gut-Brain Peptides* e.g., Substance P (pain) *Others* e.g., Bradykinin (shock) Angiotensin II (blood pressure)	**Receptors** Nodal centers in limbic-hypothalamic, dorsal horn of spine, periacque-duck grey, testes, ovaries, gastrointestinal, immune and endocrine systems	**Hypnosis and Placebo Literature** Achterberg, 1985; Barber & Meyer, 1977; Domangue et al., 1985; Goldstein & Hilgard, 1975; Hilgard, 1977; Hilgard & Hilgard, 1975; Olness, Wain, & Ng, 1980; Rosenblatt, 1983; Rossi & Lippincott, 1992; Spruiell et al., 1983

the psychophysiological basis of mind-body healing as first proposed by the early pioneers of hypnotherapy (Ellenberger, 1970; Tinterow, 1970). Most typically this cybrenetic pathway would include four critical transition points where information is transformed between one level and another: the sociocultural, the mind-brain, the brain-body, and the cellular-genetic (see Table 7).

The processes whereby information is transformed from one form into another is usually called information transduction in biology and physics; the kinds of research now needed to fulfill the completeness criterion via hypnosis and other methods of mind-body healing have been presented in great detail elsewhere (Rossi & Cheek, 1988). Our focus on information transduction between mind, body, and the cell-gene in many of the major diagrams of this book emphasizes that we are not proposing yet another "reductive" explanation of mind, behavior, and holistic healing in terms of physiology and chemistry. Quite to the contrary, our approach is consistent with recent efforts to reformulate the foundations of biology, physics, and psychology with information theory as their common denominator (Davies, 1989; Rossi, 1992b, c; Stonier, 1990; Wheeler, 1990).

To enhance the reliability of our approaches to mind-body healing at the deepest cellular-genetic levels we need to understand the fundamental difference between *alterations in the structure of genes* via the mutations of the evolutionary process and the *modulation of gene expression* from environmental signals. Alterations in the *structure of genes* is an evolutionaly event based upon chance errors in copying the chemical structure of the gene; western science maintains that mind has absolutely nothing to do with such changes in the structure of genes. The modulation of *gene expression*, however, involves the turning on and off of certain genes by many of the same hormones and secondary messengers that encode the state-dependent processes of mind and behavior; western science maintains the possibility of mind-gene communication by this path.

The State-Dependent Encoding of Life Experience

The state-dependent encoding of life experience and mind is the psychobiological basis of hypnosis and psychoanalysis. Table 7 outlines how state-dependent memory learning, and behavior (SDMLB) operates on all levels from the sociocultural to the cellular-genetic. Further, SDMLB can be conceptualized as a psychobiological common denominator of the classical phenomenology or trauma and stress in the genesis of psychosomatic problems as well as in the therapeutic efforts of hypnosis, psychoanalysis, and the many mind-body therapies to resolve them (Rossi, 1987, 1990a, b; Rossi & Cheek, 1988). Dissociation, repression, emotional complexes, and partially reversible amnesia are all state-dependent psychological processes. The classical phenomena of hypnosis, multiple personality, neurosis, the posttraumatic stress disorders, psychosomatic symptoms, and mood disorders can all be understood as manifestations of state-dependent symptoms of mind and behavior. Under stress, certain patterns of memory, learning, and behavioral symptomatology are learned and encoded by the release of stress hormones and information substances throughout the entire mind-body. When the stress is removed, these information substances disappear and the person apparently recovers and seems symptom-free. Reintroduce stress to varying degrees and the mind-body responds by releasing the information substances that re-evoke the corresponding degree of SDMLB symptomatology.

These relationships between messenger molecules and their receptors, memory, learning, stress, and traumatically encoded mind-body problems presented throughout this volume suggest that we are now in the first stages of formulating a general and well-integrated psychobiological theory of therapeutic hypnosis, psychoanalysis, and mind-body communication and healing: Dissociation has been described as the basic mechanism of hypnosis; repression has been the central mechanism and model of psychodynamic defense in Freudian analysis; feeling-toned complexes have been the units of normal and neurotic emotional life by Jung. What has been the most puzzling about dissociation, repression, and feeling-toned complexes is that they appear to be so variable, insubstantial, and difficult to measure. We now know that much of this difficulty in measurement can be attributed to the nonlinear dynamics of the thousands of messenger molecules and their receptors interacting with hundreds of different issues throughout the brain and body containing perhaps trillions of individual cells, each with their own history encoded in state-dependent memory systems at the molecular level.

Can there be any hope, then, of recognizing some of the well-known phenomena of psychotherapy in this incredibly complex system of adaptive dynamics? It has been hypothesized (Rossi, 1990a, b) that the most vivid demonstration of how messenger molecules, particularly the neuropeptides, may be involved in most forms of psychotherapy is in the cathartic reactions. Catharsis, the dramatic emotional release of suppressed and usually traumatic state-dependent memories of significant

TABLE 7 State-dependent information transduction from the sociocultural to the cellular-genetic level and a few quotations from the research literature that epitomize the basic focus at each level (Adapted from Rossi, 1990b)

SOCIOCULTURAL

"This state/context dependence theory has other attractive features as well. It creates a bridge between a growing body of laboratory work on neurophysiology and psychopharmacology on one hand, and ethnological field studies on the other hand. It offers a better solution to the problem of rationality. It is not much weakened by the fact that participants' accounts of ritual experience are often at odds with one another, and it easily accommodates evidence that the forms of some rituals change dramatically over time." (Kiefer & Cowan, 1979, p. 55)

Frank, 1963; Kiefer & Cowan, 1979; Reus et al., 1979; Wallace, 1966

MIND-BODY

"Inasmuch as meaningful experience arises from the binding or coupling of (1) a particular state or level of *arousal* with (2) a particular symbolic *interpretation* of that arousal, experience is *state-bound* and can thus be evoked either by inducing—"naturally," hypnotically or with the aid of drugs—the particular level of arousal, *or* by presenting some symbol of its interpretation such as an image, melody or taste." (Fischer & Landon, 1972, p. 159) . . . "It is interesting to note that hormones that are known to play important roles in homeostatic regulation may also play an important role in regulating memory. This is perhaps not surprising in view of the central role of memory in adaptation." (McGaugh et al., 1984, p. 329)

Fischer, 1971a–c; Gold, Weinberger & Sternberg, 1985; Izquierdo, 1984, 1989; Izquierdo et al., 1984, 1988a,b; McGaugh, 1983, 1989; McGaugh et al., 1984; Rigter & Crabbe, 1979; Zornetzer, 1978

305

(Continued)

TABLE 7 Continued

BRAIN-BODY

"Studies of state-dependent physiology are not merely descriptive; they are essential for a complete characterization of the cellular and molecular mechanisms underlying regulatory physiology." (Lydic, 1987, p. 6) "A major conceptual shift in neuroscience has been wrought by the realization that brain function is modulated by numerous chemicals in addition to classical neurotransmitters. Many of these informational substances are neuropeptides, originally studied in other contexts as hormones, 'gut peptides,' or growth factors. Their number presently exceeds 50 and most, if not all, alter behavior and mood states. . . . Neuropeptides and their receptors thus join the brain, glands, and immune system in a network of communication between brain and body, probably representing the biochemical substrates of emotion." (Pert et al., 1985, p. 820s)

Bergland, 1985; Brush & Levine, 1989; Fackelmann, 1991; Lydic, 1987; Pert et al., 1985; Schmitt, 1984, 1986; Weingartner, 1978, 1986

CELLULAR-GENETIC

"Transient expression of genes has been observed in physiological responses to stimuli such as heat shock and hormones. . . . These observations suggest that learning and memory, like other processes of cellular differentiation, may involve a flow of information from membrane receptors to the genome. . . . By identifying the genes modulated by learning, it should be possible to characterize the cytoplasmic, and perhaps nuclear signaling systems that induce these events." (Goelet & Kandel, 1986, pp. 496–498)

Barinaga, 1992a, b; Goelet & Kandel, 1986; Kandl, 1976, 1989; Kandel & Schwartz, 1985 life events, was regarded by Freud as the most significant turning point in the development of his "talking cure." Most classical forms of psychotherapy from the rituals of native healers and shamen to encounter groups and twelve-step programs usually involve two stages: (1) an initial stage of sympathetic system arousal with elevated heart rate, respiration, sweating, shouting, tears that is typical of the emotional catharsis phase that can last from a few minutes to hours, but usually requires around 20 or 30 minutes; and (2) a relaxation phase then follows with feelings of comfort and thankfulness about the new insights received and the emotional blocks worked through.

The initial catharsis phase can be so alarming that even audiences of professional psychotherapists that have observed dramatic demonstrations have been concerned lest the patient somehow incur serious or permanent emotional harm rather than therapy. Yet the patient invariably experiences the second phase of emotional insight, comfort, and well-being. While a great deal of professional skill is in fact required to facilitate such a satisfactory therapeutic outcome, I hypothesized that the therapist may be supported by what I call *"The neuropeptide hypothesis of consciousness and catharsis."* I hypothesized that *the arousal and relaxation phases of cathartic psychotherapy and emotional insight are mediated by the release of ACTH and β-endorphin from their mother molecule, POMC (proopiomelanocortin), via the basic process of mind-body information transduction in the limbic-hypothalamic-pituitary system.* Support for this neuropeptide hypothesis of consciousness and catharis comes from recent developments in psychoendocrinology (Brush & Levine, 1989; De Wied, 1990) over the past decade. Most recently, for example, researchers documenting the ultradian and circadian rhythms of hormone and neuropeptide informational substances have said ". . . cortisol was considered to lead β-endorphin by 20 or 30 minutes. We conclude that β-endorphin is released physiologically in a pulsate manner with circadian and ultradian rhythmicity and a close temporal coupling to cortisol" (Iranmanesh et al., 1989b, p. 1019). Since cortisol is part of the informational cascade that begins with the release of ACTH, this research provides at least indirect support for the neuropeptide hypothesis of psychotherapy. More direct support would require that we continuously monitor the release of ACTH, β-endorphin, cortisol, and related informational substances during the two-step process of arousal and relaxation in cathartic psychotherapy.

Another very different messenger molecule system operating in very different tissues of the mind-body illustrating how nerves modulated by information substances can effect memory, learning, and behavior as the basis of psychological experience is the recent report of how the messenger molecule cholecystokinin (CCK-8S), a gastrointestinal hormone that is released when a good meal has been eaten, encodes memory, learning, and behavior in a state-dependent manner. The researchers (Flood, Smith, & Morley, 1987) summarize their findings as follows (p. 834):

> Our data show that both feeding and peripherally administered CCK-8S enhance memory in mice. This gastrointestinal hormone seems to produce its effect on memory by activating ascending vagal fibers. Further studies are necessary to determine if CCK-8S is responsible for the entire effect of feeding on memory, or, as appears to be the case in the regulation of feeding, if a combination of gastrointestinal hormones act synergistically to produce this effect. The concentrations of CCK-8S achieved after administration of the optimum memory enhancing dose would be well within the physiological range seen after feeding in rodents. A link may have evolved between the release of gastric peptides and memory processing in the central nervous system because of the survival advantages for an animal to remember the details of a successful food-foraging expedition.

Memory, learning, and behavior associated with the presence of the information substance CCK in the mind-body is therefore state-dependent. The association of this state-dependent learning with evolutionary processes of survival has deep implications for a new theory of the evolution of memory, learning, and ultimately, consciousness itself! Who will pursue these suggested links for creating a new view of the evolution of consciousness, meaning, and well-being? This has echoes of the pragmatic psychotherapeutic definition of "consciousness or mind as a process of self-reflection information transduction" presented earlier in Chapter 2. It has more profound implications for the current scientific enterprise to understand *"It from Bit;"* how all the basic concepts and laws of psychology, biology, and physics may be reframed so that their *"Its"* (mind, life, matter, etc.) may be understood in informational terms by using *"Bits"* as their basic common denominator (Wheeler, 1990).

The Wave Nature of Consciousness and Being

The wave nature of consciousness and being is the natural psychobiological foundation of the highly adaptive rhythms of optimal performance and healing in everyday life as well as all forms of mind-body healing. Research presented throughout this volume documents the view that all psychobiological phenomena have a natural periodicity that has been recently summarized as "the unification hypothesis of chronobiology" (Lloyd & Rossi, 1992b). These natural periodicities range from the clock-like cycles that are reset daily by light from the environment signaling the suprachiasmatic nucleus of the hypothalamus to the circadian rhythms of individual neurons that are apparently independent of any outside stimulus (Michel et al., 1993); the complex adaptive rhythms in the flow of hormones from the neuroendocrine system to all the organ and tissue systems of the body right down to the epigenetic level within each cell (Lloyd, 1992). Efforts to integrate this vast and unintegrated literature on the wave nature of mind-body communication and healing have led to systematic research on a chronobiological theory of hypnotherapeutic suggestion and holistic healing which generated a number of unique predictions that led to the following questions.

Are There Natural Periodicities in Hypnotherapy and the Many Approaches to Mind-Body Healing?   Following the author's initial outline of the clinical evidence for the associations between chronobiological data and hypnotherapeutic suggestion (Rossi, 1982, 1986a), Aldrich and Bernstein (1987) found that, as predicted, "time of day" was a statistically significant factor in hypnotic susceptibility. They reported a bimodal distribution of scores on The Harvard Group Scale of Hypnotic Susceptibility (HGSHS) in college students with a sharp major peak at 12 noon and a secondary, broader plateau around 5:00 or 6:00 P.M. Then, in a number of studies (Lippincott, 1990, 1992a, in press; Wallace, 1993), it was found that these results could be a reflection of the different optimal periods of hypnotic susceptibility in larks (people who claim to be more alert in the morning had higher hypnotic susceptibility in the evening) and owls (people who claim to be more alert in the evening were more hypnotizable in the morning). What is most significant about these studies is the realization that if the owls and larks had not been separated there would have been no significant differences in hypnotic susceptibility over time because the inverse periodic patterns of owls and larks would have canceled each other out. If future studies confirm such ultradian and circadian performance shifts in owls and larks, it will require a profound reevaluation of many previous studies on mind-body healing in general and hypnotherapeutic suggestion in particular.

Is There a Relationship Between Kleitman's Basic Rest-Activity Cycle (BRAC), Hypnotherapy and the Many Approaches to Mind-Body Communication and Healing?   The author designed a number of studies (Rossi, 1992a, 1993) to compare the therapeutic experiences of patients practicing self-hypnosis with those practicing the ultradian healing response. Similar results were found in both groups: there was an identical tendency to do self-hypnosis and ultradian healing every three hours or so throughout the day rather than every hour and a half as Kleitman's BRAC might suggest; both groups remained in their therapeutic state (self-hypnosis or ultradian healing) for about 20 minutes just as predicted from BRAC theory; both groups reported similar experiences of all the major classical hypnotic phenomena (e.g., deep relaxation and comfort with a "spontaneous" reduction of psychosomatic symptoms; tendencies toward amnesia and time distortion, daydreaming, and illusions, etc.). This apparent correspondence between the natural ultradian healing response and self-hypnosis was then replicated by a number of other investigators with varying methods and controls (Lippincott, 1990; Sanders, 1991a, b; Sommer, 1990, in press).

The existence of a "naturalistic 20-minute hypnotherapeutic trance time" is consistent with a number of earlier reports by clinicians and researchers that documented a 20-minute natural trance time in an incidental manner without recognizing its theoretical significance for chronobiological theory. Erickson, for example, mentions 20 minutes as a typical unit of trance time in a number of his clinical papers and workshops (Erickson, 1943b/1980). In one early research report he outlines how he used approximately 20 minutes for "the development of a deep trance state"; approximately another 20 minutes for "the development of a stuporous trance state"; and yet another 15 minutes for "the development of a somnambulistic state" (Erickson, 1954/1980, p. 53). A review of the literature of experimental hypnosis turned up a number of studies that could be interpreted as providing further support for a natural 15–20 minute trance time. In an early methodological study, Dorcus, Britnall, and Case (1941) compared the amount of time a group of 20 deeply hypnotizable subjects remained in trance after the hypnotist left the room with a control group who were told to simply lay down and relax. In both groups the majority of the subjects got up and left the room within 20 minutes. In two studies using control groups simulating hypnosis it was found that highly hypnotizable subjects remained in trance when they believed they were left unobserved for 10.7 and 16.5 minutes (Orne & Evans, 1966; Evans & Orne, 1971) while the simulating low hypnotizable subjects acted as if they were in trance for 25.2 minutes.

It is interesting that while none of these researchers set out to test the ultradian prediction that there is a natural 15–30 minute trance time, all their data support it. Since there is no other theory of hypnosis that would make such a prediction, the consistent observation of a 15–20 minute natural trance time in a great variety of clinical and experimental situations by many researchers working independently of each other with different theoretical perspectives provides substantial support for a chronobiological theory of therapeutic suggestion that may have important implications for many other approaches to mind-body healing.

Because ultradian psychobiological processes of self-regulation are so sensitive to psychosocial cues, they may be accessed, entrained, and therapeutically utilized by what has been traditionally called "therapeutic suggestion" even when the therapist is not aware of it. This leads to the view that the healing of stress and mind-body problems may be facilitated by utilizing the various phases of ultradian rhythms as a "window of opportunity" for optimizing the resolution of interpersonal and psychodynamic problems by many traditional schools of psychotherapy as well as by many alternative forms of holistic therapy. The ultradian healing response (Rossi & Nimmons, 1991) may be a generally unrecognized common denominator of time and rhythm in many forms of mind-body therapy such as Jacobson's progressive relaxation (1924), Benson's relaxation response (1975), biofeedback, many forms of imagery facilitating the immune response (Green & Green, 1987), and the various forms of meditation (e.g., transcendental) that usually require about 20 minutes (West, 1987). It is interesting to note that many experimental studies of psychological and holistic healing typically report that 20 minutes was used for the treatment effect (Green & Green, 1987; Rider & Achterberg, 1989) even though no theoretical rationale is ever presented for this special time period for healing. Some researchers have already provided evidence that "entertrainment mechanisms" are involved in pain reduction, potentiating the immune system, and the treatment of chronic diseases via muscle relaxation and music-mediated imagery (Rider, 1985, 1987). These therapeutic effects have been attributed to the use of imagery and relaxation on adrenal corticosteroids and "the re-entrainment of circadian rhythms" (Rider, 1985; Rider, Floyd, & Kirkpatrick, 1985).

Are the Classical Phenomena of Hypnosis Entrained Manifestations of Natural Patterns of Chronobiological Behavior That Are Characteristic of Certain Phases of Circadian and Ultradian Rhythms? While there has been a great deal of controversy about the nature of hypnotic phenomena, most modern theorists agree that the "feats of hypnosis" are all within the normal range of human behavior (Wagstaff, 1986). These researchers openly acknowledge, however, that they have no adequate theory about the source and parameters of hypnotic performance. Naish, for example, has recently summarized the situation as follows: ''As [hypnotic] susceptibility is normally assessed, a high scorer is one who *produces* the behavior, the *reason* for its production remains unknown . . . the claim was frequently made that cognitive processes are involved in the production of 'hypnotic' effects. However, the exact nature of these processes generally remained obscure'' (1986, pp. 165–166).

The chronobiological hypothesis purposes that *the source and parameters of hypnotherapeutic responsiveness may be found in that class of circadian (daily) and ultradian (more than once a day) psychobiological rhythms that are modulated by psychosocial cues* (Brown, 1991a, b; Rossi, 1982, 1986a, b; Rossi & Cheek, 1988; Rossi & Ryan, 1992). This hypothesis is consistent with Erickson's clinical findings as well as the experimental conclusions summarized by Wagstaff and Naish above. This hypothesis was assessed initially in a qualitative manner by carefully examining the written daily reports of the subjects and patients in the author's two studies reported above (Rossi, 1992a, b) and was replicated by Lippincott (1990), Sommer (1990, in press) and Sanders (1991a). Sommer and Lippincott both determined that while there were the typically wide variations in the nature of what each subject reported about the subjective aspects of their naturalistic trance experience, within their total groups virtually all the classical phenomena of hypnosis were experienced by implication as described above even though they were not directly suggested.

Summary and Overview

THE SURVEY of the psychobiology of mind-body healing presented in this book has led to a series of ever surprising insights into the changing structure of our understanding of the human condition. Let us summarize some of these insights.

1) *Information theory* is capable of unifying psychological, biological, and physical phenomena into a single conceptual framework that can account for mind-body healing, personality development, the evolution of human consciousness, and a fascinating panorama of cultural practices.

2) *Information transduction* is emerging as the key concept in our psychobiological theory of mind-body communication and healing. The basic laws of biology, psychology, and cultural anthropology are all essentially descriptions of different levels of information transduction.

3) *State-dependent memory, learning, and behavior* form the most general class of psychobiological phenomena that can be used to account for the dynamics of information transduction in humans. Classical Pavlovian and Skinnerian conditioning, as well as the psychodynamics of psychoanalysis, can be economically conceptualized as special cases of SDMLB.

4) There is no mysterious gap between mind and body. SDMLB processes encoded in the *limbic-hypothalamic and closely related systems* are the major information transducers that bridge the Cartesian dichotomy between mind and body.

5) Traditional *psychosomatic symptoms* and, perhaps, most mind-body problems are acquired by a process of experiential learning—specifically, the state-dependent learning of response patterns of Selye's General Adaptation Syndrome. Enduring mind-body problems are manifestations of these state-bound patterns of learning that are encoded within a limbic-hypothalamic system "filter" which modulates mind-body communication.

6) This limbic-hypothalamic system filter coordinates all the major channels of mind-body regulation via the autonomic, endocrine, immune, and neuropeptide systems. *Messenger molecules* (neurotransmitters, hormones, immunotransmitters, etc.) flowing through these channels are the structural in*form*ational mediators of mind-body communication and trans*form*ation.

7) Ongoing research is clarifying the precise pathways by which these messenger molecules are mediating the *mind-gene connection* that is the ultimate basis of most processes of mind-body healing via therapeutic hypnosis, the placebo response,and the traditional practices of mythopoetic and holistic medicine.

8) The new approaches to mind-body healing and therapeutic hypnosis may be conceptualized as processes of *accessing* and *utilizing* state-dependent memory, learning, and behavior systems that encode symptoms and problems and then *reframing* them for more integrated levels of adaptation and development.

9) The *ultradian healing response* is a newly developed approach to mind-body healing that is easy to learn, as people are encouraged to become more sensitive to their natural 90-minute psychobiological rhythms.

10) The *new concepts of therapeutic hypnosis* emphasize natural psychobiological processes of information transduction and SDMLB to access and facilitate the utilization of patients' own inner resources for problem-solving. This is in sharp contrast to previous methods of authoritarian suggestion, influence communication, covert conditioning, and programming in hypnosis.

The psychology of mind-body communication and healing as presented in this book thus introduces a broadly based information paradigm that is capable of integrating and expanding the scope of all previous views of illness and therapy. Much of this material is still so new that it could only be outlined in a manner that may seem intuitive and visionary; it is, however, scientifically well-documented. The art and science of reframing symptoms into signals and problems into creative functions are only beginning. It will require the dedicated efforts of all of us to gradually sift out what is of value in this work as a guide for future research, theory, and clinical practice.

References

Achterberg, J. (1985). *Imagery and healing*. Boston: Shambala.

Achterberg, J., & Lawlis, G. (1980). *Bridges of the mind/body*. Champaign, IL: Institute for Personality & Ability Testing.

Achterberg, J., & Lawlis, G. (1984). *Imagery and disease*. Champaign, IL: Institute for Personality & Ability Testing.

Ader, R. (Ed.) (1981). *Psychoneuroimmunology*. New York: Academic Press.

Ader, R. (1983). Behavioral conditioning and the immune system. In L. Temoshok, C. Van Dyke, & L. Zegans (Eds.), *Emotions in health and illness*. New York: Grune & Stratton.

Ader, R. (1985). Behaviorally conditioned modulation of immunity. In R. Guillemin, M. Cohn, & T. Melnechuk (Eds.), *Neural modulation of immunity* (pp. 55–69). New York: Raven Press.

Ader, R., Felten, D., & Cohen, N. (Eds.) (1991). *Psychoneuroimmunology* (2nd ed.). New York: Academic Press.

Alberts, B., Bray, D., Lewis, J., Raff, M., Roberts, K., & Watson, J. (1989). *Molecular biology of the cell* (2nd ed.). New York: Garland.

Aldrich, K., & Bernstein, D. (1987). The effect of time of day on hypnotizability. *International Journal of Clinical & Experimental Hypnosis, 35*(3), 141–145.

Alexander, B., Miklich, D. R., & Hershkoff, H. (1972). The immediate effects of systemic relaxation training on peak expiratory flow rates in asthmatic children. *Psychosomatic Research, 17,* 121.

Alexander, F. (1939/1984). Psychological aspects of medicine. Originally published by *Psychosomatic Medicine, 1*(1). Reprinted in 1984 by *Advances, 1*(2), 53–60.

Alexander, F. (1950). *Psychosomatic medicine*. New York: W. W. Norton.

Alexander, F., & French, T. (1948). *Studies in psychosomatic medicine: An approach to the cause and treatment of vegetative disturbances*. New York: Ronald Press.

Alkon, D. (1992). *Memory's voice*. New York: HarperCollins.

Amkraut, A., & Solomon, G. (1975). From the symbolic stimulus to the pathophysiologic response: Immune mechanisms. *International Journal of Psychiatry in Medicine, 5,* 541–563.

Anderson, C. (1992). Gene therapy researcher under fire over controversial cancer trials. *Nature, 360,* 399–400.

Andrews, V., & Hall, H. (1990). The effects of relaxation/imagery training on recurrent aphthous stomatitis. *Psychosomatic Medicine, 52,* 526–535.

Anokhin, P. (1949). Problems in higher nervous activity. *Izd. Akad. Med. Nauk SSSR,* Moscow.

Anokhin, P. (1955). New data on the afferent apparatus of the conditioned reflex. *Vop. Psikhol.,* No. 6.

Antoni, M., Esterling, B., Lutgendorf, S., Fletcher, M., & Schneiderman, N. (in press). Psychosocial stressors, herpes virus reactivation and HIV-1 infection. In M. Stein & A. Baum (Eds.), *Perspectives in behavioral medicine*. Hillsdale, NJ: Erlbaum.

Araoz, D. (1982). *Hypnosis and sex therapy*. New York: Brunner/Mazel.

Araoz, D. (1985). *The new hypnosis*. New York: Brunner/Mazel.

Arya, U. (1979). *Meditation and the art of dying*. Honesdale, PA: Himalayan International Institute.

Auerbach, J., Oleson, T., & Solomon, G. (1992). A behavioral medicine intervention as an adjunctive treatment for HIV-related illness. *Psychology & Health, 6*, 325–334.

Bailey, D., Harry, D., & Kupprat, I. (1973). Oscillations in oxygen consumption of man at rest. *Journal of Applied Physiology, 34*, 467–470.

Bakan, P. (1969). Hypnotizability, laterality of eye movements, and functional brain asymmetry. *Perceptual & Motor Skills, 28*, 927–932.

Bakan, P. (1980). Imagery, raw and cooked: A hemispheric recipe. In J. Shorr, G. Sobel, P. Robin, & J. Connella (Eds.), *Imagery* (pp. 35–53). New York: Plenum.

Balkwill, F. (1993). Improving on the formula. *Nature, 361*, 206–207.

Bandura, A. (1985). Catecholamine secretion as a function of perceived coping self-efficacy. *Journal of Counseling and Clinical Psychology, 58*(3), 406–414.

Banks, W. (1985). Hypnotic suggestion for the control of bleeding in the angiography suite. *Ericksonian Monographs, 1*, 76–88.

Barabasz, A., & McGeorge, C. (1978). Biofeedback, mediated biofeedback and hypnosis in peripheral vasodilation training. *The American Journal of Clinical Hypnosis, 21*(1), 28–37.

Barabasz, A. F., & Barabasz, M. (1989). Effects of restricted environmental stimulations: Enhancement of hypnotizability for experimental and chronic pain control. *International Journal of Clinical & Experimental Hypnosis, 37*(3), 217–231.

Barabasz, M. (1987). Trichotillomania: A new treatment. *International Journal of Clinical & Experimental Hypnosis, 35*, 146–154.

Barber, T. X. (1972). Suggested ("hypnotic") behavior: The trance paradigm versus an alternate paradigm. In E. Fromm & R. Shor (Eds.), *Hypnosis: Research development and perspectives*. New York: Aldine-Atherton.

Barber, T. X. (1978). Hypnosis, suggestions, and psychosomatic phenomena: A new look from the standpoint of recent experimental studies. *American Journal of Clinical Hypnosis, 21*(1), 13–27.

Barber, T. X. (1984). Changing unchangeable bodily processes by (hypnotic) suggestions: A new look at hypnosis, cognitions, imagining, and the mind-body problem. *Advances, 1*(2), 7–40.

Barber, T. X., & Meyer, E. (1977). Evaluation of the efficacy and neuronal mechanism of a hypnotic analgesia procedure in experimental and clinical dental pain. *Pain, 4*, 41–48.

Barinaga, M. (1992a). Knockouts shed light on learning. *Science, 257*, 162–163.

Barinaga, M. (1992b). Playing "telephone" with the body's message of pain. *Science, 258*, 1085.

Barinaga, M. (1993). Carbon monoxide: Killer to brain messenger in one step. *Science, 259*, 307.

Barnett, E. (1984). The role of prenatal trauma in the development of the negative birth experience. Paper presented at the American Society of Clinical Hypnosis Annual Meeting, San Francisco, CA.

Baron, S., et al. (1991). The interferons: Mechanisms of action and clinical applications. *Journal of the American Medical Association, 266*(10), 1375–1383.

Becker, J., Breedlove, S., & Crews, D. (Eds.). (1992). *Behavioral endocrinology*. Cambridge, MA: MIT Press.

Beecher, H. (1959). *Measurement of subjective responses: Quantitative effect of drugs*. New York: Oxford University Press.

Bein, T. (1993). Nanometre assembly lines. *Nature, 361*, 207–208.

Bennett, H. (1985). Behavioral anesthesia. *Advances, 2*(4), 11–21.

Benson, H. (1975). *The relaxation response*. New York: Avon.

Benson, H. (1983a). The relaxation response and norepinephrine: A new study illuminates mechanisms. *Integrative Psychiatry, 1*, 15–18.

Benson, H. (1983b). The relaxation response: Its subjective and objective historical precedents and physiology. *Trends in Neuroscience*, July, 281–284.

Bergland, R. (1985). *The fabric of mind*. New York: Viking.

Bernheim, H. (1956). *Suggestive therapeutives: A treatise on the nature and uses of hypnotism*. Westport, CT: Associated Booksellers. Originally published by Putnam, 1886.

Besedovsky, H. O., & del Rey, A. (1991). Physiological implications of the immune-neuro-endocrine network. In R. Ader, D. Felten, & N. Cohen (Eds.), *Psychoneuroimmunology* (2nd ed.) (pp. 589–608). San Diego, CA: Academic Press.

Besedovsky, H., del Rey, A., & Sorkin, E. (1985). Immunological-neuroendocrine feedback circuits. In R. Guillemin, M. Cohn, & T. Melnechuk (Eds.), *Neural modulation of immunity* (pp. 165–177). New York: Raven Press.

Black, I. (1975). Increased tyrosine hydroxylase activity in frontal cortex and cerebellum after reserpine. *Brain Research, 95*, 170–176.

Black, I. (1982). Stages of neurotransmitter development in autonomic neurons. *Science, 215*, 1198–1204.

Black, I. (1991). *Information and the brain: A molecular perspective*. Cambridge, MA: MIT Press.

Black, S. (1963). Inhibition of immediate-type hypersensitivity response by direct suggestion under hypnosis. *British Medical Journal*, April 6, 925–929.

Black, S. (1969). *Mind and body*. London: William Kimber.

Black, S., Edholm, R., Fox, R., & Kidd, D. (1963). The effect of suggestions under hypnosis on the peripheral circulation in man. *Clinical Science, 25*, 223–230.

Black, S., & Friedman, M. (1965). Adrenal function and the inhibition of allergic responses under hypnosis. *British Medical Journal, 1*, 562–567.

Black, S., Humphrey, J., & Niven, J. (1963). Inhibition of Mantoux reaction by direct suggestion under hypnosis. *British Medical Journal*, June 22, 1649–1652.

Blalock, E., Harbour-McMenamin, D., & Smith, E. (1985). Peptide hormones shaped by the neuroendocrine and immunologic systems. *The Journal of Immunology, 135*(2), 858s–861s.

Blankstein, J., Reyes, F., Winter, J., & Faiman, C. (1981). Endorphins and the regulation of the human menstrual cycle. *Clinical Endocrinology, 14*(3), 287–294.

Bloom, F. (1985). Neuropeptides and other mediators in the central nervous system. *The Journal of Immunology, 135*(2), 743s–745s.

Bloom, F., Lazerson, A., & Hofstadter, L. (1985). *Brain, mind, and behavior*. New York: W. H. Freeman.

Blum, G. (1967). Experimental observations on the contextual nature of hypnosis. *International Journal of Clinical & Experimental Hypnosis, 15*(4), 160–171.

Blum, G. (1972). Hypnotic programming techniques in psychological experiments. In E. Fromm, & R. Shor (Eds.), *Hypnosis: Research developments & perspectives* (pp. 359–385). Chicago, IL: Aldine-Atherton.

Bockman, D., & Kirby, M. (1985). Neural crest interactions in the development of the immune system. *The Journal of Immunology, 135*(2), 766s–768s.

Bodden, J. (1991). Accessing state-bound memories in the treatment of phobias: Two case studies. *American Journal of Clinical Hypnosis, 34*, 24–28.

Bolander, F. (1989). *Molecular endocrinology*. New York: Academic Press.

Bonneau, R., Sheridan, J., Feng, N., & Glaser, R. (1993). Stress induced modulation of the primary cellular immune response to herpes simplex virus infection is mediated by both adrenal dependent and independent mechanisms. *Journal of Neuroimmunology, 42*, 167–176.

Borbely, A., & Achermann, P. (1992). Concepts and models of sleep regulation: An overview. *Journal of Sleep Research, 1*, 63–79.

Bower, G. (1981). Mood and memory. *American Psychologist, 36*(2), 129–148.

Bowers, K. (1977). Hypnosis: An informational approach. *Annuals of the New York Academy of Sciences, 296*, 222–237.

Bowers, K., & Kelly, P. (1979). Stress, disease, psychotherapy, and hypnosis. *Journal of Abnormal Psychology, 88*(5), 490–505.

Braid, J. (1855). *The physiology of fascination of the critics criticized.* Manchester, England: Grant & Company.

Brandenberger, G. (1992). Endocrine ultradian rhythms during sleep and wakefulness. In D. Lloyd & E. Rossi (Eds.), *Ultradian rhythms in life processes: A fundamental inquiry into chronobiology and psychobiology* (pp. 123–138). New York: Springer-Verlag.

Brassfield, P. (1980). A discriminative study of the dissociative states of a multiple personality. Unpublished doctoral dissertation, United States International University.

Brassfield, P. (1983). Unfolding patterns of the multiple personality through hypnosis. *The American Journal of Clinical Hypnosis, 26*(2), 146–152.

Braun, B. (1983a). Neurophysiologic changes in multiple personality due to integration: A preliminary report. *The American Journal of Clinical Hypnosis, 26*(2), 84–92.

Braun, B. (1983b). Psychophysiological phenomena in multiple personality. *The American Journal of Clinical Hypnosis, 26*(2), 124–137.

Brewerton, D. (1992). *All About Arthritis.* Cambridge, Massachusetts: Harvard University Press.

Brodsky, V. (1992). Rhythms of protein synthesis and other circahoralian oscillations: The possible involvement of fractals. In D. Lloyd & E. Rossi (Eds.), *Ultradian rhythms in life processes: A fundamental inquiry into chronobiology and psychobiology* (pp. 23–40). New York: Springer-Verlag.

Brown, F., & Graeber, R. (Eds.). (1982). *Rhythmic aspects of behavior.* Hillsdale, NJ: Erlbaum.

Brown, P. (1991a). Ultradian rhythms of cerebral function and hypnosis. *Contemporary Hypnosis, 8,* 1, 17–24.

Brown, P. (1991b). *The hypnotic brain: Hypnotherapy and social communication.* New Haven, CT: Yale University Press.

Brush, F. R., & Levine, S. (1989). *Psychoendocrinology.* San Diego, CA: Academic Press.

Bulloch, K. (1985). Neuroanatomy of lymphoid tissue: A review. In R. Guillemin, M. Cohn, & T. Melnechuk (Eds.), *Neural modulation of immunity* (pp. 111–141). New York: Raven Press.

Cannon, W. (1932). *The wisdom of the body.* New York: W. W. Norton.

Cannon, W. (1942). Voodoo death. *American Anthropologist, 44*(2), 169–181.

Cannon, W. (1953). *Bodily changes in pain, hunger, fear and rage* (2nd ed.). Boston: Charles T. Branford Co.

Cannon, W. (1957). "Voodoo" death. *Psychosomatic Medicine, 19*(3), 182–190.

Cannon, W. (1963). *The wisdom of the body* (2nd ed.). New York: W. W. Norton.

Carich, M., & Parwatikar, S. (1992). A mind-body connection: A sex offender switch box: A brief review. *Illinois Network of the Management of Abusive Sexuality Newsletter, 5,* 2–4.

Chapman, L., Goodell, H., & Wolff, H. (1959a). Changes in tissue vulnerability induced during hypnotic suggestion. *Journal of Psychosomatic Research, 4,* 99–115.

Chapman, L., Goodell, H., & Wolff, H. (1959b). Augmentation of the inflammatory reaction by activity of the central nervous system. *AMA Archives of Neurology, 1,* 557–572.

Cheek, D. (1957). Effectiveness of incentive in clinical hypnosis. *Obstetrics & Gynecology, 9*(6), 720–724.

Cheek, D. (1959). Unconscious perception of meaningful sounds during surgical anesthesia as revealed under hypnosis. *The American Journal of Clinical Hypnosis, 1,* 101–113.

Cheek, D. (1960). Removal of subconscious resistance to hypnosis using ideometer questioning techniques. *The American Journal of Clinical Hypnosis, 3*(2), 103–107.

Cheek, D. (1962a). Ideometer questioning for investigation of subconscious pain and target organ vulnerability. *The American Journal of Clinical Hypnosis, 5*(1), 30–41.

Cheek, D. (1962b). Importance of recognizing that surgical patients behave as though hypnotized. *The American Journal of Clinical Hypnosis, 4,* 227–238.

Cheek, D. (1965). Some newer understandings of dreams in relation to threatened abortion and premature labor. *Pacific Medical & Surgical,* Nov–Dec, 379–384.

Cheek, D. (1969). Communication with the critically ill. *The American Journal of Clinical Hypnosis, 12*(2), 75–85.

Cheek, D. (1975). Maladjustment patterns apparently related to imprinting at birth. *The American Journal of Clinical Hypnosis, 18*(2), 75–82.

Cheek, D. (1976). Short-term hypnotherapy for fragility using exploration of early life attitudes. *The American Journal of Clinical Hypnosis, 19*(1), 20–27.

Cheek, D. (1978). Were you originally left-handed? *Swedish Journal of Hypnosis,* 17–25.

Cheek, D. (1981). Awareness of meaningful sounds under general anesthesia: Considerations and a review of the literature, 1959–1979. *Theoretical and Clinical Aspects of Hypnosis.* Symposium Specialists, Miami, FL.

Cheek, D., & LeCron, L. (1968). *Clinical hypnotherapy.* New York: Grune & Stratton.

Chiba, Y., Chiba, K., Halberg, F., & Cutkomp, L. (1977). Longitudinal evaluation of circadian rhythm characteristics and their circaseptan modulation in an apparently normal couple. In J. McGovern, M. Smolensky, & A. Reinberg (Eds.), *Chronobiology in allergy and immunology* (pp. 17–35). Springfield, IL: Thomas.

Ciompi, L. (1991). Affects as central organizing and integrating factors: A new psychosocial/biological model of the psyche. *British Journal of Psychiatry, 159,* 97–105.

Clawson, T. A., & Swade, R. H. (1975). The hypnotic control of blood flow and pain: The cure of warts and the potential for use of hypnosis in the treatment of cancer. *American Journal of Clinical Hypnosis, 17,* 160–169.

Clayton, D. (1992, October). The mind of a canary. *Discover,* pp. 10–11.

Coates, T., McKusick, L., Kuno, R., & Stites, D. (1989). Stress reduction training changed number of sexual partners but not immune function in men with HIV. *American Journal of Public Health, 79,* 10–11.

Cohn, M. (1985). What are the "must" elements of immune responsiveness? In R. Guillemin, M. Cohn, & T. Melnechuk (Eds.), *Neural modulation of immunity* (pp. 3–25). New York: Raven Press.

Conn, L., & Mott, T. (1984). Plethysmographic demonstration of rapid vasodilation by direct suggestion: A case of Raynaud's disease treated by hypnosis. *The American Journal of Clinical Hypnosis, 26*(3), 166–170.

Cooper, G. (1992). *Elements of human cancer.* Boston: Jones & Bartlett.

Cordes, C. (1985). Neuropeptides: Chemical cruise steers emotions. *APA Monitor, 16*(9), 18.

Cousins, N. (1979). *Anatomy of an illness as perceived by the patient.* New York: W. W. Norton.

Cousins, N. (1983). *The healing heart.* New York: W. W. Norton.

Crabtree, G. (1989). Contingent genetic regulatory vents in T-lymphocyte activation. *Science, 243*(20), 355–361.

Crasilneck, H. (1982). A follow-up study in the use of hypnotherapy in the treatment of psychogenic impotency. *The American Journal of Clinical Hypnosis, 15*(1), 52–61.

Crasilneck, H., & Hall, J. (1959). Physiological changes associated with hypnosis: A review of the literature since 1948. *International Journal of Clinical & Experimental Hypnosis, 7*(1), 9–50.

Crasilneck, H. B., & Hall, J. A. (1985). *Clinical hypnosis: Principles and applications* (2nd ed.). Orlando, FL: Grune & Stratton.

Crick, F. (1984). Memory and molecular turnover. *Nature, 312,* 101.

Crick, F., & Koch, C. (1990). Towards a neurobiological theory of consciousness. *The Neurosciences, 2,* 263–275.

Crick, F., & Koch, C. (1992, September). The problem of consciousness. *Scientific American,* pp. 153–159.

Crnic, L. (1991). Behavioral consequences of virus infection. In R. Ader, D. Felten, & N. Cohen (Eds.), *Psychoneuroimmunology* (2nd ed.) (pp. 749–769). New York: Academic Press.

Culotta, E., & Koshland, D., Jr. (1992). No news is good news. *Science, 258,* 1862–1865.

Dalton, K. (1971). Prospective study into puerperal depression. *British Journal of Psychiatry, 118,* 689–692.

Darnell, J., Lodish, H., & Baltimore, D. (1986). *Molecular cell biology*. New York: Scientific American.

Darnell, J., Lodish, H., & Baltimore, D. (1990). *Molecular cell biology*. New York: Scientific American.

Davies, P. (Ed.). (1989). *The new physics*. Cambridge, England: Cambridge University Press.

Davis, J. (1984). *Endorphins*. New York: Dial Press.

Day, M. (1964). An eye-movement phenomenon related to attention, thought and anxiety. *Perceptual & Motor Skills, 19*, 443–446.

De Chardin, T. (1959). *The phenomenon of man*. New York: Harper.

Delbruck, M. (1970). A physicist's renewed look at biology: Twenty years later. *Science, 168*, 1312–1314.

Delgado, J. (1969). *Physical control of the mind*. New York: Harper & Row.

Delgado, J., Roberts, W., & Miller, N. (1954). Learning motivated by electrical stimulation of the brain. *American Journal of Physiology, 179*, 587.

Delhounge, F., & Hansen, K. (1927). Die suggestive beeinflussbarkeit der Magen- und Pankreassekretion in der hypnose. *Dtsch. Arch. Klin. Med., 157*, 20.

Dement, W. (1965). An essay on dreams: The role of physiology in understanding their nature. In *New directions in psychology II*. New York: Holt, Rinehart & Winston.

Dement, W. (1972). *Some must watch while some must sleep*. San Francisco: Freeman.

Dement, W., & Kleitman, N. (1957). Cyclic variations in EEG readings during sleep and their relation to eye movements, body motility, and dreaming. *Electroencephalography & Clinical Neurophysiology, 9*, 673–690.

DePiano, F., & Salzberg, H. (1979). Clinical applications of hypnosis to three psychosomatic disorders. *Psychological Bulletin, 86*, 1223–1235.

De Wied, D. (1984). Neurohypophyseal hormone influences on learning and memory processes. In G. Lynch, J. McGaugh, & N. Weinberger (Eds.), *Neurobiology of learning and memory* (pp. 289–312). New York: Guilford.

De Wied, D. (1990). *Neuropeptides: Basics and perspectives*. New York: Elsevier.

Diamond, H. H. (1959). Hypnosis in children: The complete cure of forty cases of asthma. *American Journal of Clinical Hypnosis, 1*, 124–129.

Dobbin, J., Harth, M., McCain, G., Martin, R., & Cousin, K. (1991). Dytokine production and lymphocyte transformation during stress. *Brain Behavior & Immunity, 5*, 339–348.

Dohrenwend, B., & Dohrenwend, B. (Eds.). (1974). *Stressful life events: Their nature and effects*. New York: Wiley.

Domangue, B., Margolis, C., Lieberman, D., & Kaji, H. (1985). Biochemical correlates of hypnoanalgesia in arthritic pain patients. *Journal of Clinical Psychiatry, 46*, 235–238.

Dorcus, R., Britnall, A., & Case, H. (1941). Control experiments and their relation to theories of hypnotism. *Journal of General Psychology, 24*, 217–221.

Dunbar, F. (1954). *Emotions and bodily changes*. New York: Columbia University Press.

Dunlap, D., Henderson, T., & Inch, R. (1952). Survey of 17,301 prescriptions of Form Ec 10. *British Medical Journal, 1*, 292–295.

Edelson, R., & Fink, J. (1985). The immunological function of skin. *Scientific American*, June, 46–53.

Edmonston, W. (1986). *The induction of hypnosis*. New York: Wiley.

Edwards, G. (1960). Hypnotic treatment of asthma: Real and illusory results. *British Medical Journal, 2*, 492.

Eigen, M., & Winkler-Oswatitsch, R. (1992). *Steps toward life: A perspective on evolution*. Oxford, England: Oxford University Press.

Ellenberger, H. (1970). *The discovery of the unconscious*. New York: Basic.

Engel, G. (1968). A life setting conducive to illness: The giving-up-given-up complex. *Annals of Internal Medicine, 69*(2), 292–300.

Engel, G. (1971). Sudden and rapid death during psychological stress: Folklore or folkwisdom? *Annals of Internal Medicine, 74*, 771–782.

Engel, G. (1985). Spontaneous bleeding on anniversaries: The biopsychosocial model applied to a personal experience. *AOA Lecture*, University of Arizona.

Erickson, M. (1932/1980). Possible detrimental effects of experimental hypnosis. In E.

Rossi (Ed.), *The collected papers of Milton H. Erickson on hypnosis. I. The nature of hypnosis and suggestion* (pp. 493–497). New York: Irvington.

Erickson, M. (1937/1980). Development of apparent unconsciousness during hypnotic reliving of a traumatic experience. In E. Rossi (Ed.), *The papers of Milton H. Erickson on hypnosis. III. Hypnotic investigation of psychodynamic processes* (pp. 45–52). New York: Irvington.

Erickson, M. (1939/1980). Experimental demonstration of psychopathology of everyday life. In E. Rossi (Ed.), *The collected papers of Milton H. Erickson on hypnosis. III. Hypnotic investigation of psychodynamic processes* (pp. 190–202). New York: Irvington.

Erickson, M. (1943a/1980). Experimentally elicited salivary and related responses to hypnotic visual hallucinations confirmed by personality reactions. In E. Rossi (Ed.), *The collected papers of Milton H. Erickson on hypnosis. II. Hypnotic alteration of sensory, perceptual and psychophysical processes* (pp. 175–178). New York: Irvington.

Erickson, M. (1943b/1980). Hypnotic investigation of psychosomatic phenomena: A controlled experimental use of hypnotic regression in the therapy of an acquired food intolerance. In E. Rossi (Ed.), *The collected papers of Milton H. Erickson on hypnosis. II. Hypnotic alteration of sensory, perceptual and psychophysical processes* (pp. 169–174). New York: Irvington.

Erickson, M. (1943c/1980). Hypnotic investigation of psychosomatic phenomena: Psychosomatic interrelationships studied by experimental hypnosis. In E. Rossi (Ed.), *The collected papers of Milton E. Erickson on hypnosis. II. Hypnotic alteration of sensory, perceptual and psychophysical processes* (pp. 145–156). New York: Irvington.

Erickson, M. (1943d/1980). Investigation of psychosomatic phenomena: The development of aphasialike reactions from hypnotically induced amnesia. In E. Rossi (Ed.), *The collected papers of Milton H. Erickson on hypnosis. II. Hypnotic alteration of sensory, perceptual and psychophysical processes* (pp. 157–168). New York: Irvington.

Erickson, M. (1948/1980). Hypnotic psychotherapy. In E. Rossi (Ed.), *The collected papers of Milton H. Erickson on hypnosis. IV. Innovative hypnotherapy* (pp. 35–48). New York: Irvington.

Erickson, M. (1952/1980). Deep hypnosis and its induction. In E. Rossi (Ed.), *The collected papers of Milton H. Erickson on hypnosis. I. The nature of hypnosis and suggestion* (pp. 139–167). New York: Irvington.

Erickson, M. (1954/1980). Pseudo-orientation in time as a hypnotherapeutic procedure. In E. Rossi (Ed.), *The collected papers of Milton H. Erickson on hypnosis. IV. Innovative hypnotherapy* (pp. 397–423). New York: Irvington.

Erickson, M. (1960a/1980). Breast development possibly influenced by hypnosis: Two instances and the psychotherapeutic results. In E. Rossi (Ed.), *The collected papers of Milton H. Erickson on hypnosis. II. Hypnotic investigation of sensory, perceptual and psychophysical processes* (pp. 203–206). New York: Irvington.

Erickson, M. (1960b/1980). Psychogenic alteration of menstrual functioning: Three instances. In E. Rossi (Ed.), *The collected papers of Milton H. Erickson on hypnosis. II. Hypnotic investigation of sensory, perceptual and psychophysical processes* (pp. 207–212). New York: Irvington.

Erickson, M. (1961/1980). Historical note on the hand levitation and other ideomotor techniques. In E. Rossi (Ed.), *The collected papers of Milton H. Erickson on hypnosis. I. The nature of hypnosis and suggestion* (pp. 135–138). New York: Irvington.

Erickson, M. (1963/1980). Hypnotically oriented psychotherapy in organic brain damage. In E. Rossi (Ed.), *The collected papers of Milton H. Erickson on hypnosis. IV. Innovative hypnotherapy* (pp. 283–311). New York: Irvington.

Erickson, M. (1964/1980). The "surprise" and "my-friend-John" techniques of hypnosis: Minimal cues and natural field experimentation. In E. Rossi (Ed.), *The collected papers of Milton H. Erickson on hypnosis. I. The nature of hypnosis and suggestion* (pp. 340–359). New York: Irvington.

Erickson, M. (1967/1980). Further experimental investigation of hypnosis: Hypnotic and nonhypnotic realities. In E. Rossi (Ed.), *The collected papers of Milton H. Erickson on hypnosis. I. The nature of hypnosis and suggestion* (pp. 18–82). New York: Irvington.

Erickson, M. (1977/1980). Control of physiological functions by hypnosis. In E. Rossi (Ed.), *The collected papers of Milton H. Erickson on hypnosis. II. Hypnotic alteration of sensory, perceptual and psychophysical processes* (pp. 179–191). New York: Irvington.

Erickson, M. (1980a). Provocation as a means of motivating recovery from a cerebrovascular accident. In E. Rossi (Ed.), *The collected papers of Milton H. Erickson on hypnosis. IV. Innovative hypnotherapy* (pp. 321–327). New York: Irvington.

Erickson, M. (1980b). *The collected papers of Milton H. Erickson on hypnosis, 4 Volumes.* Edited by Ernest L. Rossi. New York: Irvington.

Erickson, M. (1980c). The hypnotic alteration of blood flow: An experiment comparing waking and hypnotic responsiveness. In E. Rossi (Ed.), *The collected papers of Milton H. Erickson on hypnosis. II. Hypnotic alteration of sensory, perceptual and psychophysical processes* (pp. 192–195). New York: Irvington.

Erickson, M. (1985). Memory and hallucination, Part I: The utilization approach to hypnotic suggestion. Edited with commentaries by Ernest Rossi. *Ericksonian Monographs, 1*, 1–21.

Erickson, M., & Rossi, E. (1974/1980). Varieties of hypnotic amnesia. In E. Rossi (Ed.), *The collected papers of Milton H. Erickson on hypnosis. III. Hypnotic investigations of psychodynamic processes* (pp. 71–90). New York: Irvington.

Erickson, M., & Rossi, E. (1976/1980). Two-level communication and the microdynamics of trance and suggestion. In E. Rossi (Ed.), *The collected papers of Milton H. Erickson on hypnosis. I. The nature of hypnosis and suggestion* (pp. 430–451). New York: Irvington.

Erickson, M., & Rossi, E. (1979). *Hypnotherapy: A exploratory casebook.* New York: Irvington.

Erickson, M., & Rossi, E. (1980). The indirect forms of suggestion. In E. Rossi (Ed.), *The collected papers of Milton H. Erickson on hypnosis. I. The nature of hypnosis and suggestion* (pp. 452–477). New York: Irvington.

Erickson, M., & Rossi, E. (1981). *Experiencing hypnosis: Therapeutic approaches to altered states.* New York: Irvington.

Erickson, M., Rossi, E., & Rossi, S. (1976). *Hypnotic realities.* New York: Irvington.

Evans, F. (1977). The placebo control of pain: A paradigm for investigating non-specific effects in psychotherapy. In J. Brady, J. Mendels, W. Reiger, & M. Orne (Eds.), *Psychiatry: Areas of promise and advancement* (pp. 215–228). New York: Spectrum.

Evans, F. (1981). The placebo response in pain control. *Psychopharmacology Bulletin, 17*, 72–76.

Evans, F. (1985). Expectancy, therapeutic instructions, and the placebo response. In L. White, B. Tursky, & G. Schwartz (Eds.), *Placebo: Theory, research, and mechanism* (pp. 215–228). New York: Guilford.

Evans, F., & Orne, M. (1971). The disappearing hypnotist: The use of simulating subjects to evaluate how subjects perceive experimental procedures. *The International Journal of Clinical & Experimental Hypnosis, 19*, 277–296.

Ewer, T. C., & Stewart, D. E. (1986). Improvement in bronchial hyperresponsiveness in patients with moderate asthma after treatment with a hypnotic technique: A randomized controlled trial. *British Medical Journal, 293*, 1129–1132.

Ewin, D. (1974). Condyloma acuminatum: Successful treatment of four cases by hypnosis. *American Journal of Clinical Hypnosis, 17*(2), 73–78.

Ewin, D. (1978). Clinical use of hypnosis for attenuation of burn depth. In F. H. Frankel & H. S. Zamansky (Eds.), *Hypnosis at its bicentennial* (pp. 155–162). New York: Plenum.

Ewin, D. (1979). Hypnosis in burn therapy. In G. Burrows, D. Collison, & L. Dennerstein (Eds.), *Hypnosis 1979* (pp. 269–275). Amsterdam, NY: Elsevier/North-Holland Biomedical Press.

Ewin, D. (1980). Constant pain syndrome: Its psychological meaning and cure using hypnoanalysis. In H. J. Wain (Ed.), *Clinical hypnosis in medicine.* Chicago, IL: Year Book Medical.

Ewin, D. (1986a). Emergency room hypnosis for the burned patient. *American Journal of Clinical Hypnosis, 29*(1), 7–12.

Ewin, D. (1986b). The effect of hypnosis and mental set on major surgery and burns. *Psychiatric Annals, 16*(2), 115–118.

Ewin, D. (1992). Hypnotherapy for warts (verruca vulgaris): 41 consecutive cases with 33 cures. *American Journal of Clinical Hypnosis, 35*, 1–10.

Fackelmann, K. A. (1991). Randy reptiles: Curious clockwork spurs sex drive in snakes. *Science News, 139*, 300–301.

Feher, S., Berger, L., Johnson, J., & Wilde, J. (1989). Increasing breast milk production for premature infants with a relaxation/imagery audiotape. *Pediatrics, 83*, 57–60.

Felten, D., Felten, S., Carlson, S., Olschowka, J., & Livnat, S. (1985). Noradrenergic and peptidergic innervation of lymphoid tissue. *The Journal of Immunology, 135*(2), 755s–765s.

Field, T., Morrow, C., Valdeon, C., Larson, S., Kuhn, C., & Schanberg, S. (1993). Massage reduces anxiety in children and adolescent psychiatric patients. *Journal of the American Academy of Child & Adolescent Psychiatry, 31*, 125–131.

Finkelstein, S., & Greenleaf, H. (1982–83). Cancer prevention: A three-year pilot study. *The American Journal of Clinical Hypnosis, 25*(2–3), 177–187.

Fischer, R. (1971a). Arousal-statebound recall of experience. *Diseases of the Nervous System, 32*, 373–382.

Fischer, R. (1971b). The "flashback": Arousal-statebound recall of experience. *Journal of Psychedelic Drugs, 3*, 31–39.

Fischer, R. (1971c). A cartography of ecstatic and meditative states. *Science, 174*, 897–904.

Fischer, R., & Landon, G. M. (1972). On the arousal state-dependent recall of "subconscious" experience: Stateboundedness. *British Journal of Psychiatry, 120*, 159–172.

Flood, J., Smith, G., & Morley, J. (1987). Modulation of memory processing by cholecystokinin: Dependence on the vagus nerve. *Science, 236*, 832–834.

Foss, L., & Rothenberg, K. (1987). *The second medical revolution: From biomedicine to infomedicine.* Boston: Shambala.

Frank, J. (1963). *Persuasion and healing.* New York: Schocken Books.

Frankel, F. (1985). Personal communication. (Also reported by P. Bagne in *Omni*, April 1985, p. 122.)

Freud, S. (1956). *Collected papers.* Edited by Ernest Jones. New York: Basic.

Frick, D. (1976). Immediate hypersensitivity. In H. Fudenberg (Ed.), *Basic and clinical immunology* (pp. 204–224). Los Altos, CA: Lange Medical Publications.

Friedman, M., & Ulmer, D. (1984). *Treating type A behavior and your heart.* New York: Ballantine.

Friedman, S. (1972). On the presence of a variant form of instinctual regression: Oral drive cycles in obesity-bulimia. *Psychoanalytic Quarterly, 41*, 364–383.

Friedman, S. (1978). A psychophysiological model for the chemotherapy of psychosomatic illness. *The Journal of Nervous & Mental Diseases, 166*, 110–116.

Friedman, S., Kantor, I., Sobel, S., & Miller, R. (1978). On the treatment of neurodermatitis with a monoamine oxidase inhibition. *The Journal of Nervous & Mental Diseases, 166*, 117–125.

Fromm, E., & Shor, R. (Eds.) (1979). *Hypnosis: Research development and perspectives* (2nd ed.). Chicago, IL: Aldine-Atherton.

Gabel, S. (1988). The right hemisphere in imagery, hypnosis, REM sleep, and dreaming. *Journal of Nervous and Mental Disease, 176*, 323–331.

Gage, D. (1983). Mood state-dependent memory and the lateralization of emotion. Unpublished doctoral dissertation, Catholic University of America.

Ganong, W. (1985). *Review of medical physiology* (12th ed.). Los Altos, CA: Lange Medical Publications.

Garfinkel, A. (1983). A mathematics for physiology. *American Journal of Physiology, 245*, R455–R466.

Garfinkel, A., & Abraham, R. (1992). Phase plots of temporal oscillations. In D. Lloyd & E. Rossi (Eds.), *Ultradian rhythms in life processes.* New York: Springer-Verlag.

Gazzaniga, M. (1967). The split brain in man. *Scientific American, 217*, 24–29.

Gazzaniga, M. (1985). *The social brain: Discovering the networks of the mind.* New York: Basic.

Gendlin, E. (1978). *Focusing.* New York: Everest House.

Gentry, W. (Ed.). (1984). *Handbook of behavioral medicine*. New York: Guilford.

Gerson, M., Payette, R., & Rothman, T. (1985). Microenvironmental factors in phenotypic expression by enteric neurons: Parallels to lymphocytes. In R. Guillemin, M. Cohn, & T. Melnechuk (Eds.), *Neural modulation of immunity* (pp. 221–252). New York: Raven Press.

Ghanta, V., Hiramoto, R., Solvason, H., & Spector, N. (1985). Neural and environmental influences on neoplasia and conditioning of NK activity. *Journal of Immunology, 135*(2), 848s–852s.

Gill, M., & Brenman, M. (1959). *Hypnosis and related states*. New York: International Universities Press.

Gilligan, S., & Bower, G. (1984). Cognitive consequences of emotional arousal. In C. Izard, J. Kagan, & R. Zajonc (Eds.), *Emotions, cognitions, and behavior*. New York: Cambridge Press.

Gladue, B., Boechler, M., & McCaul, K. (1989). Hormonal response to competition in human males. *Aggressive Behavior, 15*, 409–422.

Glaser, R., Kennedy, S., Lafuse, W., Bonneau, R., Speicher, C., Hillhouse, J., & Kiecolt-Glaser, J. (1990). Psychological stress-induced modulation of interleukin 2 receptor gene expression and interleukin 2 production in peripheral blood leukocytes. *Archives of General Psychiatry, 47*, 707–712.

Glaser, R., & Kiecolt-Glaser, J. (1991). Modulation of the cellular immune response. *Clinical Immunology Newsletter, 11*, 101–105.

Glaser, R., Kiecolt-Glaser, J., Bonneau, R., Malarkey, W., & Hughes, J. (1992). Stress-induced modulation of the immune response to recombinant hepatitis B vaccine. *Psychosomatic Medicine, 54*, 22–23.

Glaser, R., Kiecolt-Glaser, J., Speicher, C., & Holliday, J. (1985). Stress, loneliness, and changes in herpes virus latency. *Journal of Behavioral Medicine, 8*, 249–260.

Glaser, R., Lafuse, W., Bonneau, R., Atkinson, C., & Kiecolt-Glaser, J. (in press-a). Stress-associated modulation of proto-oncogene expression in human peripheral blood leukocytes. *Behavioral Neuroscience*.

Glaser, R., Pearson, G., Bonneau, R., Esterling, B., Atkinson, C., & Kiecolt-Glaser, J. (in press-b). Stress and the memory T-cell response to the Epstein-Barr virus. *Health Psychology*.

Glaser, R., Pearson, G., Jones, J., Hillhouse, J., Kennedy, S., Mao, H., et al. (1991). Stress-related activation of Epstein-Barr virus. *Brain Behavior & Immunity, 5*, 219–232.

Glaser, R., Rice, J., Sheridan, J., Fertel, R., Stout, J., Speicher, C., et al. (1987). Stress-related immune suppression: Health implications. *Brain Behavior & Immunity, 1*, 7–20.

Glaser, R., Thorn, B., Tarr, K., Kiecolt-Glaser, J., & D'Ambrosio, S. (1985). Effects of stress on methyltransferase synthesis: An important DNA repair enzyme. *Health Psychology, 4*, 403.

Glass, L., & Mackey, M. (1988). *From clocks to chaos: The rhythms of life*. Princeton, NJ: Princeton University Press.

Globus, G. (1972). Periodicity in sleep and in waking states. In M. Chase (Ed.), *The sleeping brain*. Los Angeles: Brain Research Institute.

Globus, G., Phoebus, E., & Moore, C. (1970). REM "sleep" manifestations during waking. *Psychophysiology, 7*, 308.

Goelet, P., & Kandel, E. (1986). Tracking the flow of learned information from membrane receptors to genome. *Trends in Neuro Sciences, 9*(10), 492–499.

Gold, P. (1984). Memory modulation: Neurobiological contexts. In G. Lynch, J. McGaugh, & N. Weinberger (Eds.), *Neurobiology of learning and memory* (pp. 374–382). New York: Guilford.

Gold, P., Weinberger, N., & Sternberg, D. (1985). Epinephrine-induced learning under anesthesia: Retention performance at several training testing intervals. *Behavioral Neuroscience, 99*(4), 1019–1022.

Goldman-Rakic, P. (1988). Topography of cognition: Parallel distributed networks in primate association cortex. *Annual Review of Neuroscience, 11*, 137–156.

Goldstein, A., & Hilgard, E. (1975). Lack of influence of the morphine antagonist naloxone on hypnotic analgesia. *Proceedings of the National Academy of Science, U.S.A., 72*, pp. 2041–2043.

Goldstein, L., Stoltzfus, N., & Gardocki, J. (1972). Changes in interhemispheric amplitude relationships in EEG during sleep. *Physiology & Behavior, 8*, 811–815.

Goodkin, K., et al. (1992). Active coping style is associated with natural killer cell cytotoxicity in asymptomatic HIV-1 seropositive homosexual men. *Journal of Psychosomatic Research, 36*, 635–650.

Gorczynski, R., Macrae, S., & Kennedy, M. (1982). Conditioned immune response associated with allogenic skin grafts in mice. *Journal of Immunology, 129*, 704–709.

Gordon, H., Frooman, B., & Lavie, P. (1982). Shift in cognitive asymmetries between wakings from REM and NREM sleep. *Neuropsychologica, 20*, 99–103.

Gorton, B. (1957). The physiology of hypnosis, I. *Journal of the American Society of Psychosomatic Dentistry, 4*(3), 86–103.

Gorton, B. (1958). The physiology of hypnosis: Vasomotor activity in hypnosis. *Journal of the American Society of Psychosomatic Dentistry, 5*(1), 20–28.

Gould, S., & Tissler, D. (1984). The use of hypnosis in the treatment of herpes simplex II. *American Journal of Clinical Hypnosis, 26*, 171–174.

Graham, K., & Pernicano, K. (1976). *Laterality, hypnosis and the autokinetic effect.* Paper presented at the meeting of the American Psychological Association, Washington, DC.

Gravitz, M. A. (1981). The production of warts by suggestion as a cultural phenomenon. *American Journal of Clinical Hypnosis, 23*, 281–283.

Gray, C., Engel, A., Konig, P., & Singer, W. (1992). Synchronization of oscillatory neuronal responses in cat striate cortex: Temporal properties. *Visual Neuroscience, 8*, 337–47.

Green, M., Green, R., & Santoro, W. (1988). Daily relaxation modifies serum and salivary immunoglobulins and psychophysiologic symptom severity. *Biofeedback & Self-Regulation, 13*, 187–200.

Green, R., & Green, M. (1987). Relaxation increases salivary immunoglobulin A. *Psychological Reports, 61*, 623–629.

Greenberg, R. (1973). Anti-expectation techniques in psychotherapy: The power of negative thinking. *Psychotherapy: Theory, Research and Practice, 10*, 145–148.

Groer, M., Shekleton, M., & Kant, K. (1979). *Basic pathophysiology.* St. Louis, MO: C. V. Mosby.

Gruen, W. (1972). A successful application of systematic self-relaxation and self-suggestions about postoperative reactions in a case of cardiac surgery. *International Journal of Clinical and Experimental Hypnosis, 20*, 141–151.

Guillemin, R. (1978). Peptides in the brain: The new endocrinology of the neuron. *Science, 202*, 390–402.

Gur, R., & Gur, R. (1974). Handedness, sex, eyedness, and moderating variables in relation to hypnotic susceptibility and functional brain symmetry. *Journal of Abnormal Psychology, 83*, 635–643.

Guyon, A. (1981). *Textbook of medical physiology.* New York: Saunders.

Hahn, R. (1985). A sociocultural model of illness and health. In L. White & B. Tursky (Eds.), *Placebo: Theory, research, and mechanisms* (pp. 167–195). New York: Guilford.

Haley, J. (1963). *Strategies of psychotherapy.* New York: Grune & Stratton.

Haley, J. (1985). *Conversations with Milton H. Erickson* (3 vols.). New York: Triangle Press.

Hall, H. (1982–83). Hypnosis and the immune system: A review with implications for cancer and the psychology of healing. *The American Journal of Clinical Hypnosis, 25*(2–3), 92–103.

Hall, H., Mumma, G., Longo, S., & Dixon, R. (1992a). Voluntary immunomodulation: A preliminary study. *International Journal of Neuroscience, 63*, 275–285.

Hall, H., Minnes, L., Tosi, M., & Olness, K. (1992b). Voluntary modulation of neutrophil adhesiveness using a cyberphysiologic strategy. *International Journal of Neuroscience, 63*, 287–297.

Hall, N., & Goldstein, A. (1985). Neurotransmitters and host defense. In R. Guillemin, M. Cohn, & T. Melnechuk (Eds.), *Neural modulation of immunity* (pp. 143–156). New York: Raven Press.

Hall, N., McGillis, J., Spangelo, B., & Goldstein, A. (1985). Evidence that thymosins and other biologic response modifiers can function as neuroactive immunotransmitters. *The Journal of Immunology, 135*(2), 806s–811s.

Hall, N., & O'Grady, M. (1991). Psychosocial interventions and immune function. In R. Ader, D. Felten, & N. Cohen (Eds.), *Psychoneuroimmunology* (2nd ed.) (pp. 1067–1080). New York: Academic Press.

Hampson, E. (1990a). Estrogen-related variations in human spatial and articulatory-motor skills. *Psychoneuroendocrinology, 15*, 97–111.

Hampson, E. (1990b). Variations in sex-related cognitive abilities across the menstrual cycle. *Brain & Cognition, 14*, 26–43.

Hampson, E., & Kimura, D. (1992). Sex differences and hormonal influences on cognitive function in humans. In J. Becker, S. Breedlove, & D. Crews (Eds.), *Behavioral endocrinology* (pp. 357–400). Cambridge, MA: MIT Press.

Harding, E. (1955). *Woman's mysteries ancient and modern*. New York: Pantheon.

Harris, G. (1948). Neural control of the pituitary gland. *Physiological Review, 28*, 139–179.

Hartland, J. (1966). *Medical and dental hypnosis*. London: Bailliere, Tindall, & Cassell.

Hawkins, R., & Kandel, E. (1984). Steps toward a cell-biological alphabet for elementary forms of learning. In G. Lynch, J. McGaugh, & N. Weinberger (Eds.), *Neurobiology of learning and memory* (pp. 385–404). New York: Guilford.

Hebb, D. (1949). *The organization of behavior. A neuropsychological theory*. New York: Wiley.

Hebb, D. (1963). The semi-autonomous process, its nature and nurture. *American Psychologist, 18*, 16–27.

Heijnen, C., Kavelaars, A., & Ballieux, R. (1991). Corticotropin-releasing hormone and proopiomelanocortin-derived peptides in the modulation of immune function. In R. Ader, D. Felten, & N. Cohen (Eds.), *Psychoneuroimmunology* (2nd ed.). 429–446. San Diego, CA: Academic Press.

Heisenberg, W. (1989). *Encounters with Einstein*. Princeton, NJ: Princeton University Press.

Henry, J. (1982). Circulating opioids: Possible physiological roles in central nervous function. *Neuroscience & Biobehavioral Reviews, 6*, 229–245.

Hilgard, E. (1977). *Divided consciousness: Multiple controls in human thought and action*. New York: Wiley.

Hilgard, E. (1984). Book review of *The collected papers of Milton H. Erickson on hypnosis. The International Journal of Clinical & Experimental Hypnosis, 32*(2), 257–265.

Hilgard, E., & Hilgard, J. (1975). *Hypnosis in the relief of pain*. Los Altos, CA: Kaufman.

Hilgard, E., & Marquis, D. (1961). *Conditioning and learning*. New York: Appleton-Century-Crofts.

Hillhouse, J., Kiecolt-Glasser, J., & Glasser, R. (1991). Stress associated modulation of the immune response in humans. N. Plotnikoff et al. (Eds.), *Stress and immunity* (pp. 3–27). Caldwell, NJ: Telford Press.

Hillman, J. (1983). *Healing fiction*. Barrytown, NY: Hill Press.

Hokama, Y., & Nakamura, R. (1982). *Immunology and immunopathology*. Boston: Little, Brown, & Co.

Holland, J., Holyoak, K., Nisbett, R., & Thagard, P. (1986). *Induction: Processes of inference, learning, and discovery*. Cambridge, MA: MIT Press.

Holroyd, K., & Lazarus, R. (1982). Stress, coping and somatic adaptation. In L. Goldberger & S. Breznitz (Eds.), *Handbook of stress* (pp. 21–35). New York: Free Press.

Hopkins, J., Marcus, M., & Campbell, S. (1984). Postpartum depression: A critical review. *Psychological Bulletin, 95*(3), 498–515.

Hornig-Rohan, M., & Locke, S. (1985). *Psychological and behavioral treatments for disorders of the heart and blood vessels: An annotated bibliography* (Vol. 1). New York: Institute for the Advancement of Health.

Hudgins, C. (1933). Conditioning and voluntary control of pupillary light reflex. *Journal of General Psychology, 8,* 3.

Hull, C. (1933). *Hypnosis and suggestibility: An experimental approach.* New York: Appleton-Century.

Hunter, T. (1987). A thousand and one protein kinases. *Cell, 50,* 823–829.

Ikemi, Y., & Nakagawa, S. (1962). A psychosomatic study of contagious dermatitis. *Kyushu Journal of Medical Science, 13,* 335–350.

Ingham, S. (1938). Some neurologic aspects of psychiatry. *Journal of the American Medical Association, 111,* 665.

Iranmanesh, A., Lizarralde, G., Johnson, M., & Veldhuis, J. (1989b). Circadian, ultradian, and episodic release of B-endorphin in men, and its temporal coupling with cortisol. *Journal of Clinical Endocrinology & Metabolism, 68*(6), 1019–1026.

Iranmanesh, A., Veldhuis, J., Johnson, M., & Lizarralde, G. (1989a). 24-hour pulsatile and circadian patterns of cortisol secretion in alcoholic men. *Journal of Andrology, 10,* 54–63.

Irwin, M., Daniels, M., Smith, T., Bloom, E., & Weiner, H. (1987). Impaired natural killer cell activity during bereavement. *Brain, Behavioral Immunology, 1,* 98–104.

Ischlondsky, N. (1955). The inhibitory process in the cerebrophysiological laboratory and in the clinic. *Journal of Nervous and Mental Diseases, 121,* 5–18.

Isenberg, S., Lehrer, P., & Hochron, S. (1992). The effects of suggestion and emotional arousal on pulmonary function in asthma: A review and a hypothesis regarding vagal mediation. *Psychosomatic Medicine, 54,* 192–216.

Izquierdo, I. (1984). Endogenous state-dependency: Memory depends on the relation between the neurohumoral and hormonal states present after training at the time of testing. In G. Lynch, J. McGaugh, & N. Weinberg (Eds.), *Neurobiology of learning and memory* (pp. 65–77). New York: Guilford.

Izquierdo, I. (1989). Different forms of post-training memory processing. *Behavioral & Neural Biology, 51,* 171–202.

Izquierdo, I., Netto, C., Chaves, M., Pereira, M., & Siegfried, B. (1988a). The organization of memories into "files." In J. Delacour & C. Levy (Eds.), *Systems with learning and memory abilities.* Amsterdam: Elsevier.

Izquierdo, I., Netto, C., Dalmaz, D., Chaves, M., Pereira, M., & Siegfried, B. (1988b). Construction and reconstruction of memories. *Brazilian Journal of Medical & Biological Research, 21,* 9–25.

Izquierdo, I., Souza, D., Dias, R., Perry, M., Carrasco, M., Volkmer, N., & Netto, C. (1984). Effect of various behavioral training and testing procedures on brain B-endorphin-like immunoreactivity and the possible role of D-endorphin in behavioral regulation. *Psychoneuroendocrinology, 9*(4), 381–389.

Jacobson, A., Hackett, T., Surman, O., & Silverberg, E. (1973). Raynaud's phenomenon: Treatment with hypnotic and operant technique. *Journal of the American Medical Association, 225,* 739–740.

Jacobson, E. (1924). The technique of progressive relaxation. *Journal of Nervous & Mental Disorders, 60,* 568–578.

Janet, P. (1889). *L'automatisme psychologique.* Paris: Felix Alcan.

Janet, P. (1907). *The major symptoms of hysteria.* New York: Macmillan.

Johnson, R. F. Q. (1989). Hypnosis, suggestion, and dermatological changes: A consideration of the production and diminution of dermatological entities. In N. P. Spanos & J. F. Chaves (Eds.), *Hypnosis: The cognitive-behavioral perspective* (pp. 297–312). Buffalo, NY: Prometheus Books.

Johnson, R. F. Q., & Barber, T. X. (1978). Hypnosis, suggestions, and warts: An experimental investigation implicating the importance of "believed-in efficacy." *American Journal of Clinical Hypnosis, 20,* 165–174.

Jones, J. F., & Straus, S. E. (1987). Chronic Epstein-Barr virus infection. *Annual Review of Medicine, 38,* 195–209.

Jouvet, M. (1973). Telencephalic and rhonbencephalic sleep in the cat. In W. Webb (Ed.), *Sleep: An active process* (pp. 12–32). Glenview, IL: Scott Foresman.

Jouvet, M. (1975). The function of dreaming: A neurophysiologist's point of view. In M. Gazzaniga & C. Blakemore (Eds.), *The handbook of psychobiology.* New York: Academic Press.

Jung, C. (1910). *Jb. Psychoanal. Psychopath. Forschgg. II*(1) p. 363.

Jung, C. (1929/1984). *Dream analysis* (William McGuire, Ed.) (Bollingen Series, XCIX). Princeton, NJ: Princeton University Press.

Jung, C. (1950). *The symbolic life. Vol. XVIII. The collected works of Carl G. Jung* (R. F. C. Hull, Ed.). (Bollingen Series XX). Princeton, NJ: Princeton University Press.

Jung, C. (1960). *The structure and dynamics of the psyche. Vol. III. The collected works of Carl G. Jung.* (R. F. C. Hull, Trans.) (Bollingen Series XX). Princeton, NJ: Princeton University Press.

Jung, C. (1976). *The visions seminars.* Book 1, Part 7. Zurich, Switzerland: Spring Publications.

Kandel, E. (1976). *Cellular basis of behavior.* San Francisco: Freeman.

Kandel, E. (1989). Genes, nerve cells, and the remembrance of things past. *Journal of Neuropsychiatry, 1*(2), 103–125.

Kandel, E., & Schwartz, G. (1985). *Principles of neural science* (2nd ed.). New York: Elsevier.

Kaneko, Z., & Takahashi, N. (1963). Psychometric studies on chronic urticaria. *Folia Psychiatrica et Neurologica Japonica, 17,* 16–24.

Kaufmann, S. (1993). *Origins of order: Self-organization and selection in evolution.* Oxford, England: Oxford University Press.

Kayser, R. (1895). Die exacte messung der luftdurchgangigkeit der nasa. *Archi fuer Laryngologie und Rhinologie, 3,* 101–120.

Keller, S., Schleifer, S., & Demetrikopoulos, M. (1991). Stress-induced changes in immune function in animals: Hypothalamo-pituitary-adrenal influences. In R. Ader, D. Felten, & N. Cohen (Eds.), *Psychoneuroimmunology* (2nd ed.) (pp. 771–788). San Diego, CA: Academic Press.

Kemeny, M., Cohen, F., Zegans, L., & Conant, M. (1989). Psychological and immunological predictors of genital herpes recurrence. *Psychosomatic Medicine, 51,* 195–208.

Kemeny, M., Duran, R., Weiner, H., Taylor, S., Visscher, B., & Fahey, J. (1990). *Chronic depression precedes a decline in CD4 helper/inducer T cells in HIV positive men.* Unpublished manuscript.

Kiecolt-Glaser, J., Dura, J., Speicher, D., Trask, O., & Glaser, R. (1991). Spousal caregivers of dementia victims: Longitudinal changes in immunity and health. *Psychosomatic Medicine, 53,* 345–362.

Kiecolt-Glaser, J., & Glaser, R. (1986). Psychological influences on immunity. *Psychosomatics, 27*(9), 621–624.

Kiecolt-Glaser, J., & Glaser, R. (1988). Psychological influences on immunity: Implications for AIDS. *American Psychologist, 43*(11), 892–898.

Kiecolt-Glaser, J., & Glaser, R. (1991). Stress and immune function in humans. In R. Ader, D. Felten, & N. Cohen (Eds.), *Psychoneuroimmunology* (2nd ed.) (pp. 849–868). San Diego, CA: Academic Press.

Kiecolt-Glaser, J., Kennedy, S., Malkoff, S., Fisher, L., Speicher, C., & Glaser, R. (1988). Marital discord and immunity in males. *Psychosomatic Medicine, 50,* 213–229.

Kiecolt-Glaser, J., Stephens, R., Lipetz, P., Speicher, C., & Glaser, R. (1985). Distress and DNA repair in human lymphocytes. *Journal of Behavioral Medicine, 8,* 311.

Kiefer, C., & Cowan, J. (1979). State/context dependence and theories of ritual. *Journal of Psychological Anthropology, 2*(1), 53–58.

Kimble, D. (1965). *Learning, remembering and forgetting. Vol. I. The anatomy of learning.* Palo Alto, CA: Science & Behavior Books.

Kimble, D. P. (1992). *Biological psychology* (2nd ed.) (pp. 392–423). Orlando, FL: Harcourt Brace Jovanovich.

Kissilef, H., Pi-Sunyer, F., et al. (1981). C-terminal octapeptide of cholecystokinin decreases food intake in man. *The American Journal of Clinical Nutrition, 34,* 154–160.

Klein, R., & Armitage, R. (1979). Rhythms in human performance: One-and-a-half-hour oscillations in cognitive style. *Science, 204,* 1326–1328.

Kleitman, N. (1963). *Sleep and wakefulness* (2nd ed.). Chicago, IL: University of Chicago Press.

Kleitman, N. (1969). Basic rest-activity cycle in relation to sleep and wakefulness. In A. Kales (Ed.), *Sleep: Physiology and pathology* (pp. 33–38). Philadelphia, PA: Lippincott.

Kleitman, N. (1970). Implications of the rest-activity cycle: Implications for organizing activity. In E. Hartmann (Ed.), *Sleep and dreaming* (pp. 13–14). Boston: Little, Brown.

Kleitman, N. (1992). The basic rest-activity cycle—32 years later: An interview with Nathaniel Kleitman at 96. Interviewed by E. Rossi. In D. Lloyd & E. Rossi (Eds.), *Ultradian rhythms in life processes* (pp. 303–306). New York: Springer-Verlag.

Klopfer, B. (1957). Psychological variables in human cancer. *Journal of Projective Techniques, 21,* 331–340.

Knobil, E., & Hotchkiss, J. (1985). The circhoral gonadotropin releasing hormone (GnRH) pulse generator of the hypothalamus and its physiological significance. In H. Schulz & P. Lavie (Eds.), *Ultradian rhythms in physiology and behavior* (pp. 32–40). New York: Springer-Verlag.

Koch, C. (1992, November). What is consciousness? *Discover,* pp. 95–98.

Kogan, G. (1980). *Your body works: A guide to healthy energy and balance.* Berkeley, CA: Transformation Press.

Kosslyn, S. M., & Koenig, O. (1992). *Wet mind: The new cognitive neuroscience.* New York: Free Press.

Kreinheder, A. (1979). The call to individuation. *Psychological Perspectives, 10*(1), 58–65.

Kripke, D. (1982). Ultradian rhythms in behavior and physiology. In F. Brown & R. Graeber (Eds.), *Rhythmic aspects of behavior* (pp. 313–344). Hillsdale, NJ: Erlbaum.

Kripke, D. (1984). Critical interval hypothesis for depression. *Chronobiology International, 1*(1), 73–81.

Kripke, D., Mullaney, D., & Fleck, P. (1985). Ultradian rhythms during sustained performance. In H. Schulz & P. Lavie (Eds.), *Ultradian rhythms in physiology and behavior.* New York: Springer-Verlag.

Kroger, W., & Fezler, W. (1976). *Hypnosis and behavior modification: Imagery conditioning.* Philadelphia, PA: Lippincott.

Kuriyama, K. (1990). Prolonged hypnosis in psychosomatic medicine. In D. C. Hammond (Ed.), *Handbook of hypnotic suggestions and metaphors* (pp. 242–244). New York: W. W. Norton.

LaBerge, S. (1985). *Lucid dreaming.* Los Angeles: Tarcher.

Lachman, S., & Goode, W. (1976). *Hemispheric dominance and variables related to hypnotic susceptibility.* Paper presented at the meeting of the American Psychological Association.

Langley, J. (1878). On the physiology of the salivary secretion. *Journal of Physiology, 1,* 340–369.

Langton, C. (Ed.). (1989). *Artificial life* (Vol. VI). Redwood City, CA: Addison-Wesley.

Langton, C., Taylor, C., Farmer, J., & Rasmussen, S. (Eds.). (1992). *Artificial life II.* Redwood City, CA: Addison-Wesley.

Lankton, S. (1987). The scramble technique. *Ericksonian Monographs, 2,* in press.

Lankton, S., & Lankton, C. (1983). *The answer within: A clinical framework of Ericksonian hypnotherapy.* New York: Brunner/Mazel.

Lattal, K. (1992). B. F. Skinner and psychology: Introduction to the special issue. *American Psychologist, 47,* 1269–1272.

Lazarus, A., & Mayne, T. (1991). Relaxation: Some limitations, side effects, and proposed solutions. *Psychotherapy, 27,* 261–266.

Lazarus, R., & Folkman, S. (1984). Coping and adaptation. In W. Gentry (Ed.), *Handbook of behavioral medicine* (pp. 282–325). New York: Guilford.

Leckie, F. (1964). Hypnotherapy in gynecological disorders. *International Journal of Clinical & Experimental Hypnosis, 12,* 121–146.

LeCron, L. (1954). A hypnotic technique for uncovering unconscious material. *Journal of Clinical & Experimental Hypnosis, 2,* 76–79.

Leonard, G. (1981). *The silent pulse.* New York: Bantam.

LePage, K., Schafer, D., & Miller, A. (1992). Alternating unilateral lachrymation. *American Journal of Clinical Hypnosis, 34,* 255–260.

LeShan, L. (1977). *You can fight for your life.* New York: Evans & Co.

Levy, S. (1992). *Artificial life.* New York: Pantheon.

Lewin, R. (1992). *Complexity: Life at the edge of chaos.* New York: Macmillan.

Lewis, J., & Sarbin, T. (1943). Studies in psychosomatics. *Psychosomatic Medicine, 5,* 125.

Lewis, T. (1927). *The blood vessels of the human skin and their responses.* London: Shaw & Sons.

Lex, B. (1974). Voodoo death: New thoughts for an old explanation. *American Anthropologist, 76,* 818–823.

Li, Y., & Goldbeter, A. (1992). Pulsatile signaling in intercellular communication. *Biophysics Journal, 6,* 161–171.

Lichtstein, D., & Atlan, H. (1990). The "cellular state": The way of regain specificity and diversity in hormone action. *Journal of Theoretical Biology, 145,* 287–294.

Lienhart, J. (1983). Multiple personality and state-dependent learning. Unpublished doctoral dissertation, U.S. International University, San Diego, CA.

Lightfoot, J. J. (1992). The art of healing, the science of drama: How acting may affect the immune system. *Advances, 8*(4), 66–69.

Lippincott, B. (1990, March 24–28). *Testing two predictions of the ultradian theory of therapeutic hypnosis.* Paper presented at 32nd Annual Scientific Meeting and Workshops on Clinical Hypnosis, Orlando, FL.

Lippincott, B. (1991, April 14–18). *Owls and larks in hypnosis: An experimental validation of the ultradian theory of hypnotic susceptibility.* Paper presented at the 33rd Annual Scientific Meeting of the American Society of Clinical Hypnosis, St. Louis, MO.

Lippincott, B. (1992a). Owls and larks in hypnosis: Individual differences in hypnotic susceptibility relating to biological rhythms. *American Journal of Clinical Hypnosis, 34,* 185–192.

Lippincott, B. (1992b). Owls and larks in hypnosis: Age regression and analgesia. Unpublished manuscript.

Lippincott, B. (1992c). The nasal cycle and hypnosis: A brief communication. Unpublished manuscript.

Lippincott, B. (in press). The temperature rhythm and hypnotizability: A brief report. *Contemporary Hypnosis.*

Liu, W., Standen, P., & Altkenhead, A. (1992). Therapeutic suggestions during general anesthesia in patients undergoing hysterectomy. *British Journal of Anesthesiology, 68,* 277–281.

Lloyd, D. (1992). Intracellular time keeping: Epigenetic oscillations reveal the functions of an ultradian clock. In D. Lloyd & E. Rossi (Eds.), *Ultradian rhythms in life processes: A fundamental inquiry into chronobiology and psychobiology* (pp. 403–405). New York: Springer-Verlag.

Lloyd, D., & Edwards, S. (1984). Epigenetic oscillators during the cell cycles of lower eucaryoats are coupled to a clock: Life's slow dance to the music of time. In L. Edmunds (Ed.), *Cell cycle clocks* (pp. 27–46). New York: Marcel Dekker.

Lloyd, D., & Edwards, S. (1987). Temperature-compensated ultradian rhythms in lower eukaryotes: Timers for cell cycles and circadian events? In J. Pauly & L. Scheving (Eds.), *Advances in chronobiology, Part A* (pp. 131–151). New York: Alan R. Liss.

Lloyd, D., & Rossi, E. (1992a). *Ultradian rhythms in life processes: A fundamental inquiry into chronobiology and psychobiology.* New York: Springer-Verlag.

Lloyd, D., & Rossi, E. (1992b). Epilogue: The unification hypothesis of chronobiology-psychobiology from molecule to mind. In D. Lloyd & E. Rossi (Eds.), *Ultradian rhythms in life processes: A fundamental inquiry into chronobiology and psychobiology* (pp. 403–405). New York: Springer-Verlag.

Lloyd, D., & Stupfel, M. (1991). The occurrence and functions of ultradian rhythms. *Biological Review, 66,* 275–299.

Locke, S. E. (1986). *Psychological and behavioral treatments for disorders associated with the immune system: An annotated bibliography* (Vol. 2). New York: Institute for the Advancement of Health.

Locke, S., & Hornig-Rohan, M. (Eds.). (1983). *Mind and immunity: Behavioral immunology: An annotated bibliography 1976–1982.* New York: Institute for the Advancement of Health.

Locke, S., Kraus, L., Leserman, J., Hurst, M., Heisel, S., & Williams, R. (1984). Life change stress, psychiatric symptoms, and natural killer-cell activity. *Psychosomatic Medicine, 46,* 441–453.

Ludwig, A. (1983). The psychobiological functions of dissociation. *The American Journal of Clinical Hypnosis, 26*(2), 93–99.

Ludwig, A., Brandsma, J., Wilbur, C., Benfeldt, F., & Jameson, D. (1972). The objective study of a multiple personality. *Archives of General Psychiatry, 26,* 298–310.

Luparello, T. J., Leist, N., Lourie, C. H., & Sweet, P. (1970). The interaction of psychologic stimuli and pharmacologic agents on airway reactivity in asthmatic subjects. *Psychosomatic Medicine, 32,* 509–512.

Luria, A. (1966). *Higher cortical functions in man* (H. Teuber & K. Pribram, Trans.). New York: Basic.

Lydic, R. (1987). State-dependent aspects of regulatory physiology. *FASEB Journal, 1*(1), 6–15.

Lynch, G., McGaugh, J., & Weinberger, N. (Eds.). (1984). *Neurobiology of learning and memory.* New York: Guilford.

Maclean, D., & Reichlin, S. (1981). Neuroendocrinology and the immune process. In R. Ader (Ed.), *Psychoneuroimmunology* (pp. 475–519). New York: Academic Press.

Malinow, R., Schulman, H., & Tsien, R. W. (1989). Inhibition of postsynaptic PKC or CaMKII blocks induction but not expression of LTP. *Science, 245,* 862–865.

Manyande, A., Chayen, S., Priyakumar, P., Smith, C., Hayes, M., Higgens, D., Kee, S., Phillips, S., & Salmon, P. (1992). Anxiety and endocrine responses to surgery: Paradoxical effects of preoperative relaxation training. *Psychosomatic Medicine, 54,* 275–287.

Margolis, C. (1982–83). Hypnotic imagery with cancer patients. *The American Journal of Clinical Hypnosis, 25*(2–3), 128–134.

Margolis, C., Domangue, B., Ehleben, C., et al. (1983). Hypnosis in the early treatment of burns: A pilot study. *American Journal of Clinical Hypnosis, 26,* 9–15.

Margules, D. (1979). Beta-endorphin and endoloxone: Hormones of the autonomic nervous system for conservation or expenditure of bodily resources and energy for anticipation of famine or feast. *Neuroscience & Biobehavioral Review, 3,* 155–162.

Margulis, L., & Sagan, D. (1991). *Microcosmos: Four billion years of evolution from our microbial ancestors.* New York: Simon & Schuster.

Margulis, L., & Schwartz, K. V. (1988). *Five kingdoms: An illustrated guide to the phyla of life on earth* (2nd ed.). New York: W. H. Freeman.

Marijuan, P. (1991). Enzymes and theoretical biology: Sketch of an informational perspective of the cell. *BioSystems, 25,* 259–273.

Marini, J., Sheard, M., Bridges, C., & Wagner, E. (1976). An evaluation of the double-blind design in a study comparing lithium carbonate with placebo. *Acta Psychiatrica Scandinavica, 53,* 343–354.

Markowitz, A. (1985). *Change of life: Dreams and the menopause.* Toronto, Canada: Inner City Books.

Marrack, P., & Kappler, J. (1986, Feb.). The T cell and its receptor. *Scientific American, 254*(2), 36–45.

Maslow, A. (1962). *Toward a psychology of being.* New York: Van Nostrand.
Mason, A. (1952). A case of congenital ichthyosiform erythrodermia of Brocq treated by hypnosis. *British Medical Journal, 2,* 422–423.
Mason, A. (1955). Ichthyosis and hypnosis. *British Medical Journal, 2,* 57.
Mason, A. (1963). Hypnosis and allergy. *British Medical Journal, 13,* 1675–1676.
Mazziotta, J., Phelps, M., Carson, R., & Kuhl, D. (1982). Tomographic mapping of human cerebral metabolism: Auditory stimulation. *Neurology, 32,* 921–937.
McDaniel, J. (1992). Psychoimmunology: Implications for future research. *Southern Medical Journal, 85,* 388–397.
McFadden, E. R., Luparello, T., Lyons, H. A., & Bleecker, E. (1969). The mechanism of action of suggestion in the induction of acute asthma attacks. *Psychosomatic Medicine, 31,* 134–143.
McGaugh, J. (1983). Preserving the presence of the past: Hormonal influences on memory storage. *American Psychologist, 38*(2), 161–173.
McGaugh, J. (1989). Involvement of hormonal and neuromodulatory systems in the regulation of memory storage. *Annual Reviews of Neuroscience, 12,* 255–287.
McGaugh, J., Liang, K., Bennett, C., & Sternberg, D. (1984). Adrenergic influences on memory storage: Interaction of peripheral and central systems. In G. Lynch, J. McGaugh, & N. Weinberger (Eds.), *Neurobiology of learning and memory* (pp. 313–332). New York: Guilford.
McGaugh, J. L., Martinez, J. L., Jr., Jensen, R. A., Hannan, T. J., Vasquez, B. J., Messing, R. B., Liang, K. C., Brewton, C. B., & Spiehler, V. R. (1982). Modulation of memory storage by treatments affecting peripheral catecholamines. In C. Ajmone Marsan & H. Matthies (Eds.), *Neuronal plasticity and memory formation.* New York: Raven Press.
McGillis, J., Mitsuhashi, M., & Payan, D. (1991). Immunologic properties of substance P. In R. Ader, D. Felten, & N. Cohen (Eds.), *Psychoneuroimmunology* (2nd ed.) (pp. 209–224). San Diego, CA: Academic Press.
McGlashan, T., Evans, F., & Orne, M. (1969). The nature of hypnotic analgesia and placebo response to experimental pain. *Psychosomatic Medicine, 31,* 227–246.
Meares, A. (1982–83). A form of intensive meditation associated with the regression of cancer. *The American Journal of Clinical Hypnosis, 25*(2–3), 114–121.
Meares, A. (1990). Deep, meditative trance: The approach of Ainslie Meares, M.D. In D. C. Hammond (Ed.), *Handbook of hypnotic suggestions and metaphors* (pp. 160–162). New York: W. W. Norton.
Mejean, L., Bicakova-Rocher, A., Kolopp, M., Villaume, C., Levi, F., Debry, G., et al. (1988). Circadian and ultradian rhythms in blood glucose and plasma insulin of healthy adults. *Chronobiology International, 5*(3), 227–236.
Mello, C., Vicario, D., & Clayton, D. (1992). Song presentation induces gene expression in the songbird forebrain. *Proceedings of the National Academy of Science, 89,* 6818–6822.
Melnechuk, T. (1985). Neuroimmunology: Crossroads between behavior and disease. Reports on selected conferences and workshops. *Advances, 2*(3), Summer, 54–58.
Merleau-Ponty, M. (1963). *The structure of behavior* (A. Fisher, Trans.). Boston: Beacon Press.
Meyers, R., & Sperry, R. (1953). Interocular transfer of a visual form discrimination habit in cats after section of the optic chiasm and corpus callosum. *Anatomical Record, 115,* 351–352.
Michel, S., Geusz, M., Zaritsky, J., & Block, G. (1993). Circadian rhythm in membrane conductance expressed in isolated neurons. *Science, 259,* 239–241.
Miller, G., Galanter, E., & Pribram, K. (1960). *Plans and the structure of behavior.* New York: Henry Holt.
Mills, J., & Crowley, R. (1986). *Therapeutic metaphors for children and the child within.* New York: Brunner/Mazel.
Mindell, A. (1982). *Dreambody.* Los Angeles: Sigo Press.
Mindell, A. (1985a). *River's way: The process science of the dreambody.* Boston: Routledge & Kegan Paul.

Mindell, A. (1985b). *Working with the dreaming body*. Boston: Routledge & Kegan Paul.

Mishkin, M. (1982). A memory system in the monkey. *Phil. Trans. R. Soc. Lond., B298*, 85–95.

Mishkin, M., Malamut, B., & Bachevalier, J. (1984). Memories and habits: Two neural systems. In G. Lynch, J. McGaugh, & N. Weinberger (Eds.), *Neurobiology of learning and memory* (pp. 65–77). New York: Guilford.

Mishkin, M., & Petri, H. (1984). Memories and habits: Some implications for the analysis of learning and retention. In S. Squire & N. Butters (Eds.), *Neuropsychology of memory* (pp. 287–296). New York: Guilford.

Moll, A. (1898). *Hypnotism*. New York: Scribner's Sons.

Montgomery, G. (1989). Molecules of memory. *Discover, 10*(12), 46–55.

Moore, L., & Kaplan, J. (1983). Hypnotically accelerated burn wound healing. *The American Journal of Clinical Hypnosis, 26*(1), 16–19.

Moore-Ede, M. C., & Czeisler, C. A. (Eds.). (1984). *Mathematical models of the circadian sleep-wake cycle*. New York: Raven Press.

Morimoto, R., Tissières, A., & Georgopoulos, C. (Eds.). (1990). *Stress proteins in biology and medicine*. Cold Spring Harbor, NY: Cold Spring Harbor Laboratory Press.

Morris, D. (1992). The place of pain. *Advances, 8*(2), 3–24.

Morris, J., & Beck, A. (1974). The efficacy of antidepressant drugs: A review of research (1958 to 1972). *Archives of General Psychiatry, 30*, 667–674.

Moruzzi, I., & Magoun, H. (1949). Brain stem reticular formation. *Electroencephalography & Clinical Neurophysiology, 1*, 455–473.

Mrazek, D., & Klinnert, M. (1991). Asthma: Psychoneuroimmunologic considerations. In R. Ader, D. Felten, & N. Cohen (Eds.), *Psychoneuroimmunology* (2nd ed.) (pp. 1013–1035). San Diego, CA: Academic Press.

Munck, A., Guyre, P., & Holbrook, N. (1984). Physiological actions of glucocorticoids in stress and their relation to pharmacological actions. *Endocrinological Review, 5*, 25–37.

Munoz, A., Carey, V., Saah, A., Phair, J., Kingsley, L., Fahey, J., et al. (1988). Predictors of decline in CD4 lymphocytes in a cohort of homosexual men infected with human immunodeficiency virus. *Journal of Acquired Immune Deficiency Syndrome, 1*, 396–404.

Murry, E., & Mishkin, M. (1985). Amygdalectomy impairs crossmodal association in monkeys. *Science, 228*, 604–606.

Nadel, L., & Stein, D. (Eds.). (1992). *1991 lectures in complex systems*. Reading, MA: Addison-Wesley.

Naish, P. (Ed.). (1986). *What is hypnosis? Current theories and research*. Philadelphia: Open University Press, Milton Keynes.

Nauta, W. (1964). Some efferent connections of the prefrontal cortex in the monkey. In J. Warren & K. Akert (Eds.), *The frontal granular cortex and behavior*. New York: McGraw-Hill.

Nauta, W. (1972). Neural associations of the frontal cortex. *Acta Neurobiologiae Experimentalis, 32*, 125–140.

Nauta, W., & Domesick, V. (1980). Neural associations of the limbic system. In A. Beckman (Ed.), *Neural substrates of behavior*. New York: Spectrum.

Nauta, W., & Feirtag, M. (1979). The organization of the brain. *Scientific American, 41*, 78–105.

Nemiah, J., Freyberger, H., & Sifneos, P. (1976). Alexithymia: A view of the psychosomatic process. In D. Hill (Ed.), *Modern trends in psychosomatic medicine. Vol. III*. London: Butterworth, pp. 430–439.

Newton, B. (1982–83). Introduction: Hypnosis and cancer. *The American Journal of Clinical Hypnosis, 25*(2–3), 89–91.

Nicolis, G. (1989). Physics of far-from-equilibrium systems and self-organization. In P. Davis (Ed.), *The new physics*. New York: Cambridge University Press.

Noll, R. B. (1987, October). *Assessment of physiological and behavioral correlates of hypnosis: Warts as a model*. Paper presented at the 38th Annual Scientific Meeting of the Society for Clinical and Experimental Hypnosis, Los Angeles, CA.

Nugent, W., Carden, N., & Montgomery, D. (1984). Utilizing the creative unconscious in the treatment of hypodermic phobias and sleep disturbance. *The American Journal of Clinical Hypnosis, 26*(3), 201–205.

Olds, J. (1977). *Drives and reinforcements: Behavioral studies of hypothalamic functions.* New York: Raven Press.

Olds, J., Anderson, M., McPhie, D., Staten, L., & Aldon, D. (1989). Imaging of memory-specific changes in the distribution of protein knase C in the hippocampus. *Science, 245,* 866–869.

Olds, J., & Milner, P. (1954). Positive reinforcement produced by electrical stimulation of septal area and other regions of rat brain. *Journal of Comparative & Physiological Psychology, 47,* 419–427.

Olness, K., & Conroy, M. (1985). A pilot study of voluntary control of transcutaneous PO_2 by children. *International Journal of Clinical & Experimental Hypnosis, 33*(1), 1–5.

Olness, K., Wain, H., & Ng, L. (1980). Pilot study of blood endorphin levels in children using self-hypnosis to control pain. *Developmental & Behavioral Pediatrics, 1*(4), 187–188.

Orne, M. (1962). The social psychology of the psychological experiment: With particular reference to demand characteristics and their implications. *American Psychologist, 17,* 776–783.

Orne, M. (1972). On the stimulating subject as a quasi-control group in hypnosis research: What, why and how? In E. Fromm & R. Shor (Eds.), *Hypnosis: Research development and perspectives.* Chicago, IL: Aldine-Atherton, pp. 399–443.

Orne, M. (1974). Pain suppression by hypnosis and related phenomena. In J. Bonica (Ed.), *Pain.* New York: Raven Press.

Orne, M., & Evans, F. (1966). Inadvertent termination of hypnosis with hypnotized and simulating subjects. *The International Journal of Clinical & Experimental Hypnosis, 14,* 61–78.

Ornstein, R. (1973). *The psychology of consciousness.* New York: Viking.

Ornstein, R., & Thompson, R. (1984). *The amazing brain.* Boston: Houghton Mifflin.

Orr, W., Hoffman, H., & Hegge, F. (1974). Ultradian rhythms in extended performance. *Aerospace Medicine, 45,* 995–1000.

Osowiec, D. (1992). *Ultradian rhythms in self-actualization, anxiety, and stress-related somatic symptoms.* Unpublished doctoral dissertation, California Institute of Integral Studies.

Overton, D. (1968). Dissociated learning in drug states (state-dependent learning). In D. Effron, J. Cole, J. Levine, & R. Wittenborn (Eds.), *Psychopharmacology: A review of progress, 1957–1967* (pp. 918–930). Public Health Service Publications, 1836. U.S. Government Printing Office, Washington, DC.

Overton, D. (1972). State-dependent learning produced by alcohol and its relevance to alcoholism. In B. Kissen & H. Begleiter (Eds.), *The biology of alcoholism. Vol. II. Physiology and behavior* (pp. 193–217). New York: Plenum.

Overton, D. (1973). State-dependent learning produced by addicting drugs. In S. Fisher & A. Freedman (Eds.), *Opiate addiction: Origins and treatment* (pp. 61–75). Washington, DC: Winston.

Overton, D. (1978). Major theories of state-dependent learning. In B. Ho, D. Richards, & D. Chute (Eds.), *Drug discrimination and state-dependent learning* (pp. 283–318). New York: Academic Press.

Palmblad, J. (1985). Stress and human immunologic competence. In R. Guillemin, M. Cohn, & T. Melnechuk (Eds.), *Neural modulation of immunity* (pp. 45–53). New York: Raven Press.

Papez, J. (1937). A proposed mechanism of emotion. *Archives of Neurology & Physiology, 38,* 725–744.

Pardue, M., Feramisco, J., & Lindquist, S. (1989). *Stress-induced proteins.* New York: Liss.

Peavey, B. (1982). Biofeedback assisted relaxation: Effects on phagocytic immune function. Unpublished doctoral dissertation, North Texas State University, Denton, TX.

Peavey, B., Lawlis, F., & Goven, A. (1985). Biofeedback-assisted relaxation: Effects on phagocytic capacity. *Biofeedback & Self-Regulation, 10,* 33–47.

Pennebaker, J., Kiecolt-Glaser, J., & Glaser, R. (1988a). Disclosure of traumas and immune function: Health implications for psychotherapy. *Journal of Consulting Psychology, 56,* 239–245.

Pennebaker, J., Kiecolt-Glaser, J., & Glaser, R. (1988b). Confronting traumatic experience and immunocompetence: A reply to Neale, Cox, Valdimarsdottir, and Stone. *Journal of Consulting Psychology, 56,* 638–639.

Perelson, A. S. (1988a). *Theoretical immunology* (Vol. 1). Redwood City, CA: Addison-Wesley.

Perelson, A. S. (1988b). Toward a realistic model of the immune system. In A. Perelson (Ed.), *Theoretical immunology* (Vol. 2) 377–401. Redwood City, CA: Addison-Wesley.

Perry, C., Laurence, J., D'eon, J., & Tallant, B. (1988). Hypnotic age regression techniques in the elicitation of memories: Applied uses and abuses. In H. Pettinati (Ed.), *Hypnosis and memory* (pp. 128–154). New York: Guilford.

Pert, C. (1986). Emotions in body, not just in brain. *Brain/Mind Bulletin, 11*(4), 1.

Pert, C., Ruff, M., Spencer, D., & Rossi, E. (1989). Self-reflective molecular psychology. *Psychological Perspectives, 20*(1), 213–221.

Pert, C., Ruff, M., Weber, R., & Herkenham, M. (1985). Neuropeptides and their receptors: A psychosomatic network. *The Journal of Immunology, 135*(2), 820s–826s.

Peters, C. (1978). *Tell me who I am before I die.* New York: Rawson.

Phelps, M., & Mazziotta, J. (1985). Positron emission tomography: Human brain function and biochemistry. *Science, 228,* 799–809.

Pincus, D., DiCicco-Bloom, E., & Black, I. (1992). Neuropeptide regulation of neuronal development. In I. A. Hendry & C. E. Hill (Eds.), *Development, regeneration and plasticity of the autonomic nervous system* (pp. 267–303). Switzerland: Harwood Academic.

Platonov, K. I. (1959). *The word as a physiological and therapeutic factor.* Moscow: Foreign Languages Publishing.

Poirel, C. (1982). Circadian rhythms in behavior and experimental psychotherapy. In F. Brown & R. Graeber (Eds.), *Rhythmic aspects of behavior* (pp. 363–398). Hillsdale, NJ: Erlbaum.

Prank, K., Harms, H., Kayser, C., Brabant, G., Olsen, L., & Hesch, R. (1991). Information transfer in hormonal systems. In E. Mosekilde & L. Mosekilde (Eds.), *Complexity, chaos, and biological evolution.* New York: Plenum.

Pribram, K. (1965). Proposal for a structural pragmatism: Some neuropsychological considerations of problems in philosophy. In B. Wolman & E. Nagle (Eds.), *Scientific psychology: Principles and approaches* (pp. 426–459). New York: Basic.

Pribram, K. (1971). *Languages of the brain: Experimental paradoxes and principles in neuropsychology* (3rd ed.). New York: Brandon House.

Pribram, K. (1976). Problems concerning the structure of consciousness. In G. Globus, G. Maxwell, & I. Savodnik (Eds.), *Consciousness and the brain: A scientific and philosophical inquiry* (pp. 798–809). New York: Plenum.

Pribram, K. (1979). Behaviorism, phenomenology and holism in psychology: A scientific analysis. *Journal of Social & Biological Structure, 2,* 65–72.

Pribram, K. (1980). Cognition and performance: The relation to neural mechanisms of consequence, confidence, and competence. In A. Routtenberg (Ed.), *Biology of reinforcement: Facets of brain stimulation reward* (pp. 11–36). New York: Academic Press.

Pribram, K. (1986). The cognitive revolution and mind/brain issues. *American Psychologist,* in press.

Pribram, K. (1991). *Brain and perception: Holonomy and structure in figural processing.* Hillsdale, NJ: Erlbaum.

Pribram, K., Lassonde, M., & Ptito, M. (1981). Classification of receptive field properties in cat visual cortex. *Experimental Brain Research, 43,* 119–130.

Prigogine, I., & Stengers, I. (1984). *Order out of chaos: Man's new dialogue with nature.* New York: Bantam.

Putnam, F. (1982, October). Traces of Eve's faces. *Psychology Today,* p. 8.

Putnam, F. (1985). Dissociation as a response to extreme trauma. In R. Kluft (Ed.),

Childhood antecedents of multiple personality. Washington, DC: American Psychiatric Press.

Putnam, F. (1992). Using hypnosis for therapeutic abreactions. *Psychiatric Medicine, 10,* 51–65.

Rama, S., Ballentine, R., & Ajaya, S. (1976). *Yoga and psychotherapy: The evolution of consciousness.* Honesdale, PA: Himalayan International Institute of Yoga Science & Philosophy.

Rank, O. (1924/1952). *The trauma of birth.* (Published in German in 1924; published in English in 1952) New York: R. Brunner.

Rapp, P. (1979). An atlas of cellular oscillators. *Journal of Experimental Biology, 81,* 281–306.

Rapp, P. (1987). Why are so many biological systems periodic? *Progress in Neurobiology, 29,* 261–273.

Rasmussen, D. (1986). Physiological interactions of the basic rest-activity cycle of the brain: Pulsatile luteinizing hormone secretion as a model. *Psychoneuroendocrinology, 2(4),* 389–405.

Reinberg, A., Gervais, P., & Ghata, J. (1977). Chronobiologic aspects of asthma. In J. McGovern, M. Smolensky, & A. Reinberg (Eds.), *Chronobiology in allergy and immunology* (pp. 36–63). Springfield, IL: Thomas.

Remien, R., Rabkin, J., Williams, J., & Katoff, L. (1992). Coping strategies and health beliefs of AIDS longterm survivors. *Psychology and Health, 6,* 335–345.

Reus, V., Weingartner, H., & Post, R. (1979). Clinical implications of state-dependent learning. *American Journal of Psychiatry, 136(7),* 927–931.

Reynolds, C. (1987). Flocks, herds, and schools: A distributed behavioral model. *Computer Graphics, 21,* 25.

Rider, M. (1985). Entrainment mechanisms are involved in pain reduction, muscle relaxation, and music-mediated imagery. *Journal of Music Therapy, 22(4),* 183–192.

Rider, M. (1987). Treating chronic disease and pain with music-mediated imagery. *Arts in Psychotherapy, 14(2),* 113–120.

Rider, M., & Achterberg, J. (1989). Effect of music-assisted imagery on neurotrophils and lymphocytes. *Biofeedback & Self-Regulation, 14(3),* 247–258.

Rider, M., Floyd, J., & Kirkpatrick, J. (1985). The effect of music, imagery, and relaxation on adrenal corticosteroids and the re-entrainment of circadian rhythms. *Journal of Music Therapy, 22(1),* 46–58.

Rider, M., & Weldin, C. (1990). Imagery, improvisation, and immunity. *The Arts in Psychotherapy, 17,* 211–216.

Rigter, H., & Crabbe, J. (1979). Modulation of memory by pituitary hormones. *Vitamins and Hormones, 37.* New York: Academic Press.

Rosenberg, S., & Barry, J. (1992). *The transformed cell: Unlocking the mysteries of cancer.* New York: Putnam/Chapmans.

Rosenberg, S., et al. (1985). Observations on the systemic administration of autologous lymphokine-activated killer cells and recombinant interleukin-2 to patients with metastic cancer. *New England Journal of Medicine, 23(3B),* 1485–1492.

Rosenblatt, M. (1983). Neuropeptides: Future implications for medicine. *Medical Times,* November, 31–37.

Rosenzweig, M., & Bennett, E. (1984). Basic processes and modulatory influences in the stages of memory formation. In G. Lynch, J. McGaugh, & N. Weinberger (Eds.), *Neurobiology of learning and memory* (pp. 263–288). New York: Guilford.

Ross, J. (1989). The turnover of messenger RNA. *Scientific American, 260,* 48–55.

Rossi, E. (1972/1985). *Dreams and the growth of personality: Expanding awareness in psychotherapy* (2nd ed.). New York: Brunner/Mazel.

Rossi, E. (1973/1980). Psychological shocks and creative moments in psychotherapy. In E. Rossi (Ed.), *The collected papers of Milton H. Erickson on hypnosis. IV. Innovative hypnotherapy* (pp. 447–463). New York: Irvington.

Rossi, E. (1977). The cerebral hemispheres in analytical psychology. *Journal of Analytical Psychology, 22,* 32–51.

Rossi, E. (1981). Hypnotist describes natural rhythms of trance readiness. *Brain/Mind Bulletin*, March, p. 1.

Rossi, E. (1982). Hypnosis and ultradian cycles: A new state(s) theory of hypnosis? *The American Journal of Clinical Hypnosis, 25*, 21–32.

Rossi, E. (1985). Unity and diversity in Ericksonian approaches: Now and in the future. In J. Zeig (Ed.), *Ericksonian psychotherapy. Vol. I. Structures* (pp. 15–30). New York: Brunner/Mazel.

Rossi, E. (1986a). Altered states of consciousness in everyday life: The ultradian rhythms. In B. Wolman & M. Ullman (Eds.), *Handbook of altered states of consciousness* (pp. 97–132). New York: Van Nostrand.

Rossi, E. (1986b). Hypnosis and ultradian rhythms. In B. Zilbergeld, G. Edelstien, & D. Araoz (Eds.), *Hypnosis questions and answers* (pp. 17–21). New York: W. W. Norton.

Rossi, E. L. (1986c). *The Psychobiology of mind-body healing*. New York: W. W. Norton.

Rossi, E. (1987a). Mind/body connections and the new language of human facilitation. In J. Zeig (Ed.), *The evolution of psychotherapy*. New York: Brunner/Mazel.

Rossi, E. (1987b). From mind to molecule: A state-dependent memory, learning, and behavior theory of mind-body healing. *Advances, 4*(2), 46–60.

Rossi, E. (1989a). Mind-body healing, not suggestion, is the essence of hypnosis. *American Journal of Clinical Hypnosis, 32*, 14–15.

Rossi, E. (1989b). Archetypes as strange attractors. *Psychological Perspectives, 20*, 4–14.

Rossi, E. (1990a). Mind-molecular communication: Can we really talk to our genes? *Hypnos, 17*(1), 3–14.

Rossi, E. (1990b). From mind to molecule: More than a metaphor. In J. Zeig & S. Gilligan (Eds.), *Brief therapy: Myths, methods and metaphors* (pp. 445–472). New York: Brunner/Mazel.

Rossi, E. (1990c). Mind-molecular communication: Can we really talk to our genes? *Hypnos, 17*(1), 3–14.

Rossi, E. (1991). The wave nature of consciousness. *Psychological Perspectives, 24*, 1–10.

Rossi, E. (1992a). Periodicity in self-hypnosis and the ultradian healing response: A pilot study. *Hypnos, 19*, 4–13.

Rossi, E. (1992b). What is life? *Psychological Perspectives, 26*, 6–22.

Rossi, E. (1992c). The wave nature of consciousness: A new direction for the evolution of psychotherapy. In J. Zeig (Ed.), *The evolution of psychotherapy: The second conference* (pp. 216–235). New York: Brunner-Mazel.

Rossi, E. (1992d). The chronobiological theory of therapeutic suggestion: Towards a mathematical model of Erickson's naturalistic approach. Invited address at *The 12th International Congress of Hypnosis*, Jerusalem, Israel, July 29 (in press, to be published by The International Society of Hypnosis.)

Rossi, E. (1992e). Reality, stress and imagination in temporal isolation experiments: An interview with Rütger A. Wever. In D. Lloyd & E. Rossi (Eds.), *Ultradian rhythms in life processes: A fundamental inquiry into chronobiology and psychobiology* (pp. 323–337). New York: Springer-Verlag.

Rossi, E. (1993). A clinical-experimental exploration of Erickson's naturalistic approach: A pilot study of ultradian time and trance phenomena. *Hypnos, 20*, 10–20.

Rossi, E., & Cheek, D. (1988). *Mind-body therapy: Ideodynamic healing in hypnosis*. New York: W. W. Norton.

Rossi, E., & Cheek, D. (1990). Ideomotor healing of burn injuries. In D. C. Hammond (Ed.), *Handbook of hypnotic suggestions and metaphors* (p. 233). New York: W. W. Norton.

Rossi, E., & Jichaku, P. (1992). Creative choice in therapeutic and transpersonal double binds. In E. Rossi & M. Ryan (Eds.), *Creative choice in hypnosis* (pp. 225–253). New York: Irvington.

Rossi, E., & Lippincott, B. (1992). The wave nature of being: Ultradian rhythms and mind-body communication. In D. Lloyd & E. Rossi (Eds.), *Ultradian rhythms in life processes: A fundamental inquiry into chronobiology and psychobiology* (pp. 371–402). New York: Springer-Verlag.

Rossi, E., & Nimmons, D. (1991). *The 20-minute break: Using the new science of ultradian rhythms.* Los Angeles: Tarcher.

Rossi, E., & Ryan, M. (Eds.). (1986). *Mind-body communication in hypnosis: Vol. 3. The seminars, workshops, and lectures of Milton H. Erickson.* New York: Irvington.

Rossi, E., & Ryan, M. (Eds.). (1992). *Creative choice in hypnosis: Vol. 4. The seminars, workshops, and lectures of Milton H. Erickson.* New York: Irvington.

Roszman, T., Cross, R., Brooks, W., & Markesbery, W. (1985). Neuroimmodulation: Effects of neural lesions on cellular immunity. In R. Guillemin, M. Cohn, & T. Melnechuk (Eds.), *Neural modulation of immunity* (pp. 95–109). New York: Raven Press.

Roth, J., LeRoith, D., Collier, E., Weaver, N., Watkinson, A., Cleland, C., & Glick, S. (1985). Evolutionary origins of neuropeptides, hormones, and receptors: Possible applications to immunology. *The Journal of Immunology, 135*(2), 816s–819s.

Ruff, M., Martin, B., Ginns, E., Farrar, W., & Pert, C. (1987). CD4 receptor binding peptides that block HIV infectivity cause human monocyte chemotaxis. *FEBS Letters, 211*(1), 17–22.

Sachar, E. (1969). Psychological homeostasis and endocrine function. In A. Mandell & M. Mandell (Eds.), *Psychological strategies in man.* New York: Academic Press.

Sagan, C. (1977). *The dragons of Eden: Speculations on the evolution of human intelligence.* New York: Random House.

Salk, J. (1969). Immunological paradoxes: Theoretical considerations in the rejection or retention of grafts, tumors, and normal tissue. *Annals of New York Academy of Science, 164*(2), 365–380.

Saltz, E. (1973). Higher mental processes as the bases for the laws of conditioning. In F. McGuigan & D. Lumsden (Eds.), *Contemporary approaches to conditioning and learning.* New York: Wiley.

Sanders, S. (1991a, April 14–18). Self-hypnosis and ultradian states: Are they related? Paper presented at the 33rd Annual Scientific Meeting of The American Society of Clinical Hypnosis, St. Louis, MO.

Sanders, S. (1991b). *Clinical self-hypnosis: The power of words and images.* New York: Guilford.

Sapolsky, R. (1990, January). Stress in the wild. *Scientific American,* pp. 116–123.

Sapolsky, R. (1992a). *Stress, the aging brain, and the mechanisms of neuronal death.* Cambridge, MA: MIT Press.

Sapolsky, R. (1992b). Neuroendocrinology of the stress response. In J. Becker, S. Breedlove, & D. Crews (Eds.), *Behavioral endocrinology.* Cambridge, MA: MIT Press.

Sapolsky, R., & Ray, J. (1989). Styles of dominance and their endocrine correlates among wild olive baboons. *American Journal of Primatology,* 1–13.

Sarbin, T., & Coe, W. (1972). *Hypnosis: A social psychological analysis of influence communication.* New York: Holt, Rinehart, & Winston.

Sawaguchi, T., & Goldman-Rakic, P. (1991). D1 dopamine receptors in prefrontal cortex: Involvement in working memory. *Science, 8,* 947–950.

Schafer, D. (1975). Hypnosis use on a burn unit. *The International Journal of Clinical and Experimental Hypnosis, 23,* 1–14.

Scharrer, E., & Scharrer, B. (1940). Secretory cells within the hypothalamus. *Research Publications of the Association of Nervous & Mental Diseases.* New York: Hafner.

Schiffer, R., & Hoffman, S. (1991). Behavioral sequelae of autoimmune disease. In R. Ader, D. Felten, & N. Cohen (Eds.), *Psychoneuroimmunology* (2nd ed.) (pp. 1037–1066). New York: Academic Press.

Schmitt, F. (1984). Molecular regulators of brain function: A new view. *Neuroscience, 13,* 991–1001.

Schmitt, F. (1986). Chemical information processing in the brain: Prospect from retrospect. In L. Iversen & E. Goodman (Eds.), *Fast and slow signaling in the nervous system* (pp. 239–243). New York: Oxford University Press.

Schneck, J. (1948). Psychogenic cardiovascular reaction interpreted and successfully treated with hypnosis. *Psychoanalytical Review, 35,* 14–19.

Schneider, J., Smith, W., & Witcher, S. (1983). The relationship of mental imagery to white blood cell (neutrophil) function: Experimental studies of normal subjects. Uncirculated mimeographs. Michigan State University, College of Medicine. East Lansing, MI.

Schneider, J., Smith, W., & Witcher, S. (1984). The relationship of mental imagery to white blood cell (neutrophil) function in normal subjects. Paper presented at the 36th Annual Scientific Meeting of the International Society for Clinical & Experimental Hypnosis, San Antonio, TX, October 25th.

Schreiber, F. (1973). *Sybil*. Chicago, IL: Regnery.

Scott, M. (1960). *Hypnosis in skin and allergic diseases*. Springfield, IL: Thomas.

Seligman, M. (1975). *Helplessness: On depression, development, and death*. New York: Freeman.

Seltzer, L. (1985). *Paradoxical strategies in psychotherapy*. New York: Wiley.

Selye, H. (1936). A syndrome produced by diverse noxious agents. Cited in *The stress of life*. (1976). New York: McGraw-Hill.

Selye, H. (1974). *Stress without distress*. New York: Signet.

Selye, H. (1976). *The stress of life*. New York: McGraw-Hill.

Selye, H. (1982). History and present status of the stress concept. In L. Goldberger & S. Breznitz (Eds.), *Handbook of stress* (pp. 7–20). New York: Macmillan.

Shands, H. (1969). Integration, discipline, and the concept of shape. *Annals of New York Academy of Science, 164*(2), pp. 578–587.

Shannahoff-Khalsa, D. (1991). Lateralized rhythms of the central and autonomic nervous systems. *International Journal of Psychophysiology, 11*, 225–251.

Shannon, C., & Weaver, W. (1949). *The mathematical theory of communication*. Urbana: University of Illinois Press.

Shapiro, A. (1971). Placebo effects in medicine, psychotherapy and psychoanalysis. In A. Begin & S. Garfield (Eds.), *Handbook of psychotherapy and behavior change*. New York: Wiley.

Shavit, Y. (1991). Stress-induced immune modulation in animals: Opiates and endogenous opioid peptides. In R. Ader, D. Felten, & N. Cohen (Eds.), *Psychoneuroimmunology* (2nd ed.) (pp. 789–806). New York: Academic Press.

Shavit, Y., Terman, G., Martin, F., Lewis, J., Liebeskind, J., & Gale, R. (1985). Stress, opioid peptides, the immune system, and cancer. *The Journal of Immunology, 135*(2), 834s–837s.

Sheehan, P., & Perry, C. (1976). *Methodologies of hypnosis*. Hillsdale, NJ: Erlbaum.

Shor, R. (1959). Hypnosis and the concept of the generalized reality-orientation. *American Journal of Psychotherapy, 13*, 582–602.

Shorr, J., Sobel, G., Robin, P., & Connella, J. (1980). *Imagery: Its many dimensions and applications*. New York: Plenum.

Shors, T., Weiss, C., & Thompson, R. (1992). Stress-induced facilitation of classical conditioning. *Science, 257*, 537–539.

Siegman, A., & Feldstein, S. (Eds.). (1985). *Multichannel integrations of nonverbal behavior*. Hillsdale, NJ: Erlbaum.

Silberman, E., Putnam, F., Weingartner, H., Braun, B., & Post, R. (1985). Dissociative states in multiple personality disorders: A quantitative study. *Psychiatry Research, 15*, 253–260.

Silberner, J. (1985). A new look at arthritis origins. *Science News, 127*(23), 358–359.

Simon, C., Brandenberger, G., & Follenius, M. (1987). Ultradian oscillations of plasma glucose, insulin, and C-peptide in man during continuous enteral nutrition. *Journal of Clinical Endocrinology & Metabolism, 64*, 669–674.

Simonton, O., Simonton, S., & Creighton, J. (1978). *Getting well again*. Los Angeles: Tarcher.

Sizemore, C. (1977). *I'm Eve*. New York: Harcourt Brace Jovanovich.

Smith, E., Harbour-McMenamin, D., & Blalock, J. (1985). Lymphocyte production of endorphins and endorphin-mediated immunoregulatory activity. *The Journal of Immunology, 135*(2), 779s–782s.

Smith, G., & McDaniel, S. (1983). Psychologically mediated effect on the delayed hyper-sensitivity reaction to tuberculin in humans. *Psychosomatic Medicine, 46,* 65–73.

Smith, G., McKenzie, J., Marmer, D., & Steele, R. (1985). Psychologic modulation of the human immune response to varicella zoster. *Archives of Internal Medicine, 145,* 2110–2112.

Smith, R. (1991). The immune system is a key factor in the etiology of psychosocial disease. *Medical Hypotheses, 34,* 49–57.

Snyder, S. (1980). Brain peptides as neurotransmitters. *Science, 209,* 976–983.

Snyder, S. H., & Bredt, D. S. (1992). Biological roles of nitric oxide. *Scientific American, 266*(5), 68–77.

Solomon, G. (1985). The emerging field of psychoneuroimmunology with a special note on AIDS. *Advances, 2*(Winter), 6–19.

Solomon, G., & Amkraut, A. (1981). Psychoneuroendocrinological effects on the immune response. *Annual Review of Microbiology, 35,* 155–184.

Solomon, G., Kemeny, M., & Temoshok, L. (1991). Psychoneuroimmunologic aspects of human immunodeficiency virus infection. In R. Ader, D. Felten, & N. Cohen (Eds.), *Psychoneuroimmunology* (2nd ed.) (pp. 1081–1113). New York: Academic Press.

Sommer, C. (1990, March 24–28). *The ultradian rhythm and the common everyday trance.* Paper presented at the 32nd Annual Scientific Meeting, Orlando, FL.

Sommer, C. (1993). Ultradian rhythms and the common everyday trance. *Hypnos, 20,* 135–144.

Spanos, N., & Coe, W. (1992). A social-psychological approach to hypnosis. In E. Fromm & M. Nash (Eds.), *Contemporary hypnosis research.* New York: Guilford.

Spanos, N., Strenstrom, J., & Johnston, J. (1988). Hypnosis, placebo, and suggestion in the treatment of warts. *Psychosomatic Medicine, 50,* 245–260.

Spanos, N., Williams, V., & Gwynn, M. (1990). Effects of hypnotic, placebo, and salicylic acid treatments on wart regression. *Psychosomatic Medicine, 52,* 109–114.

Sperry, R. (1964). The great cerebral commissure. *Scientific American, 210,* pp. 42–52.

Spiegel, D. (1991). A psychosocial intervention and survival time of patients with meta-static breast cancer. *Advances, 7*(3), 10–19.

Spiegel, D., Bierre, P., & Rootenberg, J. (in press). Hypnotic alteration of somatosensory perception. *American Journal of Psychiatry.*

Spiegel, D., Bloom, J., Kraemer, H., & Gottheil, E. (1989, October 14). Effect of psychosocial treatment on survival of patients with metastatic breast cancer. *Lancet,* pp. 888–891.

Spiegel, D., & King, R. (1992). Hypnotizability and CSF HVA levels among psychiatric patients. *Biological Psychiatry, 31,* 95–98.

Spiegel, H., & Spiegel, D. (1978). *Trance and treatment.* New York: Basic.

Spruiell, G., Steck, C., Lippencott, C., & King, D. (1983). Failure of naloxone to modify the depth of hypnotic trance. *Experientia, 39*(7–12), 763–764.

Stein, M. (1985). Bereavement, depression, stress, and immunity. In R. Guillemin, M. Cohn, & T. Melnechuk (Eds.), *Neural modulation of immunity* (pp. 29–53). New York: Raven Press.

Stein, M., Keller, S., & Schleifer, S. (1985). Stress and immunomodulation: The role of depression and neuroendocrine function. *The Journal of Immunology, 135*(2), 827s–833s.

Stein, M., Schiavi, R., & Camerino, M. (1976). Influence of brain and behavior on the immune system. *Science, 191,* 435–440.

Stein, M., Schleifer, S., & Keller, S. (1981). Hypothalamic influences on immune re-sponses. In A. Ader (Ed.), *Psychoneuroimmunology* (pp. 429–447). New York: Academic Press.

Stephenson, J. (1978). Reversal of hypnosis-induced analgesia by naloxone. *Lancet,* (28097), 991–992.

Sternbach, R. (1982). On strategies for identifying neurochemical correlates of hypnotic analgesia. *International Journal of Clinical & Experimental Hypnosis, 30*(3), 251–256.

Stewart, J. (1981). Brain ACTH-endorphin neurones as regulators of central nervous sys-tem activity. In K. Brunfeldt (Ed.), *Peptides, 1980* (pp. 774–779). Copenhagen, Den-mark: Scriptor.

Stewart, J., Krebs, W., & Kaczender, E. (1971). State-dependent learning produced with steroids. *Nature, 216*, 1233–1234.

Stonier, T. (1990). *Information and the internal structure of the universe.* New York: Springer-Verlag.

Straus, S. E. (1988). The chronic mononucleosis syndrome. *Journal of Infectious Disease, 157*, 405–412.

Stryer, L. (1988). *Biochemistry* (3rd ed.). New York: W. H. Freeman.

Taylor, R. (1992, June 7). A lot of "excitement" about neurodegeneration. *Science*, pp. 1380–1381.

Teitlebaum, H. (1954). Spontaneous rhythmic ocular movements: Their possible relationships to mental activity. *Neurology, 4*, 350–354.

Temoshok, J., & Dreher, H. (1992). *The type C connection.* New York: Random House.

Temoshok, L. (1991). Malignant melanoma, AIDS, and the complex search for psychosocial mechanisms. *Advances, 7*, 20–28.

Temoshok, L. (1992). Emotions and health outcomes: Some theoretical and methodological considerations. In H. D. Traue & T. W. Pennebaker (Eds.), *Emotion, inhibition, and health.* Toronto: Hogrefe & Huber.

Thigpen, C., & Cleckley, H. (1957). *The three faces of Eve.* Kingsport, TN: Kingsport Press.

Thompson, R., et al. (1984). Neuronal substrates of learning and memory: A "multiple-trace" view. In G. Lynch, J. McGaugh, & N. Weinberger (Eds.), *Neurobiology of learning and memory* (pp. 137–164). New York: Guilford.

Timbury, M. C. (1991). *Medical virology.* New York: Churchill Livingstone.

Tinterow, M. (1970). *Foundations of hypnosis.* Springfield, IL: C. Thomas.

Tinterow, M., & Rossi, E. (1992). *The future of therapeutic hypnosis: Expanding the suggestion domain.* Paper presented at the 34th Annual Scientific Meeting and Workshops on Clinical Hypnosis, Las Vegas, NV, April 4–8.

Tinterow, M., & Rossi, E. (in press). The future of therapeutic hypnosis: Expanding the suggestion domain. *American Journal of Clinical Hypnosis.*

Todorov, I. (1990). How cells maintain stability. *Scientific American, 263*, pp. 66–75.

Travis, J. (1993). A stimulating new approach to cancer treatment. *Science, 259*, 310–311.

Trijsburg, R., van Knippenberg, F., & Rijpma, S. (1992). Effects of psychological treatment on cancer patients: A critical review. *Psychosomatic Medicine, 54*, 489–517.

Trum, L., & Ritchie, J. (1992). The transformations model: The decoding of symptomatic states. Unpublished manuscript.

Tsien, R. (1993, January 25). As interviewed by Franklin Hoke in "Confocal microscopy: Viewing cells as 'wild animals'." *The Scientist*, pp. 17–19.

Tsuji, Y., & Kobayshi, T. (1988). Short and long ultradian EEG components in daytime arousal. *Electroencephalography & Clinical Neurophysiology, 70*, 110–117.

Tyler, T., Perkins, A., & Harris, K. (1989). The development of long-term potentiation in hippocampus and neocortex. *Neuropsychologia, 27*, 31–39.

Ullman, M. (1947). Herpes simplex and second degree burn induced under hypnosis. *American Journal of Clinical Hypnosis, 103*, 828–830.

Ullman, M. (1959). On the psyche and warts. I. Suggestion and warts: A review and comment. *Psychosomatic Medicine, 21*, 473–488.

Vaihinger, H. (1911). *Philosophy of the as-if.* Translated by C. K. Ogden in 1924. London: Routledge.

van Cauter, E., Desir, D., Decoster, C., Fery, F., & Balasse, E. (1989). Nocturnal decrease in glucose tolerance during constant glucose infusion. *Journal of Clinical Endocrinology and Metabolism, 69*(3), 604–611.

Vance, M., & Thorner, M. (1989). Fasting alters pulsatile and rhythmic cortisol release in normal man. *Journal of Endocrinology and Metabolism, 68*(6), 1013–1018.

van der Kolk, B. (1987). *Psychological trauma.* Washington, DC: American Psychiatric Press.

van der Kolk, B., Greenberg, M., Boyd, H., & Krystal, J. (1985). Inescapable shock, neurotransmitters, and addiction to trauma: Toward a psychobiology of post-traumatic stress. *Biological Psychiatry, 20*, 314–325.

van der Kolk, B., & van der Hart, O. (1991). The intrusive past: The flexibility of memory and the engraving of trauma. *American Imago, 48,* 425–454.

Van Ostade, X., et al. (1993). Human TNF mutants with selective activity on the p55 receptor. *Nature, 361,* 266–269.

Van Ree, J., Jolles, J., & Verhoeven, W. (1990). In D. de Wied (Ed.), *Neuropeptides: Basics and perspectives* (pp. 313–351). New York: Elsevier Science.

Veldhuis, J. (1992). A parsimonious model of amplitude and frequency modulation of episodic hormone secretory bursts as a mechanism for ultradian signalling by endocrine glands. In D. Lloyd & E. Rossi (Eds.), *Ultradian rhythms in life processes: A fundamental inquiry into chronobiology and psychobiology* (pp. 139–172). New York: Springer-Verlag.

Veldhuis, J., Christiansen, E., Evans, W., Kolp, L., Rogol, A., & Johnson, M. (1988). Physiological profiles of episodic progesterone release during midluteal phase of the human menstrual cycle: Analysis of circadian and ultradian rhythms, discrete pulse properties, and correlations with simultaneous luteinizing hormone release. *Journal of Clinical Endocrinology & Metabolism, 67*(1), 116–123.

Veldhuis, J., Iranmanesh, A., Lizarralde, G., & Johnson, M. (in press). Amplitude modulation of a burst-like mode of cortisol secretion gives rise to the nyctohemeral glucocorticord rhythm in man. *American Journal of Physiology.*

Veldhuis, J., & Johnson, M. (1988). Operating characteristics of the hypothalamo-pituitary-gonadal axis in men: Circadian, ultradian, and pulsatile release of prolactin and its temporal coupling with luteinizing hormone. *Journal of Clinical Endocrinology & Metabolism, 67*(1), 116–123.

Veldhuis, J., King, J., Urban, R., Rogol, A., Evans, W., Kolp, L., & Johnson, M. (1987). Operating characteristics of the male hypothalmo-pituitary-gonadal axis: Pulsatile release of testosterone and follicle-stimulating hormone and their temporal coupling with luteinizing hormone. *Journal of Clinical & Endocrinological Metabolism, 65,* 65–929.

Wadden, T., & Anderton, C. (1982). The clinical use of hypnosis. *Psychological Bulletin, 91*(2), 215–243.

Wagstaff, G. (1986). Hypnosis as compliance and belief: A socio-cognitive view. In P. Naish (Ed.), *What is hypnosis? Current theories and research* (pp. 57–84). Philadelphia: Open University Press, Milton Keynes.

Wahlestedt, C., Pich, E. M., Koob, G. F., Yee, F., & Heilig, M. (1993). Modulation of anxiety and neuropeptide Y-Y1 receptors by antisense oligodeoxynucleotides. *Science, 259,* 528–531.

Wain, H., Amen, D., & Oetgen, W. (1984). Hypnotic intervention in cardiac arrhythmias. *The American Journal of Clinical Hypnosis, 27*(1), 70–75.

Wakeman, J., & Kaplan, J. (1978). An experimental study of hypnosis in painful burns. *The American Journal of Clinical Hypnosis, 21,* 3–12.

Waksman, B. (1985). Neuroimmunomodulation of homeostasis and host defense. *Journal of Immunology, 135*(2), 862s.

Waldrop, M. (1992). *Complexity: The emerging science at the edge of order and chaos.* New York: Simon & Schuster.

Walford, R. (1983). *Maximum lifespan.* New York: Avon.

Wallace, A. (1966). *Religion. An anthropological view.* New York: Random House.

Wallace, B. (1993). Day persons, night persons, and variability in hypnotic susceptibility. *Journal of Personality and Social Psychology, 64,* 827–833.

Warner, R. (1992). Cyclicity of vocal activity increases during conversation: Support for a nonlinear systems model of dyadic social interaction. *Behavioral Science, 37,* 128–138.

Watkins, J. (1978). *The therapeutic self.* New York: Human Sciences Press.

Watkins, J. (1980). The silent abreaction. *International Journal of Clinical & Experimental Hypnosis, 28,* 101–113.

Watzlawick, P. (Ed.). (1984). *The invented reality.* New York: W. W. Norton.

Weeks, G., & L'Abate, L. (1982). *Paradoxical psychotherapy: Theory and practice with individuals, couples, and families.* New York: Brunner/Mazel.

Wehr, T. (1982). Circadian rhythm disturbances in depression and mania. In F. Brown & R. Graeber (Eds.), *Rhythmic aspects of behavior*. Hillsdale, NJ: Erlbaum.

Weinberger, N., Gold, P., & Sternberg, D. (1984). Epinephrine enables Pavlovian fear conditioning under anesthesia. *Science, 223,* February 10, 605–607.

Weiner, H. (1972). Presidential address: Some comments on the transduction of experience by the brain: Implications for our understanding of the relationship of mind to body. *Psychosomatic Medicine, 34*(4), 355–380.

Weiner, H. (1977). *Psychobiology and human disease*. New York: Elsevier.

Weiner, H. (1991). Social and psychobiological factors in autoimmune disease. In R. Ader, D. Felten, & N. Cohen (Eds.), *Psychoneuroimmunology* (2nd ed.) (pp. 955–1011). New York: Academic Press.

Weingartner, H. (1978). Human state dependent learning. In B. Ho, D. Richards, & D. Chute (Eds.), *Drugs discrimination and state-dependent learning* (pp. 361–382). New York: Academic Press.

Weingartner, H. (1986, January). Memory: The roots of failure. *Psychology Today*, pp. 6–7.

Weingartner, H., Miller, H., & Murphy, D. (1977). Mood state-dependent retrieval of verbal associations. *Journal of Abnormal Psychology, 86,* 276–284.

Weingartner, H., & Murphy, D. (1977). Brain states and memory. *Psychopharmacological Bulletin, 13,* 66–67.

Weinstein, E., & Au, P. (1991). Use of hypnosis before and during angioplasty. *American Journal of Clinical Hypnosis, 34,* 29–37.

Weisbuch, G. (1991). *Complex systems dynamics*. Redwood City, CA: Addison-Wesley.

Weitzenhoffer, A. (1971). Ocular changes associated with passive hypnotic behavior. *The American Journal of Clinical Hypnosis, 14,* 102–121.

Weitzenhoffer, A. (1982). In search of hypnosis. *International Journal of Clinical & Experimental Hypnosis, 30*(2), 210–211.

Welch, W. (1990). The mammalian stress response: Cell physiology and biochemistry of stress proteins. In R. Morimoto, A. Tissieres, & C. Georgopoulos (Eds.). *Stress proteins in biology and medicine*. Cold Spring Harbor, NY: Cold Spring Harbor Laboratory Press.

Werntz, D. (1981). Cerebral hemispheric activity and autonomic nervous function. Unpublished doctoral dissertation, University of California, San Diego.

Werntz, D., Bickford, R., Bloom, F., & Shannahoff-Khalsa, D. (1981). Selective cortical activation by alternating autonomic function. Paper presented at the Western EEG Society Meeting, February 12, Reno, NV.

Werntz, D., Bickford, R., Bloom, F., & Shannahoff-Khalsa, D. (1982a). Alternating cerebral hemispheric activity and lateralization of autonomic nervous function. *Human neurobiology, 2,* 225–229.

Werntz, D., Bickford, R., & Shannahoff-Khalsa, D. (1982b). Selective hemispheric stimulation by unilateral forced nostril breathing. *Human neurobiology, 6,* 165–171.

West, M. (Ed.). (1987). *The psychology of meditation*. Oxford: Clarendon Press.

Wever, R. A. (1984). Toward a mathematical model of circadian rhythmicity. In M. Moore-Ede & C. Czeisler (Eds.), *Mathematical models of the circadian sleep-wake cycle* (pp. 17–79). New York: Raven Press.

Wever, R. (1988). Order and disorder in human circadian rhythmicity: Possible relations to mental illness. In D. Kupfer, T. Monk, & J. Barchas (Eds.), *Biological rhythms and mental disorders*. New York: Guilford.

Wever, R., & Rossi, E. (1992). The sleep-wake threshold in human circadian rhythms as a determinant of ultradian rhythms. In D. Lloyd & E. Rossi (Eds.), *Ultradian rhythms in life processes: A fundamental inquiry into chronobiology and psychobiology* (pp. 307–322). New York: Springer-Verlag.

Wharram, B., Fitting, K., Kunkel, S., Remick, D., Merritt, S., & Wiggins, R. (1991). Tissue factor expression in endothelial cell/monocyte cocultures stimulated by lipopolysaccharide and/or aggregated IgG. *The Journal of Immunology, 146,* 1437–1445.

Wheeler, J. (1990). Information, physics, quantum: The search for links. In W. Zurek

(Ed.), *Complexity, entropy and the physics of information* (pp. 3–28). Redwood City, CA: Addison-Wesley.

White, L., Tursky, B., & Schwartz, G. (1985). *Placebo: Clinical implications and new insights.* New York: Guilford.

Wickramasekera, I. (Ed.) (1976). *Biofeedback, behavior therapy and hypnosis.* Chicago, IL: Nelson-Hall.

Wickramasekera, I. (1985). A conditioned response model of the placebo effect: Predictions from the model. In L. White, B. Tursky, & G. Schwartz (Eds.), *Placebo, theory, research, and mechanisms* (pp. 255–287). New York: Guilford.

Wiener, N. (1948). *Cybernetics, or control and communication in the animal and the machine.* New York: Wiley.

Williams, J. (1974). Stimulation of breast growth by hypnosis. *Journal of Sex Research, 10,* 316–326.

Winfree, A. T. (1980). *The geometry of biological time.* New York: Springer-Verlag.

Wolberg, L. (1947). Hypnotic experiments in psychosomatic medicine. *Psychosomatic Medicine, 9,* 337–342.

Wolkowitz, O., et al. (1990). Cognitive effects of corticosteroids. *American Journal of Psychiatry, 147*(10), 1297–1303.

Woodman, M. (1984). Psyche/soma awareness. *Quadrant, 17*(2), 25–37.

Wurtman, R., & Anton-Tay, F. (1969). The mammalian pineal as a neuroendocrine transducer. *Recent Progress in Hormone Research, 25,* 493–513.

Wybran, J. (1985). Enkephalins, endorphins, substance P, and the immune system. In R. Guillemin, M. Cohn, & T. Melnechuk (Eds.), *Neural modulation of immunity* (pp. 157–161). New York: Raven Press.

Yanovski, A. (1962). The feasibility of alteration of cardiovascular manifestations in hypnosis. *The American Journal of Clinical Hypnosis, 5,* 8–16.

Zeig, J. (1980a). Symptom prescription and Ericksonian principles of hypnosis and psychotherapy. *The American Journal of Clinical Hypnosis, 23*(1), 16–22.

Zeig, J. (1980b). Symptom prescription techniques: Clinical applications using elements of communication. *The American Journal of Clinical Hypnosis, 23*(1), 23–33.

Zeig, J. (Ed.). (1985). *Ericksonian psychotherapy. Vol. I. Structures.* New York: Brunner/Mazel.

Zilboorg, G., & Henry, G. (1941). *A history of medical psychology.* New York: W. W. Norton.

Zornetzer, S. (1978). Neurotransmitter modulation and memory: A new neuropharmacological phrenology? In M. Lipton, A. di Mascio, & K. Killam (Eds.), *Psychopharmacology: A generation of progress.* New York: Raven Press.

Index